Roots of Ancient
Greek Civilization

Roots of Ancient Greek Civilization
The Influence of Old Europe

HARALD HAARMANN

McFarland & Company, Inc., Publishers
Jefferson, North Carolina

LIBRARY OF CONGRESS CATALOGUING-IN-PUBLICATION DATA

Haarmann, Harald.
Roots of ancient Greek civilization : the influence
of old Europe / Harald Haarmann.
    p.   cm.
Includes bibliographical references and index.

ISBN 978-0-7864-7827-9 (softcover : acid free paper) ∞
ISBN 978-1-4766-1589-9 (ebook)

1. Greece—Civilization—To 146 B.C. 2. Bronze age—Europe.
3. Culture—Origin. 4. Social evolution. I. Title.
DF220.H16 2014   938—dc23   2014030267

BRITISH LIBRARY CATALOGUING DATA ARE AVAILABLE

© 2014 Harald Haarmann. All rights reserved

*No part of this book may be reproduced or transmitted in any form
or by any means, electronic or mechanical, including photocopying
or recording, or by any information storage and retrieval system,
without permission in writing from the publisher.*

On the cover: Statue of Athena © Jun He/Dreamstime.com

Printed in the United States of America

*McFarland & Company, Inc., Publishers
Box 611, Jefferson, North Carolina 28640
www.mcfarlandpub.com*

Table of Contents

Introduction. Athens: Cradle of Democracy? ... 1

1. European Tradition Versus Afrocentrism
    The Reality Behind the Myth of "Black Athena" ... 9

2. What the Greeks Learned from Their Predecessors
    Wine and Olive Cultivation, Pottery and Metallurgy ... 40

3. Greek Immigrants and Native Europeans in Southeastern Europe
    Contact of Cultures, Fusion of Languages and Ways to Remember the Past ... 73

4. Seafaring, Trade and Commerce
    Trade Networks in the Early Greek World ... 111

5. Ingredients of Pan-Hellenic Identity
    Sacred Places, Rituals and Festivities ... 127

6. Pre-Greek Origins of the Arts
    The Muses and Their Doings from Old Europe to Classical Antiquity ... 162

7. Old European Bases of Social Egalitarianism in Greek Society
    Social Networking and the Making of Democratic Governance ... 183

Epilogue. The Long Trail of Old Europe and Its Aftermath in Western Civilization ... 221

Bibliography ... 225

Index ... 237

Introduction
Athens: Cradle of Democracy?

Every generation has to connect with its heritage from antiquity in its own way. Over and over again stereotyping views about how people of the modern age absorbed the achievements of the ancients, of the Greeks and Romans, are repeated in school education and in university courses. It is high time to abandon outworn teachings and to adopt a new vision of antiquity, and to reconsider the long-standing influence of classical culture on the western world. New findings and insights in classical studies, in archaeology and in historical linguistics call for a recognition of the achievements of pre–Greek cultures from which the ancient Greeks profited.

One of the major prerequisites of a critical revision is the development of a fresh and balanced approach to the exploration of the fabric of Greek civilization and its major institutions, of which democratic governance is one. Such an approach is presented in this study, with the intention to outline the contours of a new paradigm for the study of antiquity. For this purpose, a data bank has been established by the author, with information on the language and the cultural features of the pre–Greek population. The rich material of this data bank provides the basis for the construction of new knowledge about intercultural relations in antiquity.

The Western canon of political history advocates the notion that democracy is an invention of the ancient Greeks who blessed the world with a novel model of governance. Was the democracy that was introduced in the fifth century BCE an invention? If democracy were a true invention then this form of governance would deserve to be called a product of Greek ingenuity. The impulses for this kind of political rule could come neither from ancient Egypt (with its pharaohs and their absolute power) nor from Mesopotamia (with its autocratic rulers from Babylon and Assyria). If we can rule out foreign influence from outside Europe, did the idea for citizen participation in political decision-making originate in the sociocultural environment of the Greek settlements or was there perhaps an older tradition that the Greeks continued and elaborated? This is in fact the case. But from whom could the Greeks possibly have inherited democratic rule?

The canon of Western thought has it that the impulses could not possibly have come from the past because the only known form of governance of the ancients was kingship, like in the Mycenaean city states of the second millennium BCE. Seemingly, the circle is closed and the only conclusion that is left points in the direction of classical antiquity shining with the ingenuity of those who created Greek civilization. This assessment of the idea of democracy and its implementation as a Greek invention, given by representatives of the movement of Enlightenment, has dominated European historiography and political reasoning since the eighteenth century. However, this is a myth, and there is good reason to set out on a quest in search of the reality behind this myth.

When the early Greek tribes settled what came to be called Hellas, they encountered the Pelasgians, descendants of the ancient indigenous population (i.e., the Palaeo-Europeans or native Europeans) who, with respect to their culture and language, differed markedly from the immigrating Greeks. The newcomers absorbed much of the ancient knowledge of the pre–Greek population and the impact of the culture of the ancients on Greek civilization became manifested in the transfer of advanced technologies and of markers of high culture, for example, the know-how of wine cultivation, smelting techniques in metallurgy, architecture, shipbuilding, ancient rituals and theatrical performances. The Greeks assimilated many expressions associated with the arts and crafts, in the process of their adoption. Those borrowed terms of pre–Greek origin were integrated in the lexical structures of ancient Greek and, in Greek transformation, they were transferred to the cultural vocabulary of our modern languages. Among those linguistic indicators of the pre–Greek substratum are well-known terms such as *anchor, aroma, olive, ceramics, chemistry, chimney, mechanics, metal, hymn, lyre, myth, psyche, theater, wine* and others.

The Greeks also became familiar with the system of communal self-administration and land lease that was practiced by the Pelasgians. At the time when Cleisthenes (born ca. 570 BCE; date of death unknown), through his reforms, established democratic rule in Athens (in 507 BCE) he could model this form of government on the traditional system of self-governance in the village communities, the demes (*demoi* in Greek). Knowledge-construction based on communal experience became essential for Cleisthenes's reforms. Cleisthenes was well aware that the model of communal governance practiced by the villagers had stood the test of time. Whether he was conscious or not that the administrative system of the demes was a heritage from the pre–Greek era is a question still unanswered.

Innumerable studies have been published on the emergence of Greek democracy and most of them follow the mainstream of Western thought since the Age of Enlightenment in the eighteenth century, that is, advocating the notion of democracy as a Greek innovation. For instance, Josiah Ober elaborates on "democracy and knowledge" (2008) in a way as to unilaterally associate the concept of knowledge-construction with purely Greek thought and experience. Seemingly, Ober is not aware of the perseverance of pre–Greek traditions which shaped knowledge-construction in Greek antiquity to a remarkable extent. Equally one-sided is Charlotte Higgins's recent approach that culminates in a generalizing statement about the impact of "Greek" civilization on our modern culture: "It's all Greek to me" (2010). As to her verdict caution is called for, and, in response, a more sophisticated view may be offered as a corrective: "Not all is Greek that looks like Greek."

If we take democracy as a starting point for our investigation of Greek civilization we soon become aware that the origins of this institution cannot be rightly understood in isolation from other institutions of Greek antiquity. The functioning of democratic governance was part of a network of social and cultural activities in ancient Greek society. Those who engage in the study of Greek democracy are advised to analyze the whole range of cultural patterns that participated in the formation of Greekness. It is the scope of this book to highlight the pre–Greek sources of Greek civilization and to illuminate how the idea and practice of democratic governance are rooted in the social order of pre–Greek society. The network of pre–Greek traditions that gave profile to Greek institutions is much more extensive than what is known so far. Of the many facets of Greek civilization that have had a bearing on our modern cultures, the idea and practice of democracy are perhaps the most visible signs of perpetuation.

In our days, democracy is the most widespread, the most popular and the most debated model of governance in the world. The current economic and financial crisis makes us pause and revise the potential of democratic governance. There are those who call for more democracy, for more direct participation of citizens in democratic decision-making, for more public transparency of political processes, for more public control over financial resources. And there are others who favor the option of less democracy in a sense as to streamline government decision-making by reducing the authority of democratic bodies such as the parliament to interfere, to minimize state control of private business and financial markets and to practice an overall liberal policy with less control over the economy, either by state or communities. It turns out that democratic rule encounters manifold quandaries and pitfalls that make this business rather cumbersome.

In view of the heavy burden that an inflated bureaucracy puts on governmental management in populous states such as India, the USA or Russia, it seems that we have touched the ceiling with what can be achieved with a democratic order. The question so far has remained unanswered as to whether we will be able to master the economic and financial challenges that we are facing—given the limitations, set by the democratic mechanism, for the range of action of governments in individual states—or whether we will fail in backing up majority decisions and in making their contents come to bear. Nobody can yet foresee whether or not democracy, as we know it, has a chance to survive into future generations. Anyway, we can hardly escape the insight that a famous dictum about democracy, given in recent history, holds true. According to Winston Churchill, democracy is "the worst form of government except all those other forms that have been tried from time to time" (*Hansard*, November 11, 1947).

In the history of governance democratic rule did not persist uninterruptedly. In many countries where it was once introduced, it disappeared after a while and, in some states, it was renewed in modern times. According to the canon of Western education since the Age of Enlightenment the ancient Greeks are credited with the introduction of democracy. Democratic rule in the Athenian state lasted not even two centuries before the Macedonians took over power in Athens and, thereafter, the city was ruled by Macedonian kings (Osborne 1996: 292*ff*). Later, the status of the Greek regions changed from that of Roman colonies to that of provinces under Byzantine imperial rule. The Ottoman Turks kept Greece in a tight colonial grip until the Greeks, in the war of independence of 1823, freed themselves of foreign sovereignty. It is noteworthy, though, that the newly formed Greek state which was acknowledged in 1832 was a kingdom, not a democracy in the style of classical antiquity. The reintroduction of democratic governance in Greece is a phenomenon of the modern age.

There is only one state in the world where democratic governance has persisted once it had been introduced. This is true for the USA. The Constitution of 1789 has been in force ever since, albeit with alterations in the form of 27 amendments of later periods. During a longer span of time, democracy in the consolidating USA was a matter of white people— of white male citizens, to be correct. Women's suffrage (i.e., the right to vote) was secured by the 19th amendment of the Constitution as late as 1920. The USA was not the first country to grant women the right to vote. New Zealand (1893), Australia (1902; explicitly excluding Aboriginal women who have been allowed to vote since 1962), Finland (1906) and other countries were forerunners in this regard.

In the early decades of democratic history in North America, society in the USA shared with ancient Athenian democracy a highly undemocratic property: the "right" of citizens to slaveholding. The former African American slaves were freed as late as the 1860s, and the indigenous peoples of the USA, the Amerindians, had to wait even longer before they were considered equal U.S. citizens. An Equal Rights Amendment of the Constitution is still pending.

The fact that democratic order has persisted in the USA may be, to some extent, due to the high degree of public representation of those who initiated the movement in the 1770s and to their memory in American historiography (Barthelmas 2003). There were numerous attempts, in the Americas (Peru, New Granada/Colombia, Haiti) and in Europe (the Netherlands, Switzerland, Ireland, Italy, Spain, the Rhineland) between 1770 and 1810, to set in motion revolutionary mechanisms. But they all differed significantly from the U.S. model.

> Except for the American Revolution which followed a different pattern, all these revolutions were orchestrated by tiny batches of mostly strikingly unrepresentative editors, orators, pamphleteers, and professional agitators or renegade nobles, like Mirabeau and Volney—and practically never businessmen, lawyers, or office-holders. These entirely unrepresentative intellectuals captured a mass following by seizing on and amplifying popular protest arising from widespread discontent into a formidable political force. The leaders of the French Revolution of 1788–92 were socially completely marginal, and heterogeneous as well as unrepresentative; all they had in common was their ideological standpoint, and here the "revolution of reason" was strikingly cohesive, especially after the pro–British, anti-*philosophique* moderate *monarchiens*—great devotees of moderate Enlightenment—were ousted from the National Assembly in October 1789 [Israel 2012: 15*f*].

The attitude of the representatives of the anti–British campaign striving for independence in North America was not unanimous with respect to their evaluation of the Greek model of democracy. Some emphasized the weaknesses of Athenian democracy: the exclusion of women from public affairs, politics as the business of "unChristian" slaveholders and, the hero cult, the excessive self-glorification of the Greeks in their military campaigns. Others hailed Athenian democracy as a haven of virtues such as the love of liberty. The perspective of American intellectuals of the eighteenth century differed markedly from that of their European contemporaries, and this for good reason.

> What Americans heard about classical Athens would inevitably carry a special valence, for unlike eighteenth-century Europeans concerned about the possible decadence of their large nation-states, Americans shared with the inhabitants of Renaissance Italy a real opportunity to resurrect the classical polis. They decided against it. There was no lack of glowing generalizations about ancient states in eighteenth-century America. William Smith maintained that the history of Greece and Rome might justly be called "the History of Heroism, Virtue and Patriotism"; John Adams insisted that the best governments of the world had all been mixed and cited Greece, Rome, and Carthage as examples. Levi Hart praised the "public spirited, patriotic men whose hearts glowed with the love of liberty" to whom the great states of classical antiquity owed their stature. Under scrutiny, however, the eventual collapse of all the ancient states was alleged against them, most particularly in Greece, and still more particularly in Athens [Roberts 1994: 179].

Switzerland is commonly considered to be the European country with the oldest, still functioning tradition of democratic rule. However, there is considerable confusion as to the date when this tradition came into existence. The old Helvetian Confederation was no democracy. It was a union of regional states that were each governed by aristocratic élites. The first Helvetian Republic was founded in 1798, as a "daughter republic" according to the French model. This republic was dissolved in 1803. Thus, the democratic tradition was interrupted and only reinstated at a later date. The Confoederatio Helvetica was established, as a federal state with democratic governance, in 1848. The Swiss Constitution has been extensively reconstructed twice (in 1874 and 1999). For the longest time in the history of the Helvetian Confederation, women had no right to vote or be voted in elections. In a plebiscite of 1971, women were granted the right to vote and to become active political citizens. It took as late as 1990 until this right was implemented in all cantons of the country (Mesmer 2007).

In many other countries, democracy made its appearance in earlier stages of history, but its existence was only temporary. Democratic governance was practiced in medieval Novgorod (Kljuchevskij 1994). There, democracy was ousted and tsarist rule established once the city had been conquered by the Muscovite state in 1478. Russia saw the reemergence of democracy as late as 1991 when the former Soviet Union was dissolved and the new Russian state came into being. Although only an intermezzo of political history, democratic rule was exercised in Italy at different times, and it was always abandoned and substituted by kingship or imperial autocratic rule. The Roman Republic lasted from ca. 470 to 27 BCE when Augustus assumed power as the first Roman emperor. In medieval Italy, democracy was exercised in various city states such as Amalfi, Pisa, Genoa, and Venice (Bragadin 2010). The Republic of Venice, called La Serenissima, ceased to exist after Napoleon had conquered the city in 1797. To the great disappointment of Garibaldi who led the insurgents in the wars of unification and who became the hero of the Italian national movement, the national state of the Italians, in 1861, chose a king to be its leader. In Italy, democracy is a phenomenon of the twentieth century.

France is another example for a tradition of democratic governance with interruptions. The Revolution of 1789 brought about a radical political change, with the abolition of kingship and the introduction of a democratic rule. The protagonists of the revolutionary movement modeled the new order according to the organization of the Roman Republic, modeled on the Athenian democracy. The spirit of the old Roman Republic that had been celebrated by Roman historians such as Livy and Tacitus also inspired the revolutionaries who overthrew the Ancien Régime in France.

> This idealized version of the Roman Republic was the Rome appropriated by the revolutionaries. Robespierre's often extravagant rhetoric extended to a self-aggrandizing and self-pitying comparison of himself with the Gracchi, two brothers famous as populist agrarian reformers in the Roman Republic, whose death by violence he accurately predicted for himself. François-Emile Babeuf, another revolutionary politician and conspirator, adopted the name Caius Gracchus and called himself "Tribun du peuple," recalling the office of tribunus plebis, tribune of the plebs or people, held by both Caius Sempronius Gracchus and his older brother Tiberius Sempronius Gracchus. This was more than an empty gesture: Babeuf advocated a "protocommunist" system of modified land distribution which derived from the proposals of the Gracchi [Vance 1997: 24*f*].

As in Greek and Roman antiquity, in the French democratic system, there was no place for women as active citizens. One of the activists of the revolutionary movement, Olympe de Gouges, publicized a "Déclaration des droits de la femme et de la citoyenne" ("Declaration of Rights of the Woman and Female Citizen") in 1791. The male members of the National Assembly opposed and spun an intrigue against her. Olympe was accused of treason, put on trial, sentenced to death, and her life ended under the guillotine in 1793 (Scott 1996). She was not the only woman who engaged in politics. There were other women "who risked their lives in the American and French revolutions, only to discover the patriarchal character of the Enlightenment, which was never meant for them" (Spretnak 1997: 225). French women remained barred from politics until 1946 when their right to vote became anchored in the French Constitution.

Napoleon interrupted the course of democratic governance in France when he declared himself emperor in 1804. After Napoleon had been forced into exile in 1815, the Ancien Régime (Old Regime)—the Bourbon monarchy—was restored. The state of the French tilted between republic and empire, and the principles of state rule shifted several times. In 1958, the Fifth Republic replaced the weak Fourth Republic. A marker of modern French democracy is the strong mandate for the presidency.

Democratic governance is known from history books to have been devised by the ancient Greeks. In 1993, the 2,500th anniversary of the birth of democracy was lavishly celebrated, with a banquet in London's Guildhall, organized by the Classical Society. It is true that, in 507 BCE, Cleisthenes carried out radical reforms which included a reorganization of the tribal system and of the demes (village communities) as the basic political unit. Cleisthenes put a model of governance to work that lasted for 185 years before it was abandoned and autocratic rule reinstated. There had been kings and tyrants ruling before the time of Cleisthenes, and kings and tyrants ruled after the demise of democracy. And yet, there must have been something very special about this model of governance that, more than two thousand years later, Europeans started to look back to antiquity and Athenian democracy in nostalgia.

Since the Age of Enlightenment and the two successful revolutions—the declaration of independence of the former British colonies in North America in 1776 and the French revolution of 1789—democracy has been celebrated as an icon, as the megasymbol of freedom. As for the origins of democracy, mythical ideas have flourished throughout the ages because "democracy, like any other movement, needs its founding myth. It needs an ancient pedigree and worthy heroes. And who could be more ancient or more worthy than Cleisthenes the Alcmaenid?" (Davies 1996: 131).

There are myths that carry the wisdom of the ancients, and there are myths that only tell fanciful stories. Which kind is the founding myth celebrating Cleisthenes as the father of democracy? There is good reason to look for the reality behind this myth. Those who search for earlier manifestations of democratic ideas will encounter Solon (ca. 630—558 BCE) and the reforms he devised in 594 BCE. However, it only took a few years before Solon's reforms were brushed aside and Peisistratus established himself as tyrant in Athens. For those who are unwilling to accept Cleisthenes as the father of democracy Solon may appear to be a better candidate for this role. Anyway, whether Cleisthenes or Solon, we are left with the sixth century BCE as the period when democracy was introduced. Perhaps we have to do with two variants of a founding myth, and there are worthy heroes in both.

Democracy in antiquity is not the only institution of Western civilization whose beginnings have been associated with a certain timeframe as to become conventional knowledge, transmitted through education and scholarship. Another such institution is the English parliament, its origins traditionally dated to the thirteenth century. Since we live in a time when ever more attention is paid to long-term processes of cultural evolution and sociopolitical advancement, it is not surprising that the exploration of the past is yielding insights that call for a revision of earlier assessments. Recently, the date for the beginnings of the English parliament has been revised.

> Modern writing on the origins of the English parliament generally takes the thirteenth century as its starting point. It was then that the word moved into common usage, while the thing itself acquired its later constitution of king, lords, and commons within a comparable pan–European context of rising representative institutions. This study has taken a different (...) approach in attempting to show that parliament's ultimate origins lay much further back, with the great assemblies which first appeared under Aethelstan in the tenth century and which may in turn, like so many early English institutions, have had Carolingian antecedents [Maddicott 2010: 440].

How about democracy? When searching for the cultural heritage of those who exercised democracy before the Greeks we make the encounter of the ancient cultures of the Bronze Age, those that are still older than the Mycenaean-Greek city states. Actually, in order to reach the stage when democratic governance came into being, we have to dig still deeper into the layers of pre–Greek history. The search for the origins of democracy takes us into the Neolithic and Copper Ages of southeastern Europe which span several millennia, from the seventh to the fourth millennia BCE.

To those who adhere to the canon of Western cultural history, this search for prolonged continuity of a major Western institution may sound strange. Skeptics may defy any association of any Greek institution with ancient pre–Greek cultures in the region claiming that the knowledge about Bronze Age history is too scarce to allow comparisons, not to speak of cultural continuity from older ages. In fact, the Bronze Age is no longer dark, as it was still half a century ago (Runnels and Murray 2001). The same is true for the Copper Age, and research on the culture of the early Neolithic agriculturalists in Europe has been extensive. During the past two decades new information about the ancient cultures has been produced by archaeology, anthropology and other disciplines, and many new insights call for a revision of stereotyping notions and for the construction of new knowledge about pre–Greek cultures (Bintliff 2012: 46*ff*).

Neolithic society in southeastern Europe has been intensely investigated and novel findings about the governance of agrarian communities facilitate the reconstruction of continuity of social patterns from ancient times through antiquity. The trail of democratic rule in the village communities of Greece in the sixth century BCE starts from communal self-administration in the Neolithic settlements. The spirit of social solidarity in village communities of the old days persisted into Greek antiquity (Haarmann 2013a).

This is a big claim that demands substantial evidence and this will be produced in this study. The trail of democratic governance that will be mapped out here is no isolated phenomenon of continuity. In fact, the infrastructure of ancient Greek civilization is permeated with elements from pre–Greek times. In a wide array of domains, from agriculture to metalworking and religion, pre–Greek influence can be documented. The features and activities of the goddess Athena, herself of pre–Greek origin, may serve as an allegory for the multifaceted legacy from earlier periods of cultural history. In all the domains of activity that are highlighted for Athena in Greek mythology, pre–Greek heritage is manifested, starting with olive cultivation which, according to myth, was introduced by Athena to the people of Attica and of which the goddess is hailed as patron. Vital functions of democratic governance are also linked to Athena (see Chapter 7). How this is all intertwined and functioning as a network of mutual relationships under the overarching cover of democratic governance will be highlighted in the following.

The influx from pre–Greek times fused with genuinely Greek traditions and, in the cultural memory of the ancient Greeks, formed an organic whole that we know as classical

Greek civilization. And yet, the Greeks themselves were aware that they owed much of their cultural achievements to their predecessors who had lived in Greece before them. The Greeks called the pre-Greek population of Greece Pelasgians, and there are accounts in early Greek historiography (i.e., in the *Histories* of Herodotus) how the Pelasgians assimilated to Greek language and became Hellenes in the process. The Pelasgians represented the youngest cultural stage of what had persisted since the Neolithic, and they became mediators between the world of Old Europe and the era of Hellas. Seemingly, democracy is the best known of the Greek institutions and, at the same time, the one of whose pre-Greek origins we are still ignorant.

In order to perceive the magnitude of cultural fusion that occurred during the Bronze Age, the democratic tradition has to be illuminated in light of the mainstream of continuity from Old Europe to classical antiquity. In his/her quest to pinpoint stages of this fusion the modern observer will encounter many elements that our education tells us are Greek and the names for which look Greek. And yet, in a new perspective of cultural chronology, these elements are much older and date to pre-Greek times. The investigation of the fusion in question leads us to conclude that Greek civilization of antiquity was a true mosaic culture that was comprised of many different components, partly genuinely Greek and to a great extent foreign that were assimilated and integrated. The foreign elements obviously had a quality that made them worth adopting and, within Greek culture, these elements added to the useful knowledge on which Greek society of the archaic period could draw to elaborate the sophisticated civilization of the classical age.

Among the experiences that the Greeks distilled from the heritage of their predecessors was the principle of communal self-governance (Haarmann 2013a: *69ff*). Since this principle had been functioning from the Neolithic era onward, it had proved its usefulness already at the time when the early Greeks became acquainted with it. In the Greek village communities (demes), the guidelines for communal administration persisted as they had been practiced by the pre-Greek population, the Pelasgians. The ancient Greeks were aware of the usefulness of the democratic principle and their view was in concord with a mindset that is known from the Navajo Indians who bring it to the point in their assessment of the essence of life: *sa'ah naagháí bike's hózhóón*, "the beauty of life created by application of teachings that work."

1

European Tradition Versus Afrocentrism

The Reality Behind the Myth of "Black Athena"

The Greeks did not found Athens. This city is much older. The date of the foundation of Athens is not certain. Archaeological evidence for human presence on the Acropolis and in nearby areas points to the fourth millennium BCE but there may have been a small settlement already in the fifth millennium BCE. Anyway, the beginnings of Athens predate the coming of the Greeks by more than one thousand years. Athens is not just any Greek settlement. It is the one that is studied best of all, and, in its long history, a continuum of inhabited space over thousands of years is reflected, from the late Copper Age up to the present (Antonaccio 1994: 100). For the longest span of time of its history Athens has offered a space for Greek culture to unfold, a culture that experienced its formative period under the immense impact of the culture of the pre–Greek population that inhabited many places where Greeks later settled, Athens for one. The impact of the older culture was channeled via social contacts of the Greeks with their predecessors, and this was true not only for Athens but for the whole region that became known as Attica in antique sources.

The Greeks did not record their own history in a way modern historians do. When the father of Greek historiography, Herodotus (ca. 484–424 BCE), compiled his *Histories*, his accounts about the early history of the Greeks were in the form of myths. The ancient Greeks did not know anything for sure about the remote times when their ancestors interacted with the indigenous people. And yet, the Greeks were aware that they followed certain ancient customs that they had adopted from the native Europeans whom they called Pelasgoi ("those living in the neighborhood; neighbors," derived from *pelas*, "nearby"). The indigenous Athenians, the Pelasgoi, worshipped various local divinities, and the Greeks continued their cults. In Athens, there were several goddesses, and these divine figures fused into one which was mighty Athena. In the Greek name of the city, the multiplicity of divinities is still recognizable: Athenai (plural form of Athena, literally "the Athenas").

The major place to worship Athena was the Acropolis, the high rock formation that dominates the view over the city. The name by which we know this place, Acropolis, is a composite name (i.e., *akros*, "highest, topmost" + *polis*, "city," corresponding to English "uptown" or German *Hochstadt*). The rock formation in the central part of Athens has been called Acropolis since the fourth century BCE. But this is not the oldest name. The native Europeans had their own name for it, and they called it Krana(a) "the rock." One of the names for Athens that is found in antique sources is Kranaa polis ("rocky city" or "city of the rock"). The Athenians were sometimes called Kranaoi "the rock people," and an adjectival

The Acropolis of Athens (aerial view) (photograph by Nikos Daniilidis).

form (i.e., *kranaos*, "hard, rocky") is preserved in ancient Greek (Beekes 2010: 770). So, for the ancients the Acropolis was known as "THE rock" or "the Sacred Rock" (Valavanis 2013: 18). In Greek mythology, the name of one of the mythical kings of Athens is given as Kranaos (Gantz 1993: 234). In the cultural memory of the Greeks the old name is still resounding, and it has been revived in various contexts (e.g., in the name of a publisher, "Krene" Editions, in Athens).

When the pre–Greek sources of Greek civilization will be mapped out in the following, Athens and the Athenian city-state are in the focus of attention. The significance of the city and of the historical region of Attica is paramount for the formation of civic institutions in Greek antiquity and for the Greeks' appreciation of ancient traditions. There are many reasons for the outstanding role of Athens.

> Athens stands out because of a number of related factors: the exceptional size of the city (at least a quarter of a million people in the whole of Attica, the area around Athens), its unusual wealth (not just from tribute paid by other Greeks in the fifth century, but from its rich silver mines, and the situation of its port, Piraeus, as an important entrepôt), its military power, its unparalleled erection of inscriptions, its attraction as a cultural center, and the canonization of the city and its writers by later Greeks and Romans [Johnstone 2011: 8].

Athena as Multi-Talented Patron of a Mosaic Culture

Athena had already been residing on the Acropolis when the Indo-European migrants arrived and settled down because "the common name of the city and the goddess is certainly prehellenic" (Valavanis 2013: 11). That means that Athena was a pre–Greek divinity whose cult the Greeks took over from the Pelasgians. In reality, the Greeks joined the Pelasgians in their worship, and they continued to venerate Athena after the Pelasgians had assimilated and ceased to exist as a distinct ethnic group. In mythology, the goddess Athena chose the Greeks as her people, arranged for them to have a strong king and she became the patron of the city and of all of Attica. On a metaphorical level, Athena's persistence from ancient times onward can be seen as reflecting the persistence of a cultural current that did not disintegrate under the overlay of Greek customs and preferences.

In Greek myths—as in literature and in public life—competition assumed a pivotal role for the direction of progress, and this also extended to the world of the gods (Fisher and van Wees 2011: 85*ff*). Pre-Greek Athena won a competition over a strong Indo-European opponent, which was Poseidon. According to myth, Kekrops, the first mythical king of Athens to rule the city, had challenged Athena and Poseidon to engage in a competition about who could offer the Athenians the best gift. Athena made an olive tree sprout on the slope of the Acropolis and taught the Greeks the know-how of olive cultivation. Poseidon, in turn, offered the Athenians the horse, the typical animal of the Indo-European pastoralists. Kekrops decided that Athena's gift was worth more than Poseidon's horse (Gantz 1993: 234). So Athena became the unrivaled mistress of the city. Oil from the sacred tree was given as a prize to the victors in the competitions on the occasion of the great festival, the Panathenaia.

> In a dramatic gesture, the most coveted prize at the Panathenaia is sacred olive oil which continues to flow from the original moment when Athens' autochthonous king-founder adjudicated between Poseidon and Athena and found in favour of the goddess. The very token of Panathenaic victory is thus not only a materially valuable object for the victor, but the political capital for the Athenian *polis* of oil from the very trees which literally sprouted from Kekrops' judgment [Brown 2012: 148].

As the patron of olive cultivation, the goddess Athena was revered as Athena Moria. The association of olive cultivation with a pre–Greek divinity is conclusive since this domain of agriculture was already practiced by the native Europeans and later adopted by the Greeks (see Chapter 2).

In the cultural memory of the Greeks, Athena's status was conceived as that of a primordial goddess who had resided on the Acropolis since times immemorial. Indeed, Athena forms part of the mythical substratum which had been functioning before the arrival of the Greeks. A linguistic sign of the high age of the goddess cult in the region is reflected in her name: the suffix -*n* in Athena is a pre–Greek formative element (Katičić 1976: 51). Pre-Greek origin is attested linguistically also in the word designating the olive, *elaia*, for which no Indo-European cognate root can be given. Athena is known as the virgin goddess who never marries and remains without a child of her own. Although unmarried Athena gets along well with men and even helps them with their endeavor. For instance, she gives Odysseus advice how to build his ship. The epithet intrinsically linked to the goddess is *parthenos* which means "young unmarried woman." The origin of this word is as pre–Greek as is the name (i.e., Athena) with which it is associated (Beekes 2010: 1153).

The most typical attribute of Athena is the owl. There were various species of owls in ancient Greece and they all have their own name. Athena's owl was not any of those owls but only a certain species, of small size. The name for this little owl is *glaux* in ancient Greece, and the close association of this particular species shows in the scientific name given in Latin (i.e., Athene noctua). Since the name of the goddess is of pre–Greek coinage, it can hardly be surprising to learn that a pre–Greek lexical root has been identified for *glaux*. In addition to *glaux*, other derivatives from this borrowed root can be found in the Greek vocabulary, for instance *glaukos* ("blueish, green color"). In epic literature and poetry, Athena is described as "owl-eyed" (*glaukopis*), which may have referred both to the color of her eyes and to her sharp gaze. In the *Iliad* and in the *Odyssey* this attribute (i.e., owl-eyed) is referred to dozens of times.

Identifying the Pre-Greek Population, Their Area of Settlement and Their Language

Indo-European (Helladic) tribes who arrived from the north "merged with the indigenous population, which tradition holds were the Pelasgians" (Servi 2011: 12). The newcomers settled down in what was called Hellas in antiquity, and they became the neighbors of those people who had inhabited the land before them. Those people whom the Greeks encountered upon their arrival were the descendants of the indigenous European population, the Palaeo-Europeans. Already in antiquity, there was an awareness among the Greeks that their predecessors were not akin to them. Herodotus (writing his nine-volume *Histories* in the fifth century BCE), called the father of historiography, was the first to state that the Pelasgians were non–Greek and that the Athenians descended from them.

> Herodotus not only elides the autochthony myth—the basis of many Athenian essentialist claims—but also reports that the Athenians were originally Pelasgian (I.57–58).... The Pelasgians are judged to be barbarians on the basis of their language, which according to Herodotus is non–Greek [Lape 2010: 152*f*].

In a more general view, Herodotus points to Pelasgian origins for all Greeks except the Dorians (*Histories* I.56.3–58). This may be paraphrased as meaning that Herodotus was conscious of the wide spread of the pre–Greek population in the regions of Hellas. Language is a prominent vehicle of culture and Herodotus perceives language shift as a major marker in the assimilation process of the pre–Greek population into the community of Greek-speaking people. "If therefore all the Pelasgians (spoke) this way [that is, their own language], then the Attic people (*to Attikon ethnos*), being Pelasgic, must have changed their language too at the time when they became part of the Hellenes" (*Histories* I.57.3).

The native European (Pelasgian) population left many traces of their former existence, and not only an extensive layer of lexical borrowings in ancient Greek (see Chapter 2). Modern human genetics has managed to pinpoint the gene pool of the pre–Greek population which extends on both sides of the Aegean Sea. The people that lived there left their genetic "fingerprints," and these testify to an ethnic identity distinct from that in surrounding areas. In the genetic map, a distinct genomic profile is discernible which the geneticists call the "Mediterranean outlier" in southeastern Europe, with its core area on both sides of the Aegean Sea and with gradients extending into Ukraine (Cavalli-Sforza 1996: 63). This is a so-called local genetic "outlier" because it differs markedly from surrounding patterns.

In his archaeological and cultural interpretation of genotypes, Cavalli-Sforza relates the Mediterranean genotype to the geographical dispersal of the Greek population during the period of colonization in the eastern Mediterranean, that is, to the early first millennium BCE. This assumption is repeated in Cavalli-Sforza (2000: 119*f*). However, on closer inspection of the geographical profile of this genetic outlier, it becomes apparent that the contours of the Mediterranean genotype do not coincide with the historical boundaries of the Greek population.

The area covered by the inner genetic gradient of the genotype (1) extends far beyond the geographical limits of historical Greek settlement. Greeks never settled in regions located in present-day Serbia, Albania or Bosnia-Hercegovina; they never settled inland in Bulgaria or Romania and only established colonies on the coast; they did not settle as far east as central Anatolia either, though the inner gradient extends that far eastward. Even in the western part of Anatolia, on the eastern coast of the Aegean Sea, the Greek population was concentrated in urban centers and settled in rural areas only in very small numbers. But the genetic profile of the region must have been shaped by a large population.

Taking the spread of the second gradient of the genetic outlier (2), the assumed connection of the Mediterranean genotype with Greek settlement becomes even more improbable. Furthermore, what explanation could there be for the radical difference between the Greek genotype and the genetic profiles of the neighboring Indo-European populations other than that the former represented a substantial substratum in a region of divergent ethnic stock? A comparison with the profiles of other principal genetic components shows that the gradients which cover the southern Pontic zone form a consistent belt stretching on either side of the Bosporus, without any significant profile of the Greek stock occurring (see Cavalli-Sforza et al. 1994: 292*ff*).

There is a more plausible explanation for the geographical spread of this genotype and this is that it reflects the stratum of the pre–Greek population. In all probability, the Mediterranean genotype documents the density of ancient non–Indo-European settlements in the Balkans and in Greece. From an anthropological perspective, it becomes apparent that the population around the Aegean Sea on the European side and on the Asian side of the southern Pontic zone (that is the area bordering the southern coast of the Black Sea) was ethnically homogeneous, which does not exclude the possibility of cultural and/or linguistic diversity.

Indo-European populations moved into parts of these areas during the third millennium BCE and, to some extent, the migration movement can be traced archaeologically. The final result, the set-

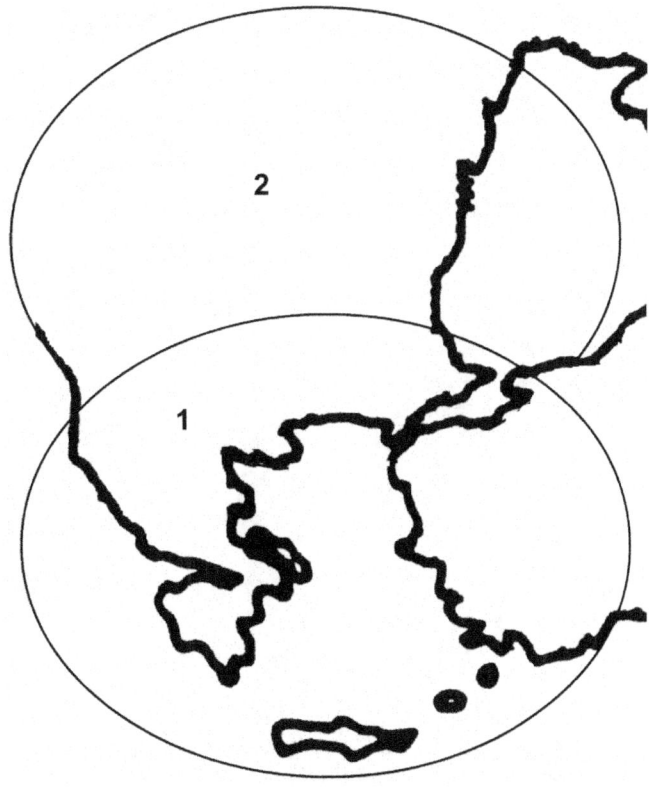

The core area of the Mediterranean genotype (author's collection).

Above and opposite: Ancient settlements and historical landscapes in mainland Greece, Asia Minor and in the Aegean archipelago: (a) Mainland Greece and western Aegean; (b) Eastern Aegean and western coast of Asia Minor (originally published in *Greece and the Hellenistic world*, edited by John Boardman, Jasper Griffin and Oswyn Murray. Oxford: Oxford University Press, 1988. Used by permission of Oxford University Press).

tlements of the early Greeks, is known from historical times and comparative studies of ancient Greek dialects allow some assumptions about early tribal divisions. It is not easy to include all the necessary data (illustrating the physical nature of the landscape as well as features of the settled space) for an overall view of the Greek cultural sphere. In the academic literature one finds excellent maps of the physical properties of Greece (e.g., in Isager and Skydsgaard 1995: 12 and 13), and there are many maps available which illustrate the distribution of settlements, either on a smaller scale—that is, focusing on mainland Greece (e.g., in Fine 1983 or Barringer 2008: 10)—or on a larger scale—that is, surveying Greek city-states and colonies around the Mediterranean and the Black Sea (e.g., in Osborne 1996: 120).

Those maps where physical features of the geographical regions, the division of historical landscapes and the distribution of settlements (distinguishing between political centers, city-states, and rural settlements) are integrated, are rare exceptions, such as the one found in the handbook edited by Boardman et al. (1988).

In addition to their genetic "fingerprints" the Palaeo-European population of southeastern Europe left linguistic traces of their presence. The non–Indo-European elements which can be identified in the names of places (toponymy), rivers (hydronymy) and phenomena of the natural environment form part of the most ancient onomastic residue. Characteristic of the onomastic roots of non–Indo-European origin are certain suffixes (i.e., *-ss*, *-nd*, *-nth*). The formative element *-ss* is common to all these names: Assa (Macedonia), Bubassos (Caria), Passa (Thrace), Sardessos (Troad), Termessos (Pisidia), Kabassos (Lycia), Larissa (Thessaly), etc. (Otkupshchikov 1973: 7*ff*, 20*ff*).

Certain onomastic roots occur in names on either side of the Aegean:

European side	Asian side
Alos (Thessaly)	Alinda (Caria)
Bargos (Illyria)	Bargasa (Caria)
Kurba (Crete)	Kurbasa (Caria)
Leba (Macedonia)	Lebinthos (Caria)
Oinoe (Attica)	Oinoanda (Lycia)
Passa (Thrace)	Passanda (Caria)
Prinos (Argolid)	Prinassos (Caria)
Sardos (Illyria)	Sardessos (Troad)
Sindos (Macedonia)	Sinda (Pisidia)
Tegea (Arcadia)	Tegessos (Cyprus)

In an onomastic survey of the wider Aegean region, the distribution of names containing these formative elements points to a balanced dispersal in Europe and Asia. In the Aegean archipelago and in the Balkans, we find a total of 181 names compared with 175 names in Asia Minor. A high concentration of these pre–Greek names can be observed in the historical areas of Caria, Crete, Thrace, Thessaly, Macedonia and Troy. The onomastic material of pre–Greek origin is most evident on the islands and in the coastal areas of the Aegean Sea, e.g., Arakynthos (names of mountains in Aetolia, Boeotia and Attica), Tiryns (gen. Tirynthos, town in Argolis), Titaresios (river in Thessaly), Ordymnos (mountain on Lesbos), Mykonos (island in the Cyclades), Kameiros (city on Rhodos), and Skiathos (island in the Cyclades) (Katičić 1976: 42*ff*).

It is noteworthy that the pre–Greek names include many designations for towns and cities.

> From this fact can be concluded that the speakers of Greek found at their arrival the Aegean urbanization already in full development. This observation fits well with the inference from archaeological evidence according to which the first peak of urban life in the Aegean World was reached already in the Early Bronze Age, whereas Greek-speaking tribes invaded the area only at the beginning of the Middle Bronze Age [Katičić 1976: 55].

The Pelasgians spoke their own language and they had their own culture, and both were different from how the ancestors of the Greeks spoke and from their customs. Until recently, the investigation of Pelasgian language and culture was treated as a special field of Indo-European studies because the majority of scholars were convinced that the pre–Greek population of Greece must have been of Indo-European ethnic stock. Many attempts have been made to identify Pelasgian as a distinct branch of Indo-European while as many attempts have been made to deny this. The contributions of Georgiev (1966) and Hester (1966) are illustrative for the contradicting standpoints as manifested in the older literature. More recent documentation can be found in the discussion presented in a volume edited by Bammesberger and Vennemann (2004).

Those who adhere to the notion of Pelasgian being an old form of Indo-European in the Balkans assume a separate set of sound changes by which proto–Indo-European words would have developed to form the lexical elements of the Pelasgian vocabulary. The opponents of the Indo-European hypothesis point at the existence of formative elements (i.e., suffixes) that cannot be explained as stemming from Indo-European and to the fact that, in many of the pre–Greek lexical items, the assumed sound changes cannot be applied at all or are only manifested in a rather fragmentary way. And yet, despite insurmountable barriers separating the adherents of the two schools of scholarship, there seems to be agreement as to the identification of the pre–Greek stratum with a distinct ethnic group, that is, with the Pelasgians. "Such a people, as the speakers of the newly discovered Pre-Greek language have been, can ... very confidently be identified with the Pelasgians of ancient literature" (Katičić 1976: 77).

Those who advocate an Indo-European affiliation for Pelasgian have to deal with the problem of how to differentiate between a pre–Greek substratum of Pelasgian (i.e., Indo-European) origin and another layer of pre–Greek lexical borrowings in Greek that point to an indigenous non–Indo-European language which is identified under different names in the etymological dictionaries and scholarly literature, as Aegean, Mediterranean or Old European. None of the Indo-European scholars denies the independence and divergence of that ancient language from the Indo-European phylum.

In light of the hopeless reconstructions of an alleged Indo-European affiliation for Pelasgian, it is conclusive to identify this pre–Greek language as non–Indo-European, and this insight opens the path for a comparative investigation of Aegean and Pelasgian as affiliated languages. Ever more linguistic material has been collected and investigated which allows for a definite statement about the characteristic features of Pelasgian. Beekes, in the introduction to his monumental *Etymological dictionary of Greek* (2010: xlii), makes a categorical statement: "Pre-Greek is non–Indo-European." This scholar is not the first to make a case for Pelasgian being of Old European (i.e., non–Indo-European) affiliation, but he may be the last who has to do that. In another context, Beekes calls for the demise of the notion of Pelasgian as an Indo-European language:

> The "Pelasgian" theory has done much harm, and it is time to forget it. The latest attempt was Heubeck's "Minoisch-Mykenisch" (discussed by Furnée [1972] 55–66), where the material was reduced to some ten words; the theory has by now been tacitly abandoned [Beekes 2010: xvi].

Beekes has broadly documented the phonetic and morphological structures of the substrate language, based on a scrutinous analysis of the early lexical borrowings in ancient Greek. If Pelasgian, as a non–Indo-European language, is related to the linguistic layer of the indigenous Palaeo-European population then we can distinguish between an older form of Palaeo-European and a younger form which is Pelasgian. Roughly, the older form of Palaeo-European would represent the language of the early agrarian population in southeastern Europe and would be associated with the Neolithic and Copper Ages (i.e., spanning a period from the sixth to the fourth millennia BCE). The younger form of Palaeo-European, Pelasgian, would be associated with the people of the Bronze Age in the third and second millennia BCE. The transformation from the older to the younger form might have been a prolonged process that started already in the fourth millennium BCE.

The motivation for linguistic change may be sought in the sociopolitical turbulences resulting from the intrusions of people from the Eurasian steppe (Anthony 2007, Haarmann 2012). In a third wave of out-migrations that began in the late fourth millennium BCE, Indo-European pastoralists from the Eurasian steppe moved south and west. The movement lasted for several centuries and, during that period, the Indo-Europeans infiltrated into most of southeastern Europe and came to dominate the major areas where Old European civilization once flourished.

The changes of customs and religious life did not arise all of a sudden, and it is not reasonable to assume that the new social order would have completely replaced the older one. The pre–Indo-European civilization did not disintegrate under the Indo-European overlay, but patterns of a selective continuity are successively derived from the ancient foundations. This continuity is anchored in a kaleidoscope of domains, of material culture as well as in spiritual conceptualizations. Key technologies of crafts such as pottery, metallurgy, architecture, ship-building and others were adopted by the Greeks together with pertinent elements of their terminologies.

And this is true also for religious and spiritual concepts that persisted—via various transformations—into classical antiquity. In fact, "the Old European sacred images and symbols were never totally uprooted; these most persistent features in human history were too deeply implanted in the psyche" (Gimbutas 1989: 318). This statement made by Gimbutas is crucial because it points at the heart of the problem of cultural continuity in the horizon of time. It is noteworthy that, for the key term *psyche* ("life; vitality; soul") in ancient Greek, no cognate parallels can be found in other Indo-European languages. In addition to being isolated the phonetic structure of this expression points to pre–Greek origin (Beekes 2010: 1671*f*). This means that the idea of *psyche* had been conceptualized by the pre–Greek population and that the Indo-European immigrants to the region showed themselves impressed and adopted the idea together with the word for it from their predecessors.

How to Approach the Question of Foreign Influence During the Formative Process of Greek Culture? Separating Constructive Evidence from Untenable Speculations

Those who devoted themselves to the study of ancient Greece during the Age of Enlightenment soon became aware that Greek civilization is not homogeneous but comprised of different layers: an older one with roots in the remote past and a more modern one that was constructed on top of it.

It is known that the Germans discovered, at the dawn of speculative idealism and of romantic philology (in the last decade of the eighteenth century, at Jena, among Schlegel, Hölderlin, Hegel, and Schelling), that Greece, in reality, had been double: there had been a Greece of measure and of clarity, of theory and of art (in the proper sense of these terms), of "beautiful form," of virile, heroic rigor, of law, of the City, of the light of day; and a buried Greece, nocturnal, somber (or too blindly bright), the archaic, savage Greece of group rituals, of bloody sacrifices and collective intoxications, of the cult of the dead and of the Earth Mother—in short, a mystical Greece, on which the other, not without difficulty, was raised (through the "repression" of the mystical one), but which always remained silently present right up to the final collapse, particularly in tragedy and in the mystery religions [Lacoue-Labarthe and Nancy 1990: 300*f*].

What the intellectuals of the Age of Enlightenment could not know is that the two major layers in Greek civilization represent the elements from two different cultures that eventually fused into the organic whole we know as "Greek," or as Charlotte Higgins put it: "It's all Greek to me" (2010). It took well into the twentieth century before archaeology, historiography and historical linguistics managed to illuminate the characteristic features of the pre–Greek cultures of the Bronze Age and of the still older Copper Age. Those cultures contributed to the fabric of Greek civilization, and in ways reaching beyond the extension of the archaic layer that had already been noticed by representatives of the Enlightenment. To them all of Greek culture of the classical era was of purely Greek coinage, regardless of the age of its layers.

Since the Age of Enlightenment the academic discourse about the fabric of ancient Greek civilization has produced a kaleidoscope of diverse and contradicting approaches. What strikes the eye of anyone who follows the currents of scholarly investigation is the presence of covert ideological underpinnings in the statements about Greek antiquity and conclusions about the origins of major institutions of classical culture. The history of classical studies is illustrative of intellectual currents that are strongly oriented at the European zeitgeist of different periods.

In the early nineteenth century, the Hellenophiles—representatives of the Romantic movement—produced the stereotype of the Greek miracle, with the victory of logos over mythical thought, and the theoretical construct of Greek culture as of purely European coinage. Such Eurocentric ideas dominated the study of Greek philosophy and literature well into the twentieth century. Under the impression of progress made in archaeology of the ancient Near and Middle East another zeitgeist challenged the Eurocentric mindset that had been mobilized by the Romantics, and that crystallized around the slogan "ex oriente lux" ("the light from the east"). Archaeologists told the Europeans that pottery-making and metal-working were brought to Europe from the Near East, and scholars engaged in writing research determined that the Greek alphabet was derived from the Phoenician script.

The Europeans had always been aware of the historical contacts of the Greeks with ancient Egypt and these contacts had always been on the agenda of scholars studying the Ptolemaic era in Egypt and possible influences of Egyptian art on Greek art of the archaic period. And yet, the study of the Greek-Egyptian relations remained in the shadow of the mainstream along the lines of "ex oriente lux." Things changed in the 1980s when Martin Bernal published the first volume of his "Black Athena" (1987). Bernal was not the first to speculate about Egyptian influences on Greek culture but he was the first to make his case in an aggressive and polemic way without precedent. Bernal's radical approach aroused the attention of the academic public in a way it could not have been imagined without the emotional load it carries.

Black Athena on Trial

The main thrust of Martin Bernal's culture theory is ideologically motivated, with factual evidence in short currency. From the contents of his works, it becomes clear that the attribute "black" in the main title (i.e., "Black Athena") is synonymous with "ancient Egyptian" rather than referring to black in the meaning of African black.

Undoubtedly, the roots of various Egyptian institutions and cultural traditions (e.g., the worldview of the ruler of divine descent, the pharaoh, as a reflection of African sacred kingship) are to be sought in the prehistory of the black African populations. On the other hand, perhaps more cultural patterns are of local Egyptian coinage and developed without influence from the heritage of black African cultures (e.g., writing technology, monumental architecture, the creation of new gods and goddesses). It is noteworthy that the black Nubians who lived in the south of Egypt learned the crafts of writing and of pyramid-building from the Egyptians, and not vice versa.

A significant marker of distinction, and separation, of the ancient Egyptians from the black populations of Africa is language. Ancient Egyptian is affiliated with the Afrasian (Afroasiatic) phylum and unrelated to the languages of the black populations which belong to other language families (i.e., Niger-Congo, Nilo-Saharan); (Beekes 2011: 5*f*). Since language is a prominent vehicle to construct culture and knowledge, ancient Egyptian civilization created its own specific blend of cultural heritage.

Bernal intentionally chose a provocative title for his work, to stir up the Europeans who, in their Eurocentric bias, had created a fanciful image of Greek antiquity and the origins of its civilization. In the zeitgeist of nationalism of the nineteenth century, the concept of "national culture" was idealized as an independent entity, and high esteem was given to those cultures with a long history, along the lines of "the older and purer, the more precious." National cultures in Europe were categorized accordingly and, when it came to the evaluation of Greek civilization, a fabric of idealized Hellenism emerged, glorifying Greek ingenuity and hailing the purity and originality of Greek cultural traditions.

This construct of pure and original Greek civilization was more a reflection of intellectual preoccupations of the national cultures of Europe rather than a factual reconstruction of life in antiquity. In fact, this fabric was so attractive that many writers, poets and philosophers preferred to live with their fanciful dreams rather than get acquainted with the reality of Greek traditions: "They turned to the Hellenic ideal with such exultation that they refused to taint it with any experience. Winckelmann, Schiller, Hölderlin, Hegel, and Nietzsche never visited Greece" (Lambropoulos 1993: 57).

Bernal's attack is directed against the self-contained way in which the image of ancient Greek civilization was distorted by European cultural chauvinism. Calling those who advocated Eurocentrism "racists"—as Bernal (1987: 201*ff*) does—means barking up the wrong tree. The Eurocentrics who hailed the purity of Greek civilization applied the same categories to the cultures of other "old nations" like the Germans, French, English or Russians. Since Bernal's intention is to provoke he applies the recipe to fight the devil with Satan, and he advocates the opposite extreme of what he stands up against. According to this logic anyone who is not an Afrocentric is a racist. With this distortion as guideline Bernal crosses the line that divides serious scholarship from ideology.

> Bernal's main strategy [...] has invited, and perhaps even insures, however, the opposite of his intended effect of lessening European cultural arrogance. He pays attention and gives stature to

Egypt and Phoenicia only in relation to a later and different Western culture. Thus *Black Athena* succumbs to exactly the Eurocentrism it was written to combat [MacLean Rogers 1996: 452].

The enlightened scholars of classical antiquity, starting with Gottfried Wilhelm Leibniz in the early eighteenth century, have never negated Near Eastern and Egyptian influences on Greek culture and language, but critical scholarship has always known to make a distinction between cultural exchange among equal partners, on the one hand, and the foundational impact of one culture on the formation of another, on the other. That means, critical scholarship has kept a balance and avoided extreme positions because neither the purely Eurocentric nor Bernal's Afrocentric doctrine can serve as a viable orientation for explaining the fabric of Greek civilization.

Arguably, most students of Greek antiquity of the nineteenth century were caught in the Eurocentric zeitgeist. Speaking of zeitgeist, this holds true for the position of Bernal himself.

> Bernal's project is an admirable and interdisciplinary one of challenging notions of cultural identity in a metanarrative of European origins. He brings past and present together in attacking the racism and anti-semitism of entrenched authorities, but on the basis of another metanarrative of cultural influence and social change which is ironically quite compatible with what he criticises [Shanks 1996: 91].

The elaboration of his Afrocentric theory of classical culture falls in a period (i.e., the late 1970s and early 1980s) when fundamental changes in the academic world of archaeology and culture studies were under way. One major innovation in archaeology was the application of dendrochronological dating methods (i.e., tree-ring dating) to calibrate older radiocarbon (i.e., C 14) dates for reaching reliable connections with absolute time. The new cultural chronology for European prehistory was something of a revolution (see Anthony 2009a: 31*ff* for absolute chronology). What had been thought of as spanning a time of some hundreds of years turned out to have lasted several thousands of years. The new chronology opened the view into the depth of prehistory that had previously been blurred.

Archaeologists learned that agriculture spread to southeastern Europe from western Asia already around 7000 BCE (Cunliffe 2008: 88*ff*), some two thousand years earlier than the beginnings of food production in the Nile valley. Marija Gimbutas deserves the merit to have mapped out the civilization of the early (pre–Greek) agriculturalists of Europe, for whose regional cultures she used the blanket term "Old Europe" (Gimbutas 1982, 1991). The validity of the concept "Old Europe" (corresponding to the more recent name "Danube civilization") has been confirmed in recent studies (e.g., Anthony 2007, 2009b, Haarmann 2007, 2011a) and evidence has been produced to illustrate that Old Europe developed foundational institutions of high culture at a time when Egyptian civilization as we know it did not yet exist.

Among the markers of the Danube civilization which flourished from ca. 5500 BCE to ca. 3500 BCE were an extended network of trade relations, a sophisticated belief system (with refined religious concepts and practices centering on a supreme female divinity), advanced technologies such as pottery-making, weaving and metal-working (copper since the sixth millennium BCE and gold since the fifth millennium BCE). The web of communication systems was highly varified, with a vivid cultural symbolism and notational systems. One system served for rendering numbers, the other was an archaic form of writing, referred to as "Old European script" (Haarmann 1995) and also as "Danube script" in recent scholarly literature (e.g., Marler 2008, Merlini 2009, Haarmann 2010).

This pre–Greek (that is, pre–Indo-European) civilization declined under the impact of Indo-European culture whose bearers came from the steppes of southern Russia and intruded into southeastern Europe in the fourth millennium BCE (Anthony 2007). Old European traditions were gradually overformed on the mainland, but they reached the islands in the Aegean Sea in a cultural drift, giving rise to the Minoan civilization of ancient Crete (of the third and second millennia BCE) which, in turn, decisively shaped the profile of Mycenaean-Greek culture of the second millennium BCE. Even on the mainland, many Old European features are retained in the culture of the Pelasgians.

From the standpoint of the newly established cultural chronology of southeastern Europe, the foundational institutions of which classical Greek civilization is comprised find their origins in cultural layers that predate the rise of civilizations in ancient Egypt and in Mesopotamia. The fact that one gives emphasis to the indigenous (= European) roots of pre–Greek civilization does not stand in opposition to considerations about Afroasiatic influences in Greek culture. Crucial for any assessment of such influences is the proper correlation of the phases of Egyptian and Mesopotamian influence with the cultural chronology of Europe. Bernal fails to establish such a correlation, and he does not consult the pertinent scholarly literature that informs about Old Europe and the achievements of the pre–Greek population.

Already early in the nineteenth century there was an awareness among open-minded academic people in Europe that there had been a constant seepage of Egyptian and Near Eastern influence in Greek culture. Evidence for Oriental influence dates to the second millennium BCE. The knowledge of such influences appears in a new light when assigned its proper place in the cultural chronology.

Since the times of the New Kingdom in Egypt's dynastic history (ca. 1550–1295 BCE), Egyptian cultural influence radiates far from the heartland into other Mediterranean civilizations. Wherever and in whatever form the Egyptian influence is manifested in the Greek world, it is received by a culture that had grown from ancient roots already at a time before the diffusion of Egyptian cultural impulses. This is true for the Minoan culture in Crete and for the Mycenaean-Greek culture on the mainland. Greek civilization of the archaic and classical period (eighth to fourth centuries BCE) is an offspring of traditions that reach back in time—via the ancient Aegean cultures and the Pelasgian culture—to the Danube civilization, which makes Greek civilization the grandchild of Old Europe. Its fabric is that of a true conglomerate or mosaic, with a fusion of indigenous and "imported" constituents.

The scenario of how this mosaic culture came into being will be highlighted in a variational approach by illustrating the infrastructure of classical Greek culture and its various constituents rather than by reflecting exclusively on the single concept "roots."

Assessing the Egyptian Linguistic Influence in Ancient Greek

Bernal dedicates the third volume of "Black Athena" (2006) to the discussion of the linguistic impact of Egyptian on the Greek language which, according to the Afrocentric view, is allegedly massive. The extensive survey of reconstructed Egyptian roots for Greek expressions, however, lacks an "anchor." Bernal cannot explain how hundreds of borrowings would have entered the Greek vocabulary without any well-established interaction between the people that spoke the languages in contact. While the presence of the elements of the pre–Greek substratum in the Greek lexicon can be explained through social interaction and cultural exchange between the Greeks and the local agrarian population living in the region that was to become their homeland, the alleged flow of Egyptian terms is not anchored, for the simple reason that there was no intensive interaction between Egyptians and the populations of Europe in the third millennium BCE, which, according to Bernal's claims, is the decisive time-frame for massive borrowing.

Serious scholarship does not negate the presence of Semitic and Egyptian loanwords in Greek. However, less than 30 words are widely acknowledged to have been adopted from Semitic sources, and the transfer of some 40 Egyptian borrowings into Greek is of a relatively late date. "The Egyptian words in Greek are on the whole fewer and later than the Semitic words. A high percentage are confined to the Greek spoken in Egypt in Hellenistic and Roman times; others are merely quoted as foreign words by late Greek authors" (Jasanoff and Nussbaum 1996: 188).

Most of the expressions are elements that enriched the cultural vocabulary of the Greek language (e.g., Greek *elephas* "elephant" or *ibis* "ibis bird"), but they do not form part of the basic vocabulary which would be a precondition for demonstrating the validity of the Afrocentric theory. A number of special terms of Egyptian origin remained isolated in written sources and did not enter the everyday spoken language of the Greeks. Therefore, these lexical elements do not feature in the vocabulary of the koine (common language).

Only few of the Egyptian loanwords were in wider use, such as the terms for ebony (*ebenos*), papyrus (*papyros*) or gum (*kommi*). The expression with the widest range of practical use was perhaps *chartes* which was transmitted, via Greek, into our modern languages, developing meanings in manifold transformations (e.g., English *card,* French *carte* "card," Spanish *carta* "letter," German *Karte* "map," etc.) and derivations (e.g., Italian *cartolina,* Russian *kartochka* "postcard" etc.).

Egyptian borrowings in ancient Greek (with references to the entries in Beekes' *Etymological dictionary,* 2010):

abramis "(a kind of) fish (mullet)" (5*f*)
aon (aiona) "(a kind of) garment" (187)
aron "(a kind of) plant (arum italicum)" (136)
bakanon "brassica napus oleifera" (194)
baris "Egyptian boat, (a kind of) raft" (202)
basanos "touchstone, examination, inquiry (by torture), agony" (203)
bassara "fox," "dress of a bacchante (from the skin of a fox)" (204*f*)
bikos "vase with handles," also a measure (215)
borassos "growing spadix of the date with immature fruit" (226)
boreus "mullet" (251)
boubastis "groin" (possibly coined after the Egyptian goddess Bubastis) (229)
bynetos "Egyptian garment" (249)
champsai Egyptian name of crocodiles (1613)
chartes "papyrus leaf, roll," "thin plate (metaphor.)" (1615*f*)
chenosiris Egyptian name of "ivy" (1625)
ebenos "ebony (tree)" (368)
elephas "ivory, elephant tusk," "elephant" (409*f*)
erpis "wine" (463)

(h)yllos the Egyptian *ichneumon* (glossed as "tracker"), "pharaoh's rat," name of a fish (1530)
ibis "ibis" (575)
kalasiris "Egyptian garment with tassels or fringes at the bottom" (622)
kanopikon "kind of cake" (637)
kiborion "seed-vessel of the Egyptian water lily" (693)
kiki "castor oil," which is oil from the "wondertree" (ricinus communis)
koïx "(a kind of) palm (hyphaena thebaica)" (731*f*)
kommi "gum" (744)
kouki name of a palm-like tree (hyphaena thebaica)
koukouphas Egyptian name of the epops "hoopoe (upupa epops)" (763)
mnasion name of an Egyptian waterplant (cyperus esculentus) (960)
nitron "sodium carbonate, soda, natron" (1022)
othone "delicate cloth, linen, sheet, canvas" (1051)
othonna "greater celandine (chelidonium maius)" (1052)
phennesis "priest of Isis" (1561)
phoinix name of a mythical bird, worshipped in Egypt (1584)
phosson a coarse linen garment used in Egypt (1602)
psagdes name of an Egyptian ointment (1657)
rops Egyptian word for "ship" (1297*f*)
seseli "small hartwort (tordylium officinale)" (1321)
sphigx (+ variants) "sphinx" (1431*f*)
stimi "powdered antimony, kohl, black make-up" (1406)
tereites a musical instrument in Egypt (1468)
zythos "Egyptian beer" (503)

The general impression of this list of lexical borrowings is a far cry from Bernal's claimed massive influx of Egyptian in Greek. In order to make his case Bernal applies a blunt strategy, that is, crafting an Egyptian etymology for Greek words that cannot be securely demonstrated to have Indo-European cognates. This attempt results in numerous fabrications that remain outside the frame of historical development and violate the principles of Greek sound changes. In addition, single words are analyzed without giving any clue as to their embedding in cultural history.

Illustrative of this is Bernal's way of treating geographical terms and place-names. He proposes an Egyptian origin for the name Olympos and related names (Bernal 2006: 361). The most famous of the various mountains in Greece that are called Mount Olympus is the one in Thessaly that was perceived as the home of the gods. The most famous derivation from the basic term Olympos is of course the name for the holy precinct, Olympia, in the western Peloponnese. Bernal does not explain the motivation why a foreign name for a geographical formation would be adopted and he does not relate to the most typical feature of borrowed place-names, namely that they belong to the substrate. "Positively, one can say that landscape terms are frequently borrowed from a substrate language" (Beekes 2010: xlii).

The precondition for this type of borrowing to occur is that those who adopt a substrate term had predecessors who inhabited the region before them and spoke the substrate language. The persistence of geographical terms from a substrate language is a well-known phenomenon throughout the world. This is true for thousands of place-names in many countries and even for the names of big cities or parts of them. Manhattan is such a name which was given to the island by the local Amerindians before the arrival of the white people who retained it. Another example is the name for the Russian capital, Moscow; the original form is Moskova. This is the name by which the Finno-Ugrian tribes called the place before the Russians took over. Rome (Ruma) was founded by Etruscans and London (Londinium) is a Celtic place-name in Roman (i.e., Latin) disguise.

However, in the case of Bernal's imagined settings of Greek-Egyptian contacts the substrate theory does not work, and this because Egyptians never inhabited the places where Greeks later settled. There are no traces of an Egyptian élite ruling over Greek cities—not to speak of any sizable portion of common Egyptian population—since no indicators of any Egyptian presence have been found in Greece. Elsewhere, evidence for an Egyptian presence is documented for all areas where Egyptian rule had been exercised outside Egypt. This is true for Nubia in the south and for Palestine and Syria in the north. Indicators that illustrate Egyptian presence are the following:

- Urban dwellings or farm houses—No remnants of Egyptian houses or urban quarters have been found anywhere in Greece.
- Egyptian graves—In Greece, there is not a single Egyptian grave.
- Monumental architecture—In all areas where Egyptian power was dominant for a certain period, the remnants of temples have been unearthed. The vicinity of a temple was a conditio sine qua non for Egyptian communal life to function. This was of highly symbolic value. According to ancient Egyptian worldview, the winged goddess Ma'at had a pivotal role for sustained community life in that she held the balance for the Egyptian way of life. Ma'at was the personification of the right way, of righteousness and the customary law, of the conventions of social behavior as they were handed down from the ancestors (Assmann 1990). It was common belief among the Egyptians that everybody in the sphere of Egyptian culture would virtually inhale the spirit of Ma'at with every breath an Egyptian took. To this end, it was essential that a temple, a crystallizing focus of Egyptian-ness, was close from which the spirit of Ma'at would irradiate.

In Greece, there was not a single Egyptian temple that would have served this purpose. It was not necessary to erect Egyptian-style temples because there was no Egyptian population that would have been in need of them.

Looked at from whatever standpoint, Bernal's claim of an Egyptian presence in Greece cannot be substantiated and has to be rejected as unfounded. In view of the lack of any alleged Egyptian substrate influence, explanations for the hundreds of non–Greek place-names that are found all over Greece have to be sought outside the frame of Bernal's speculations. It is conclusive to relate those names to the pre–Greek substrate, to the language spoken by the Pelasgians (see the list of pre–Greek names in the foregoing). In addition to the names for places, rivers, landscapes and their formations, there is a broad layer of lexical elements of pre–Greek origin in the Greek vocabulary referring to the natural environment; e.g., *thalassa* ("sea"), *potamos* ("river"), *petra* ("stone, rock").

The Prominent Women of Greek Mythology and Their Pre–Greek Ancestresses

What strikes the eye of everybody who engages in the study of ancient Greek mythology is the abundance of female divinities. This impression holds true not only with respect to the classical era, that is from the fifth century BCE onward, but also for the remote past. The pantheon of the Mycenaean Greeks in the second millennium BCE was as peopled by female divinities.

> The most noticeable characteristic of Mycenaean Greek religion is the preponderance of female deities. The most important of these is Po-ti-ni-ja /Potnia/ as both the mother of the Earth and the protectress of animals. Her sanctuaries are to be found in different places and from their names she becomes known as A-ta-na-po-ti-ni-ja /Athanai Potniai/, Da-pu-ri-to-jo-po-ti-ni-ja / Laburinthoio Potnia/ [Ilievski 2000: 365].

The preponderance of goddesses in Greek mythology stands in stark contrast to the male-dominated pantheon of Proto-Indo-European coinage (Mallory and Adams 2006: 408*ff*). When the early Greeks absorbed the cultural heritage of the native Europeans they also adopted the cults of female deities. The magnitude of this process of adaptation to non–Indo-European cult life may be reflected in a pertinent deviation of Greek terminology from the nomenclature in most other branches of Indo-European. This concerns the key term "god." It is noteworthy that

> at an early stage the Greeks seem to have dropped the term *deiwós*, "god," attested in nearly all branches of the Indo-European family, which is a derivative of IE *dyew-/diw-*, which denoted the bright sky or the light of day. Instead they opted for *theós*, originally "having the sacred," cognates of which have been recognized in Armenian and, rather recently, in Lycian, Lydian and Hieroglyphic Luwian. The change must have happened at an early stage of Greek history, as it had already taken place in Mycenaean times, the oldest period for which we have evidence regarding the gods of ancient Greece [Bremmer 2010: 1].

Indeed, the concept "having the sacred" (*theos*, rendered as *te-o* in Linear B texts of the Mycenaean era) applies to the whole range of pre–Greek divinities—most of them chthonic (i.e., earthbound)—that were integrated into the Greek pantheon, but any association with the bright sky and the light of day does not reflect their true nature. The gods of the native Europeans were not distant and they did not people the sky; the pre–Greek divinities were all-present and everything living was imbued with their spirit.

The heritage of the "strong women" is reflected in the goddess cults of classical antiquity. All major achievements of Greek civilization and elementary concepts of Greek worldview are associated with goddesses (Haarmann and Marler 2008: 48*f*):

- Demeter: the patron of agriculture (the Grain Mother);
- Hestia: the guardian of the hearth and the household;
- Artemis: the patron of nature and of wildlife;
- Themis: the goddess of customary law and righteousness;
- Dike: the goddess of justice;
- Eirene: the divine guardian of peace;
- Eunomia: the goddess of lawful government;
- Athena (A-ta-na in Mycenaean Linear B texts): the super goddess, the patron of technologies such as pottery (the potter's icon was Athena's owl), ship-building and weaving, the patron of justice, of the arts and science. As a protectress, Athena watched over the safety of Athens and the well-being of its citizens. The main temple on the acropolis in Athens, the Parthenon, was dedicated to her.

The Parthenon, with its monumental measures (length: 69.5 m, width: 30.9 m, height: 13.7 m), was the masterpiece of the architect Pheidias, and it was built between 447 and 438 BCE, with work on the decorations (i.e., friezes) continuing until 432 BCE.

Top and above: The Parthenon temple on the Acropolis: (a) A view of the west side (photograph by Hans R. Goette); (b) Reconstruction of the west pediment showing scenes of the contest of Athena and Poseidon (reconstruction by E. Berger; Faltkarte III, upper section, drawing by Miriam Cahn; E. Berger, "Parthenon-Studien: Zweiter Zwischenbericht, *Antike Kunst* 20 [1977], 124–141. Falttafel III, Zeichnung: Miriam Cahn; reproduced with permission).

The Parthenon was not referred to by this name until the fourth century; prior to that time, building accounts designate it as *ho neos*, the temple, a generic term, but beginning in the fourth century, it was called the Parthenon or *hekatompedos*. Both Parthenon and *hekatompedos* are terms used for parts of the building in the fifth-century inscriptions, but not to refer to the whole [Barringer 2008: 63].

Inside the temple, a colossal statue of Athena was erected. It measured 12.2 m in height. This chryselephantine figure (made of gold and ivory) was crafted over a wooden frame. In the palm of her right hand, Athena held the statue of the goddess Nike which was 1.8 m high. Originally, a golden serpent coiled at the goddess' right foot but it was later removed and placed inside the aegis, the shield. The statue rested upon a base (length: 8 m, depth: 4.1 m) that was decorated with painted marble figures.

The association of the snake with Athena, the pre–Greek goddess, is no coincidence. The symbolism of the snake in connection with a female divinity is of high age, going back at least to the Neolithic in southeastern Europe (Gimbutas 1989: 121*ff*). In ancient Greece and throughout the ancient Aegean cultures "[t]here is scarcely a divinity with which [the snake] is not in some way associated" (Bevan 1986/I: 261).

As in the case of the Greek language, which is permeated with elements of pre–Greek origin also, Greek mythology is comprised of genuinely Indo-European and non–Indo-European divinities. Before their out-migrations from the Eurasian steppe the Indo-European pastoralists knew only a few goddesses, and these occupied rather marginal niches in the pantheon which was otherwise dominated by male gods. Among them was a pastoral god who persists in Greek mythology, as Pan, in the same function (Haarmann 2012: 34*f*).

> The only goddesses which may be safely assumed to be proto–Indo-European are those which are not only mythologically comparable with one another but which are linguistically cognate as well. There are few such goddesses, and they represent largely natural phenomena [dawn, sun maiden, earth] with slight personification [Dexter 1997: 231].

In light of the scarce documentation of old Indo-European goddesses one may wonder how the Greeks came to venerate so many female divinities. The only explanation for this phenomenal transformation of Indo-European mythology is that the Greeks got acquainted with a worldview that was centered around divine femininity, gradually got accustomed to it and eventually adopted its major features to become their own. Surprising as it may seem this overall fusion process of pre–Greek divinities with figures of Indo-European coinage to form the organic whole of the Greek pantheon is a still neglected field of research even among specialists of Greek religion (see Henrichs 2010 for such a void).

The question remains: which direction did the impulses for such kind of cultural process come from? Was the source Old European or Egyptian? Bernal places Athena at the center of his Afrocentric speculations which prompts reflections on the origins of this goddess. According to Bernal's claim, the Greek goddess Athena is a figure that was coined on an Egyptian model, and he gives several potential "candidates" of Egyptian goddesses that allegedly inspired the creation of the Greek Athena.

The first is the goddess Nephthys (Bernal 1991: 99*f*). This juxtaposition is difficult to perceive since a comparison of the two goddesses reveals quite differing functions for each. The Egyptian goddess was married and had a child with Osiris while Athena was venerated as the eternal virgin who sought the company of men but never got involved with them. Nephthys is the goddess of the realm of the dead and the patron of birth-giving, both functions that Athena never had.

Next is the goddess Neit (Bernal 2006: 563*f*). Neit was the local patron of Sais in the Nile Delta. She was venerated as a goddess of the river and the sea. As a primordial goddess, Neit is the mother of the sun god Ra. As a goddess of the underworld Neit shares important functions with Nephthys. In the late phase of pharaonic Egypt, Neit becomes the patron of kingship who bestows the regalia upon the pharaoh. All these functions lack resemblance with Athena and her role in Greek mythology.

The statue of Athena Parthenos (reconstruction) (author's collection).

Athena is neither of Egyptian nor of black African origin and, being the daughter of an ancient Palaeo-European divinity, she is as old as any of the Egyptian goddesses. In order to understand Athena's role in the web of mythological relations it is necessary to illustrate the position of Greek goddesses in the Greek pantheon ("circle of divinities"). A closer inspection reveals that female divinities are the most ancient figures of Greek mythology and date to pre-Greek times. A goddess is even at the very heart of the Greek myth of origin. The prominence that female divinities enjoy in Greek mythology is unknown to the Egyptian tradition which, therefore, cannot be seen as the source of the former.

The mainstream Greek cosmogonical myths (i.e., myths of origin) are collected in the epic work *Theogony*, composed by the Greek poet Hesiod around 700 BCE, although there are other cosmogonies categorized as "deviant" (Gantz 1993: 739*ff*). Among the "deviant" cosmogonies is the so-called "Pelasgian" myth of pre-Greek origin which is of high age. According to this version, the first divinity to emerge from the primordial chaos is Eurynome ("wide wandering"), the goddess of all things, whose first task is to divide heaven from the eternal waters. She cannot find a place to rest, so she wanders south on the waves.

Eurynome is followed by the north wind, Boreas, who takes the form of a snake. His longing for a female companion culminates in a sexual union with the goddess who becomes pregnant. Eurynome experiences a metamorphosis, turns into a water fowl and places an egg on a patch of land. From this egg emerge all the things of this world, living and non-living. In this version, the central position of the goddess as creator of the world is indicative of the pre-Greek origin of the cosmogonic myth. Moreover, Eurynome originally presided over Olympus before she is dethroned by Zeus and the other Greek Olympians.

With respect to the cultures of the Aegean islands, the pre-Indo-European heritage of the goddess cult is best known from ancient Crete with its Minoan civilization that flourished in the second millennium BCE. The opinions of scholars are divided over the fabric of Minoan religion. Some assume the presence of one mighty female divinity while others reconstruct a pantheon of gods and goddesses. Even if Minoan religion knew various divinities, the prominence of female deities among them remains striking. "That a powerful goddess of nature was the chief deity of the Minoans ... has never been seriously questioned" (Marinatos 1993: 147).

When one relates the linguistic evidence of a pre-Greek formative element in Athena's name (i.e., the suffix *-n*) to the kaleidoscope of functions of Athena and to the history of her cult practices then any claim about Afroasiatic origins becomes void.

Another strong female figure occupies a key role in the world of agriculture. Basic conceptualizations about fertility in a spirited world, related to the soil that produces crops, to animals that were raised as cattle and to women as givers of life, persisted in many agrarian communities into the times of classical antiquity. In some religious traditions, the mindset of early sedentary people still echoes. This is true for the cult of the Greek goddess Demeter, the Grain Mother, and her festivities. The name of the goddess is a hybrid compound, constructed of a pre-Greek expression for "earth," *de-*, and the expression *meter* "mother" (of Indo-European coinage).

A clear reference to Demeter in her association with the cultivation of grain is given by Homer in his epic *Iliad* (XIII 322, XXI 76, V 500) which was compiled in the eighth century BCE. In the cult practices of Demeter, the pig (particularly the suckling pig) played a prominent role. When the crops were sown in autumn, the festival of Thesmophoria was held in honor of Demeter. The Thesmophoria "give an impression of extraordinary antiquity" (Burkert 1985: 13). During this festival, which was performed and attended by women only, piglets, among other votive gifts, were offered to the goddess.

Another festival, called Skirophoria, was also associated with Demeter. Virgins received figurines of suckling pigs (Greek *skira*), and these were left after the ceremonies in the shrine dedicated to Demeter. In the rites of the Eleusinian Mysteries, the pig was the basic symbol of purification.

The traditions of these strong women of Greek mythology lived on and later fused with the cult of the Virgin Mary who absorbed the authority of the ancient goddesses and attracted their worshippers. Among those Greek divinities whose features were absorbed by Mary, Athena may be the most revered: "By the time the Parthenon of Athens was dedicated to Mary as Mother of God in the sixth century, she had taken on many of the images and honours of the ancient goddesses as well as moving into many of their temples" (Shearer 1996: 118).

Albeit her pre–Greek origin, Athena was assimilated by the Greeks and integrated as a member of their pantheon on equal footing with the Olympian goods of Indo-European coinage. Athena shared with the other Greek gods basic properties (Henrichs 2010: 29*ff*):

- immortality ("First and foremost, Greeks gods are immortal (*athanatoi* or *aien eontes*). Immortality is the ultimate benchmark of their divinity");
- anthropomorphism ("In myth as well as cult Greek gods could assume non-human shapes and appear as animals, for instance as lions, bulls, horses, bears, birds or snakes. But the cases in which gods adopt a theriomorphic form are negligible compared to the overwhelming number of instances in which they appear in human shape");
- power ("The most ubiquitous quality that defines a Greek god is divine power (*dynamis*). Of all the divine qualities, it is by far the hardest to define, in part because it does not manifest itself in the abstract and because its concrete manifestations can take so many different forms. Like most other religions, including all Mediterranean religions, Greek religion imagines its gods as powerful by definition").

These properties of Greek divinities may have decisively contributed to the longevity of these figures, in cultural memory, beyond antiquity. Of all the female deities that were once venerated in antiquity, the prominent women of Greek mythology live on in manifold transformations—often in their Roman equivalents (Demeter as Ceres, Athena as Minerva or Iustitia, Aphrodite as Venus, etc.)—as ingredients of Western civilization, with many allusions to them in the visual arts and in literature.

The Question of Continuity: Cultural Traditions from Old Europe to the Ancient Aegean and into Later Periods

The pre–Indo-European civilization did not disintegrate under the Indo-European overlay, but patterns of a selective continuity are successively derived from the ancient foundations. This continuity is anchored in a kaleidoscope of domains, of material culture as well as in spiritual conceptualizations. Key technologies of crafts such as pottery, metallurgy, architecture, ship-building and others were adopted by the Greeks together with pertinent elements of their terminologies. And this is true also for religious and spiritual concepts that persisted—via various transformations—into classical antiquity. The figure of Athena around which Bronze Age traditions crystallize illustrates the decisive phase of transition from the late Bronze Age to the Iron Age. Pre-Greek Athena does not stand alone since also the archaeology of other divinities of pre–Greek times (e.g., Hera) confirms the grand theme of continuity of artifact production and of mentifacts (cultural and religious concepts). Cultic continuity

> includes the megaron on the acropolis of Tiryns, supposedly reconstructed to house a cult of Hera which continued a palace-based religion, besides the cult of Athena on the Athenian Acropolis, which also takes up a palace cult. The same scenario is proposed for Athena at Mycenae. The assumption that citadel sanctuaries carried on palace-centred Mycenaean cult is ultimately based on the presumed divinity of the Mycenaean king, grounded in two Homeric passages (Iliad 6. 546–51, Odyssey 7. 80–1) [Antonaccio 1994: 88*f*].

The vivid continuity of Old European features in later periods (i.e., the Aegean Bronze Age) has given rise to the idea that the Minoan civilization of ancient Crete (third and second millennia BCE) and the Pelasgian culture on the continent (second millennium BCE) were daughters of the Old European mother culture.

A Matrix of Spheres of Knowledge That Was Transmitted from Old Europe to Ancient Greece

If the cultures of the Minoans and Pelasgians were the daughters of Old Europe, then Greek civilization of antiquity is the grandchild, and a bright and shining one. The items of cultural heritage of pre–Greek (i.e., Old European) origin that were absorbed by the Greeks were, so to speak, "marked" since not only the things were adopted but also their pre–Greek names were integrated into the vocabulary of ancient Greek.

The conditions for intensive contacts of the native Europeans with the Indo-European migrants who entered Greece from the North unfolded during the Bronze Age. This is the Helladic era that begins around 3100 BCE (Early Helladic) and ends around 1050 BCE (Late Helladic) (Manning 2010: 23). Within the frame of Helladic absolute chronology (i.e., Helladic I—beginning ca. 3100 BCE; Helladic II—beginning ca. 2200 BCE; Helladic III—beginning ca. 1700 BCE), the Middle Helladic period (Helladic II) is the decisive phase for Pelasgian-Greek interaction.

In the course of the Middle Helladic period (from late third to early second millennia BCE), interaction between the two (ethnically distinct) groups resulted in a prolonged process of linguistic fusion when the linguistic systems in contact experienced contact-induced interferences. These interferences are manifested in elements from the substrate language that were transmitted, together with items of ancient knowledge, to various spheres of Greek civilization:

- overall concepts of knowledge-construction (including key terms such as *myth*, *psyche*, *sophia* and others)
- practical knowledge: conditions of daily life; arranging things in the living space; work in the household (cooking meals, baking bread, etc.; *amora* "sweet cake" (fine wheat flour boiled with honey), *thalamos* "inside room at the back of a house," "room for women," *klibanos* "baking-oven")
- cultural knowledge: relationship between the human space and nature; the place of human beings in the *oikos* (home) and *demos* (village community); the role of cults in human affairs (*hestia* "hearth, fireplace," *grymeia* "bag or chest for old clothes," *karkaris* "load of firewood")
- customary knowledge: the ways of Themis; observing festivals (*heorte* "feast, religious festival," *thiasos* "procession," *threskeuo* "to perform or observe religious customs")
- knowledge and know-how of crafts: weaving, house construction, ploughing etc. (*atraktos* "spindle," *plinthos* "brick, air-brick," "square building-stone," *laion* "ploughshare")

- specialized knowledge: pottery, working metal, ship-building (*keramos* "potter's earth, clay," *chalkos* "ore, copper," *agkyra* "anchor")
- technological know-how: how to build and operate a furnace; how to build a trap for hunting (*gaggamon* "small round net for catching oysters," *mechane / machine* (Dor.) "means, tool, device, machine," *chymeia / chemeia* "the art of alloying metals, alchemy")
- ritual knowledge: the role of Hestia; various private cults (for the home) and communal cults; the state cult of Athena in Athens; observing sacrificial rites (*pelanos* "sacrificial cake (liquid flour dough, flour pulp, honey and oil)," *sphazo* "to slaughter (by cutting the throat), sacrifice")
- intergenerational knowledge: remembering the past; grave culture, ancestor cult (*kokuai* "forefathers," *kterea* "gifts for the dead, sacrifice," *hosia* "customary law, inherited from the ancients, to be observed in the present and future")
- social and communal knowledge: social networks, communal administration, concepts of status and function (*anax* "lord, ruler," originally "overseer of ritual activities," *prytanis / protanis* (Aeol.) "foreman, chief of affairs," *prytan* (title of a leading official, in Athens member of the governing committee of the council)
- intimate knowledge: terminology of body parts and functions (*kikke* "sexual intercourse," *mastos* "mother breast," *sabyttos* "shaving for ornamentation [of female genitals]")
- mythopoetic knowledge: myths of origin, relationships between human beings, heroes and divinities (Elusion the abode of the Blessed after death, (H)elene daughter of Zeus and Leda, a personification of the Minoan goddess of vegetation, connected with the tree cult, (h)eros "hero; lord"; several feminine formations (*heroïne, heroïssa,* etc.)
- economic know-how: network of terms in various domains (agriculture, horticulture, animal husbandry); (*kropion* "sickle, scythe," *lathyros* "pulse, chickling (lathyrus sativus)," *sitos* "corn (especially wheat)," *bdallo* "to milk (cows)," *killix* "cow with one twisted horn," *oisype* "greasy extract of sheep's wool")
- trade and commerce: (*drakhme/darkhma* "drachm" (weight and coin), *kapelis* "female merchant," *medimnos* "grain measure")
- ecological knowledge: weather conditions; vegetation cycle, forms of landscape (*asterope / sterope / astrape* "lightning," *isthmos* "strait of sea (especially with respect to the strait of Corinth); spit of land, small entry," Notos "South(west) wind which brings mist and wetness," *ombros* "rain, shower," "thunderstorm," "rainwater")
- medicinal knowledge, knowledge of treatment and cure: traditional ways of healing (e.g., boiling leaves for medicinal liquids); (*ballis* a medical plant, *pharmakon* "healing medicine, healing herb," *phibaleos* "a fig suitable for curing"

There is evidence for pre–Greek influence in all the spheres mentioned above. It is no exaggeration to state that Greek civilization of antiquity would not have achieved the level of cultural and technological advancement that it indeed achieved without the foundational backing of the preceding cultural strata. When the Mycenaeans set out to sea to engage in overseas trade their culture was permeated with Old European elements, irradiating the wisdom of the ancients.

Greek Culture Throughout the "Dark Ages"

The political supremacy of the Mycenaean city-states declined in the course of the twelfth century BCE. On the Greek mainland, a period of cultural disorientation seems to have begun, and literacy in Linear B was abandoned. During those times of social unrest and political instability, many Greeks migrated from the mainland to Cyprus, taking with them urban lifeways and their cultural traditions.

The lack of literary sources and the scarcity of archaeological artifacts between the eleventh and ninth centuries BCE produced the puzzle of what scholars previously used to call the "Dark Ages." This term is awkward and it is nowadays used with quotation marks or avoided altogether. Even on the mainland the decline of Mycenaean rule was not followed by a total disruption in cultural tradition. In the visual arts of archaic Greece (eighth century BCE), in their form, style and motifs, the legacy of the Mycenaean era can be clearly perceived.

There were no "Dark Ages" in Cyprus, and cultural development there is characterized by a continuity of cultural forms, including writing. Contacts between Cyprus and the Greek mainland continued even after the decline of Mycenaean power. The contacts of the eleventh century BCE were of mutual advantage, with the transfer of Mycenaean traditions to the island (e.g., decoration of Cyprian pottery with motifs of the Late Helladic IIIC period such as pictures of warriors and Mycenaean–style weaponry) and with Cyprian stimulations of a mainland iron industry and the import of a Cyprian innovation, "something of a revolution in pottery, the formation of a very distinct style known as protogeometric" (Osborne 1996: 28).

In the cultural environment of Cyprus, Mycenaean patterns did not cease to exist, persisting instead until well into the first millennium BCE. The remainders of Mycenaean cultural persistence in Cyprus can be traced for several centuries, and "it becomes evident that during the first millennium BC the Cypriotes cherished their Mycenaean ancestry and tradition and preserved or revived elements of Mycenaean culture even at times of foreign-oriental domination in the island" (Karageorghis 1962: 77).

In the bilingual milieu of ancient Cyprian and Greek cultural interference, literacy in the Cypriot-Syllabic script evolved from the eleventh century BCE onwards, until it was challenged by the Greek alphabet in the sixth century BCE, eventually being replaced by it in the third century BCE. Cyprus was not only a striking exception to the stereotyping notion of the "Dark Ages" in the Mycenaean-Greek hemisphere, it also played an active part in the perpetuation of the old Aegean heritage and its proliferation in the Mediterranean world into the archaic period of the eighth to sixth centuries BCE.

The Tradition of the Bull Cult in the Mediterranean and the Originality of the Minoan Bull Games

The strings of cultural continuity that have been identified, in scholarly works since the 1980s, for European cultural history from the Neolithic to the Bronze Age and beyond seem to have been ignored by Bernal. His discussion of the role of the bull as a mythical animal in Mediterranean cultures reflects this lack of information. Bernal claims that, during the period between the documentation of bull horns in sanctuaries of Çatalhöyük in Anatolia of the seventh millennium BCE and the appearance of the bull motif in Minoan art (second millennium BCE), there is no evidence for continuity in the region (Bernal 1991: 166). In fact, there is ample evidence in the imagery of Old Europe (e.g., bull figurines, the picture of a bull's head carved on a bone plate, the motif of the horns of consecration); (see Gimbutas 1991: 98*ff*, 244*ff* for bull symbolism and bucrania). Bernal's conclusion, based on his imagined lacuna of visual evidence, is that, during that time, Egyptian influence comes to bear and, ultimately, inspires the Cretan tradition of the bull games.

These bull games are documented in the famous bull-leaping fresco in a courtyard of the Minoan palace of Knossos (see figure below). For over a hundred years, the scene depicted in this fresco has puzzled experts and lay persons alike. Some see the leaping as the act of an individual actor, separate from the other actors. In fact, few have thought of a choreography involving several actors, three to be precise, as they are depicted in the fresco. If the actor who clings to the horns had the intention to perform a salto mortale and land on the bull's back, an accurate landing would hardly be possible, given the unpredictable and accidental motion of the bull's head.

It is important to keep in mind that the scene does not depict the action in a realistic manner. Instead, "the artistic depictions concentrate on the essence of the feat, which consists of outwitting the bull, rendering him almost ridiculous by turning his potency into a vehicle for display of human skill" (Marinatos 1993: 218*f*). The participation of three human figures in the scene speaks for a reconstruction of bull leaping as a coordinated choreography, with several actors performing.

The depiction of three acrobats (i.e., A, B, C) corresponds to a staged choreography. Acrobat A is the first to approach the bull, trying to hold its head down by clinging to its horns. Such a motion is still typical of the Portuguese tradition of an non-bloody bull fight.

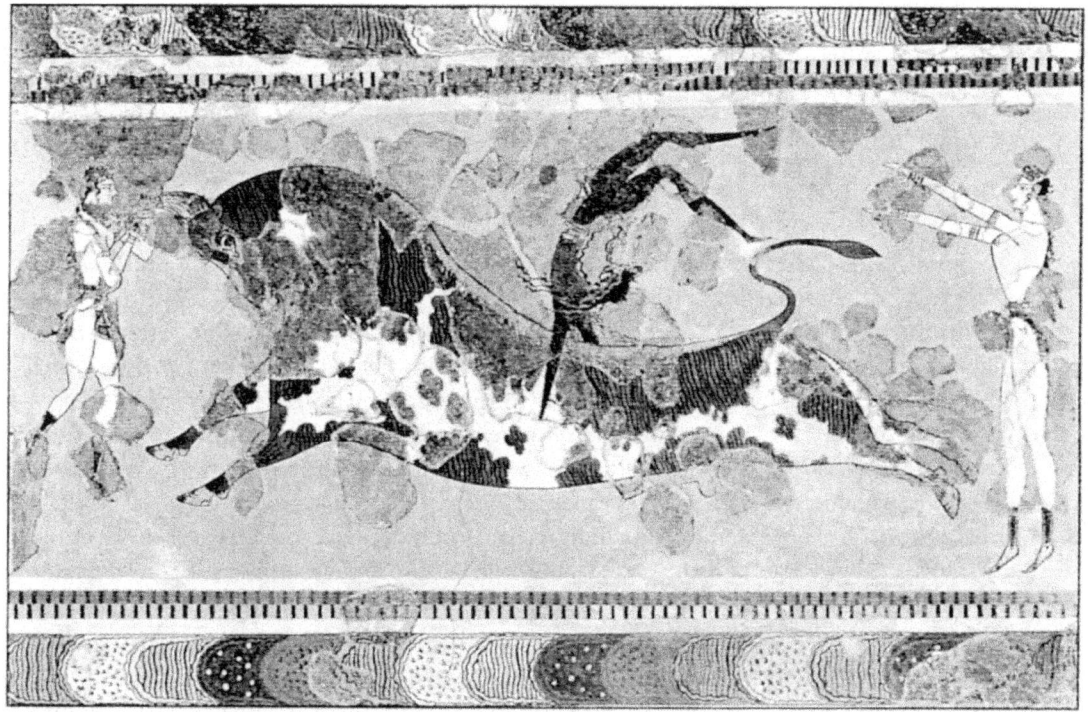

A   B   C

The bull-leaping fresco from the Minoan palace of Knossos (ancient Crete; 2nd millennium BCE) (author's collection).

Pressing down the bull's head is an important precautionary action, the purpose of which is to keep the dangerous sharp ends of the horns out of reach of the level where they could harm acrobat B, who is the next to act. He waits for the right moment to leap over the bull's head while this is held down by acrobat A. Acrobat B performs an extended leap, lands on the back of the bull, and uses the thrust of the motion to jump over the animal to land on his feet. Acrobat C will assist him to land safely. Leaping over a bull (or a cow) is a ceremonial action still performed during festivities in southern France.

Once the leap has been successfully performed, acrobat A loosens his grip on the bull's horns so that the animal can run freely. The acrobats then gather in a slightly changed order. Acrobat B remains behind the bull while acrobat C takes the role of the one to cling to the bull's horns. Acrobat A, for her part, waits for a favorable moment to leap over the bull. Depending on the physical resources and skills of the acrobats, or on the requirements of the ritual, a choreography of this type could be performed in repetitive sequences for a shorter or longer duration of time.

In whatever way one may interpret the bull-leaping performance, this action that formed part of religious rituals was a Minoan invention, and there is nothing comparable in the mythological tradition of the bull and its sacrifice in ancient Egypt. The find of the picture of a leaping bull at Avaris in the eastern Delta region, the capital of the Hyksos who ruled over Egypt during the second intermediate period (ca. 1650–1550 BCE), which shows resemblance with the Cretan fresco, cannot be overrated in its significance as a possible source for the Minoan tradition, as Bernal has it. Rather, this parallel documents to the vivid trade relations and cultural exchange between two civilizations, each with its own indigenous roots, capable of absorbing additional and manifold impulses from its neighbors.

Trade Relations Vis-à-vis Colonization in the Mediterranean Regions

Trade goods of Egyptian origin are literally strewn in the areas around the Mediterranean Sea. In the archaeological record, one finds Egyptian miniature sculptures, among them the popular motif of the scarabee, the dung-rolling bug, that was considered a sacred symbol of eternity by the Egyptians. His obsession with Egyptian grandeur makes Bernal forcefully argue for Egyptian political power in the regions with Egyptian trade goods, or even for colonization. It is hazardous to exclusively interpret trade relations as an indicator of colonial power. Some examples may illustrate such misconception.

The archaeological record of the settlements near the southern coast of the Baltic Sea—in what is nowadays Polish and Lithuanian territory and dating to the early centuries of our era—shows an abundance of Roman coins. It would be absurd to interpret this concentration of wealth as an indicator of Roman colonial presence in the area. The coins stem from the vivid trade relations which the Romans entertained along the amber route across central Europe to obtain the highly valued raw material (Sidrys 2001).

Another case of the wide spread of items of value without any connection to a colonial history is the abundance of Arabic silver coins found in the medieval settlements of northwestern Russia and in Scandinavia. These regions were never colonized by Arabs. The coins were brought to northern Europe by Viking traders. The connection with the Arab-controlled markets was established along the river Volga which was called the "route to the Arabs" by the Vikings (Darkevič 1986: 231).

Trade goods are indeed a measure of exchange, but not forcefully an indicator of colonization. Trade relations emerge when there are articles to be exchanged, and there has to be a consensus about their value, among providers of such articles and those who are interested in obtaining them. The ancient Egyptians could extend their trade network under two conditions: (i) they possessed the resources and the know-how to offer goods of value for people outside Egypt, and (ii) there existed cultures outside Egypt that were advanced enough to offer goods for exchange themselves. The reason for the wide spread of Egyptian trade goods throughout the Mediterranean region is the presence of advanced civilizations that had quality goods to offer in exchange for Egyptian goods.

Among the prominent trading partners of Egypt in the second millennium BCE was Keftiu which is the Egyptian name for ancient Crete. Keftiu is mentioned in Egyptian texts which made Bernal jump to the conclusion that Minoan Crete must have been an Egyptian colony. Except for an abundance of Egyptian trade goods there are no signs for any colonization in Crete. Bernal makes a case for Egyptian colonization also for the Greek mainland. Bernal (2006: 564) makes the claim that Athens was allegedly founded as "the daughter city of Sais," the important trading port in the western area of the Nile delta. It is perhaps superfluous to state that this claim can by no means be substantiated by any archaeological evidence.

On the contrary, there is evidence for the presence of foreigners from the Aegean islands, from Crete in particular, in Egypt. They might have come as traders or artisans who offered their professional skills to Sesostris II (nineteenth century BCE), king of the twelfth dynasty. There is another clue to the understanding of what kind of relationship existed between Egypt and ancient Crete: Minoan pottery (especially Kamares ware) dating to the nineteenth–seventeenth centuries BCE.

> Kamares ware would appear to have two major sources in Crete—the palaces at Knossos and Phaistos. However, the route and method of entry for this pottery into Egypt has given occasion for much discussion, and several possible routes have been suggested. These include the journey from Crete to a Delta port and then on to Memphis or another centre by an inland river route; from Crete to Cyrene and thence along the North African coast to the Nile Delta; or from Crete to the Syrian coast, sometimes passing via Cyprus, and following the coasts of Anatolia and Palestine to the Nile Delta [David 1986: 181].

There is something intriguing about the Minoan pottery in Egypt, and that is, it was obviously so fashionable that its style was imitated by Egyptian potters using local clay. This says something about the nature of the trade relations between Egypt and Minoan Crete as equal partners.

Key Technologies in the Greek World as Achievements without Egyptian Patronage

The rulers of Egypt waged many wars with their southern neighbors, the Nubians, over political supremacy in the region and, eventually, they conquered Nubia and established colonial rule. The Egyptian presence in Nubia brought key technologies to that country, among them Egyptian-style architecture and ceramic ware. The Nubians later adopted the hieroglyphic script for writing their local language, Meroitic (Millet 1996).

The Egyptians never attempted to occupy Minoan or Greek territory, they never established colonial rule there and, consequently, there is no evidence for the transfer of Egyptian technologies (i.e., architectural techniques and styles, writing) as the typical markers of foundational influence.

Architecture

Basic architectural forms were developed, independently, in Egypt and in the Minoan-Mycenaean world and, later, the two regions experienced an exchange of inspiring influences moving either direction. There is no echo of a one-way irradiation of Egyptian technical know-how into the Aegean. On the contrary, the idea has been entertained that perhaps the most typical Minoan type of architecture, the layout of a labyrinth, might have been imitated in Egypt.

> In architectural and artistic terms, the Middle Minoan and Middle Kingdom Periods saw a perhaps constant exchange of ideas and techniques. It has been suggested that some architectural connections existed during this period, and that these were perhaps evidenced in buildings such as the Labyrinth built by Amenemmes III [eighteenth century BCE] at Hawara, which later visitors compared to the Labyrinth of Minos at Knossos [David 1986: 182].

Writing Technology

The ancient Aegean scripts (i.e., Cretan hieroglyphics, Linear A, Linear B) and their derivations (i.e., Cypro-Minoan, Cypriot-Syllabic) find their inspiration in the much older tradition of the Danube script (Haarmann 2011b: 139*ff*). As such these scripts are unrelated to the writing systems that were in use in ancient Egypt (i.e., hieroglyphs, Hieratic, Demotic). The name "hieroglyphics" for one of the Cretan scripts refers to the use of picture symbols as signs of writing and to the religious function of this kind of writing, but the Cretan hieroglyphs are not historically related to the Egyptian type of hieroglyphics (Haarmann 1995: 96*ff*).

The alphabetic script was not transferred to the Greek world from Egypt either but this specialized technology was elaborated in the Near East and reached Crete with Phoenician trade goods in the tenth century BCE. The Greeks had known literacy before adopting the Phoenician script which was a more precise tool for rendering the sound structure of language in comparison to the older Aegean forms of syllabic writing. The Greek alphabet emerged in the eighth century BCE, in the bicultural and bilingual milieu of contacts between Greeks and Minoans in Crete (Haarmann 1995: 131*ff*). The early development of the various local variants of the Greek script is unrelated to the tradition of contemporary literacy in Egypt.

In light of the history of writing technology Bernal's Afroasiatic speculations lose any weight. Had there been Egyptian occupation of Greek territory and had Greek civilization emerged amidst Egyptian cultural patronage then Egyptian hieroglyphic writing would have been introduced for writing Greek. Dominance of Egyptian writing was the rule in those areas under Egyptian political control, Nubia for one. Contrary to what would be expected from an Afroasiatic impact on Greek civilization it was Greek alphabetic writing that came to dominate literacy in Egypt, eventually replacing the older tradition of hieroglyphic writing. In the aftermath of the conquests of Alexander the Great in the fourth century BCE, the Greek alphabet became known in the Near East and in Egypt.

With the expansion of Greek culture and language during the Hellenistic era, the Greek script eventually was adopted to write the Egyptian language (in its late phase of development). The alphabet that was elaborated for the local language in Egypt at the time when Christianity spread in the Nile valley is known as the Coptic script, with its signs derived from Greek letters. The adoption of alphabetic writing based on the Greek model did not only bring Greek letters to Egypt but also some other significant innovations.

> The Coptic script represents a distinct break with earlier Egyptian writing systems by its general abandonment of pictographic characters, substituting instead the 24 letters of the Greek alphabet.... By adopting the Greek alphabet, Coptic entails several further innovations in Egyptian writing. Contrary to earlier preferences [...], standard Coptic is written from left to right. More importantly, Coptic is the only native script of Egypt to indicate vowels [Ritner 1996: 287*ff*].

The name "Coptic" reflects the Greek name for the Egyptians, Aigyptioi. The Coptic alphabet was used in Egypt to write religious texts in the Christian tradition until the advent of Arabic language and alphabet in the seventh century CE. As a spoken language, Coptic declined in the late Middle Ages. As a sacred language of the Coptic church, it continues to be used for reading religious literature.

2

What the Greeks Learned from Their Predecessors

Wine and Olive Cultivation, Pottery and Metallurgy

The Europeans experienced the fundamental economic transition from the lifeways of Mesolithic hunter-gatherers to plant production in Neolithic agrarian communities between 7000 and 6500 BCE (Cunliffe 2008: 88–101). The earliest evidence for agriculture comes from Thessaly in northern Greece. By ca. 5500 BCE, the native Europeans (Palaeo-Europeans) had adopted agrarian lifeways throughout the Balkan peninsula. Like their ancestors who had practiced hunting and gathering, the early agriculturalists organized themselves in groups, only that these groups were sedentary village communities.

The agriculturalists did not abandon all the traditions of their ancestors once they had become sedentary. Many old traditions were kept up, such as the production of figurines and old shamanistic rituals related to the celebration of the vegetation cycle and fertility of animals, plants and human beings. The construction of culture among the agriculturalists was motivated by the same universal principle that activates organizational skills in humans and promotes cultural activities elsewhere (after Tomasello 2004: 1): (a) the creation and use of conventional symbols, (b) the creation and use of complex tools and other instrumental technologies, (c) the creation of and participation in complex social organizations and institutions. It is of little importance whether the "social" is seen as generating culture or as forming part of it. The main issue is that "a society's intellectual developments cannot be divorced from its concrete historical and social contexts" (McCarthy 1996: 107).

Culture is intrinsically associated with those who construct it and, in the present study, the fabric of culture is understood in its widest possible composition, being comprised of

- its material basis, artifacts (e.g., stone tools, architecture, technologies),
- its network of social relationships, symbolizing in-group solidarity among the members in the community (e.g., kinship relations, social groupings with professional specialization and/or social hierarchies, forms of administration),
- its collective technologies of communication (ranging from the symbolism of landscape to notational systems such as numerology and writing),
- its entire constructive potential originating amidst communal life (from handicraft to music, art and oral/written literature),
- its systems of shared values and beliefs (worldview, mythology, religious cults),
- its collective knowledge and stored memory, mentifacts (as virtual and practical knowl-

edge and as instructions given from one generation to the next to safeguard cultural continuity).

In the lifeways and worldview of prehistoric people were encapsulated the capacities for cultural, social and technological advance, and it was only a matter of time how these capacities would come to bear (Lewis-Williams and Pearce 2005). The most essential precondition for a complex system such as culture to come into existence and to persist is the accumulation of knowledge which the individuals share and, in a concerted way, use to organize themselves in their living space. Knowledge-construction is a resource which provides the foundation for the build-up of any culture. At the same time, constructing knowledge is the driving force to keep culture functioning. Prehistory is a period of incubation when human skills and capacities experienced a dynamic process of refinement and specialization.

Recent findings in the field of culture theory emphasize the overall significance of cultural memory. Some scholars emphasize the crucial role of writing for the preservation of cultural knowledge (e.g., Assmann 2007). Others view cultural memory in a wider perspective, also including the mythopoetic traditions in illiterate societies (e.g., Haarmann 2007). In a wider sense, cultural memory, as a mnemonic device, is central to all modes of interpretation of civic institutions and their functioning in the horizon of time. In order to understand the experimenting process out of which emerges civilization in the sense of "high culture," due credit has to be paid to the impact of cultural memory. Cultural memory which works as a motor of cultural identification in individuals and, in a collective sense, in any given cultural environment, is a continuously accumulating mechanism.

Ancient Knowledge, Ancient Know-how, Ancient Reasoning: Exploring the Old European Connection

For some mysterious reason cultural development in Neolithic Europe was swifter than in Anatolia, Mesopotamia or Egypt. The cultural activities of the early agriculturalists in the region made progress in a way as to eventually create the world's oldest high culture. The term "Old Europe" might evoke connotations of something old-fashioned or even primitive in the minds of some but its essence reflects in fact just the opposite. Some 7000 years ago, Old Europe (or the Danube civilization, respectively) represented the most advanced society of the Old World, and it flourished at a time when the ancient civilizations of Egypt and Mesopotamia did not yet exist.

What makes the world of Old Europe very special is the fact that it produced some of the key technologies which characterize any high culture and which were transferred to subsequent cultures, to ancient Greek civilization for one. This insight contrasts with the canon of Western education according to which we are trained, in the school curriculum and at university level, that the major achievements of high culture originated in the Near East and were transferred from there to Europe to civilize the barbarians. This is a myth. Let's have a look at the reality behind the myth:

EARLY MONUMENTAL ARCHITECTURE

The significance of sacred spaces is evidenced both for foraging and for agrarian communities. At Lepenski Vir in the area of the so-called Iron Gate in the Danube Valley (near

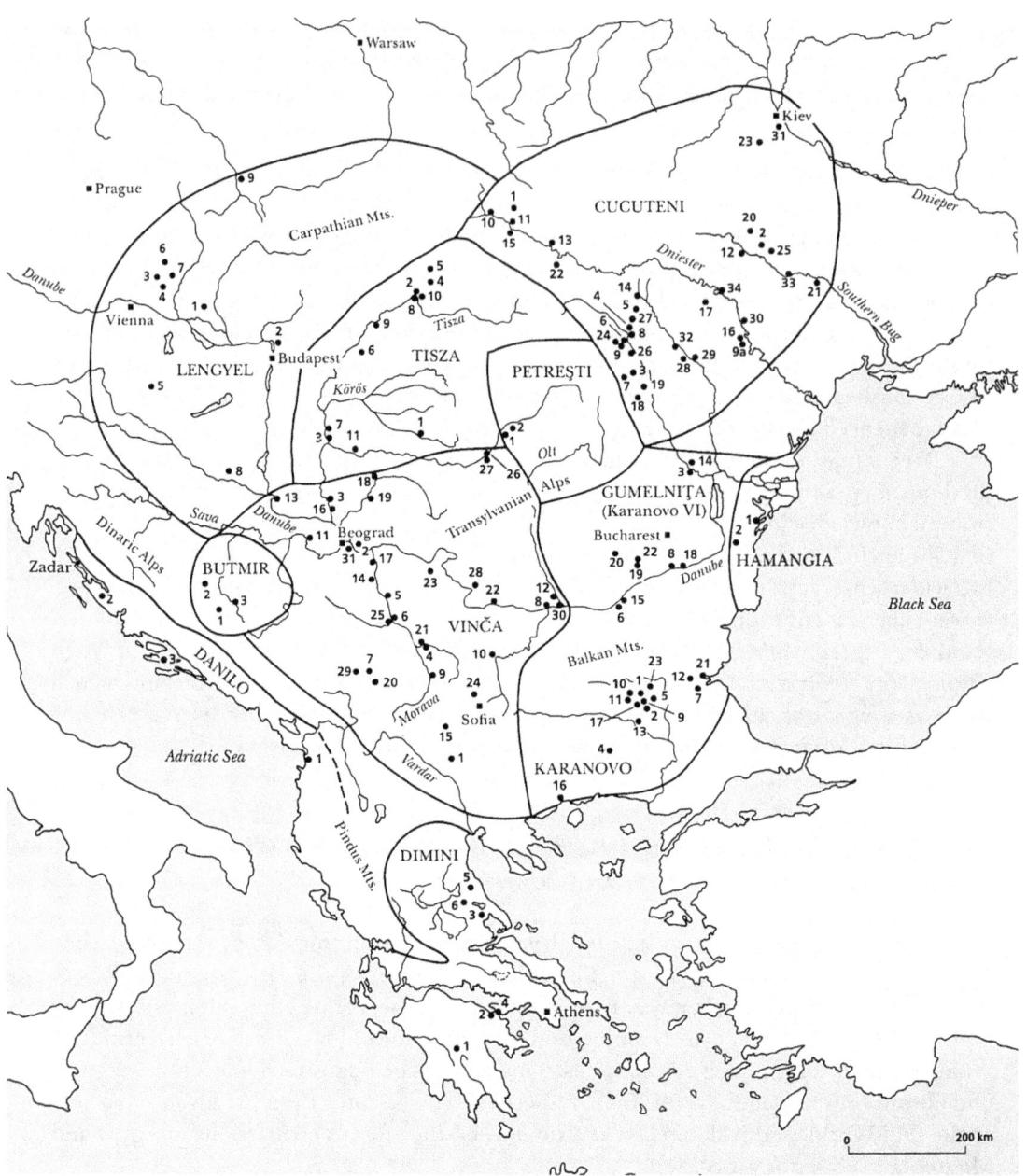

The cultural regions of the Danube civilization (Old Europe) (originally published in *The language of the goddess: Unearthing the hidden symbols of Western civilization* by Marija Gimbutas. San Francisco: Harper & Row, 1989. Used with permission of the Institute of Archaeomythology).

Map of the Late Neolithic, Chalcolithic, and Copper Age, East-Central Europe

I. Vinča Culture

1. Anza IV, C Macedonia; Early Vinča settlement
2. Banica at Belgrade, N Yugoslavia; stratified settlement
3. Beletinci, Novi Sad, N Yugoslavia; settlement
4. Crnokalačka Bara; settlement
5. Čuprija, Supska, C Yugoslavia; settlement
6. Drenovac, Svetozarevo, C Yugoslavia; settlement
7. Fafos, Kosovo Metohije, S Yugoslavia; settlement
8. Farcașu de Sus, SW Romania; settlement
9. Gradac, C Yugoslavia; settlement
10. Gradešnica (II), Vraca, NW Bulgaria; stratified settlement
11. Gomolava, Sremska Mitrovica, N Yugoslavia; large tell site; Vinča deposits on bottom
12. Hotărani, Olt, SW Romania; settlement
13. Jela Odžaci, NW Yugoslavia; settlement

14. Krameniti Vinogradi, Aradac, Servia, C Yugoslavia; settle-ment
15. Leskovica, SE Yugoslavia; destroyed settlement
16. Matejski Brod, Zrenjanin, N Yugoslavia; settlement
17. Medvednjak, Smederevska Palanka, C Yugoslavia; settlement
18. Parța, R. Termeș, Timișoara, W Romania; settlement
19. Potporanj, Vršac, N Yugoslavia; settlement
20. Predionica, Priština, Kosovo-Metohije, S Yugoslavia; settlement
21. Radacje, Niš, SE Yugoslavia; settlement
22. Rast, Dolj, SW Romania; settlement
23. Rudna Glava, E Yugoslavia; copper mines
24. Slatino, Klustendil, W Bulgaria; settlement
25. Svetozarevo (see Drenovac)
26. Tartaria, Club, W Romania; settlement
27. Turdaș, Cluj, W Romania; settlement
28. Vădăstra, SW Romania; stratified settlement tell
29. Valač, Kosovska Mitrovica, S Yugoslavia; settlement
30. Verbicioara, Dolj, SW Romania; settlement
31. Vinča, 14 km east of Belgrade; stratified tell; complete sequence of Vinča culture; Starčevo deposits at the bottom

II. Karanovo IV–VI (Gumelnița) Culture

1. Azmak, Stara Zagora, C Bulgaria; stratified tell
2. Bereketskaja Mogila, Stara Zagora, C Bulgaria; large tell site
3. Brailița, lower Siret, S Moldavia, Romania; settlement
4. Devetashka Cave, Plovdiv, C Bulgaria; cave sanctuary
5. Djadevo, Nova Zagora, C Bulgaria; large tell, numerous strata
6. Hotnica, lower Danube, N Bulgaria; sanctuary
7. Goljamo Delčevo, E Bulgaria; stratified settlement site
8. Gumelnița, lower Danube, south of Bucharest, Romania; stratified settlement tell
9. Lovets, Stara Zagora, C Bulgaria; settlement
10. Kalojanovets, Nova Zagora, C Bulgaria; settlement
11. Karanovo IV–VI, Nova Zagora, C Bulgaria; stratified settlement tell
12. Ovčarovo, Trgovište, NE Bulgaria; stratified settlement tell
13. Pazardžik, Plovdiv, C Bulgaria; settlement
14. Radașeni, S Moldavia, Romania; settlement
15. Ruse, lower Danube, N Bulgaria; settlement
16. Sitagroi I–III, Drama Plain, NE Greece; stratified settlement tell
17. Sulica, Stara Zagora, C Bulgaria; settlement
18. Sultana, lower Danube, S Romania; settlement
19. Tangiru, south of Bucharest, Romania; stratified settlement tell
20. Teiu, SE Romania; settlement tell
21. Varna, E Bulgaria; cemetery
22. Vidra at Bucharest, Romania; settlement tell
23. Yasatepe, C Bulgaria; settlement tell

III. Hamangia Culture

1. Baia, E Romania; cemetery
2. Cernavoda, E Romania; cemetery

IV. Petrești Culture

1. Pianul de Jos, Transylvania; settlement
2. Petrești, Transylvania; settlement

V. Cucuteni Culture

1. Bilcze Zlote, upper Dniester, W Ukraine; settlement
2. Brinzeni-Tsiganka, Moldavia; settlement
3. Buznea, Piatra Neamț, Moldavia, NE Romania; settlement
4. Cucuteni near Tirgu-Frumoș, d. of Iași, NE Romania; stratified settlement
5. Dragușeni at Botoșani, upper Prut, Moldavia, NE Romania; settlement
6. Frumușica at Piatra Neamț, Moldavia, NE Romania; settlement
7. Ghělaești-Nedeia district of Peatra Neamț, Moldavia, NE Romania; settlement and sanctuary
8. Habașești near Tirgu-Frumoș, Moldavia, NE Romania; settlement
9. Izvoare, district of Bacău, Moldavia, NE Romania; stratified settlement
9a. Karbuna, lower Dniester, Soviet Moldavia; large deposit of copper artifacts in a vase
10. Koshilivtsi (Koszyłowce), upper Dniester, W Ukraine; settlement
11. Kriszczatek, Bukovina, upper Dniester; settlement
12. Krutoborodintsi W Ukraine; settlement
13. Kuka Vrublevetskaya, upper Dniester, W Ukraine; settlement
14. Miorcani, Botoșani, Moldavia, NE Romania; settlement
15. Nezvisko, upper Dniester, W Ukraine; settlement (above Linear Pottery stratum)
16. Novye Ruseshty I, Kishenev, Soviet Moldavia; settlement
17. Petreni, M. Dniester, W Ukraine; settlement
18. Podei, Tirgu Ocna, NE Romania; settlement
19. Poduri Dealul Ghîndaru, Bacău, Moldavia, NE Romania; stratified
20. Popudnya, near Uman,' W Ukraine; settlement (temple model)
21. Sabatinivka, lower Bug, W Ukraine; temple
22. Șipenitsi (German: Schipenitz), upper Dniester, W Ukraine; settlement
23. Staraja Buda, SE of Kiev, Ukraine; settlement
24. Tirpești, district of Tg. Neamț, upper Siret, Moldavia, NE Romania; settlement
25. Tomashevka, middle So Bug, W Ukraine; settlement
26. Traian-Dealul Fîntînilor, R. Siret, Moldavia, NE Romania; settlement; and Traian-Dealul Viei; settlement
27. Trușești at Botoșani, between Siret and Prut, Moldavia, NE Romania; settlement
28. Valea Lupului, M. Prut, district of Iași, Moldavia, NE Romania; settlement
29. Valeni, Moldavia, NE Romania; settlement
30. Varvarovka, district of Kishenev, Soviet Moldavia; settlement
31. Veremie, south of Kiev, W Ukraine; settlement
32. Vladeni, north of Iași, Moldavia, NE Romania; settlement
33. Vladimirivka (Vladimirovka), middle So Bug (Boh), W Ukraine; settlement
34. Vykhvatintsi, Rybnitsa, upper Dniester, W Ukraine; cemetery

VI. Lengyel Culture

1. Abraham, W Slovakia; settlement

2. Aszód, north of Budapest; settlement and cemetery
3. Hluboké Mašuvky, Znojmo, Moravia, Czechoslovakia; settlement
4. Křepice, Brno, Moravia, Czechoslovakia; settlement
5. Sé, Szombately, W Hungary; settlement
6. Střelice, Znojmo, Moravia, Czechoslovakia; settlement
7. Tešetice-Kyjovice, Brno, Moravia, Czechoslovakia; settlement
8. Zengővárkony, SW Huntary; settlement
9. Jordanów, Dzierżoniów, district of Wroclaw, Silesia

VII. *Culture groups in the Tisza basin: lower Tisza (Tisza culture proper); upper Tisza (Meolithic Bükk, Copper Age Polgár, and Bodrogkeresztúr)*

1. Battonya, Szakálhát group, Tusza culture district Békés; settlement
2. Bodrogkeresztúr; cemetery
3. Hódmesövásárhely, Tisza culture; settlement
4. Kenézlö, Borsod-Abaúj-Zemplén, Bükk culture; settlement
5. Sarazsadany-Templomdomb, district Borsod-Abaúj-Zemplén, Bükk culture; settlement
6. Polgár (see Tiszapolgár)
7. Szegvár-Tüzköves, Szentes, Tisza culture; settlement
8. Tiszadada at Kalvinháza, district of Szabolcs-Szatmár, Bükk culture; settlement
9. Tiszapolgár-Basatanya; cemetery
10. Tiszavasvári-Jozsefházá, district Szabolcs, Szatmár; Bükk culture; settlement
11. Vesztö-Mágor, Tisza culture, near Békés, E Hungary; stratified settlement tell

VIII. *Butmir*

1. Butmir at Sarajevo, W Yugoslavia; settlement
2. Nebo, NE of Sarajevo, W Yugoslavia; settlement
3. Obre II, northwest of Sarajevo, W Yugoslavia; stratified Butmir settlement

IX. *Danilo-Hvar Culture*

1. Malik, Albania; settlement
2. Smilčić, Zadar; stratified settlement
3. Hvar, cave site on the island of Hvar

X. *Dimini Culture, Thessaly and Late Neolithic of S Greece*

1. Asea, Peloponnese; settlement
2. Corinth, Peloponnese; settlement
3. Dimini at Volos, Thessaly; settlement
4. Gonia, east of Corinth; settlement
5. Rakhmani, Thessaly; settlement
6. Zarkou, Larisa, Thessaly; settlement

the border of Serbia with Romania) several of the structures undoubtedly served ritual functions. There is continuity for the use of open-air spaces for ritual purposes from pre-agrarian to agrarian society (Bonsall 2008). The combination of open and roofed spaces within one and the same holy precinct—as a type of sacred space—is an innovation of the Neolithic. This type of sacred space is what is called a sanctuary. The layout of one of the sanctuaries

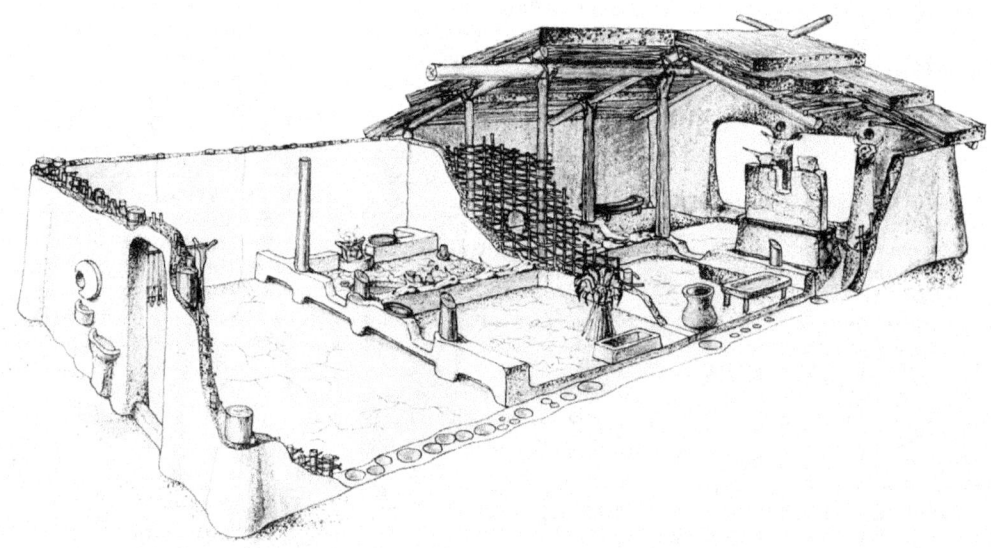

Above and opposite: The type of sanctuary with open and roofed spaces: (a) One of the sanctuaries at Parţa (Transylvania); sixth millennium BCE (courtesy of Gheorghe Lazarovici); (b) Reconstruction of the Minoan mountain sanctuary at Zakros (Crete); second millennium BCE (originally published in *The Aegean bronze age* by Oliver Dickinson. Cambridge: Cambridge University Press, 1994).

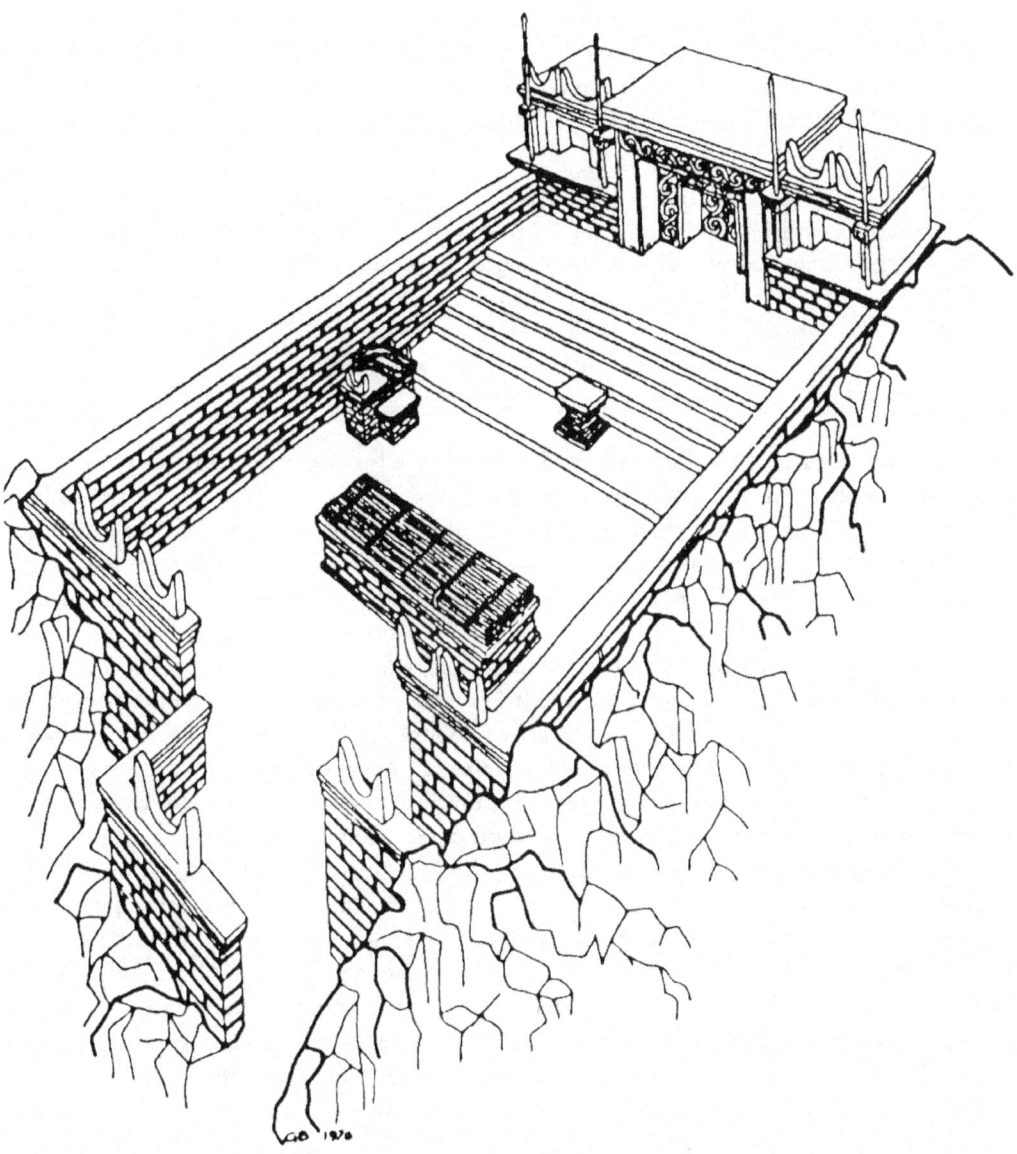

at Parța (Transylvania), with a square-shaped open-air yard and a shrine with a roof, represents a prototype that persists throughout the Neolithic and the Copper Age of Old Europe and influences architecture during the Bronze Age. In the Mycenaean period, this type of sanctuary is called *temenos* which is a term of pre–Greek origin. Evidently, the Mycenaeans adopted the architectural prototype and the term, either directly on the mainland or via the mediation of Minoan culture in ancient Crete where temenos-type sanctuaries are also known.

Urbanization

The earliest urban settlements of the Old World that emerged in the northeastern region of the Danube civilization predate the ancient Sumerian cities. The aggregation of settlements to the size of towns dates to the end of the fifth millennium BCE. The trend toward urbanization reached its peak in the first half of the fourth millennium. The largest settlements of Old Europe are found in an area between the Dnieper and South Bug rivers in southern Ukraine where the local Trypillya culture flourished.

> Between about 3700 and 3400 BC, a group of Tripol'ye C1 towns in this region reached sizes of 250 to 450 hectares, two or four times larger than the first cities of Mesopotamia.... These megatowns were located in the hills east of the South Bug river, near the steppe frontier in the southern forest-steppe ecological zone. They were the largest communities not just in Europe, but anywhere in the world [Anthony 2009a: 52].

Notational Systems and Intentional Sign Use

In Neolithic Europe we find the earliest evidence for the intentional use of abstract signs for two different notational systems. One is the notation of numbers (with the help of bars and dots), the other is the intentional use of signs for the purpose of rendering ideas in writing (Merlini 2009, Haarmann 2010). The Old European script was based on the archaic principle of logographic writing where a sign stands for a whole word (or idea, respectively). It is as yet unknown whether some of the signs could have phonetic value.

The beginnings of the two systems date to the sixth millennium BCE. This is a double world record. First, the introduction of writing technology in southeastern Europe predates similar processes in Egypt and Mesopotamia by two thousand years. Second, Europe presents the first instance in history of two parallel systems of notation, one for recording numbers and another for writing. Similar sets of dual notational systems are known from ancient Egypt and ancient Sumer, but those sign systems emerge much later than in Europe.

Writing persists into the Bronze Age (i.e., the ancient Aegean scripts), so does the sign system for writing numbers (Haarmann 1995: 49*ff*). The duality of the notational systems is abandoned when the Greeks adopted the Phoenician alphabet in the eighth century BCE. Since, in Phoenician, numbers were written with alphabetic signs also Greek letters could have numeric value. For instance, the letter alpha had the numeric value 1, the beta represented the number 2, gamma the 3, and so on. Also higher numbers were rendered with the help of letters (e.g., sigma stood for 200, chi for 600 and omega for 800); (Threatte 1996: 278). In classical Greek antiquity there was no separate sign system in use for writing numbers.

The features mentioned in the foregoing and various other properties by which Old Europe distinguishes itself from contemporary surrounding cultures are markers of civilization in the sense of high culture. The markers of civilization in Europe find their parallels in the early civilizations of Mesopotamia and Egypt, with the significant difference that the Danube civilization holds the record in that it represents the oldest known experiment with technologies that make a civilization. If the use of notational systems (i.e., visual communication and notation of numbers) says something about the intellectual capacities of their users then the native Europeans living in the Neolithic era professed a high degree of cultural evolution. In fact, they reached the stage of high culture. "The Old European system [of writing] may well have had the potential as it is conventionalised and since it exhibits an abstract ordering of its elements; some conventions may be completely fixed, while others appear only partially fixed" (Röhr 1994: 193).

The Role of Cultural Memory for the Transfer of Knowledge in the Intergenerational Chain

If Old Europe had the high standards of technological advancement and professional skills that shows in the archaeological record, the question arises to what degree were those standards kept up and how did the transfer to subsequent cultures work? The answer to these questions have to do with the ways knowledge is transmitted. Knowledge does not only provide the bricks from which culture is constructed, but knowledge is also the means by which traditions, customs and know-how is handed over—by those who have accumulated it—to future generations. When we talk about knowledge and the ways it is transmitted in the intergenerational chain, we have to be aware that the construction of knowledge is something else than collecting information. Although these two capacities of the human brain are interdependent they nevertheless unfold on different levels.

Knowledge is an integrative activity which encompasses various processes: collecting information, evaluating data and constructing second-order knowledge with it, that is reasoning with and about collected data. The act of collecting information is elementary and an essential precondition for constructing knowledge which is a higher-order process. Collected data itself is not knowledge but only the raw material for crafting it. Since their appearance in the evolutionary chain of life forms human beings have been in need to construct knowledge, for their survival in the natural environment, for group formation and social interaction, for the development of technologies, for the creation of ideas about the world and about the working of the supernatural.

In order to construct and keep functioning such a complex system of group activity and interaction that can be called culture, intimate knowledge is required about the orderly interplay of conventions of social conduct, economic resources and a wide range of in-group activities in the living-space that human beings have created. The core of shared knowledge that every individual carries in his/her mind has been termed "foundational knowledge."

> Some forms of cultural knowledge are shared by all members of a group and provide the bases for their shared worldview. This is foundational knowledge and it is likely to be learned by infants as part of primary socialization. Foundational knowledge is intersubjective in that it provides a shared framework of knowing upon which most subjective or personal knowing rests [Shore 1998:157*f*].

In order to make knowledge—essential for constructing culture—operational human beings need media for sharing items of knowledge, that is, for their transmission. Knowledge must be stored for reuse to remain operational. Not all media that serve in the transmission of knowledge have storage capacity. Spoken language facilitates the transmission of knowledge but it is not itself a medium for the storage of items of knowledge. The conditions are different with written language which serves the exchange of information and possesses storage capacity for items of knowledge to be preserved for reuse.

For categorizing items of knowledge as new items vis-à-vis items that have been learned earlier and which have been stored for reuse, cultural memory draws on a wide range of vehicles of its expression. An indispensable requirement for the working of cultural memory is the mastering of different sign systems to respond to the manifold needs of knowledge exchange and perpetuated reuse among the members of the community (e.g., heraldic or clan symbols, notation of a popular calendar, religious symbols), among them sets of meaningful symbols and/or assemblages of meaningful items of material culture. In the case of ancient civilizations, the reconstruction, by a modern observer, of their level of knowledge and technical skills can only rely on the systems of visual storage of information that the bearers of those civilizations once created for themselves because, once the ancients can no longer talk to us we have to decode what their cultural heritage keeps in store.

The relationship between knowledge-transmission and the living-conditions within a given culture is so elementary, and the variety of vehicles at the disposal of people's cultural memory to express, maintain and keep up this relationship is so vast that this range of dynamic activity may be addressed as a realm of culture in its own right, as "knowledge as culture" (McCarthy 1996). From this standpoint knowledge-construction has to be perceived as culturally specific, both in the sense of how it works and with respect to its content. "What makes knowledge a cultural entity, then, is that it is distributed to, shared with, and acquired from others" (Mokyr 2002: 7). Recent investigations in classical studies have highlighted the central role of knowledge-construction which is—in all its varieties—at the very core of the functioning of the most popular model of governance, of democracy (Ober 2008); (see Chapters 6 and 7).

It is fascinating to study the working of cultural memory and how it shapes the interplay of artifacts and associated mentifacts. What is even more fascinating is the study of processes of transmission of knowledge from one generation to the next, from one period to the subsequent layer of culture. In the course of a longer process of transition, customs, attitudes, behavioral patterns and values may readily persist despite changes in economic subsistence. If we conceptualize sociocultural transition as unfolding on a trail of cultural continuity, then we might find a clue to how useful knowledge of one period may be transmitted, in the intergenerational chain, to experience a gradual fusion with innovative ideas of a subsequent period to give shape to a novel cultural profile.

The Longevity of the Achievements of the Ancients: Domains of Pre-Greek Knowledge-Construction and How It Can Be Traced in the Lexical Borrowings of Palaeo-European Coinage in the Ancient Greek Vocabulary

The accumulated knowledge that is necessary for constructing a local culture and for shaping its individual profile is not random, but rather organized as a matrix of interrelated items in the human mind. The fabric of a culture and its level of sophistication depend on the quality of the knowledge that is collectively available to construct it. Knowledge-construction becomes part of cultural memory in the intergenerational chain, transferring cultural patterns from one generation to the next.

Another essential factor for any culture and its sustainability is the network of beliefs that govern community life. Knowledge-construction does not evolve in a vacuum. All knowledge that is used for constructing culture is integrated in a frame of beliefs and values. The relationship between knowledge and belief systems is a mutual one. On the one hand, items of knowledge are the bricks used to construct a worldview. On the other hand, once a worldview has been crafted, it will have an impact on how knowledge is retrieved and applied. There is no knowledge-construction without the "umbrella" of a worldview, and there is no worldview without applicable knowledge.

It seems unreasonable to assume any kind of "primitivism" in the ways that the early Greeks shaped their culture in contact with the native Europeans. Literacy was a cultural pattern which the early Greeks encountered already during the Bronze Age, but given the fact that the know-how of writing had shifted from Old Europe to the ancient Aegean cultures, most of the kind of learning from experience and the formation of worldview during the transitional period unfolded without the help of writing technology.

> But everything which we know about what the Greeks [...] *did* surely indicates that they had beliefs, both founded (knowledge, therefore) and unfounded, in exactly the same sense that we do. Any country maiden of pre–Platonic times *knew* quite as well as any in the Greece of the third century BC or today that milk left in the summer sun would sour faster than milk placed where it would be cooler. This is conceptual knowledge just as truly as claims about the angles of triangles. The only difference is that the classes of things unified under the concepts used in the two cases are different types of classes: of particular events or things in the former case and of abstract entities in the latter [Willard 1983: 251].

In the 1960s, spurred by folk-anthropological assessments of Western civilization, the myth of the alphabet effect was created. McLuhan's classical study *The Gutenberg Galaxy* (1962) set in motion a movement whose representatives associated the ability of abstract thinking with the elaboration of abstract writing systems, alphabetic writing in particular. That was a time when work on the decipherment of Linear B, the oldest script for rendering Greek, was not yet completed and the impact of literacy in that script on early Greek society was not yet known. When taking into consideration only the adoption of the Phoenician writing system, in the eighth century BCE, for writing Greek one might arrive at simplistic conclusions of the kind that the high degree of abstractness of the alphabet (i.e., phonographic writing according to the principle of one letter as an equivalent of one sound in the phonetic system of a given language) would have enhanced abstract thinking among the Greeks, and the impulses from using an abstract writing system would have enhanced cultural evolution and produced the achievements of the classical era. In short: the accumulation of abstract knowledge in pre–Platonic Greek society was viewed as resulting from the introduction of the alphabet. Such views were still repeated in the 1980s (e.g., Logan 1986) although, then, much information had already been available about the older phonographic script of the Greeks, Linear B.

The primary error in the discourse about the effect of alphabetic writing on culture is that the alphabet is perceived as the prototype of a phonographic system, with cultural achievements being unilaterally associated with the development and spread of this specific type of writing. It has been erroneously claimed that the alphabet distinguishes itself from other types of writing by the phonetic principle and the lineal alignment of letters, and that these properties allegedly promoted abstract thinking. In his critical analysis of older folk-anthropological literature on this issue, Watt (1989) got writing right and brought it to the point:

> There is nothing distinctively "phonetic" or "lineal" about the "phonetic alphabet," since syllabaries are just as phonetic and every bit as "lineal." And syllabaries were in use long before alphabets among the upwardly-mobile cultures of the Near and Middle East; in fact ... the Greeks themselves used a syllabary—Mycenaean or "Linear B"—from about 1600 to about 1200 [...]. So if having a "phonetic" and "lineal" writing system promotes civilization, why did the Greeks have to wait for the alphabet to cross their path? [Watt 1989: 285*f*].

The arguments of abstractness in thinking as being linked to the use of alphabetic writing fall down in light of the early history of Greek civilization which is rooted in much older layers than would be acknowledged by classical studies. There is another facet in this search for the roots of Western civilization which deserves scrutinous investigation, and this is the interplay of oral and written communication in classical antiquity, especially in Athens under the democracy.

> This point needs to be clear: there is significant overlap between the functions and features of speech and writing across a much wider range of political activities than was once believed. The Athenians realized very quickly the complementary potentiality of the two different modes of communication, the written and the oral, in the functioning of their participatory democracy. Spoken language served a very important role in their decision-making institutions, where speakers formulated orally statements amenable to critical, rational but also emotional discussions on various matters which affected their lives. But the Athenians were also aware that script could serve many additional functions. Their Assembly meetings, for example, where orality was the sole mode of communication, would be supplemented and enhanced if decisions were written down.... Hence, they employed politically patterned communicative practices drawn up jointly on speech and writing [Missiou 2011: 144*f*].

The range of knowledge that is accumulated by members in a community, associated with orality and/or literacy, covers every domain involved in the construction of a local culture, starting from the knowledge about natural phenomena (e.g., seasonal changes in the vegetation cycle) to information about the working of machines. Since classical antiquity, the high cultures of the Old World have passed on the knowledge of the existence and the functions of the six "basic machines" (the lever, screw, pulley, balance, wedge, wheel) to subsequent generations. Such knowledge has been stored in the form of oral memory and/or in writing.

In order for us to perceive the magnitude of the process of transmission of ancient knowledge—over several millennia—the various spheres of knowledge-construction in the Greek world will be mapped out where Old European influence can be traced. This influence left traces that can be identified as elements of the pre–Greek substratum.

The Fabric of the Pre-Greek Heritage in Greek Civilization: Chronological Layers of the Cultural and Linguistic Substratum

Ever since the ancestors of the Greeks, Indo-European pastoralists, migrated south from northern areas of the Balkan peninsula, they were in constant contact with the indigenous Palaeo-European population. Gradually, the former pastoralists became acquainted with the technologies, cultural patterns and customs that governed the daily life of people in the agrarian settlements.

The Indo-European tribes that moved south and changed their lifeways nevertheless preserved some of their old customs. Among these old customs was the hierarchical social order of a pastoralist society which is reflected in the male dominance of public life in Greek antiquity and in the élite status of Greek aristocracy. During the Mesolithic Age, which lasted roughly from the tenth to the eighth/seventh millennia BCE, social stratification was a rare phenomenon. "Sustained marking-out of skills and social distinctions appear to have been relatively rare in Mesolithic Europe, but instances in which some kind of socially dominant authority has arisen nonetheless exist" (Spikins 2008: 15). It is noteworthy that the instances mentioned are found in the East European Plain, in the ecological environment where ancient pastoralism emerged.

In eastern Europe, Neolithic transitions produced a trend that favored neither agrarian lifeways nor social egalitarianism. In the steppe zone of southern Russia during the early Neolithic of the seventh millennium BCE, a shift occurred from hunter-gatherer subsistence to a pastoralist economy with sheep, goats and horses (and later also cattle) as the basis of animal husbandry. Pastoralist society soon produced social stratification with the emergence of a system of clans with strong leadership, territorial control over pastures and with a warrior élite whose importance increased over time.

> The speakers of Proto-Indo-European had institutionalized offices of power and social ranks, [...] Chiefs first appeared in the archaeological record of the Pontic-Caspian steppes when domesticated cattle, sheep, and goats first became widespread, after about 5200–5000 BCE. An interesting aspect of the spread of animal keeping in the steppes was the concurrent rapid rise of chiefs who wore multiple belts and strings of polished shell beads, bone beads, beaver-tooth and horse-tooth beads, boars tusk pendants, boars-tusk caps, boars-tusk plates sewed to their clothing, pendants of crystal and porphyry, polished stone bracelets, and gleaming copper rings [Anthony 2007: 160].

The living conditions in pastoralist communities promoted the development of hierarchical structures and the rise of élite power as political control.

In their mythology, the people from the steppe kept alive the pastoralist heritage which crystallizes around the central figure of a pastoral god. Among the oldest divinities whose existence can be identified for Proto-Indo-European mythology is a pastoral god. This figure was created by the pastoralist clan groups in their original Indo-European homeland—that is, in the steppe zone stretching from eastern Ukraine through southern Russia to the northern shores of the Caspian Sea. The name of this divinity, the protector of flocks, has been reconstructed as *Pehauson* (Mallory and Adams 1997: 415). The name lives on in the form names of pastoral gods in Greek mythology (i.e., Pan) and in Old Indic (Vedic) mythology (i.e., Puṣa), and the connection between these names is widely accepted (West 2007: 281*f*). The existence of equivalents of the original name as proper names in Venetic (Puso) and Messapic (Pauso) has also been proven.

In the figure of Pan, old animistic beliefs about the oneness of all life forms persist. Pan is half-human and half-animal. According to *Homeric Hymn 19*, Pan's father was Hermes, who fell in love with the daughter of Dryops with whom he had a child who looked strange, "with its goat feet, horns, and a beard" (Gantz 1993: 110). According to the Greek writer Pindar (fifth century BCE), Pan was the companion of the Great Mother. Pan was venerated as the patron of herds and cattle and the guarantor of the fertility of goat herds (Bader 1989).

In Greek literature, the god Pan is often associated with the nymphs. In one context (the *Theogony* of Hieronymus and Hellanicus), the god Pan is equated with Zeus: "And it calls him Zeus the orderer of all and of the whole world, wherefore he is also called Pan." According to Bernabé (2010: 428), "[t]his seems to be a pun on Pan 'the universe.' The idea is consistent with the images of the god Pan with the Zodiac, which are best interpreted as representing the universe."

We have an expression in the cultural vocabulary of our modern languages which is ultimately derived from the name of the god Pan, and this is "panic" (meaning "unreasonable fear"; cf. German *Panik*, French *panique*, etc.). Panic is a contagious emotion which is supposedly induced by Pan, and the expression itself derives from the Greek adjective *panikos* meaning "of Pan."

Just like the Palaeo-Europeans, thousands of years earlier, who had adopted the agrarian package from Anatolian pioneers the Indo-Europeans migrants eventually settled down and accustomed to an agrarian way of life.

> Ancient agriculture demonstrated great continuity: there was neither any revolutionary technological innovation in agriculture nor any mechanisation, only some improvements in the tools and the methods of cultivation. No large-scale enterprises came into being in the area of the skilled crafts, and mass production hardly emerged at all [Thommen 2012: 33].

The migrants from the north blended in with their new neighbors. In the course of this process of settling down, the migrants adopted useful technologies from the indigenous people and became familiar with their lifeways to which they themselves finally accustomed. While the newcomers adopted basic technologies and tools from the native Europeans, they later added their own experience and, in the course of time, devised some innovations. This can be illustrated in the domain of technical terms associated with the plow and its parts. The Greeks did not invent the plow. This tool had been in use since the Neolithic, thousands of years before the arrival of the Indo-European migrants in Greece.

The distribution of words according to their etymology shows a network of terms, being comprised of borrowings from the substrate language and expressions of genuinely Greek coinage. The kind of plow that was used by the Greeks has been reconstructed (Drachmann 1938), and for certain of its parts, expressions from the substrate language were used. These terms are *gye / gyes* "the curved piece of wood in a plow" (Beekes 2010: 290) and *hynis / hynnis / hynne* "ploughshare" (Beekes 2010: 1532).

> There can be no doubt that the plough was symmetrical, that is to say, it could not turn the soil in the modern way; instead, it left a scratch in the soil. In other words it was an *ard*, and as such it has been in use in the Mediterranean area until our time, when it may still be found, mostly in mountainous areas [Isager and Skydsgaard 1995: 46].

In the process of interethnic relations, between native Europeans and the ancestors of the Greeks, different phases of cultural exchange can be distinguished. Although the immigrants from the North, the Proto-Greeks, came to dominate the native Europeans in their areas of settlement there was a certain driving force at work that inspired the newcomers to absorb the advanced technologies and the accumulated knowledge of the natives. When the migrants from the North entered Greece the cultivated landscape where the Palaeo-Europeans had practiced agriculture for thousands of years was unknown, strange and so

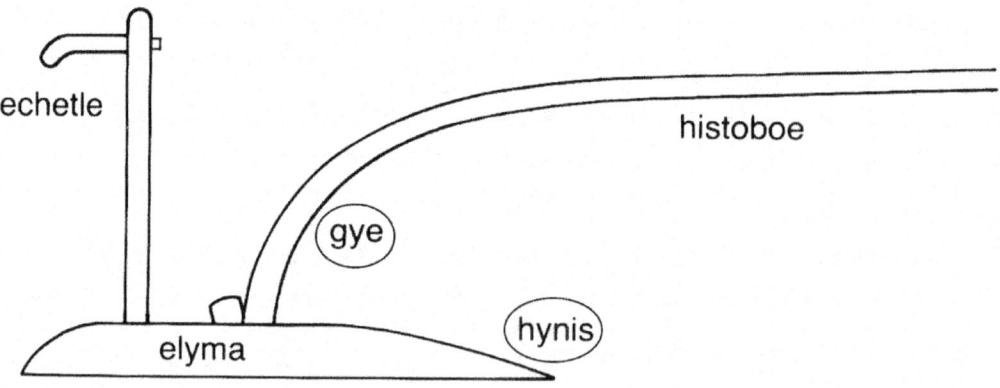

Diagram of an ancient plow and its parts (pre–Greek terms in circles) (author's collection).

different from their homeland, the Eurasian steppe. The attraction that arises from a strange advanced society for the foreigner triggers specific anthropological processes: acculturation and assimilation. It is a widely known—perhaps global—experience "that things, information, and experience acquired from distant places, being strange and different, have great potency, great supernatural power, and if attainable, increase the ideological power and political prestige of those who acquire them" (Helms 1988: 263).

Already in the northern area of the Balkan peninsula, the Indo-Europeans got acquainted with the basics of agriculture, of pottery making, metallurgy and weaving. Seemingly, also the cultivation of wine and the adoption of elementary terminology from the substrate language belong to the phase of early contacts. The cultivation of olives was practiced in the southern parts of the Balkans, and this for climatic reasons. Olives grow in the zone of dry Mediterranean climate, not in the northern zone with its wetter Atlantic climate. The Greeks got to know olive trees and their cultivation in their new homeland, Hellas. Given these ecological conditions the extant pre–Greek terminology in the domain of olive cultivation entered the Greek language in a later phase of contacts.

Given the complexity of the transitional process, involving migrational movements, interethnic contacts, cross-cultural exchange and linguistic interference, it is not possible—and perhaps not even reasonable—to draw a clear chronological dividing line between an older and a younger phase (corresponding to an older and a younger layer of borrowings from the pre–Greek substrate language). The distinction is rather floating, with certain influences reflecting cultural conditions of an early phase of contacts while others point to a later phase. The two phases may perhaps best be understood as gravitations on a chronological continuum, marking various stages of cultural and linguistic fusion.

On the linguistic level, the fusion process of Old European elements and those of genuinely Greek (i.e., Indo-European) fabric did not only produce a mere influx of lexical borrowings but it also resulted in the restructuring of whole terminological networks, thus reflecting a symbiotic interplay of originally foreign and indigenous items in culture and language use. Greek existed as a language from the third millennium BCE onward.

> Mycenaean Greek, the language of the Linear B tablets, is known by ca. 1300 BC if not somewhat earlier and is different enough from its Bronze Age contemporaries (Indo-Iranian or Anatolian) and from reconstructed PIE [Proto-Indo-European] to predispose a linguist to place a date of ca. 2000 BC or earlier for Proto-Greek itself [Mallory and Adams 2006: 103].

It can be assumed that the incorporation of lexical elements from the substratum was a prolonged process, starting in the period of Proto-Greek and continuing into the Mycenaean era and beyond.

The level of socioeconomic development reflected in the pre–Greek lexical borrowings—adopted by the Greeks in the course of the second millennium BCE—points to the sociocultural heritage of an agrarian population that was indigenous to the region and had practiced agriculture long before the arrival of the Indo-Europeans. There is evidence for the cultivation of vine and olive in various parts of Old Europe since the fifth millennium BCE (i.e., in Bulgaria, Macedonia, western Crete; Tomkins 2010: 33).

The distribution of lexical elements which form part of the pre–Greek substratum suggests an extended period of social interaction between pre–Greeks and Greeks. Among the loanwords are also expressions in the domain of body-part terminology (e.g., *sphyron* "ankle, foot-joint"), kinship terminology (e.g., *baia* "grandmother") and in the vocabulary of intimacy (e.g., *skyza* "lust, heat"). In addition to these sections of the borrowed vocabulary also the occurrence of verbs (e.g., *dynamai* "be mighty, potent") among the borrowings points to the fact that contact between Greeks and the pre–Greek autochthonous populations was intensive (see Haarmann 2011a: 58*ff*, 2012: 153*ff*).

The Composition of the Older Layer

It is reasonable to associate the cultural traditions mentioned in the foregoing to the older layer of the substratum since this is attested, in the archaeological record, as belonging to the period of Indo-European out-migrations from the steppe, that is to the fifth and fourth millennia BCE. The cultural and linguistic influence of the older layer was active at the time of the migratory movements of the pastoralists into southeastern Europe. That era predates the formative period of Greek ethnicity in the region that was to become known as Hellas in the first millennium BCE.

WINE CULTIVATION AND THE ROLE OF DIONYSOS

Greek civilization is known for its appreciation—and extensive consumption—of wine. It is obvious that the Greeks were fond of wine cultivation and developed this domain according to their refined gourmet taste. Greek literature abounds with praises of wine and wine festivals of which the Dionysian are the most famous. The production of and the trade with wine was a factor of prominent importance for the economy in the Greek world.

> Ancient Greece clearly had plenty of genuine experience in wine-making. Indeed, ignorance of wine was generally considered the mark of barbarians, such as the Scythians who lived in present-day Crimea (where vines were planted centuries later). Greek writers mentioned fifty varieties of grape. Some of these were continued in Roman vineyards, such as those known by the Romans as the Greco and the Grechetto. Theophrastus [fourth/third centuries BCE] talks of matching grape varieties to different types of soil and climate. Hesiod [eighth/seventh centuries BCE], the first of Greek poets, recommends early September as the best time for harvest. The Greeks believed in additives such as honey, brine and herbs, the latter producing a sort of vermouth. Theophrastus was keen on blending, suggesting that the hard, aromatic wine from Heraclea did well when mixed with Erythraean, a softer, salty wine without much bouquet. Wines probably did not last very long in ancient Greece, though Theocritus [third century BCE] speaks of drinking four-year-old wine, perhaps from Kos. And Peparethian was a well-known slow-developer, which took six years to reach maturity. But the alluring comparisons of the wine merchant were already a feature. The comic poet Hermippus talks of a mature wine 'smelling of violets, roses and hyacinths' and attributes a scent of apples to the wine from Thasos, to which ... Archestratus awarded two stars, provided it was properly aged [Mount 2010: 122*f*].

It is widely but erroneously believed that the ancient Greeks introduced the cultivation of wine to Europe. Wine cultivation is much older and dates to the times of Old Europe. In fact, wine was fermented and consumed by the ancient Danubians as early as the fifth millennium BCE. The earliest traces of wine production in Europe were found in the region of Varna, and there is still earlier evidence coming from the Caucasus, from Georgia and Armenia, where wine may have been cultivated as early as the seventh millennium BCE.

There can be no doubt that the Greeks learned the art of wine production from their predecessors, the indigenous Europeans. We find ample proof for the adoption of this specialized domain of agriculture by the Greeks in the broad layer of borrowings of Old European origin (see below). The terminology of wine cultivation in ancient Greek reflects the strong impact of Old European know-how. Key elements of the ancient terminology of wine production were adopted by the Greeks as lexical borrowings.

There is a hidden hint at the wine cultivation in the northern part of the Balkan region and the early acquaintance of Greek tribes with it in Greek mythology. The god Dionysos is the most popular figure related to wine. He is also called Bakchos (since the fifth century BCE), and this name form lives on in Roman mythology as Bacchus. Dionysos is the son of Zeus and Semele, daughter of the king of Thebes. According to tradition, Dionysos came from the north, from Thrace. The original form of his name can be reconstructed as *Diosnusos* of which the first element is Indo-European (meaning "god") and the second part refers to the name of a mountain (Nysa) on an island surrounded by the waters of the river Triton. This second element stems from the substrate language. Mount Nysa was the home of the *nysai,* nymphs of the mountain, who took care of Dionysos while he was a child. Many attempts have been made to explain the name form Dionysos entirely as of Indo-European coinage. And yet, "since all attempts to find an IE [Indo-European] etymology have failed, we have to accept that it is a foreign name" (Beekes 2010: 337).

There are other items associated with Dionysos that point to pre–Greek origins. The typical wine cup used during the festival to honor the god (the Great Dionysian Festival), the *kantharos,* is a substrate word, and the *thyrsos,* a wand made of a staff of the giant fennel (ferula communis), with a pine cone on its top, serving as a symbol of Dionysos' followers (the Bacchic maenads), also is a pre–Greek term. The Dionysiac festive procession was called *komos* (< pre–Greek).

> He it was that / drove the nursing women who were in charge / of frenzied Bacchus through the land of Nysa, / and they flung their *thyrsoi* on the ground as / murderous Lycurgus beat them with his ox- / goad [Diomedes speaking to Glaucus in Homer's *Iliad,* Book VI.132–137].

Dionysos was venerated as the god who blessed human beings with the gift of wine. He was compared, in his significance for human society, with Demeter, the Grain Mother, who blessed humankind with the know-how of plant cultivation. The combination of bread and wine was the most common of the Greek diets. In the *Bacchae* of Euripides the two benefits ("a loaf of bread, a flask of wine") and their patrons are celebrated (in Teiresias' speech).

> Two things are paramount for the human race: the goddess Demeter; she is Earth; call her by which of the two names you prefer. She nurtures humans on dry foods. The one who came later, the son of Semele, discovered the moist drink of the vine and gave it to mortals: it releases unhappy humans from sorrow, when they take their fill of the sheen from the vine, and gives sleep and oblivion of our daily misfortunes; there is no other cure for troubles [Euripides, *Bacchae* 274–83].

Contrary to Euripides' perception of the different age for the cults of Demeter and Dionysos, there is evidence that both cults were practiced already among the Mycenaean Greeks. It is very likely that the two figures, being both of pre–Greek coinage, date much further back in time.

> According to the traditional view the cult of Diónusos was taken up by the Greeks quite late, sometimes after the collapse of Mycenaean culture. Its origin was presumed to be in the "less cul-

tivated north" (Thrace), or "the decadent east" (Phrygia, Lydia).... In 1990 Greek-Swedish excavation in Khania [Crete] found a fragment KH Gq 5 with the following text: .1 Di-wi-jo-[de,] Di-we ME+Ri 209 vas + A 1; .2 Di-wo-nu-so MERI+RI [ ] 2 "to the sanctuary of Zeus to Zeus 1 amphora of honey"; "to Dionysos 2 amphoras of honey." This is absolutely certain evidence that the cult of Dionysus was practised in Mycenaean times, and theophoric personal names derived from it were also used. Thus, the Linear B texts solved the controversial problems concerning the early period of Dionysus' cult in Greece [Ilievski 2000: 367].

The substrate elements in Greek wine terminology form a highly diversified assemblage and they branch out into various subsections.

(i) Knowledge relating to the growing and handling of vines
  amamaxys "vine trained on two poles"
  ampelos "vine" (derivation ampelitawon "viticulturist," A-pe-ri-ta-wo in Linear B)
  araschades "last year's vinetwigs"
  beka "vine that grows up trees"
  bolene "grapevine"
  helinos "vine"
  ix / ips "worm that damages the vine"
  kadousa "kind of vine"
  kamax "pole to support the vine"
  klema "tendril (of the vine)"
  molax "a kind of vine (in Bithynia)"
  oreskhas "vine with grapes"
  orkhos "row of vines"
  thrinia "vine (Cretan)"
  huien "vine"

(ii) Harvesting and handling of grapes
  agerrakabos / aggerakomon "bunch of grapes"
  astaphis "dried grapes, raisins"
  botrys "bunch of grapes"
  gigarton "grape-stone"
  omphax "unripe grape"
  oron agricultural tool (piece of wood) with which bunches of grapes are crushed
  oskhai "branches full of bunches of grapes" (*oskhophoria* name of an Athenian festive day)
  pateo "to tread grapes"

rax "grape"
staphyle "grape"
strymax "wood built into a winevat for the pressing of grapes"
trygao "to gather grapes (in the vineyard)"
psithios "kind of grape"

(iii) Production of wine
  karoinon "sweet wine"
  chalis "unblended wine"
  kirros "yellow-brown (color of wine)"
  latax "drop of wine"
  lenos "trough (for pressing wine), winepress"
  oinos "wine"
  oniglin "kind of wine"
  oxos "vinegar"
  pramneios "qualification of wine"
  siraion "boiled wine"
  syphaka "new wine"
  targanon "sour wine, vinegar" (Attic)
  tryge "vintage"
  trygia "sweet wine"
  tryx "young, unfermented wine with yeast, must"

(iv) Vessels for storing wine, ladles for drawing wine
  kuathos "ladle for drawing wine"
  pithos "large, mostly earthen vessel for storing wine, which is open at the top"
  phidakne "wine jar"

The multitude of pre–Greek terms in the domain of wine cultivation is astounding. The terms adopted from the substrate language—spoken by those who cultivated wine in southeastern Europe before the Greeks—were integrated into the Greek vocabulary to form a network of specialized terminology, in close association with genuinely Greek terms.

Weaving from Old Europe to Ancient Greece: A Case Study of Long-term Continuity of a Specialized Handicraft

Progress in the development of any civilization lies with the innovative potential of its technologies. Technological advance is a function of the improvement and spread of existing techniques as well as the invention of new ones. The history of the warp-weighted loom in southeastern Europe illustrates how a very old technology (dating to the sixth millennium BCE) flourished and spread far under the conditions of an advancing society.

Weaving was among the technologies that are attested for southeastern Europe already in the Early Neolithic Age (seventh millennium BCE). Evidence for the use of the vertical loom comes from the loom weights that have been found in the southern and western parts of southeastern Europe. Barber (1991: 98) sees "connections southward into the Aegean as well as northwestward into Hungary." During the sixth millennium BCE, weaving spread throughout the whole area of the Danube civilization and into adjacent regions.

Weaving is a handicraft with a long tradition, and its primary purpose is practical. Spindle whorls and loom weights, many of them inscribed, have been unearthed in the cultural provinces of the Danube civilization extending as far as the eastern Trypillya culture in western Ukraine where the use of writing on spindle whorls persisted well into the third millennium BCE (Videiko 2003: 114*ff*). The latest specimens of inscribed whorls date to ca. 2600 BCE (in the Dnieper region).

At first sight, inscribed spindle whorls seem to deviate from the overall religious embedding of sign use in the Danube civilization, but it is exactly the religious embedding of weaving which allows for an embodied perception of this activity in ancient community life. The intention to inscribe spindle whorls may have served two purposes which both relate to the religious worldview of the ancient society. According to Winn (1981: 245) these purposes are: "(1) magical marking to ensure successful production of yarn or of the final

Inscribed loom weights from sites of the Danube civilization (courtesy of Zoia Maxim).

product fashioned from wool, or perhaps for good luck and welfare to the spinner/weaver; or (2) more formalized ritualistic marking to express devotion, requests, etc." Such functions for the use of the Danube script on spinning utensils (spindle whorls) and those for weaving (loom weights) may readily be inferred from comparisons with inscribed artifacts, related to producing textiles and dating to Greek antiquity.

Weaving was the most noble craft professed by Greek women. Classical literature abounds with references to the craft of weaving. Already in the earliest Greek texts, from Mycenaean times, women are mentioned in connection with spinning and weaving; e.g., pe-ki-ti-ra (*pektriai*) "wool-carders," a-ra-ka-teja (*alakateiai*) "spinning women," i-te-ja-o (*histeaon*, gen. plur.) "weavers," te-pe-ja "makers of te-pa (a heavy type of cloth, "rug, carpet"), we-we-si-je-ja (*werwesieiai*) "wool workers," ri-ne-ja (*lineiai*) "flax workers" (Ilievski 2000: 363).

Like all major institutions of civilization also weaving was considered to be a gift of the gods, of one goddess in particular. In Greek mythology, Athena is credited to have taught the women on earth how to produce yarn from wool and weave textiles. To honor the goddess for her gift the Athenians introduced a festival, the Great Panathenaia, and on that occasion a woven garment, a peplos, was presented to Athena.

> Once every four years, at the moment when the cranes give the signal to the Greek peasant to begin his labors (namely in mid–November), two young Athenian girls called *arrephoroi* begin weaving the peplos destined to cover the statue of Athena nine months later, on the occasion of the goddess's birthday.... The task of these female weavers ... is to weave the peplos for the ancient statue of Athena Polias, which is reputed to have fallen from the sky and was kept in the Erechtheum at the Acropolis [Scheid and Svenbro 1996: 18].

The Panathenaia was established to celebrate and enhance pan–Hellenic unity, and the weaving of a garment for the goddess may well be understood in a metaphorical sense of interlacing otherwise loosely hanging threads to produce a solid fabric where all components are intertwined, and this fabric is a united Greek society. A similar spirit governed ritual performances at Olympia where a garment was woven to cover the statue of Hera in her temple (Connelly 2007: 43; see Chapter 6).

The figure of Athena, the multitalented goddess, produced many myths and stories about her doings. In connection with weaving, some very human emotions are revealed in her divine character, namely of envy and wrath. In a tale that has come down to us through the works of Roman writers, of Vergil (G 4.246–47) and of Ovid (Met 6.5–145), Arachne challenges the goddess Minerva (the Roman equivalent of Athena) and calls for a competition of the two to demonstrate who is the most skillful weaver. After the two women have finished weaving their textiles Athena inspects Arachne's work and has to admit that this fabric is perfect without any flaw. The goddess gets furious with envy and turns Arachne into a spider so that she may continue weaving in the air (Gantz 1993: 86).

The terminology related to weaving developed over a long span of time and proliferated according to specializations that occurred on the long trail from Old Europe to ancient Greece. This terminology may serve to illustrate the multifaceted patterns of integration and linguistic fusion. It is noteworthy that the ancient Greek vocabulary contains an abundance of borrowings that survived from pre–Greek times. These borrowings of non–Indo-European origin are not isolated in the lexicon but have been integrated into the language, forming a broad layer of terminology that is symbiotically interconnected with expressions based on Indo-European cognates.

In the lexical structures, two integrational patterns can be discerned that attest to the symbiotic interplay of elements from two linguistic systems, the substrate language and Greek:

- Terminology with complementary representation of pre–Greek (non–Indo-European) and Greek expressions (with cognates in other Indo-European languages). The terminology relating to weaving contains some expressions of Indo-European origin and others of pre-Indo-European origin; the expressions are complementary rather than synonymous (Barber 1991: 280): Greek *lenos* / pre–Greek *mallos* "wool"; Greek *netho* / pre–Greek *klotho* "to spin"; Greek *atraktos* / pre–Greek *elakate* "spindle"; Greek *stemon* / pre–Greek *etrion* "warp"; Greek *histopodes* / pre–Greek *keleontes* "loom uprights"; Greek *pene* / pre–Greek *rhodane* "weft," etc.
- Terminology of different origin, with a duality of pre–Greek and Greek terms with specific meanings (Barber 1991: 278*f*):

Greek *histos* "loom," *antion* "cloth beam," *pleko* "to plait," *hyphaino* "to weave," etc. pre–Greek *merinthos* "thread," *laiai* / *agnythes* "loom-weights," *spondylos* "spindle whorl," *kanon* "heddle bar," *kairos* "shed bar," *stypo* "to scutch," etc.

The complex patterns in which pre–Greek terms interact with Greek expressions of Indo-European coinage may serve as a metaphor for the process of fusion that ultimately produced the fabric of classical Greek culture with its multiple pre–Greek sources.

> Clearly some of the new textile vocabulary of the Greeks came from the people and language(s) of the southern Aegean. On the basis of semantics, I would suspect that at least some of the "unknown" and C(C)V Ch-groups [word structures with consonant (+ consonant) + vowel + Chi] of loans were coming specifically from the central Balkans, from the region that developed the warp-weighted loom and its products so richly in the Neolithic and Bronze Age—from the region of the "Old Europeans." But whatever the precise origin of the languages, here among the textile terms of Greek we can see them casting some remarkably distinctive shadows [Barber 1991: 281].

Pottery, Ceramic Production and the Potter's Wheel

Technological advancement in pottery making can be measured in terms of the progress and specialization in the domain of firing techniques (i.e., pyrotechnology). Once pots and more precious ceramic vessels can be fired at high temperatures in furnaces where the temperatures can be controlled, this advancement makes progress possible also in the local development of metallurgy which requires the development of pyrotechnology. There can be no refined casting or alloying of metal without a parallel advance in the production of pottery. "As a fire craft the pottery production opened the humans' way to discover other important technologies such as metalworking or metallurgy" (Gligor et al. 2007: 114).

In fact, pyrotechnology in connection with the firing of pottery made fast progress in southeastern Europe, reaching its most advanced stages in the Vinca complex (see Gligor et al. 2007: 121*ff* for the development of Old European pyrotechnology in the domain of ceramic production). Advancement can also be measured in terms of the devices that are at the potter's disposal. The earliest evidence for a device whose function corresponds to that of a potter's wheel form part of the archaeological record of a workshop in Moldova, Varvarovka, dated to around 4000 BCE (Gimbutas 1991: 122*f*). Evidence for the use of the potter's wheel in Mesopotamia is slightly younger (Nissen 1988: 46).

Pre-Greek borrowings in the terminology of Greek pottery-production abound:

(i) Materials, utensils and facilities for pottery production
   argillos "white clay"
   kaminos "furnace for smelting, baking, burning"
   keramos "potter's earth, clay," "earthen vessel, jar; wine jar," "pottery"

(ii) Types of ceramic ware
   ambix "spouted vessel"
   arakis / arakten "bowl"
   aryballos "globular oil flask"
   bout(t)is "vase in the form of a frustum of a cone"
   bytine "flask or chamberpot"
   gabena "small vessel; cup, bowl"
   distropon "vase for libation"
   kakkabe "three-legged pot"
   kalyx / kalykos "cup" ("calyx of a flower; rosebud," "husk, shell, pod," "ornament of a woman [metaphor]")
   kantharos ("(dung-)beetle (scarabaeus pilularius)"), "drinking cup (metaphor)"
   karchesion "drinking vessel which is narrower in the middle"
   kaukos "cup"
   kelebe "vase with a big opening, mixing bowl"
   kernos "earthen vase with nipples all around, used in mystery cults"
   kotilion "vessel (to preserve things)"
   kotyle / kotylos "bowl, dish, small cup," (a measure for liquids and dry materials, "socket, especially of the hip-joint," "cymbals")
   kypellon "bulbous drinking vessel, beaker, goblet"
   lagynos "flask with a small neck" (a measure)
   lebes "kettle, cauldron" (monetary unit)
   lekythos "casket for oil or perfume"
   mathalis "cup used as a measure"
   pelargos "earthen vessel" ("stork")
   pithos "large, mostly earthen vessel for storing wine, which is open at the top"
   tryblion "drinking vessel (of unknown shape and varying size)" (a measure of capacity)
   hyrche "earthen vessel used for salting fish (etc.)"; cf. Latin urceus, urna
   phiale / phiele "flat vessel, flat bowl for drinking and/or sacrificing," "dish for cooking and to preserve ashes"
   phidakne / pithakne "wine jar"

Some of these ancient Greek expressions of pre–Greek origin made it into the cultural vocabulary of our modern languages. The English adjective ceramic (first recorded in 1850) was borrowed from Greek *keramikos* (derived from *keramos*). Other cultural terms in this domain are much older in English. For instance, English chalice (recorded since ca. 1300) which was borrowed through Anglo-Norman chalice from Latin *calix* (acc. *calicem*). The Romans had adopted this expression from Greek *kalyx* (*calyx*). Chalice replaced an older Middle English expression *calice* which was borrowed from a northeastern variant of Old French, and this also reflects Latin calix. There is a third variant of this word in English, and this is Old English *celic* (recorded in the ninth century), this being a direct borrowing from Medieval Latin (Barnhart 2002: 157*f*).

Metallurgy: A Technological Breakthrough in the Sixth Millennium BCE

The earliest evidence for the smelting of copper, the first metal used in history, comes from southern Serbia and dates to ca. 5400 BCE. All finds of copper smelting in the Near

East and Egypt are of a younger date. The oldest artifacts made of gold known so far were found in the Copper Age necropolis of Varna and date to ca. 4500 BCE. There, the oldest gold treasure of humankind has been unearthed (see below).

The appearance of tools and other objects made of metal is associated with a more sophisticated level of socioeconomic organization. Working metal, even in its most elementary form (cold hammering), requires an advanced division of labor. The oldest profession in metallurgy is that of the copper smith. Working metal was something special, and the copper smith's status in early civilization must have been privileged. This can be inferred from the rise in social status of the iron smith in the societies of the Iron Age.

It is broadly accepted that the emergence of metallurgy in Europe was an independent process which was not influenced by Near Eastern traditions. "As the data stands now, it would not be unreasonable to suggest that copper-smelting began during the late sixth millennium BC in southeastern Europe and, somewhat later, in the first half of the fifth millennium BC, in Anatolia" (Pernicka and Anthony 2009: 168).

Ancient metalworking is attested for a number of cultural centers in southeastern Europe. Once metal objects came into use, their usefulness and effectiveness most probably sparked a growing demand. "Demand accelerates technological development, and progress through the metallurgical succession was relatively fast" (Tylecote 1987: 3).

One factor which stimulated demand was trade. An increase in trade can be observed from the mid-sixth millennium BCE involving shells, marble, obsidian and copper. Much later, in the third millennium BCE, a trade route was established between the Baltic region and the Aegean in which amber was exchanged for metal (Butrimas 2001). Trade also included materials needed for the production of metal objects such as ore, raw metal and scrap metal.

The Balkans are rich in ore and raw metal deposits. It is significant that the smithies are not always found at the mining sites. In the case of the early mining sites in central Bulgaria (Leskovo, Aibunar, Hristene), the workshops are found in settlements several kilometers away (Sherratt 1976: 572).

There is no evidence as yet that gold was worked as early as copper. The earliest finds of gold objects date to the mid-fifth millennium BCE. The finds in the cemetery of Varna, situated not far from Varna Lake and in close vicinity of the Black Sea coast, represent the oldest known artifacts made of gold that have so far been found anywhere in the world.

The exceptional abundance of grave goods included ritual attire ornamented with gold appliqués; gold and carnelian beads; a hat decorated with gold lamellae; earrings, necklace, and bracelets made from gold rings (Slavchev 2009: 198).

The technical skills reflected in the metal finds from the graves of Varna suggest that gold was worked much earlier in that region. Gold objects such as bracelets and ring pendants are found mainly in the Lower Danube area. It is noteworthy that gold was worked in southeastern Europe more than one and a half thousand years earlier than in Mesopotamia.

These pieces of precious metal appear to have been used almost exclusively in a ritual context. In addition, the strict distinction between richly equipped male graves and female graves which contain less goods could be indicative of a society with a social hierarchy. This observation, seemingly, contradicts the hypothesis of Old European society as an egalitarian social network. However, in one of the major burials a male and a female were interred in a joint grave which does not suggest gender difference in political power (Ivanov 1986: 38*f*).

The sudden appearance of great personal wealth, in a previously egalitarian context,

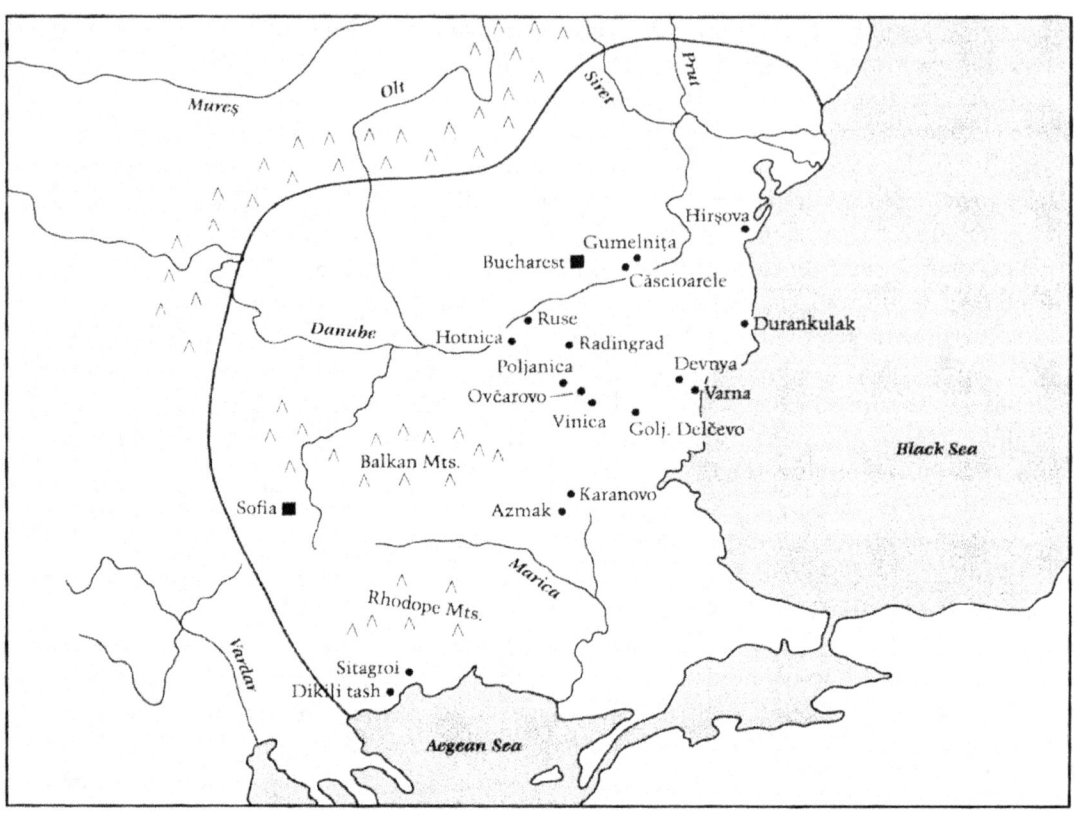

Varna and its hinterland in the fifth millennium BCE (originally published in *The civilization of the goddess* by Marija Gimbutas. San Francisco: HarperSanFrancisco, 1991. Used with permission of the Institute of Archaeomythology).

may illustrate the fusion of worldviews as a result of intensive interaction between the local population and traders from the region north of the Black Sea during the mid-fifth millennium BCE (see Gimbutas (1991: 118–121). The Suvorovo culture, which may be associated with the Kurgan I migration, flourished in the northwest Pontic and in the lower Danube as far south as northeast Bulgaria between ca. 4500 and 4100 BCE. "The [Suvorovo] culture provides evidence of the spread of steppe tribes from the east to the west and in the 'Kurgan' model of Indo-European origins is seen to reflect the first wave of Indo-Europeans from their homeland in the steppelands of the Ukraine and south Russia" (Mallory and Adams 1997: 557).

As regards the early techniques of metalworking (of copper, in particular) and their interdependence, the following step-by-step development of metallurgy in Europe has been reconstructed (Renfrew 1973: 188*ff*):

1. Simple use of native copper (as a precious material);
2. Cold hammering of native copper;
3. Annealing of native copper;
4. Smelting of copper from its ore;
5. Casting the copper in an open mold;
6. Casting in, and the use of the two-piece mold;

7. Alloying with arsenic or tin;
8. Lost-wax casting.

The sequence of techniques was not accidental. The discovery of each technique depended on knowledge of the preceding technique.

Traces of ancient terminology from pyrotechnology and metallurgy have been preserved in the vocabulary of ancient Greek.

baunos "furnace" (*banausos* "the one who knows how to operate a furnace," *banausia* "the art of using furnaces")
chymeia / chemeia "the art of alloying metals"
kibdos "metal slag"
metallon "metal"
mydros "metal mass (molten) roasted in fire"
spodos "metal ashes"

Hephaistos figure of the divine smith, god of fire:

kassiteros "tin"
psimythos "white lead"

Terminology relating to copper:

chalkos "copper"
schendyle "pair of tongs" (instrument of the *chalkeis,* the copper and bronze smiths)

The term *chalkos* is associated with *chalke / kalche* "purple snail" which is also a pre-Greek borrowing. The name for copper in Greek, thus, is derived from the reddish color of the metal. "Copper" is the original meaning of this term from the pre-Greek substrate. Bronze was produced since about 3000 BCE, and *chalkos* in ancient Greek has developed a secondary meaning, and this refers to bronze.

Terminology relating to gold:

agchouros "gold"
kollybos "small gold weight"
leros "golden ornament on women's clothes"
obryza "assaying of gold"
selaggeus "gold washer; gold refiner"

This name for gold of pre-Greek origin is the earliest term for gold in ancient Greek (Beekes 2010: 17*f*). The other term for gold, *chrysos,* also is a loanword which was borrowed from Semitic at a later period (Chantraine 2009: 1232*f*). Before the Greeks established contacts with goldsmiths of the Near East they profited from the old trade relations with the people in the northern Balkans. Most of the gold items that were found in the graves of Mycenae were manufactured of raw material that had been imported from regions north of the Danube (i.e., Transylvania) and from eastern Macedonia (Cultraro 2011: 188*f*).

The history of gold starts in the region of Varna around 4500 BCE, but the perception of the value of artifacts made of this metal differed markedly then from later periods. Since the times of metal coinage (sixth century BCE), gold was used for coins although silver dominated coinage throughout Greek antiquity. The most popular silver coin was the "Athenian owl" (see Chapter 4 for Athenian coinage). Then, precious metal was used in its material value for trading and the exchange of commodities.

The abundance of objects with ritual functions made of gold in the Varna necropolis illustrates that, in the early phase of the history of gold, this metal was related to a non-economic sphere, and it was associated with high rank of social status. The élite of Indo-European pastoralists who seized power in the Varna region faced the challenge of legitimizing its privileged status, of enhancing self-identification of the peer group, and of distancing this group from the majority, whose members do not share high social status. This challenge is even greater for a group coming as immigrants or intruders to a region where they take over political power. In the case of the takeover of power at Varna, ethnicity was an additional issue and, at the same time, a major issue, since two distinct ethnic populations were involved, Indo-European pastoralists and Palaeo-European agriculturalists.

The assemblage of artifacts made of gold in the Necropolis at Varna suggests a close link between political power and religious authority in the hands of the rulers who were buried there. Especially remarkable is grave 43, which contained gold artifacts weighing more than 1.5 kg.

> The exceptional abundance of grave goods included ritual attire ornamented with gold appliqués; [...] a bow and a quiver lined with gold, stone and copper axes; and a scepter—a stone axe whose shaft was lined with gold—suggesting that the grave belonged to the chieftain of this community. Apparently, he had religious as well as military power [Slavchev 2009: 198].

The relationship between religious authority (as symbolized by artifacts with ritual function) and military power (as manifested in weaponry of various kind)—both of which were invested in the ruler (i.e., chieftain)—is mirrored in later periods in cultural history. Some two thousand years after the Varna event, the idea of the ruler combining worldly power and priestly authority manifested itself anew in the Thracian kingship. Thracian ethnicity emerged around the middle of the third millennium BCE in the regions where the Danube civilization had once flourished and where the Indo-European pastoralists acculturated. The Thracian kings were not just autocratic rulers; they represented the institution of sacred kingship.

It is noteworthy that the abundance of gold artifacts that have been found in Thracian grave mounds (tumuli) had symbolic rather than material value to the Thracians. This mindset resembles that of the people at Varna, who furnished the graves of their rulers with symbols of élite power.

> The ancient Thracians perceived in them [gold artifacts and other precious objects] predominantly insignia, signs of social distinction and of power. The possession of a large wealth was a sign of royal power. This is precisely why the precious metal was not introduced into the economic turnover, but was used for making these material signs. [...] The task of this art was to present the dynast as *zibythides,* "shining." As with all Indo-European peoples, the aristocrats of the Thracians were also "shining" and "brilliant." [...] They [objects of art] are both a marker and arguments of the royal ideology, and task is to motivate power [Marazov 2005: 8].

It can be argued that the origins of sacred chiefdom (and of kingship) are associated with the élite of steppe pastoralists in the Varna region of 6500 years ago. Thracian ethnicity is rooted in the amalgamation of ethnic groups of Old European and Indo-European origin and it is most likely that the heritage of the king-priest was transmitted, through the channel of cultural memory, from the era of Varna into Thracian traditions.

In the Greek world, one still finds repercussions of the original appreciation of gold outside the realm of commercial considerations in the epic works of Homer. When precious metal (i.e., gold and/or silver) is referred to in the *Iliad* and the *Odyssey,* the references are commonly non-economic.

> Like silver, gold in Homer generally takes the form of artefacts…. Gold is especially associated with the gods, who may themselves be called golden and posses a large range of golden things that in the human world are not made of gold. Furthermore, the golden artefacts used by mortals are frequently associated with deity either explicitly or by their origin or by their use in ritual or by their association with immortality [Seaford 2004: 30*f*].

The idea that gold represents wealth—so typical in the classical period—did not dominate perceptions in Homer's era. Rather, it was prestige that was associated with golden artifacts. This kind of attitude lives on in some Greek myths. The story of Jason who sets out with the Argonauts to obtain the Golden Fleece is perhaps the most famous of them. The Argonauts visit Colchis where Medea, the local king's daughter, helps the adventurers to reach their goal. There is consensus among modern scholars who identify ancient Colchis with the region of Vani in western Georgia, bordering on the coast of the Black Sea.

> The tale of Jason's voyage with the Argonauts from Iolcus in Thessaly in search of the Golden Fleece, and the help he received from Medea, daughter of Aeëtes, king of Colchis, has indeed survived the centuries. It was told in antiquity, in its canonical form by Apollonius of Rhodes, and lives on today in the name of the Georgian TV channel Ayeti, in the Garden of Medea at Vani, and in the colossal bronze statue of Medea erected at the Georgian seaside resort of Batumi in 2007 [Vickers 2008: 29].

The Composition of the Younger Layer

In the southern part of the Balkans, the Greeks got acquainted with cultural patterns of the Old European heritage and with economic domains which were absent from the northern region or which had shifted, in a cultural drift, southward.

Olive Cultivation: Economy and Mythology Intertwined

The wild olive (olea sylvestris) is attested for the Aegean islands and the Greek mainland already in the fourth millennium BCE but it had spread in the Mediterranean area much earlier. The native Europeans already distinguished various species and subspecies of olive trees because they had different names for them (see below). Olives are easier to cultivate than vines because olive trees can grow on soil that would be otherwise not suitable for agriculture. Antique sources inform us that olive trees grew on the margins of land that was used for the production of grain and as vineyards. The domesticated olive tree (olea europaea) produces more olives and, thus, more oil although olives can be harvested from both the wild and the domesticated species. From the works of Xenophon (fifth century BCE) and of Theophrastos (fourth century BCE) we know that domesticated olive trees were generated by grafting on a wild olive tree (*kotinos*). The word for grafting in ancient Greek is *moleuo / molouein* ("to cut off and transplant the shoots of trees; to engrave the offshoots") which is of pre–Greek origin. Another practice was to cut down an old tree from whose stump would sprout new shoots to form a new tree.

The Greeks adopted the know-how of olive cultivation, together with key elements of its terminology, from the Pelasgians and they learned by experience that olive trees can become very old. "Once the olive tree has taken root, it can grow to a very old age. Theophrastus says that normally the tree will reach an age of about two hundred years (HP 4.13.5), but he knows of specimens which are presumably much older, such as Athene's sacred olive tree on the Acropolis and the sacred wild olive tree in Olympia (HP 4.13.2)" (Isager and Skydsgaard 1995: 38).

Olives and olive oil have been characteristic ingredients of the Greek cuisine as we know it since antiquity and this cuisine finds its origins in the Old European heritage of earlier millennia. In the archaic era (eighth and seventh centuries BCE), Greek aristocratic families established their wealth and influence through the trade with olive oil. The Greeks also learned the know-how of scented oil from their predecessors, and aromatic olive oil ranged among the most prestigious commodities, highly appreciated by the urban population of classical antiquity.

The olive tree and its fruits were perceived by the Greeks as gifts of the gods, of Athena in particular, and sacred olive trees grew in the precincts of many sanctuaries. The exact location and the history of the sacred olive tree on the Acropolis are shrouded in mythological allusions. Myth has it that the Persians who conquered Athens and devastated the Acropolis in 480 BCE cut down the sacred olive tree but Athena made it sprout again from its stump. Pausanias, in the second century CE, claims to have seen the sacred tree on a slope of the Acropolis. Olive leaves became the symbol of the victors in the sportive competitions at Olympia, and wreaths of olive twigs were given to the victorious maidens of the Heraia contest and also to the male athletes of the Olympics.

The olive tree was celebrated during festive events. The most significant festival in which the olive tree was in focus was the Panathenaia. This festival was celebrated in the month of Hekatombaion which corresponds to July/August of the modern calendar.

> As Athene's special tree, the olive played an important part at the Panathenaia where the prize was oil from Athene's sacred olive trees. This festival was one of the greatest of the year and had no specific relationship with agriculture; it was a sort of national festival. It took place in the first month of the year [midsummer was the beginning of the year according to the Attic calendar]. That was the time when patriotic sentiments ran high along with the festival celebrating the synoikism [festival to celebrate the communal spirit] of Athens [Isager and Skydsgaard 1995: 166].

The Panathenaia festival celebrated the cult of Athena and of her special tree. This festival is of great antiquity and its beginnings may well date to the founding of the city of Athens in the fourth millennium BCE. The focus was always on the religious performance, regardless of the political input during the times of democratic governance in Athens (see Chapter 7).

> From before the democracy, in the seventh and sixth centuries, and during the democracy in the fifth and fourth centuries ... the Panathenaic procession persisted as a form of ritual that defined the Athenian community as a collection of individuals who dwelt in the same land and worshipped the same goddess. In other words, it realized religious citizenship, and this religious citizenship did not change as the political definition of citizenship in democratic Athens evolved [Maurizio 1998: 316].

Greek terminology of olive cultivation is permeated with expressions of pre–Greek origin:

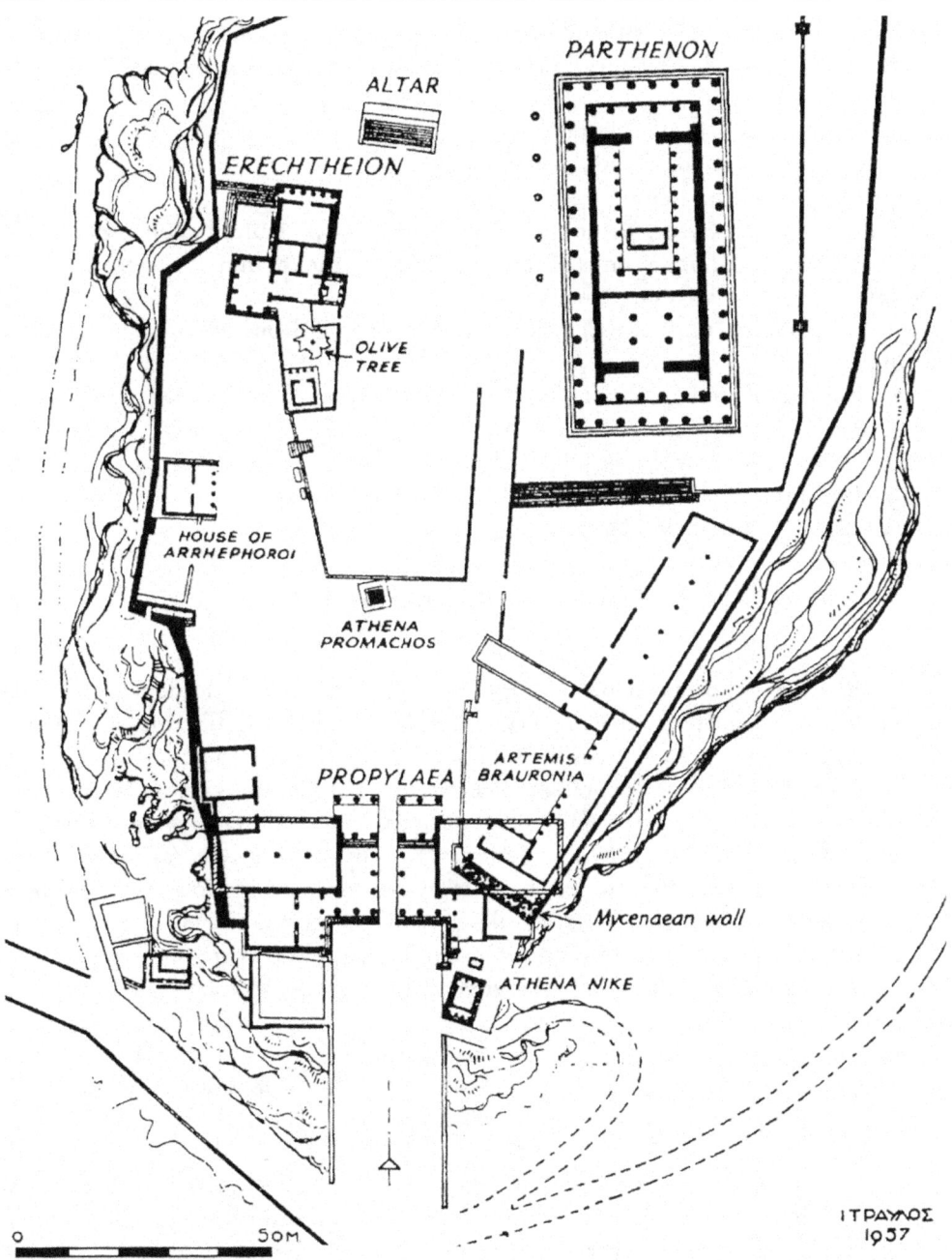

The Acropolis in Athens with the major temples dedicated to Athena (the Parthenon, the temples of Athena Promachos and Athena Nike) and the location of the sacred olive tree near the Erechtheion (courtesy of the British Museum).

agrippos "wild olive (Laconian)"
amergo "to pluck (of olives, flowers)"
babren "sediment of olive-oil (Macedonian)"
egkris "cake made of oil and honey"

eiresione "an olive or laurel twig adorned with red and white bands and decorated with fruits" (as a symbol of fertility); "a song when carrying this twig around," "wreath (of honor)"
elaia "olive (tree)"
elpos / elphos "olive oil, rendered fat, abundance"
koletrao "to trample on (a term from oil preparation)"
kotinos "wild olive"; *kotinas* "fruit of the wild olive," "(olive) grafted upon a wild olive"
kroupezai "wooden shoes to press olives (or to indicate the rhythm of a dance)"
moriai name of holy olives in Athens
omphax / omphakos "unripe (e.g., grape, olive)" ("young girl [metaphor]," "undeveloped nipple [poet]")
oron "agricultural tool (piece of wood) with which bunches of grapes (or olives) are crushed"
premadie "(kind of) olive"
stemphylon "mass of olives from which the oil has been pressed"
phyla / phylie "(kind of) wild olive"

THE PRE-GREEK GOD ASKLEPIOS AND THE HEALING SKILLS OF THE ANCIENTS

As with other important achievements of Greek civilization also the domain of healing and medicine are associated with a divinity. According to the mythical tradition, Asklepios is the god of healing. His attribute is the snake, which has remained a popular visual motif in the logos of pharmacies to the present. The parentage of Asklepios is somehow obscure. All antique sources agree that Asklepios is the son of Apollo, but different women are named as mothers (Gantz 1993: 91*f*). In some sources, Koronis is mentioned as the mother of Asklepios while, in others, the mother's name is given as Arsinoe. In Homer's *Iliad* (4.193–94, 218–19), Asklepios learns the skills of healing from Cheiron who also provides his apprentice with medicines. The name of the god of healing, Asklepios, is as pre-Greek as his skills. His master Cheiron is a mythical being, a centaur. Greek *kentauros* is a borrowing from the substrate language.

Asklepios was appreciated as a great healer and sacred spaces were dedicated to him. One is found on the Acropolis in Athens. "As we know from the inscribed double-sided relief housed in the Acropolis Museum, the sanctuary of Asclepius on the South Slope was founded by an Athenian citizen, Telemachus, in 420/419 BC" (Servi 2011: 81). Perhaps the most important sanctuary of Asklepios was the one at Epidauros in the northeastern part of the Peloponnese. Among the methods of cure that were practiced at Epidauros was one in which medicinal healing and psychological input are intertwined. Patients who came to Epidauros in search of cure were advised to sleep in the sanctuary and to collect information about the cure for their illnesses from their dreams.

> After certain ritual cleansings, the sick would spend the night in a special building, the *enkoimeterion* (sleeping ward), where the god would appear in their dreams and suggest the treatment they should follow. Not excluding surgery and drug treatment completely, therapy at the Asclepieion relied mainly on the patient's shattering psychical experience, the shock of having come into direct contact with the supernatural—an experience which, in psychogenic and nervous disorders especially, must have given immediate and impressive results [Iakovidis 1985: 130].

Music as therapy—an idea favored by Pythagoras and his followers—was also a preferred mode of cure for patients. It is purported that "Pericles is brought out of his severe melancholia by his daughter's song (Pericles: 5.1.44–95)" (Brumble 1998: 358). In one of the epithets of Asklepios' father, Apollo, there is an allusion to music as therapy: pre–Greek *paian / paianos* "choral song, hymn"; "physician, savior (epithet of Apollo)."

> The Cretans were generally connected to the performance of the healing paean, which Thaletas [a seventh-century poet and musician from Gortyn in Crete], for example, imported to mainland Greece, a tradition which may have had some basis in fact, as Paia(w)on is attested at Mycenaean Knossos (KN V 52.2, C 394.4) [Bachvarova 2009: 37].

The lifespan of the divine patron of medicine ends dramatically. For some time Asklepios experiments with the healing of death. When Zeus is told that Asklepios is making plans for raising someone from Hades, the Underworld, he gets furious because he considers the aspirations of Asklepios a sacrilege. As a punishment Zeus strikes down Asklepios with his thunderbolt.

The Greeks' veneration for this god illustrates their awareness for the values of traditional medicine and, at the same time, their appreciation of the medicinal knowledge of their Pelasgian masters. The native Europeans had accumulated useful knowledge of medicinal plants and herbs and, in the vocabulary of ancient Greek, we find traces of it in the form of borrowings from the pre–Greek substrate language. The native Europeans knew about diseases of human beings and domestic animals, and they had developed methods to cure them. The Indo-European pastoralists certainly had their own experiences with healing, but the early Greeks encountered an advanced level of medicinal knowledge among the Pelasgians. The Greeks profited greatly from the medicinal knowledge of the ancients and they preserved many of the pre–Greek terms, among them some that have been transferred to the medicinal vocabulary of our modern languages (e.g., gangrene, lethargy, cholera, pharmacy).

(i) Bodily functions as medicinal indicators
blenna "mucous discharge (myxa)"
koruza "mucous discharge from the nostrils, rheum"
lemphos "mucous discharge from the nostrils"
spatile / patile "thin excrement"
chorion "skin enclosing the foetus, afterbirth"
odis / (plur.) *odines* "throes of birth, that which is born (out of pains)" ("strain [metaphor]")

(ii) Diseases, defects, wounds, inflammation
agchilops "swelling which obstructs the lacrymal duct"
aspalax / spalax "mole (sphalax typhus)"
boubon "groin," "swollen gland"
bragchos / baragchos "hoarseness, angina"
gagglion "tumor on a tendon, or the head"
gaggraina "gangrene (an illness that eats away the flesh)"
dothien / dothion "small abscess"
(h)elmis "intestinal worm, parasitic worm"
erysipelas "skin disease"
eschara "scab, eschar on a wound by burning (medic)"
epialos "ague, ague from fever"
kanthyle / konthelai "swelling, tumor"
kedmata "chronical limb-diseases"
kordyle / skordyle / korydylis "tumor, swelling"
lethargos "lethargy, lethargic fever"
liminthes "intestinal worms"
nokar / nokaros "lethargy, coma (absence of the soul)"
poros / pouros "stone (in the bladder, the kidneys, etc.)"

rodigges / rotigges "spots bloodshot by hitting; bruises"
sabakos "damaged, rotten (of inner organs)"
siphlos / sipalos / siphnos "crippled, lame"
smodix / modix "bloodshot, bruise, bloody weal"
staphyle "swollen uvula, uvula inflammation"
tagge "(kind of) tumor" ("rancid smell")
pharygx / pharyx "throat disease" ("throat, gorge, larynx, windpipe")
phausigx / phaustigx "blister from burns, blister"
phlyktaina "blister, pustule"
phoides / phodes "blister from burns"
cholera "cholera (disease of the stomach which causes vomiting and diarrhea)," "vomit, nausea"
psydrax / psydrakion "pustule, blister (on the head, on the eyelid, on the nose, on the tongue)"
oteile / otella (Aeol.) "wound (especially referring to close combat)"

(iii) Medicinal plants and herbs; healing; cure

achalion a plant used as medicament
ballis a medical plant
throna a medicine and charm ("flowers [as a decoration in woven tissues and embroidery]")
kerais medical name of the wild radish
orontion "cuckoo-pint (plant used as a remedy against jaundice)"
skiggos lizard that is used as medicine (Asia Minor)
pharmakon "healing or harmful medicine, healing or poisonous herb; drug; poisonous potion, magic potion"
phibaleos a fig suitable for curing

(iv) Items of medicinal care
keiria "bandage (for wounds)"

According to the canon of Western civilization, Hippocrates from the island of Cos is regarded as the father of medicine. This most famous doctor of the Greeks lived in the latter half of the fifth century BCE and he is hailed by Plato in his work *Phaedrus*. The most extensive collection of Greek medical texts is the *Hippocratic Corpus* that was compiled between ca. 420 and ca. 370 BCE. Despite the association with Hippocrates' name he authored only a few texts in this corpus, the others having been collected from other doctors. In the *Corpus*, traditional healing is appreciated alongside experimental medicine, and one also finds religiously motivated methods for cure such as prayers and incantations.

> The Hippocratic doctors did not perform dissections on corpses—Aristotle was possibly the first scientist to do this methodically—so, perhaps inevitably, they tended to be rather obsessed by the body's surface: temperature, discharges, urine, mucus, and suchlike [Higgins 2010: 133].

Apparently, this tradition of giving a diagnosis about the state of health based on an analysis of bodily functions was adopted by the Greeks as an Old European heritage. Among the borrowed items of medicinal terminology there are various expressions for discharges (see under i).

Greek medicine developed in a milieu of gender-oriented conceptions about the nature of men and women. The doctors made their observations and gave their diagnoses according to common stereotypes held by the ancient Greeks. There was a widespread consciousness of gender distinction, with men representing the active and forming part in society and with the capacity to control bodily functions and emotions. The female counterpart was viewed as being inferior to men, being less capable of controlling bodily functions and having less control over their emotions. This view was shared by Aristotle and other intellectuals of antiquity (Dean-Jones 1994: 37*ff*).

> Generally the Hippocratic doctors believed that the wet and spongy nature of women was precisely what was inferior about them. Their wetness, the result of sedentary lifestyles according to several treatises [...], was positively pathological and made them susceptible to specific kinds of illness, especially reproductive problems [...] [Foxhall 2013: 73].

Hippocrates set standards and priorities for medicine in antiquity, both for the Greek and the Roman traditions:

> Hippocrates and subsequent writers in the same tradition—Galen, Oribasius and, writing in Latin, Celsus—saw medicine as having three main departments, to do with regimen (*diaita,* of which diet is an important element), to do with drugs (pharmacy, some of which are also foodstuffs) and to do with surgery [Craik 1995: 388].

It is noteworthy that Hippocrates was aware of the long-term experience with foodstuff and nutritious plants that stood behind the Greek tradition of choosing the right diet: "In my view, our present *diaitemata* (ways of regimen) were discovered and devised and evolved over a long period of time" (Hipp. VM 3).

Health was a key issue among the Greeks, and they spent much time with diet regimes and caring for their bodies:

> By the late fifth century, health had become almost an obsession in Greek society. Widespread general interest in medicine is reflected in medical treatises aimed at a lay audience, as well as in numerous literary sources, such as the medically sophisticated description of the plague by Thucydides, and the frequent appearance of medical themes and allusions in Attic comedy and tragedy. Plato describes Hippocrates as well known in *Protagoras,* portrays the physician Eryximachus in society in the *Symposium,* and parodies Hippocratic theories of sex determination in that same dialogue [Demand 1994: 33].

The Greeks were conscious about their diet, and they were as conscious about physical exercise to ensure the balance of the bodily conditions. The idea that a sound mind resides in a sound body was well familiar in Greek antiquity. As one of the popular institutions to take care of one's body, the Greeks maintained gymnasiums which more or less corresponded, in function, to our modern gyms. There was one marked difference, though, when comparing a gym in ancient Greece with one of our times. In the Greek gym one would find only young men and they would be naked. Women were excluded. The word for "naked" in Greek is *gymnos.*

> Greek youths exercised in the nude quite naturally as an expression of freedom and delight in the physical world, the sunshine on their backs, the warm breeze rustling through the olive groves which surrounded the gymnasium, the sparkling water from the nearby spring, for gymnasiums were often situated near a sacred grove or spring. Their nudity was not simply a matter of a benign climate, it was a cultural lack of inhibition—and one which was soon to disappear. Already in the Roman Republic nudity began to be viewed as unseemly and likely to lead to disorderly conduct [Mount 2010: 57*f*].

It is reasonable to assume that the native Europeans already had some kind of a moral code concerning the relationship between the patient and the healer. What might have been transmitted, through cultural memory, in the intergenerational chain was not written down. At least there are no traces of any written text that would contain something similar in content to what we encounter, as an advice for doctors, in the *Hippocratic Corpus:*

> Practise two things in your dealings with disease: either help or do not harm the patient. There are three factors in the practice of medicine: the disease, the patient and the physician. The physi-

cian is the servant of the science, and the patient must do what he can to fight the disease with the assistance of the physician [*Epidemics* 1].

Arguably, there are two significant contributions to medicine that we owe the ancient Greeks. One is the abundance of medicinal terms of Greek coinage with which the professional vocabulary of modern medicine is saturated. The other is the moral code the items of which are encapsulated in the text of the Hippocratic oath. It is noteworthy that, in its original version, the text makes reference to the linkage of healing and religious life (see allusions to divinities such as Apollo and Asklepios, to the chastity of the physician's behavior).

* * *

I swear by Apollo the healer, by Asclepius, by Health and all the powers of healing, and call to witness all the gods and goddesses that I may keep this Oath and Promise to the best of my ability and judgement.

I will pay the same respect to my master in the Science as to my parents and share my life with him and pay all my debts to him. I will regard his sons as my brothers and teach them the Science, if they desire to learn it, without fee or contract. I will hand on precepts, lectures and all other learning to my sons, to those of my master and to those pupils duly apprenticed and sworn, and to none other.

I will use my power to help the sick to the best of my ability and judgement; I will abstain from harming or wronging any man by it.

I will not give a fatal draught to anyone if I am asked, nor will I suggest any such thing. Neither will I give women means to procure an abortion.

I will be chaste in my religious life and in my practice.

I will not cut, even for the stone, but I will leave such procedures to the practitioners of that craft.

Whenever I go into a house, I will go help the sick and never with the intention of doing harm or injury. I will not abuse my position to indulge in sexual contacts with the bodies of women or of men, whether they be freemen or slaves.

Whatever I see or hear, professionally or privately, which ought not to be divulged, I will keep secret and tell no one.

If, therefore, I observe this Oath and do not violate it, may I prosper both in my life and in my profession, earning good repute among all men for all time. If I transgress and forswear this Oath, may my lot be otherwise.

The Hippocratic Oath (from *It's all Greek to me: From Homer to the hippocratic oath, how ancient Greece has shaped our world* **by Charlotte Higgins. New York: Harper Collins: 137).**

3

Greek Immigrants and Native Europeans in Southeastern Europe

Contact of Cultures, Fusion of Languages and Ways to Remember the Past

In the course of the third millennium BCE (during late Helladic I and Helladic II), the Indo-European migrants who had infiltrated Greece and who came to establish continuous contacts with the indigenous population experienced a process of ethnic transition. It is reasonable to assume that this is the formative period for the matrix of cultural and linguistic influences from the substrate in ancient Greece. The outcome of this process was the formation of a distinct Greek (Hellenic) identity that set the Greeks aside from other historical peoples of Indo-European affiliation, of the Italic tribes in the west, the Thracians in the north, the Hittites in the east.

We do not know many details about the conditions of life when the pre–Greek population entered a prolonged process of assimilation that eventually culminated in the total integration of the indigenous people into Greek culture and language. Anyway, there are echoes of an early awareness among the Greeks about cultural and linguistic diversity in the countries around the Aegean Sea. There also was an early awareness that languages can mix, resulting from intensive contacts. An early instance of this awareness is found in Homer's epic work *Odyssey* where the hero explains to Penelope the diversity of languages in Crete: "Every language is mixed with others; there live Achaeans, there great-hearted native Cretans, there Cydonians, and Dorians dwelling in threefold location, and noble Pelasgians" (*Odyssey* 19.175*ff*).

In some of the ancient sources, the issue of ethnic and linguistic assimilation of the native Europeans is addressed as "the Pelasgians becoming Hellenes" (e.g., Herodotus in his *Histories* I.57.3). It is noteworthy that, in the fifth century BCE, some Athenian writers observe that their language use is characterized by the admixture of elements from other languages. For example, the author called "Old Oligarch" whose work was discovered among manuscripts of Xenophon, gives the following statement: "Hearing every kind of language, they have taken something from each; the Greeks individually rather use their own language, way of life, and type of dress, but the Athenians use a mixture from all the Greeks and non–Greeks" (*Constitution of Athens* 2. 8).

The Greeks are known for their proverbial "unwillingness to learn other languages" (Thomas 1996: 240). And yet, the ancient Greeks noticed that their own language, when in contact with foreign tongues (*phonai barbaroi, glossai barbaroi*), adopted words from them: "The Greeks, especially those living among the barbarians, have taken many words from the barbarians." (Plato *Kratylos* 409 E). What Plato remarks about the effects of Greeks in contact with foreign languages is compatible with the situation in mainland Greece where the early Greeks lived, as neighbors, in continual social interaction with the natives, the Pelasgians. Modern research in the domain of contact linguistics has produced many insights into recent processes of acculturation and linguistic assimilation of minority groups into a majority population (Janse 2002, Haarmann 2006). Those insights allow for some elementary reconstructions also for the conditions of interaction of the Pelasgians with the Greeks, for phases of their bilingualism, for boundary-crossing of linguistic systems and for "the hybridization of two very different culture systems" (Gimbutas 1991: 401).

Reflections of these differences clearly show in the meanings and values which the native Europeans and the Indo-European newcomers associated with elementary symbols.

	Old European	*Indo-European*
The Color Black	Color of fertility and Mother Earth	Color of death and of the God of Death and the Underworld, called "Black God" (in Slavic and Baltic mythology)
The Color White	Color of bone, symbolic of death related to yellow, gold, amber, marble, alabaster	Color of the God of the Shining Sky, related to yellow, gold, amber
The Serpent	Benevolent snake, symbol of life energy in humans, animals and plants; stimulating and protecting the life powers of the family and domestic animals; poisonous snake an epiphany of the Goddess of Death	Symbol of evil, especially lurking in whirlwinds; epiphany of the God of Death and the Underworld, adversary of the Thunder God
The Sun	Symbol of regeneration and one of the manifestations of the Goddess of Regeneration	The dominant symbol of the Indo-Europeans: life-giving symbol associated with the God of the Shining Sky who is a year-god representing the birth of the sun, the young sun (spring), the triumphant sun (summer), and the old sun (autumn)
The Horse	Nonexistent in pre–Indo-European Europe	Sacred animal and epiphany of the main gods; white or gray—epiphany of the Gods of the Shining Sky, Twins, and Moon God; black—the epiphany of the Good of Death and the underworld; mare—epiphany of the Dawn Goddess; gods are portrayed riding horses, or horses pull their chariots

Symbols with contrasting values in Old European and Indo-European mythologies (originally published in *The civilization of the goddess* by Marija Gimbutas. San Francisco: HarperSanFrancisco, 1991. Used with permission of the Institute of Archaeomythology).

A major precondition for the investigation of the pre–Greek impact on Greek civilization—from the viewpoint of interethnic relations between the native Europeans (descendants of the bearers of the Danube civilization) and the Indo-European immigrants to the region of Attica who blended in with the natives—is the awareness that Attica had a Bronze Age population and that their settlements continued into the era of the Greeks. The existence of pre–Greek settlements in Bronze Age Greece has been common knowledge among scholars for decades.

> Athens and parts of Attica had been inhabited for millennia before recorded history began. Remains of pottery produced by Neolithic man have been discovered on the northern and southern slopes of the Acropolis and also in the district which ultimately became the agora of historical Athens. There is evidence for habitation throughout the whole Bronze (Helladic) Age [Fine 1983: 176].

The existence of pre–Greek settlements in what the Greeks came to call Hellas set conditions for interethnic relations and cultural contacts. And yet, the agenda of the contacts between Indo-Europeans and native Europeans, starting with the arrival of the early Greeks, is still poorly understood.

The Indo-European Migrants, Their Warrior Class and Their Élite Status

Three factors had a decisive effect on the process of migration and the occupation of land that had been inhabited by the native Europeans (ancient Danubians) by the immigrating Indo-Europeans. Those settlers who established themselves in their new homeland formed local élites and eventually came to dominate the indigenous population. And these immigrant settlers brought with them their Indo-European vocabulary of power relations (Mallory and Adams 2006: 267) which is preserved in the ancient Greek language: *agos* "leader," *aosseo* "follower, companion," *tagos* "leader," *amphipolos* "servant," *skeptron* "scepter (symbol of power)," *ktaomai* "to procure."

The migratory movement—the third migration of people out from the Eurasian steppe (between 3100 and 2800 BCE) directed to the south—was populous (Mallory and Adams 1997: 339*ff*, Anthony 2007: 321*ff*, Haarmann 2006: 166*ff*).

The early Indo-Europeans are known for their warrior class and the early Greeks who infiltrated Greece in the third millennium BCE were well organized in terms of military capacity. The early Greeks had inherited the cult of their heroes from their ancestors. For a long time, the origins of the hero cult had been shrouded in speculation and guesswork. Its emergence has only recently been associated with the takeover of the trade center of Varna around 4500 BCE (Haarmann 2012: 99*ff*). The abundance of copper axes in the graves of the Varna Necropolis is a striking feature. It was unusual in the burial culture of Old Europe for the grave goods in a single grave to include a multitude of axes, as was the case with graves of males at Varna.

The majority of the axes are of copper, and this underscores the importance which this type of artifact had for the deceased during his lifetime. Along with finds of axes, a number of spearheads made of copper have been found. It can be reasonably concluded that the abundance of weapons made of metal reflect the *zeitgeist* of an early warrior élite. The Varna graves point to the earliest manifestation of weaponry as status symbols for a ruling class.

The archaeology of cultures in the Russian steppe zone has produced new evidence

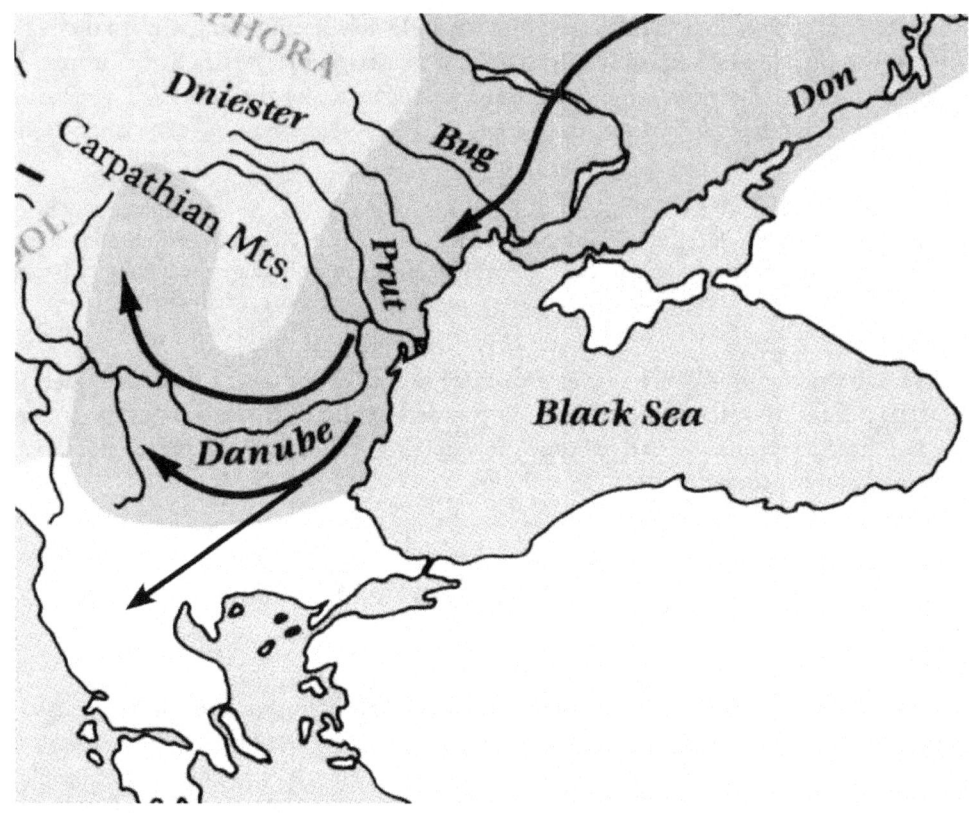

The southern movement of pastoralists in the third millennium BCE (originally published in *The civilization of the goddess* by Marija Gimbutas. San Francisco: HarperSanFrancisco, 1991. Used with permission of the Institute of Archaeomythology).

Copper axes from the Varna Necropolis (courtesy V. Slavchev).

that points to the existence of warriors as separate units in Mesolithic communities. Finds of weapons as grave good "suggest a society consisting of large male-dominated social aggregations, which included an important segment of military-oriented bands (particularly in the steppe, where food resources were scarce)" (Dolukhanov 2008: 298).

Cohesion within the warrior class was enhanced by kinship—belonging to the same lineage or clan—which is a powerful link in group formations of warriors. The kinship principle of the warrior class is well known from the major successor of the Varna society, Thracian culture. The role of kinship is believed to have been a factor in the effectiveness of the Thracian army. "Fighting in groups with your relatives and neighbours at your side improves an army's cohesiveness and valour" (Webber 2011: 137).

The importance of the warrior élite as a social body is well known from historical times. The warriors constituted one of the major pillars of society among Indo-European peoples. In the works of Homer and the other epic poets, one can discern a far-distant echo of the image of the Indo-European warrior and his path to glory. In the story told about Achilles (Akhilleus) in Homer's *Iliad* (I 280, 352, 414, XX 206, etc.) is revealed the true mythical embedding of this figure which was not historical (albeit his projection into the Mycenaean era and into the Trojan war), and it is apparent that the accounts about the hero's youth and his bravery "reflect the institution of Indo-European warrior initiation, perhaps even of Indo-European mythical narration" (Graf 1993: 74).

The warrior élite played an important role in the tripartite paradigm that can be reconstructed for Indo-European mythology and society. The principle of tripartition manifested itself in local Indo-European mythologies which date to periods after proto–Indo-European branched out of into local cultures. Such local mythologies give key insights into the original essence of mythical thought. The intrinsic connection between myth and society becomes evident as "the myths of a people were not only to some extent ciphers of their (often archaic) social structures, but they also reinforced social behaviour and served as divine charters for political realities" (Mallory 1989: 130).

The paradigm of tripartition was elaborated by Georges Dumézil in the 1930s and 1940s. The findings of earlier studies are accumulated in his major work of the 1950s (Dumézil 1958). Regardless of the criticism that has been articulated during the past half-century, Dumézil's basic arguments have retained their validity. However, a serious challenge to the idea of tripartition has arisen in the form of an attempt to distinguish a fourth dimension, which seems to have already existed in the oldest example of social differentiation, that in Vedic society in India.

The major categories of distinction were (1) *brahmanas* (the priests as a social élite), (2) *ksatriyas* (the warriors as protectors of the community), (3) *vaisyas* (the majority of the population, herders and cultivators), (4) *sudras* (indigenous inhabitants of India whose social status was considered inferior to that of Aryans). The difference between the members of the first three categories and the fourth was ethnic in nature, with three social categories reserved for Aryans and the fourth as a blanket term for the indigenous non–Aryan population of India, that is, for those people who had already inhabited the country before the arrival of the Aryans.

There are two major populations who were considered to be *sudras* by the early Aryans. The Dravidians consisted of more than 30 ethnic groups and were the more populous, numbering more than 200 million people. The other category of *sudras* were the Adivasi, the most ancient population of the Indian subcontinent. The Adivasi, who descended from the first modern humans who reached India from the west, are nowadays split up into some 30 smaller groups that are scattered in mountainous areas of central India and in remote and isolated communities in eastern India.

A tripartite system can be reconstructed for the Varna society, and this reconstruction draws on evidence from grave goods in the Necropolis. At least three categories of graves can be distinguished: (i) the graves of chiefs or rulers, (ii) the graves of warriors and/or nobles, (iii) the graves of ordinary people. From the available evidence, it is difficult to say whether a fourth category comparable to the Vedic *sudras* existed. In any event, as an example of a non–Indo-European population (i.e., the native Europeans) being ruled by an Indo-European élite, Varna was characterized by interethnic relations similar to those that obtained in Vedic India.

As evidenced in the major Indo-European traditions, the tripartite distinction of major concepts of mythological significance reflects a concrete distinction in the social hierarchy. The three categories symbolize the ruling élite, the warrior class and the ordinary herders or cultivators. The distinction between the social classes is reflected in color symbolism. The priestly function is associated with the color white and the warrior class with red (i.e., Indo-Iranian, Hittite, Celtic, Roman). The symbolic color of the ordinary class was blue, brown or black.

The tripartite system with its major categories (i.e., sovereignty, guardianship and subsistence/fertility) is the basic formula for sustained community life in the Indo-European mythical worldview, an ideology which manifests itself in the belief systems and in the conventions of social conduct of the great majority of Indo-European cultures. It is also clearly discernible in ancient communities, with Vedic society representing the most archaic of the recorded Indo-European societies (Mallory and Adams 1997: 119*f*).

In line with the tripartite distinction of social categories, concepts of a tripartite division of activities in community life exist, with sovereignty represented by sacral and juridical (law-giving) functions, with guardianship as the domain of martial traditions (i.e., the activities and ideologies of warriors), and with subsistence represented by the raising of livestock and food production:

1. The first function of sovereignty is represented by a priestly stratum of society which maintains both magical-religious and legal order. The gods associated with the sovereign function are often presented as a pair reflecting the dual aspect: the Indic god Varuna and the Norse god Odin correspond to the religious aspect, while the gods Mitra and Tyr correspond to the legal aspect.
2. The second function, which was ascribed to the warrior stratum and involved the use of both aggressive and defensive force, was associated with the war-gods Indra, Mars and Thor.
3. The third function involved fertility and sustenance, and was ascribed to the herder-cultivators. In this case, the mythic personages usually take the form of divine twins, one closely associated with horses and the other a female figure, for example, the Indic Asvins (horseman) and Sarasvati, the Greek Castor and Pollux with Helen, the Norse Frey, Freyr and Njörth.

There are difficulties associated with assigning divinities to the three functions, given that the function of individual mythical figures may have changed over time. This presents difficulties for the reconstruction of the fabric of local mythologies.

For example, the role of the Indian goddess Sarasvati is ambiguous and her functional identity depends on various criteria of mythological context (Coleman 2007: 908). Due to her early roles as river goddess and mother goddess, Sarasvati is associated with the third function of sustenance of life and fertility. At a later stage in the evolution of religious concepts, Sarasvati assumed a role connected with the first function. She was the daughter of Brahma and later became his wife, as she was equally intelligent and personified the ultimate wisdom. In her role as the goddess of the arts, Sarasvati can be compared with the Greek goddess Athena. Sarasvati is credited with the invention of the sacred language of Sanskrit and of its Devanagari script. And in one of her roles—as the protector who kills the demon Ahi—Sarasvati can even be assigned to the second function.

The tripartite functionality of divinities also includes a threefold distribution of sacrificial animals. In the early Indic tradition, for instance, animals were selected by species according to the function of the deity being venerated (Puhvel 1978):

Divinities	*Animal species for sacrifice*
Function 1	sheep or hornless ram (offered to a priestly deity)
Function 2	horse or bull (offered to the warrior-god)
Function 3	goat or pig (offered to deities with "ordinary" status)

Elite Recruitment and the Beginnings of Language Politics

The Indo-European migrants who moved into southeastern Europe came to dominate in the areas where they finally settled down. In view of the ethnic, cultural and linguistic differences between them and the native Europeans, the newcomers were in need to legitimize their status as a ruling élite. Many examples of the mythical legitimization of élite power are known from history. The Norman conquest of England and the Frankish invasion of Gaul provide examples of immigrant groups exalting their own ethnicity after assuming power: "the idea that racial identity operates as a causal force in history commences with the old European myths of invasion and conquest, the Normans over the Saxons in England and the Germanic or Trojan Franks over the Gauls in France" (Lape 2010: 143).

The Franks legitimized their conquest of northern Gaul as a privilege to which they were entitled by their noble descent. Similarly, the Normans believed there was a causal link between their conquest of England and their supposed noble status. In fact, there are much earlier examples of such arguments.

In the context of Indo-European culture, the earliest known example of the self-exaltation of an élite group is the Aryan pastoralists from Central Asia who invaded the Punjab in northern India around 1700 BCE. The invaders came from the area of the Sintashta culture (east of the Ural Mountains in Central Asia), which has been identified as the most likely location of the Aryan (i.e., Indo-Iranian) homeland. At first, Aryan warriors were called to India by local Dravidian rulers as allies in military conflicts. Soon, the Aryan warrior élites assumed control and claimed territory for themselves. In this way, an élite of Aryan (Indo-European) origin came to exercise political power over a non–Aryan (Dravidian) majority. Aryan identity was fundamentally linked to ritual and language. "If a person sacrificed to the right gods in the right way using the correct forms of the traditional hymns and poems, that person was an Aryan" (Anthony 2007: 408).

And yet, there was another aspect to being an Aryan that had to do with the expression of self-esteem. In the compilation of hymns and prayers that originated between 1500 and 1300 BCE called the *Rig Veda,* we find a formulaic ending of many hymns that refers to rituals and sacrifices, as well as to the public feasting that accompanied the funeral of an important person: "Let us speak great words as men of power in the sacrificial gathering" (*Rig Veda* 2.12, 2.23, 2.28). These figures of speech may be understood as a strategy to set Aryans apart from Dravidians and as an expression of group cohesion among those who were in power.

Those who are in power seek to legitimize their status by drawing on their noble descent. This becomes apparent in the variety of meanings that are associated with the name "Aryans" and which include ethnic connotations. Old Indic *árya-* is someone who is faithful to the Vedic religion and practices a lifeway according to the social conventions that this religion stipulates. The idea of nobleness is contained in two related expressions: *arí-* meaning "kinsman; a faithful devoted person; attached to, faithful" and *aryá-* meaning "kind, true, noble, devoted, favorable" (Mallory and Adams 1997: 213).

It can be assumed that the Aryan mindset had developed over a longer period of experienced time in a context of élite self-identification in the hierarchical clan system of steppe pastoralists and that the same mindset had already dominated the ideological framing of élite power at Varna and, later, the immigrants to Greece professed the same kind of attitude as to the anchoring of their dominant status in mythical legitimization. Far-distant repercussions of these early manifestations of legitimization may be discerned in the Greek myths of origin, of the Athenians and Spartans in particular (see Chapter 5).

The encounter of the native Europeans with the immigrants produced patterns of a complex social networking, resulting in extensive biculturalism and bilingualism. The native Europeans kept their mother tongue (i.e., Pelasgian, the substrate language) as first language and adopted the Indo-European dialect transferred to Greece by the migrants as second language. Bilingualism must have also been a major model of communication for the early Greeks, who would have picked up at least some of the language used by those with whom they lived as neighbors. Otherwise, the transfer of hundreds of borrowings from the substrate language into the Greek vocabulary would remain unexplained and lack motivation.

The process of shift, from the native Pelasgian language to Indo-European, unfolded in various phases:

Phase 1: The adoption of the language of the élite as second language.

(The population which experiences the language shift constitutes a majority, as compared with the élite minority; the process of language shift occurs in the absence of any state authority; the adoption of the élite language occurs without regular teaching, that is, as uncontrolled language acquisition; the medium of shift is speech and literacy is not involved.)

Phase 2: Emergence of an extended speech community (among the native   population) with the new language as second language.

(The élite language has a prestige which the ordinary language of the majority does not have.)

Phase 3: Increasing significance of the demographic factor, with the emergence of specifically local patterns of shift resulting from increasing demographic pressure during the course of a further extension.

(Language shift involves processes of linguistic fusion, during the course of which the vanishing language of the majority leaves traces in the structures of the élite-induced language that comes to dominate.)

Phase 4: Acceptance of the élite language as first language and abandonment of the former local native language.

(Language shift is supported by a shift in attitude, with the élite language assuming the role of an identity marker for the majority.)

The completion of the process of language shift with phase 4 marks the wholeness of what may be termed élite recruitment of language. The process of Indo-Europeanization that had started at Varna continued to unfold as a consequence of the migration of Indo-European tribes to the south, and the establishment of new local élites followed a pattern that repeated itself over and over again wherever Indo-Europeans migrated.

There is some documentary evidence from Crete about the relationship of early Greeks and native Minoans in the second millennium BCE. The coming of Mycenaean Greeks to Crete was facilitated by the disastrous eruption of the volcano on the island of Thera (modern Santorini) in the Cycladic archipelago around 1625 BCE which caused a tsunami that destroyed the Minoan fleet on the northern coast of Crete. After the backbone of the Minoan thalassocracy, their fleet, had been annihilated, the Mycenaeans succeeded in occupying the northern part of Crete where they established themselves as the ruling élite over the native islanders. In the Linear B texts from the archives in the palaces of Knossos and Chania one can observe a distinction of personal names in two groups. One is the group of the "collectors," the other that of the "shepherds."

> If we compare the names of the "collectors," men belonging to the ruling class with the exception of a few [...], are easily recognizable as Greek, the situation with the names of the "shepherds," people from the social class of middle rank, is the opposite. More than half of them (200, i.e., 57 percent) are without identification. A large number of them are very likely of non–Greek origin, born of the inhabitants of the pre–Greek population which continued to dwell in Crete together with the conquerors, the Mycenaean Greeks [Ilievski 2000: 355].

An ethnographic comparison with another example of élite recruitment in the context of stateless society may serve to illustrate more details of a process which, in the case of Pelasgian-Greek contacts, is shrouded in prehistory without surviving documentary sources. The spread of Germanic languages among Celtic tribes in the southeast of Britain in the fifth and sixth centuries CE provides a view on complex social interaction, with ethnic, cultural and linguistic features strongly overlapping.

When addressing the overlap of the ethnic, cultural and linguistic matrices in early medieval Britain one has to be aware of the problems posed by historical designations such as "Anglo-Saxon" (Reynolds 1985). A closer inspection of the terminology in question suggests

> that our modern usage of the term Anglo-Saxon is deeply flawed and ambiguous. The term Anglo-Saxon arose on the continent in the 8th century as a way of describing the Germanic inhabitants of Britain: the English Saxons as opposed to the Saxons still in Germany. In Britain itself, the terms Angli and Saxones were to some extent interchangeable, but were usually used to signify one or another subgroup by the Germanic inhabitants themselves, while the Britons and Irish regarded them all alike as Saxons (and still do). It was only in the 9th century that the compound term "Anglo-Saxon" was used within England, and this was soon replaced in the 10th century by the simple term English. Nevertheless, scholars today refer to the Anglo-Saxons in both a cultural and chronological sense to cover the Germanic inhabitants of Britain from the 5th century to the Norman conquest. This signifies a great deal more uniformity and ethnicity than actually existed at the time [Henson 2006: 35].

When talking about fusion processes in Britain we have to deal with various ethnic processes. The process of fusion within the network of intertribal contacts of the invading Germanic tribes resulted in those Germanic tribes assuming a new identity (i.e., from Angles and Saxons to Anglo-Saxon). The other fusion process concerns the intermingling of local Insular Celtic populations with the Germanic immigrants.

Roman rule in Britain ended with the withdrawal of the Roman army in 410 CE. The Roman administration and military no longer had the resources to cope with the instability caused by continuous raiding by Germanic pirates in the coastal areas of southeastern Britain. After the Romans departed, the indigenous Celts and the Romanized offspring of interethnic marriages between natives and Roman settlers were left to their own devices. The raids turned into waves of invasions of Germanic tribes that landed on the shore and moved further inland. A vacuum of political power existed for a time, which was gradually filled by Germanic élite groups that established themselves in the newly conquered territory (Salway 1993: 291*ff*).

During a prolonged process that lasted from the fifth to the seventh centuries CE, the British (Insular Celts) gradually experienced a shift to the language of the élite. Since no detailed documentary evidence of the shift has survived, the dynamics of the shift can only be deduced from its result: complete assimilation. In the case of the region of Kent in the extreme southeast of Britain, experts believe a three-generation model of replacement of British speech by Germanic dialects is most likely (Henson 2006: 120). According to this model, the language shift was completed by the mid-sixth century CE. In regions further inland and further north (i.e., Wessex, Bernicia, Elmet), it seems probable that a timespan greater than three generations would have been required for the language shift to occur. In the case of Wessex and Bernicia, it is believed that the shift from Celtic to Germanic was completed in the seventh century CE.; and in the case of Elmet, in the first half of the eighth century CE.

In the regions where early contact between Celts and Germanic tribes occurred, the number of British names for places and rivers is greater than in the areas that were conquered later by the Anglo-Saxon kings. Administration would have been more firmly under the control of the Anglo-Saxons in the border regions of Anglo-Saxon rule than in the regions in the east, where élite power initially functioned without the institutions of state organization.

> British villages would find themselves in contact with English speaking clergy, most likely English speaking estate officials, English speaking merchants and by this period English speech in such towns as preserved urban functions. Their situation would thus be different to their cousins in the east of Britain, in the 5th and 6th centuries, whose speech might leave more of an impact on place-names [Henson 2006: 121].

Greeks and Native Europeans (Pelasgians) in Contact: Biculturalism and Bilingualism in Bronze Age Greece

It can be inferred that the conditions of the original contact situation of two independent languages and cultures in contact (Pelasgian vs. Greek) soon produced patterns of biculturalism and bilingualism, with Pelasgians becoming familiar with Greek social conduct and adopting Greek as second language. Most probably, bilingualism was a prerequisite for the

Pelasgians to successfully communicate with those who had the upper hand in the political control over the region, and the need to learn the others' language—in addition to one's native tongue—was felt more strongly among the Pelasgians than among the Greeks.

In the course of repeated and intensive interaction, the two linguistic systems, Pelasgian and Greek, experienced phenomena of boundary-crossing, with Pelasgian expressions and phrases "slipping" into the Greek language used by the bilingual people and by the two linguistic codes crossing over (i.e., code-switching). When two languages are used in a way that their codes cross over, then features of the one may shift to become ingredients of the other. That is the starting point for the shifting of words, elements of word formation, sentence patterns and even patterns of phonetic articulation from one language to the other. In spoken language, processes of such shifting are unintentional and unfold in a kind of chaotic way. That means that there were no regular sound equivalents how loanwords were adopted and integrated, and many words of pre–Greek origin appear in several variants in the Greek vocabulary, that is, not in a standardized form (see Beekes 2010: xxv*ff* for variational patterns of consonants and vowels).

As for an example of a substrate word that became integrated into the ordinary language of the Greeks in multiple variants, *kidaphos* (*kidaphe* and *ki(n)daphios,* respectively, meaning "fox") can be mentioned. Variation is also typical of words that are well known from Greek antiquity and which we might take, mistakenly, for expressions of Indo-European coinage. In fact, their sound structure and their variation point to the substrate language. This is true for the term *drachme* ("drachm") that also appears as *darchma* in the sources. Originally, drachm was a term for a certain weight. Its use as the most common monetary unit in the Athenian state is a secondary and later development (see Chapter 4).

It is not known how many generations of Pelasgians interacted in a bicultural and bilingual environment before they eventually abandoned their native language and experienced a shift to Greek. During this prolonged process also the Greek language experienced change. Since Pelasgian culture was not inferior to Greek culture, the Pelasgian language, with so much ancient knowledge encapsulated in it, certainly enjoyed prestige as a vehicle of ancient civilization. The many cultural borrowings of pre–Greek origin that were adopted by the Greeks speak in favor of Pelasgian as a source of enrichment for the ancient Greek vocabulary.

Social Relations as Reflected in Borrowed Terms from the Substrate Language: The Vocabulary of Social Interaction and Intimacy

Can we reach beyond conjecture regarding Pelasgian-Greek relations during the Middle and Late Bronze Age and how intensive these were? Indeed, there are archaeolinguistic indicators that may serve to highlight the quality of Pelasgian-Greek social interaction.

In the vast array of substrate elements in ancient Greek certain domains play a pivotal role for marking intensity of social relations.

Social events:

aiklon "evening meal at Sparta"
choros "round dance," "band of dancers," "dancing-place," "choir"
eranos "meal on joint account, meal of friends," "contribution, benefactory society"
(h)eorte "feast, religious festival"

kothon "drinking utensils (Laconian)," "drinking-bout, feast"
melpo / melpomai "to celebrate with song and dance"
phiditia / philitia "collective meal of the Spartans," "the place where this meal is consumed"
Thargelia / Targelia Ionic-Attic festival
thoine / thoina "meal, banquet, feast"

Entertainment:

balbis "rope indicating start and finish of the race-course, turning post"
chelichelone a girls' game in which the participants form a ring around a player called *chelone*
kerynos "throw of the dice"
kikkasos name for an obol, "cast of the dice"
kondax "gambling game, played with a blunt dart"
kottabos / kossabos (Ionian) name of a game in which the player throws the rest of the wine from a cup
kybos "dice," "eyes of the dice" ("cubus [metaphor for a dice-like object]," "dice-like block of stone or wood")
omilla a game in which nuts or similar objects were thrown in a circle, "a sociable meeting (metaphorically)"
pessos / pettos (Att.) "oval stone in board games," "gaming piece," "board game"
skaperda / skarpada a game at the Dionysia

When social relationships become close they open up into the realm of intimacy. The ancient Greek vocabulary testifies to intimate relations between native Europeans and Greeks, with the evidence of substrate elements in the domains for intimacy and body parts. The Greeks certainly were familiar with all the concepts and ideas relating to intimacy and had their own inherited vocabulary for them. What happened, though, under the impression of intensive interaction in a bilingual milieu, was that Pelasgian elements came to infiltrate spoken Greek language and partly replaced genuine Greek terms. The final result was a mosaic of genuine Greek expressions and pre–Greek loanwords which both structured these domains of language use.

> Sexual desire was a powerful instinctual drive, and a necessary one. One Greek euphemism for the penis was the "necessity." But just because it was necessary, both for the purposes of reproduction and for the experience of pleasure, that did not mean that its operations did not have to be regulated and monitored. Certain actions were indecent and contrary to the public good, and right-thinking citizens ought to disapprove of those actions and those who committed them. But there is a gulf between this kind of regulatory framework and the idea of some kinds of sexual behaviour being inherently sinful and endangering our immortal soul [Mount 2010: 101].

It is noteworthy that, in the vocabulary of intimacy, there are various terms for "penis" (i.e., *ballion, phallos, posthe*) and female genitals (i.e., *hyssakos, sabarichis*). Of these terms, the pre–Greek expression *phallos* has become the most popular term in ancient Greek which has been transferred to our cultural vocabulary. Most probably, these elements from the substrate language initially served as euphemisms and, later, transformed into established nomenclature. Among the intimate terms are two which point to women's claims to sexual pleasure independent of men's participation; see *olisbos* and *hystax* as names for dildoes.

Pre-Greek terms in the ancient Greek vocabulary of intimacy:

(i) Body-part terminology
  ballion / phallos "phallus"
  byttos / myttos "female genitals"
  gloutos / glouta "buttock"
  hyssakos / hyssax "cunnus"
  hystax "penis made of horn"
  kyssaros "anus"
  mastos "nipple," "motherbreast, breast," ("hill, height [metaphor]")
  medea "male genitals"
  olisbos "penis coriaceus (of leather)"
  oskhe / oskhea "scrotum," "sack of twins (obscene)"
  posthe "penis," "foreskin (medic)"
  sabarichis / sabariche / sarabos "vagina"
  sphrigao "to be full to bursting (especially of women's breasts)," ("to be swollen with passion or pride," "to brim with vitality")
  tramis "the narrow space between the legs (between the anus and the genitals); perineum"

(ii) Terms to express sexual stimulation, desires and activities
  chalimas "wild, lecherous woman," epithet of the Bakchai
  chidry term of sexual slang
  depho / depso "to soften (with the hand), masturbate"
  eramai "to desire, love"
  kikke "sexual intercourse"
  lekao "to have intercourse"
  machlos / machles / machlas "lascivious (of women)," "luxuriant, wild"
  myklos "lascivious, lewd"
  phruassomai / phruattomai (Attic) "to whinny for lust for life, sniff, behave impatiently (of horses)," "to be wanton (of men)"
  skeros "cunnilingus"
  skindakisai "sexual arousal at night"
  skyza "lust, heat (personified as a woman)"

Kinship Relations of Native Europeans and Greeks

Pelasgians and Greeks deepened their social contacts by establishing interethnic family ties. We do not know many details about the kinship system of the ancient Danubians, nor about that of their descendants, the Pelasgians. When summing up the findings from anthropological research in light of the archaeological evidence that has become available in recent years it is reasonable to assert that the lineages of the native Europeans were matrilineal (Anthony 2009a: 33, 39*f*, 45). This would reflect a type of kinship system which has been identified as the most ancient in the social networking of human beings: "Early human kinship was matrilineal" (Knight 2011: 61). Matrilineality enhances prominence of women in social networking, and the considerable number of pre–Greek kinship terms in ancient Greek referring to girls and women (i.e., *baia, damar, nymphe, oar, pallake, parthenos* and others) perhaps echoes such social conditions (see Chapter 7 for an analysis of the infrastructure of Old European society).

Things were different among the ancient Greeks in whose kinship system is encapsulated the heritage from their Indo-European past with its patriarchal social structures (Mallory and Adams 2006: 209*f*): *pater* "father," *pappa* (address form) "father," *homopator* "of the same father," *genetor* "procreator," *huyus* "son," *nepodes* "grandson," *anepsios* "descendant," *annis* "father's mother," *meter* "mother," *nanne, ammas, mamme* (address forms) "mother," Akko (mythical name for the nurse of Demeter) "mother," *geneteira* "procreatrix," *thygater* "daughter," *anepsia* "granddaughter," *phreter* "brother," *phratria* "brotherhood," *eor* "sister," *patros* "paternal kinsman," *patruios* "father's brother," *metros* "maternal kinsman," *daer* "husband's brother," *gambros* "sister's husband," *hekyros* "father-in-law," *hekyra* "mother-in-law," *nuos* "son's wife; brother's wife," *galos* "husband's sister," *enater* "husband's brother's wife," *pentheros* "relation," *metruia* "stepmother."

A specific term such as *enater* "makes sense if the usual social unit was an extended family of parents and married sons. The daughter-in-law in such a situation would be in need of a term to refer to her husband's brother's wives" (Mallory and Adams 2006: 216).

The aspect of male dominance in Greek society is perhaps best illustrated by the existence and functioning of phratries, of brotherhoods, which may have originated among the early Greeks as an extension of the warrior class.

> Linguistic evidence makes it almost certain that the proto–Greeks had phratries of some sort when they first entered Greece around 2000 BC The word *phrater*, with slight variations, signifies brother in the literal sense in many Indo-European languages. The fact that from Homer on the Greeks used the words *adelphos* and *kasignetos* and never *phrater* to express the idea of brother seems to prove that in very early times they abandoned using the word *phrater* in its literal sense and widened its meaning to something like brotherhood, that is, a group of people presumably connected by kinship—the meaning which it bore throughout Greek history [Fine 1983: 35].

Group cohesion within the phratries was enhanced by various rituals, among them the worship of the patrons of local phratries. It is noteworthy that, in the worship of these patrons, pre–Greek traditions of strong female divinities merge with the prominence of male Indo-European gods.

> These brotherhoods were originally perhaps aristocratic warrior bands, but once again the democratic state had reorganized them to make them open to all: every male Athenian belonged to a phratry, and it was his phratry which dominated his social life. Each phratry worshipped a male and a female god, Zeus Phratrios and Athena Phratria, at a general annual festival held in traditional localities and under local phratry control: the mixture of uniformity with a spurious diversity suggests strongly a remoulding of older institutions at a particular date. The various rites of passage of the young male Athenian were connected with this festival [Murray 1988: 202].

The social ties of kinship were at the core of Greek society although the Greeks of antiquity had a different idea about what a family is and who belongs to this social network.

> Within the framework of tribes (*phyla*) and clans (*gene*) Greek society was essentially based on the family, on the *oikos* (or household), which was composed of a combination of free people and slaves. The family was under the power of the head of the household, and it was a tightly bound unit with complex hierarchical relationships. The term *oikos* covered not only the members of the nuclear family, but the whole physical and economic unit, including property, slaves and land, and there was strict limitation of succession by inheritance.... The *oikos* was also a religious unit, which placed particular emphasis on maintaining the tombs of the family's ancestors [Dillon and Garland 1994: 373].

Once social relations among members of different ethnic groups develop, through marriage, into more permanent bonds then there is a great probability that also the network of kinship terminology experiences interferences from the languages in contact. Pre-Greek elements are well-established in this lexical domain of ancient Greek. The offspring from such unions had bicultural and bilingual identity.

> A kinship terminology is a set of a very few words (usually between twenty and thirty) that designate the relations of what we call "consanguinity" and "affinity" that a person of the male or female sex entertains with other individuals, living or dead, belonging to this person's generation or to a certain number of generations above or below him or her. Kin terms are thus linguistic

phenomena that allow individuals (and the groups to which they belong) to position themselves with regard to others in the kinship relations that characterize their society. They provide individuals with a self-representation and enable them to communicate to others their place within a set of particular social relations, and to have a representation of the place others occupy in this network without their having necessarily to be related to the speaker [Godelier 2011: 183].

There are always two sets of kinship terms, the address terms (e.g., Mom, Daddy, Grandma) and the reference terms (e.g., sister, uncle, grandchild). The former are of special interest in the context of interethnic contacts, and it is important "to consider the address terms because they are often the first to register changes in kinship relations when these are confronted with new socio-economic contexts" (Godelier 2011: 183).

The consanguinity of parents and their children in relation to citizenship in the city-state became a crucial issue in Athens under the democracy. The regulations of citizenship in the Athenian state stipulated that identity was oriented at the mother. In case the mother was a born Athenian then her children were considered Greek (with the right to Athenian citizenship), even if the father was non–Greek. Such considerations may have been valid already during the times of early Pelasgian-Greek contacts, although not formalized as in the framework for political order in the Greek polis of later periods.

The first citizenship law was passed in 451 BCE by Pericles, assigning citizenship in the Athenian state exclusively to the offspring of Athenian mothers.

> By identifying Athenian or native women as the only women capable of producing Athenian citizens, the law tapped into both gender and ethnic-national or racial categories. To put it another way, the law attached ethnic-national or racial salience to Athenian women and to their reproductive work. In this way, it created a regime of racialized reproduction [Lape 2010: 112].

Greek society was male-oriented, exclusively so with respect to public life and the access to public offices. While women were expected to engage in a permanent social relationship only with one man (this being her husband), men were allowed to have relationships with several women. In a speech of one of the most famous Athenian politicians and orators of the fourth century BCE, Demosthenes (59.122), social relationships for men, accepted by Greek society, were specified.

> Athenian men may have three women: a wife (*damar*) "for the production of legitimate children"; a concubine (*pallake*) "for the care of the body," that is to say, to have with her regular sexual relations, and a "companion" (*hetaira*) "for pleasure." To give a full account of the possible heterosexual encounters of Athenian men, we must add to the aforementioned women the prostitutes, called *pornai*, who were only occasional partners in an act that did not involve any kind of relationship [Cantarella 2005: 250].

The nomenclature of social relationships allows a reconstruction of the involvement of Greeks with native Europeans according to the status of women in a relationship. Both the terms for "wife" (*damar*) and "concubine" (*pallake*) are elements of the linguistic substratum. From this duality of pre–Greek borrowings in the language use of the ancient Greeks it may be inferred that Pelasgian women were taken by the Greeks, first as lovers, and concubines may have also become wives.

The close relations of members in the social network of a family are reflected in kinship terminology and, in this particular domain of ancient Greek, we find a considerable number of expressions which are of pre–Greek origin.

Pre-Greek terms in the domain of kinship relations (including inmates), age-group and generational distinctions, social groupings:

baia "grandmother"
damar / domortis "wife"
kokuai "forefathers"
lipernes / liphern (ountas) "deserted, orphaned"
mellax / mellakos "young boy"
meropes "human beings"
milax / mellax "age-group"
nymphe / nympha (Dorian) "bride, young lady" ("nymph [mythical being]")
oar / oaros "wife"; Linear B ideogram for woman (wo < Pre-Greek woar ?)
opuio "to marry, take as a wife," "to have sexual intercourse with (late meaning)," "to get married (of women)" (Greek < Etruscan < Mediterranean loanword)
pallake / pallakis "concubine"
parthenos / parsenos (Arcadian) "virgin, girl, young woman"
peïskos (Cretan) "offspring, son"
talis "young, nubile girl; bride"
xenos "foreigner, guest, host" ("mercenary, soldier")
xene "foreign woman" ("foreign country")

Features of Outer Appearance (Self and Other)

Daily interaction in a bicultural and bilingual environment enhances attention of the ethnic Self for the outer appearance of the ethnic Other, and this attention is reflected in patterns of linguistic interferences, that is borrowings that shift from one language to the other.

The rich imagery from Old Europe (sixth to fourth millennia BCE) illustrates many details of the outer appearance of the ancients, of their dress and, of their hairdo. There was quite some variety in the ways women adorned their hair and men cut their beards.

We do not know how the native Europeans called the various kinds of their hairdo but, from the pre–Greek borrowings for hair fashion in the vocabulary of ancient Greek, we may conclude that there was quite some variation and that the

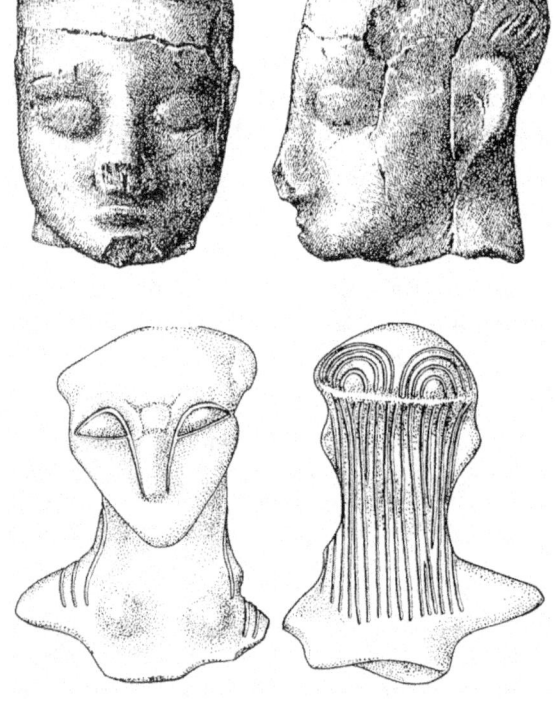

Above and following page: Heads of figurines with naturalistic design (sixth to fourth millennia BCE): (a) Hairdo of women (originally published in *The civilization of the goddess* by Marija Gimbutas. San Francisco: HarperSanFrancisco, 1991. Used with permission of the Institute of Archaeomythology); (b) Beard fashion of men (courtesy M. Videiko).

Greeks became interested and continued the customs of the ancients.

Pre-Greek borrowings in the domain of headdress and hairdo:

bostrychos "curl, lock of hair"
bystax "moustache"
hypene "moustache," "(secondarily) beard"
kikinnos "curly hair; lock of hair"
kome "hair (of the head)," ("mane [of a horse],"
 "foliage [metaphor]," "tail [of a comet]")
kommoomai "to embellish, adorn oneself"
konnos "beard," "moustache"
kottis "hairdress with long hair on the forehead"
krobylos "roll or knot of hair on the crown of the head"
mystax / mystakos "moustache" ("upper lip")
oloupho "to pluck hair"
skollys "fringe of hair," "haircut in which a tuft of hair was left on the head"
thrix "hair (bodily hair in opposition to *kome*)"

The Greeks did not practice tattooing, nor was body-painting part of their habits. Where the Greeks encountered these practices to modulate the outer appearance those people were categorized as "barbarians." Judging from the ornamentation on the bodies of many figurines that were found at the sites of the Danube civilization the modern observer can reasonably conjecture that the native Europeans knew and practiced the art of body-painting and tattooing as well as shaving intimate parts of the body for ornamentation. While certain decorative designs on figurines point to dress and accessories (e.g., necklaces, belts), other forms of ornamentation obviously have different functions and may well represent cultural symbols and motifs with religious significance that were painted or tattooed onto the skin.

As can be clearly seen, the pubic area is not spared out but attracts ornamentation as much as other body parts (i.e., breasts, thighs, buttocks). At least one form of ornamentation seems to have become popular among the Greeks once they had seen it on native European women, and this was shaving one's genitals for ornamentation. A specific term for this was adopted from the substrate language: *sabyttos / sabyttes* "shaving for ornamentation (of female genitals)" (Beekes 2010: 1300).

The Heritage of Pre-Greek Anthroponymy: Personal Names, Family Names, Tribal Names

Names are a crystallizing focus of identity, individual (personal names) and collective (ethnonyms or tribal names). "Names of all kinds have associations, flavours; they are evocative, and carry messages that are no less powerful for being ambiguous" (Wilson 1998: xi).

The native Europeans had personal names, so had the Indo-European migrants. Their

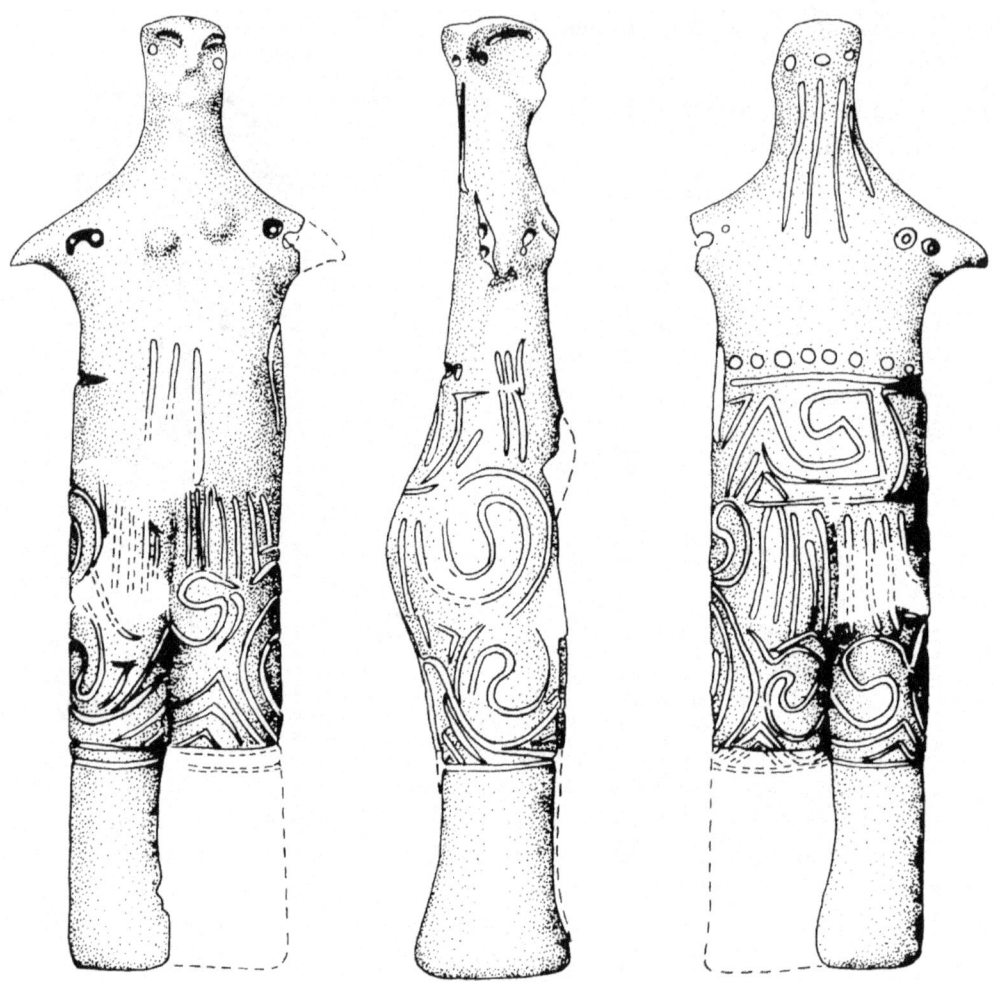

A Neolithic figurine with ornamentation resembling body painting or tattoos (fifth millennium BCE) (author's collection).

forms and variety have not come down to us directly. However, we can reconstruct some of the name forms. In the case of the names of natives this is possible on the basis of the borrowed names which the early Greeks adopted and continued, in various transformations. The personal names of genuine Indo-European coinage can be reconstructed for proto–Greek when taking into consideration Greek sound changes of proto–Indo-European.

Comparisons with other languages in southeastern Europe may help to identify names of pre–Greek origin in Greek because those relics from the substrate language have parallels in neighboring languages of Greek. Referring to the Neolithic and Copper Ages as formative periods of ancient name forms Poruciuc (1997: 218) assumes

> that it was at that time of early farming and settled life when an Aegean-Balkan onomastic system (non–Indo-European in type and matter) was being shaped. That system, in its turn, was most probably part of a vast Sprachbund [glottal union] fundamentally depending on the spreading of agriculture from the Near-East Fertile Crescent to the Aegean-Balkan world [...]. I insist: it was mainly the socio-historical context of the 6th–4th millennia BC which accounts for the roots of

an onomastic union manifest in hundreds of proper names still in use (however modified in shape, and in apparent reference) in the area under discussion.

Among the examples for convergent structures in name forms (family names) in languages of different affiliation are the following:

Microasian (Baba, Gaga, Dada, Lala, Nana, Papa, Tata)
Romanian (Baba, Gaga, Dada, Lala, Papa, Tatu)

Greek (Nannas, Babes, Navis, Panis)
Romanian (Nanas, Babes, Nanis, Panis)

Albanian (Bojk, Bukur, Bulaj, Dashe, Galea, Galan, Male, Mirja, Shuti, Zoto)
Romanian (Boicu, Bucur, Bulai, Dasu, Galea, Galan, Malea, Mirea, Sutea, Zotu)

Certain roots are common in the anthroponymy of Greek and other languages in the Balkan region. Examples of such forms are the following (according to Poruciuc 1995: 35*ff*):

An-, e.g., Mycenaean Greek A-ne-a, Illyrian Ana, Romanian Ana, Bulgarian Anko;
Ok-, e.g., Mycenaean Greek O-ke-te-u, Albanian Okiq, Romanian Ocut;
On-, e.g., Greek Onassis, Illyrian Onaion, Thracian Onakarsis, Bulgarian Onkov;
Obr-/Opr-, e.g., Mycenaean Greek O-pe-ra-no, Albanian Opari, Romanian Oprescu.

As for a method to identify names of substratal origin Poruciuc (2006: 75) states:

When a Romanian hereditary name has obvious correspondents in at least two other modern Balkan languages, we may take into consideration the probability of a substratal origin in all three [...], if the forms and affixes do not indicate exchange of a more recent date. But if credible ancient correspondents can be added to a modern Balkan triangle, then probability turns into certainty.

The impact of Old European mythological concepts on subsequent cultures was immense and proliferated to produce many items in Greek mythology. For example, this impact is reflected in the names of Greek divinities, mythic heroes and characters in epic literature (e.g., Ariadne, Asklepios, Gaia, Hephaistos, Hera, Hestia, Odysseus). The most famous of the pre–Greek mythical figures was Athena.

With respect to the conditions of Pelasgian-Greek contacts a transfer of name forms must have occurred in the early phase of intercultural exchange because some of the names of mythical personalities that appear in the epic works of the archaic period were not adopted in a unified phonetic form but show a great deal of variation. For instance, the name of the protagonist of Homer's *Odyssey* is pre–Greek: "Odysseus also had a cult, perhaps as early as the Bronze Age, and was worshiped without interruption into the historical period" (Graf 1993: 73). The well-known forms of the name (i.e., Odysseus or Odyseus) are typically only for epic literature. Other variants of this name are Olys(s)eus, Olyt(t)eus, Oliseus (in vase-inscriptions) and Oulixeus (> Latin Ulixes > engl. Ulysses).

Pre-Greek personal names that live on in Greek antiquity:

Ariadne, Atlas, Achilleus, Eirene (goddess, daughter of Zeus and Themis; "peace, time of peace"), Empousa (name of a popular phantom), Erichthonios / Erechtheus (mythical king of Athens, son of Ge), Ephialtes (name of a mythical figure, son of Poseidon and Iphimedeia ["nightmare, phantom"]), Glaukos (related to *glaux* "little owl" [Athene noctua], the attribute of Athena), (H)elene (daughter of Zeus and Leda), Kadmos / Kassmos, Penelopeia,

Peneleus (Boeotian leader), derived from *penelops / penelopos / panelops* (Aeol. Dor.) "duck or wild goose with colored neck."

Names containing a term for an animal (e.g., Penelopeia, relating to *penelops* "wild goose") may point at totemistic beliefs when a person's name was reminiscent of a mythical animal figure as founder of a lineage or kin group. Personal names associated with animals are also known from the tradition of Indo-European name-giving (e.g., Old Irish *Eochu* meaning "horse," Old Indic *Vrka-* meaning "wolf") although the preferences and selection of totem animals might have well been different among the Indo-European immigrants to southeastern Europe from those in the communities of native Europeans.

Scholars have been wondering why certain name forms that appear both in Mycenaean documents and in classical Greece had different functions. The time lapse between the two periods is more than 700 years. The names of many heroes of classical mythology are recorded as names of ordinary living people in Mycenaean times. This observation has given rise to assumptions about the formation of Greek myths in a period following the decline of Mycenaean civilization in the twelfth century BCE. However, a more thoughtful evaluation has been given recently:

> Linear B texts indicate the importance of the Mycenaean civilization for the development of Greek mythology. A great number of Greek mythological and heroic names have their parallels in Mycenaean names, e.g., A-ki-re-u /Akhilleus/, E-ko-to /Hektor/, De-u-ka-ri-jo /Deukalion/, Te-se-u /Theseus/, etc. The bearers of these names in the Linear B texts are ordinary people of the middle and lower social classes, but later, in the so-called "Dark Ages," the Greeks idealized Mycenaean society and maintained that only Mycenaean names were worthy of their heroes. The cult of these heroes originated with the emergence of urban settlements and were considered the founders of their cities. At festivals in honor of these heroes poets competed in composing poems about them [Ilievski 2000: 367*f*].

The adoption of names from one language community by another is an indicator of regular and intensive social contacts. The fact that the early Greeks integrated name patterns of Old European coinage into their onomastic system (e.g., Achilles as A-ki-re-u / Akhilleus in Linear B texts from Pylos) reflects the intensity and continuity of Pelasgian-Greek interaction. Continuity of name patterns evolved into longevity and intercultural boundary-crossing from the Bronze Age through the modern era. It is reasonable to look for the motivation of persistent name patterns in the conservatism of rural lifeways.

> I am positive that the impressive continuity of Southeast European rural life meant not only preservation of archaic traditions, but also preservation of ancient (and even prehistoric) anthroponyms, however opaque most of them may have remained (after the disappearance of the idioms that originally produced them). My conclusion is that those anthroponyms have been perpetuated—in spite of ever-changing officialdoms—due to the special strength of Southeast European peasant culture [Poruciuc 2006: 76].

Even if this statement is based on conjecture rather than on documentary proof, at least there is documentation for the persistence of name patterns from the Mycenaean era onward up to the present which spans a period of some 3,500 years. "Some Mycenaean personal names can be followed not only to classical times, but even down to the present day (cf. A-re-ka-sa-do-ro [Alexandros], Te-o-do-ra [Theodora])" (Ilievski 2000: 375).

Comparatively more is known about name patterns of Indo-European coinage than about Old European names. The continuous innovation of naming techniques and patterns makes it difficult to attribute a name pattern which may be found in more than two or three branches of Indo-European to the protolanguage. Reliable reconstructions in this area are the result of a cautious application of comparative methods. The name patterns that can reasonably be assumed to have existed already in the proto–Indo-European era show an astounding variety of forms and meanings. In addition to names associated with an animal, the following distinctions can be made:

- Names containing a term for a plant (e.g., Latin *Cicero* meaning "chickpea")
- Names "[...] expressing relationships with deities are particularly common" (Mallory and Adams 1997: 390); (e.g., Gaulish *Lugus* meaning "related to the Celtic deity Lug," *Lugudeca* meaning "chosen by Lug," *Luguselva* meaning "possessed by Lug," *Lugenicus* meaning "born of Lug")
- Names referring to attributes of deities (e.g., Old Irish *Bodb* meaning "raven," an attribute of the god Lug)
- Names referring to spiritual phenomena and to the sacred (e.g., Old Irish *Medb* meaning "intoxication," Latin *Augustus* meaning "possessed of spiritual power")
- Names referring to the concept "fame" (e.g., Old Indic *Susráva-* meaning "whose fame is wide," Greek *Sophokles* meaning "wise-famous")
- Names relating to weapons (e.g., Old Indic *Jyamagha-* meaning "who fights with a bow")
- Names containing a number (e.g., Mycenaean Greek *Qe-ta-ra-je-u,* Greek *Tetartion* meaning "fourth," Latin *Quarta,* Lithuanian *Keturai* meaning "fourth")
- Names referring to physical features (e.g., Latin *Dentatus* meaning "big-toothed," Old Norse *Grani* meaning "slender")

We do not know how the tribal groups of the Indo-European migrants referred to themselves or whether any collective name (ethnonyms) existed which referred to all members of the language community (i.e., speakers of proto–Greek). "The ethnonym is a vital component of ethnic consciousness [...] while the identity of a group is constituted in opposition to other groups rather than abstracted from the totality of its individual members [...]." (Hall 2002: 55). One has to be cautious when attempting to reconstruct a name as a marker of identity for speakers of a language that can only be described as a theoretical construct. We will never know with any certainty whether the speakers of the Greek protolanguage thought of themselves as a language community and/or a cultural community distinct from others, and whether they shared a sense of in-group solidarity. The very idea of reconstructing a linguistic and/or cultural entity called "proto-Greek" is speculative.

Some of the names of Greek tribes and historical landscapes were inherited from the native population although their role for ethnic identification of local groups remains unclear (e.g., Achaioi). The name for the historical region of Attica was not standardized in ancient Greek. The adjective Attic is rendered as Attikos, Atthikos and Athikos, and the feminine form Atthis especially referred to Attica in Greek antiquity. We can only guess whether the name of a certain tribe evoked the same consciousness of ethnic cohesion in the Bronze Age and in the Iron Age or not. Most probably, there were changes in the meaning of the name, shifting with time. This is true for cases "where the name (Achaioi) that some would apply to the whole group in the Bronze Age comes to be used in the Early Iron Age to describe subcategories of that group—i.e., the Achaians of the northern Peloponnese and Southern Italy whose claims to noble descent from personages of the Heroic Age were certainly not exclusive." (Hall 2002: 55)

Greek tribal names which are of pre–Greek origin:

Achaioi, Danaoi Greek tribe (Argos), Iones / Iaones "Ionians," Athens was also known as Kranaa polis and the Athenians as Kranaoi (derived from *kranaos* "hard, raw, rocky"), Lakedaimon town and region on the river Eurotas (original meaning perhaps "bitter water (poured over groats) which the Macedonians drink"), Lakon / Lakaina "Laconian," Makedones "Macedonians"; *makedonissa* "Macedonian woman" (derived from *makednos* "tall, slim [of trees]").

Processes of cultural exchange, of name patterns in particular, that can be observed in the context of contacts between native Europeans and early Greeks find their parallel in the Etruscan-Roman relations in Iron-Age Italy. More documentary evidence has been produced to illustrate processes of a shift to new name patterns for the Roman context than what is available for the early Greek context. It is insightful to inspect Etruscan-Roman anthroponymy for comparison.

One of the most—if not the most—complex naming system among the ancient Indo-European cultures comes from Latin. More than 300,000 inscriptions from the territory of the Roman Empire bear witness to a highly specialized form of self-identification through the choice of names.

The naming system that was in use in Roman times deviated markedly from the conventions in other Indo-European languages, and it has been suggested that the Romans adopted their threefold system from the Etruscans (Wilson 1998: 4). This system is characterized by the combination of a *praenomen* ("forename"), a *nomen* ("name") or *gentilicium*, and a *cognomen* ("nickname; additional name"). The *praenomen* was the individual's personal name; the *nomen* represented the name of the clan or lineage to which a person belonged; and the *cognomen* made reference to a specific family within the clan.

The name of every Roman citizen belonging to the upper class consisted of three elements, the *tria nomina*:

- *praenomen*

This was a personal name chosen by the parents. It usually had a meaning, though this meaning may, in some cases, have been blurred by historical sound changes (e.g., Manius referred to *mane*, meaning "born in the morning"; Lucius to *luci*, meaning "at dawn," and Marcus to the month of March)

- *gentilicium*

This name form ("middle name") was the most important constituent of the *tria nomina*. It identified the geographical or ethnic origin of the kin group and was the most important identifier in public life.

> There is evidence that the gentilicium was originally a patronymic, that is a name taken from the father's name. By the classical period, however, it was an authentic hereditary family name and indicated membership of a gens or clan. Both men and women took the gentilicium, and it was transmitted in the male line. The gens in turn derived its name from a real or supposed agnatic ancestor: [...] Fifty of the gentes were believed to be descended from the Trojans, though few of these survived into the historical period. Sixteen of the rural tribes had the names of gentes, for example Aemilia, Claudia, Cornelia, suggesting an ancient identity between them. Some of these ancient gentes remained undivided down to the time of the later Republic and they had many functions: religious, legal, social and political. They performed rites related to their clan founders [Wilson 1998: 7].

- *cognomen*

This constituent of the *tria nomina* is known from inscriptions from ca. 300 BCE but must have a much older tradition, possibly dating to the fifth century BCE. Originally, the *cognomina* related to attributes of their bearers; e.g., Cato ("prudent"), Cincinnatus ("curly-haired"), Rufus ("red-haired"), Calvus ("bald-head"). Later, *cognomina* were also associated with handicraft and professional skills, e.g., Pictor ("painter"), Faber ("smith"), Metellus ("mercenary"), Bubulcus ("good at managing oxen").

Thus, a full Roman name carried a lot of information about its owner. For example, the full name of the famous Roman orator Cicero (106–43 BCE) was Marcus Tullius Marci filius Cornelia Cicero (abbreviated as M. Tullius M.*f* Cor. Cicero).

The Romans, or at least those who came from more distinguished families, adopted this system in the seventh century BCE. Its bourgeois convenience was perhaps less significant than the snobbish implications that it made possible. As well as serving as a more discriminating name-pattern, the possession of a gentile name showed that an individual belonged to a free family of Roman citizens [Ostler 2007: 41].

In addition to the system of name-giving, the Romans also adopted name forms of Etruscan origin. Among these are the names of some famous Roman citizens, such as Caesar and Cicero. Caesar's name is associated with the town of Caere (Etruscan Caisr). This association was established during the period of the Punic wars, when one of Caesar's ancestors maintained political ties with the city as an ally against the Carthaginians.

Praenōmina (Etruscan = Roman = Abbrev.)	*Nōmina*	*Cognōmina*	
Aule = Aulus = A.	Caecilius	Caecīna	Marō
Cae = Gaius = C.	Caelius	Caesar	Perperna
Cneve = Gnaeus = Cn.	Cassius	Catilīna	Pisō
Cuinte = Quintus = Q.	Papirius	Catō	Sisenna
Kaisie = Kaeso = K.	Petrōnius	Cethegus	Varrō
Laucie = Lucius = L.	Postumius	Cicerō	Vercēnās
Marce = Marcus = M.	Vettius	Coclēs	
Puplie = Publius = P.	Volumnius	Gracchus	
Spurie = Spurius = Sp.	Lucumō		
Thefarie = Tiberius = Ti.	Maecēnās		
Tite = Titus = T.			

Roman names (*praenomina*, *nomina* and *cognomina*) of Etruscan origin (from *Ad infinitum: A biography of Latin* by Nicholas Ostler. New York: Walker & Company, 2007: 42).

The Greeks also knew a tripartite system of personal names but this was comprised of elements that differ from the Etruscan-Roman model. The introduction of the threefold naming system dates to the times of Cleisthenes' reforms: "Kleisthenes added the demotic [name of the demos, the home community] to the Athenian naming system. Thus, a fifth century Athenian's full name consisted of three elements: his own name, patronymic [name of the father, pointing to the family] and demotic" (Missiou 2011: 39).

Condiments, Spices and Special Dishes: A Glance at Pelasgian Gastronomy

The Greek cuisine offered a great variety of food stuff and dishes, and the Greeks are known for their gourmet tastes (Auberger 2010). The Greeks did not develop their cuisine from the scratch but adopted many features of the diet that had evolved over a long time, dating to pre–Greek times. When surveying the ancient Greek nomenclature of gastronomy, one gets the impression that this lexical domain is saturated with expressions from the substrate language, concerning food stuff and spices.

The assumption of pre–Greek influences in the Greek cuisine is compelling in light of the fact that the early Greeks learned the know-how of agriculture from their predecessors and adopted a broad layer of agricultural terminology, starting from the terms for cereal plants: i.e., *akte* "corn," *astachys / stachys* "ear of corn," *deai* "barley corns," *karpos* "fruits (of the earth), corn," *prokonia* "flour of barley," *sitos* "corn (especially wheat)."

There was a general awareness of the significance of the diet for the balance of the physical and mental condition, that is for the quality of life. The Greek term *diaita* had two elementary meanings: 1. "diet" (referring to food), 2. "way of life, regimen."

> Plato regards the three basic components of diet as *sitos* [a substrate word meaning "cereal food"], *oinos* [the substrate term for "wine"] and *opson* ["accompaniment"]—commonly plural, *opsa*—and this threefold view of dietary needs is expressed or briefly assumed elsewhere (as Hom. Od. 3, 480, Thuc. 1.138); *tragemata* seem sometimes to be regarded as a special kind of *opsa*, sometimes as a more luxurious adjunct to the meal, especially of a sweet kind. *Sitos* is commonly used of food generally, but also of solid food as opposed to drink (Hdt. 5.34), or cereal food as opposed to meat (Od. 9.9, 12) [Craik 1995: 391].

The Greeks ate vegetables with salt, so they could diminish the amount of food preservatives and means of conservation. Most vegetables were eaten raw or with minimal cooking. The diet included food that was available according to the season and also seafood (see Chapter 4 for a variety of seafood).

A special category of food was offered to the gods, at a domestic altar or in a public sanctuary. Very popular was the type of first-crop offering which refers to the offering of the first fruits of the earth (grain) or of the trees (olives, figs).

> The Greek term for this type of offering is *aparche,* which means "from the first." Thus the word itself has no agricultural connotation, unlike the English "first-fruits." Characteristics of the *aparche* were that it was something normally given only to the gods, or sometimes to the dead; that it was part of, or at least represented part of, something greater; and that this part was offered so as to show one's gratitude at having received the whole [Isager and Skydsgaard 1995: 169*f*].

(i) Condiments and spices
  akinos / akonos "wild basil (calamintha graveolens)"
  amarakon "marjoram (origanum majorana)"
  anethon "dill (anethum graveolens)"
  anneson "anise (pimpinella anisum)"
  anthryskon "chervil (sandix australis)"
  arkeuthos / argetos "juniper (juniperus macrocarpa)"
  aroma "condiment, aromatic plant"
  diktamnon plant name (origanum dictamnus)
  (h)orminon "sage (salvia horminum)"
  kapparis "caper plant (capparis spinosa)"
  karo "cumin (carum carvi)"

kaskandix "kind of onion"
kidalon "onion"
konile "aromatic plant (origanum, marjoram)"
koriannon / koriandron "coriander (coriandrum sativum)"
krommuon "onion (allium cepa)"
kyminon "cumin"
manyza "garlic"
marathon / marathron "fennel (foeniculum vulgare)"
minthe / mintha "mint"
molyza "garlic"
mosylon "cinnamon"
narthex / narthekos "giant fennel (ferula communis)"
okimon "basil (ocimum basilicum)"
sisymbrion "bergamot mint (mentha aquatica)"
skorodon / skordon (late) "garlic (allium sativum)"
thymon "thyme"

(ii) Special dishes (including ritual food offerings)
achaine "kind of bread, made by women for the Thesmophoria"
agathis "a mixture of sesame seeds, roasted and pounded with honey"
amora "sweet cake (fine wheat flour boiled with honey)"
basynias / basymniates kind of sacrificial cake, from the island Hecate near Delos
brathy "some herb offered to the gods"
dendalis / dandalis "kind of barley-cake"
egkris "cake made of oil and honey"
karyke "soup of blood and spices"
kachrys "parched barley"
mattue / mattua "sweet dish with all kinds of ingredients like minced meat, poultry, aromatic spices," ascribed to the Thessalians and Macedonians
myma "special dish (meat, cut up and mixed with cheese, honey, vinegar and herbs)"
myttotos / myssotos "dish, kind of paste (made of cheese, honey, garlic, etc.)"
palathe "cake made of preserved fruits"
pelanos "sacrificial cake (liquid flour dough, flour pulp, honey and oil)"
silbe "cake made of barley, sesame and poppy"
thosthai "to eat"; derivation *thosteria* "offer-food"
thrion "fig leaf," mostly as the name of a dish from eggs, milk, and honey in fig leaves

The Tradition of Visual Communication: Writing Technology from Old Europe to Mycenaean Greece

The selective transformation of Old European traditions into Aegean and Pelasgian patterns was a process of a repetitive continuity of pertinent features of the pre–Indo-European culture, rather than a fragmentization of the original entity. The continuity was repetitive in the sense that, after a time of political unrest (caused by the Indo-European out-migrations from the steppe) and after a period of cultural instability, the native European (i.e., pre–Indo-European) canon repeated itself in the Aegean civilizations and on the mainland, and its major characteristics continued to be significant as constitutive elements of Cycladic, Pelasgian, ancient Cretan (i.e., Minoan) and (Mycenaean-)Greek culture (Haarmann 1995: 57*ff*).

Cultural Memory and the Continuity of Visual Communication

A "visible" Old European tradition inspired the cultures of the ancient Aegean where writing emerged as resulting from idea diffusion in the Balkanic-Aegean cultural drift. The latest instances of the use of the Danube script come from the periphery of the area where it had flourished from the late sixth to the late fourth millennia BCE, from Ukraine and Greece. There is evidence for the habit of inscribing spindle whorls in the eastern area of the Cucuteni-Trypillya culture (in southern Ukraine) until ca. 2600 BCE. The sign inventory of Minoan Linear A owes about half of its signs (i.e., some 60) to symbols of the older Danube script. The Minoans in turn inspired the Mycenaean Greeks to write their language in a variety of their script, Linear B (Haarmann 2011b: 178*ff*).

The conditions under which the oldest of the Cretan linear scripts, Linear A, evolved cannot be compared with the emergence of original scripts in the Old World (e.g., in Mesopotamia or in ancient Egypt). Linear A definitely had a predecessor to which it is historically affiliated. The most general aspect of this historical affiliation is the memory of the existence of writing and literacy among Bronze Age people in southeastern Europe that once flourished in the Balkanic region. However fragile the documentary bridge between the decay of writing in the Danube civilization and the earliest documentation of Linear A signs around 2500 BCE in Minoan Crete may still be today, the time gap is not so dramatic as to exclude a historical relationship between the two traditions of script use via cultural memory.

There is scattered evidence which points in the direction that Old European customs continued and the memory of linear signs and their former use was kept alive by people in southern Greece. This can be concluded from the finds of two categories of leitmotif in the archaeological record from the Early Helladic II (2500–2200 BCE) and Early Helladic III periods (2200–2000 BCE), and these are terracotta figurines and linear signs on seals and on pottery.

Incised pottery from the latter half of the third millennium BCE has been excavated at various mainland sites, including Lerna, Zygouries, Orchomenos, Yialtra in Euboea and Raphina (Asketario) in Attica. The function of the signs on pottery from Orchomenos has been identified "not as decoration but to convey an arbitrary meaning" (Crouwel 1973: 104). The Early Helladic tradition is continued into the Middle Hel-

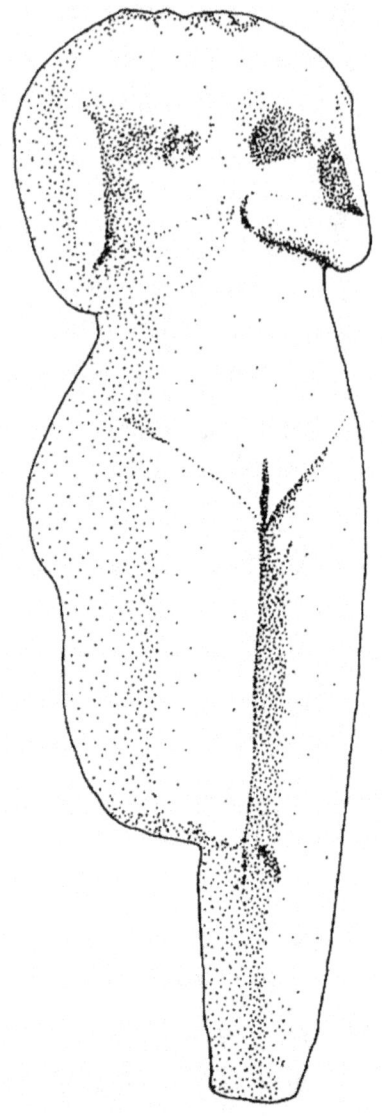

Above and following page: The continuation of Old European leitmotifs in the Bronze Age (third millennium BCE): (a) A figurine from Lerna (illustration from *Greece before history: An archaeological companion and guide* by Curtis Runnels and Priscilla M. Murray. Copyright © 2001 by the Board of Trustees of the Leland Stanford Junior University. All rights reserved: used with the permission of Stanford University Press, www.sup.org); (b) Clay seals with linear signs from Lerna (originally published in *The Aegean Bronze Age* by Oliver Dickinson. Cambridge: Cambridge University Press, 1994).

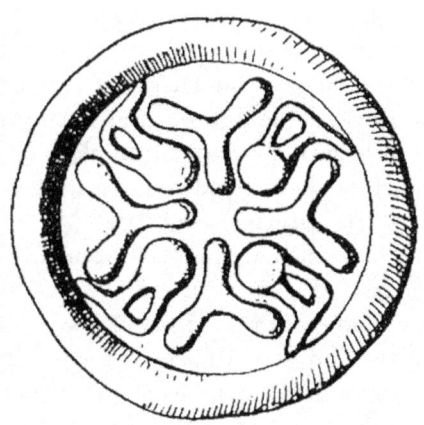

ladic period (2000–1550 BCE), and this is attested by finds of linear signs on pottery from sites including Lerna, Mycenae, Eleusis and Athens.

Balkanic-Aegean Convergences in the Domain of Writing Technology

The abundance of features linking Old European literacy to the Aegean tradition of linear writing is indicative of the persistence of his marker of early civilization in Europe. Given the importance which is generally attributed to writing, the repetitive continuity of the associated technology in the Aegean world is remarkable in that it reflects the appreciation of this technology by the native Europeans.

In the ancient Aegean world, Minoan Crete played a central role for the establishment of literacy, a cultural feature which spread as far as Cyprus and Syria in the East, and southern Italy in the West. The context of Balkanic-Aegean convergences is characterized by a range of similar patterns that are generally culture-related, and others which are associated with one of the prominent indicators of high culture: writing. Parallelisms on the European mainland and in the Aegean archipelago do not limit themselves to the visual impression of similitude of artifacts or decorative symbols, but they also embrace producing techniques in artisanship and the functional specifics of cultural patterns.

In relation to writing technology, one can observe that the transfer of knowledge from the Balkanic area into the Aegean is not limited to the perpetuation of visual forms (i.e., of individual signs in the inventory of Cretan Linear A), but it extends to the realm of organizing principles of the Cretan script. In fact, when talking about the continuity of writing from Old Europe to Minoan Crete, this includes manifold aspects of the infrastructure of writing technology and its social functions (Haarmann 1989).

The numerous similarities by which the Danube script and Cretan Linear A are characterized can by no standards be evaluated as coincidental.

> There are, perhaps, those who will be relieved to see proponents of an Old European script stuck, as it were, on the historical side of what appears to be an impassable barrier. If the script cannot be deciphered, then it will always be possible to dismiss it. But the open-minded will find its parallels to Cretan script and its own internal order and sophistication arguments sufficient not to reject it out of hand [Rudgley 1999: 70].

If we understand the perpetuation of cultural patterns from one generation to the next and from one era to the next as resulting from the working of cultural memory in human beings, then writing technology in the ancient Aegean is one of the items in that kind of memory. In the flow of ideas in Bronze Age Europe, there must have been a reminiscent knowledge that writing technology existed as a pattern of earlier civilization (on the mainland) which triggered impulses for the development of writing systems in the Aegean archipelago (Haarmann 1999: 194*ff*).

Among the remarkable peculiarities of cultural continuity in southeastern Europe from the Neolithic to the Bronze Age is the transmission of individual graphic symbols through time and space. More than sixty symbols of the Danube script persisted throughout the various periods of change from the pre–Indo-European to the Indo-European era, ultimately to be integrated into the inventory of signs of the Cretan Linear A.

Among the prominent features in the structuring of the Old European writing system is the extensive use of strokes as well as occasionally of other markers such as dots or crosses to produce variants of basic signs. This can be observed in the vast repertory of abstract

Signs of Linear A	Reference number	Old European equivalents	Reference number	Signs of Linear A	Reference number	Old European equivalents	Reference number
⊢	AB 01	Y	OE 213 a	Ψ	AB 27	Y	OE 206
+	AB 02	+	OE 130	Y	AB 31	Y	OE 205
‡	AB 03	⊤⊤	OE 203	C	AB 34	(	OE 168
↯	AB 04	↯	OE 14	∧	AB 37	∧	OE 103
T	AB 05	ǂ	OE 224	Ā	AB 38	Ā	OE 104a
AB 09	AB 09	⊍⊍	OE 19	⩟	AB 39	△	OE 161
ƒ	AB 10	⊢|	OE 69	Ā	AB 40	⟁	OE 94
⟨	AB 11	⟨	OE 222	⊹	AB 41	⊥⊥	OE 134
ǫ	AB 21	φ	OE 231	氺	AB 51	禾	OE 9
ⲕ	AB 24	ⲕ	OE 226	⟨	AB 53	⊥	OE 189
				Ħ	AB 55	⊢⊣	OE 200

Above and next page: Parallelisms in the sign inventories of the Danube script and Cretan Linear A (OE = Old European, A = Linear A, B = Linear B, AB = identical signs in Linear A and B) (author's collection).

signs where entire columns of sign variants fall under this category (see OE 76*ff* in Haarmann 1995, figure 32). The use of diacritical marks in Old Europe provides the earliest evidence for this technique in the history of writing. Outside the European cultural domain there is another ancient script which makes extensive use of the diacritical technique, this being the Indus script.

As for the question of continuity, the use of strokes and/or dots to produce sign variation is not a prominent organizational principle of linear writing in Crete. Nevertheless, the basic workings of this technique can be observed in the structuring of the Linear A system. At a later date, the diacritical technique again sees extensive application in the structuring of the chronologically latest derivative from a writing system in the Old European complex: Cypriot Syllabic (see Haarmann 1995: 109*ff*).

THE AEGEAN HERITAGE OF OLD EUROPEAN WRITING TECHNOLOGY BEYOND MINOAN LINEAR A: THE TRANSITION TO MYCENAEAN LINEAR B

The Greek-speaking people who started infiltrating mainland Greece in the third millennium BCE did not encounter the cultural institution of writing, since Old European literacy had vanished long before. However, they found the places where the Old European culture had once flourished and where, in the coastal area and in the Aegean archipelago, the descendants of the early bearers of the Danube civilization were still living. Even at those places on the mainland which had already been occupied by Indo-Europeans, the pre–Indo-European heritage was deeply rooted, not only in relics of the material and spiritual culture but also in their names (see Chapter 1 for place names and Chapter 3 for anthroponymy).

Although there is a considerable gap in the chronology of literacy between the disappearance of the Danube script and the advent of linear writing (i.e., Mycenaean Linear B) in the area of pre–Indo-European settlement, knowledge of linear writing is evidenced as early as the seventeenth century BCE. The earliest record of a Linear B inscription comes from the holy precinct of Olympia in the western Peloponnese (Godart 1995). Already much earlier, Minoan cultural goods and influence had spread throughout the northern and western parts of the Aegean archipelago, and specimens of Minoan writing (i.e., in the Linear A script) were also obtained by Greek-speaking people during the Middle Helladic era. From contact with the Minoan civilization there emerged the blend of Late

Signs of Linear A	Reference number	Old European equivalents	Reference number
⊟	AB 56	⊟	OE 201
日	AB 57	目	OE 202
⌐	AB 58	⌐	OE 52
2]	AB 60	ے	OE 230
Ŀ	AB 74	⌐,	OE 62
⁇	AB 76	⁇	OE 49
⊕	AB 77	⊕	OE 138
ᾰ	AB 80	M	OE 1
⇁	AB 81	⋀	OE 6
⇝	AB 86	⋈	OE 73
ß	AB 87	⋃	OE 53

Helladic culture which is better known from its being named after the most important political center, Mycenae, as Mycenaean culture (see Demakopoulou 1988: 22, 27 for the chronology).

The early recording of a Linear B inscription at Olympia is contemporaneous with the occupation of northern Crete by the Mycenaean Greeks or it may even predate this event. The beginnings of the Mycenaean presence on Crete are dated to the period soon after the eruption of the volcano of Thera which occurred in 1625 BCE. It seems convincing that the adaptation of Minoan Linear A and its transformation to write Mycenaean Greek had already been achieved before the arrival of Mycenaeans on Crete.

The idea of an experimenting phase with linear writing on the mainland before the middle of the second millennium BCE is supported by the fact that several signs of the Linear B system which have no equivalent in Linear A find their parallels in the Old European repertory. This is true for the signs which render the phonetic values [e], [je] and [te].

Those signs are unknown in Linear A, and the only plausible explanation for their appearance in Linear B is their continuity in the cultural complex on the mainland where the Mycenaean Greeks adopted them from a reservoir of linear signs which might have survived, as lingering traces of the once vital Old European literacy (e.g., as magical symbols or markings) and as fragmented items of cultural memory.

Such patterns of survival of motifs of an earlier script are known from India where signs of the ancient Indus script have been perpetuated among the Dravidian population of southern India in their magical symbolism (Hoeppe 2006). "One medium through which traditional motifs have passed from generation to generation all over India is the folk custom of drawing auspicious designs in courtyards and on house walls with dry or wet flour, possibly mixed with colour" (Parpola 1994: 55).

The assumption that there was a knowledge of linear signs outside the range of the Linear A system can be supported by finds on the mainland of sign usage, the origin of which is neither Linear A nor Linear B. "Numerous signs on pottery from the Early, Middle, and Late Bronze Age (3000–1500 BC) have been studied at Ayia Irini in Keos (Bikaki 1984), many of which are similar to the Old European script of Serbia and Romania" (Sampson 2009: 190).

The oldest stratum at Tiryns (i.e., Tiryns I) contains linear signs and sign groups forming short inscriptions found on various kinds of pottery, loom weights, and other objects. The linear signs from Tiryns show "general resemblance to remnants of a decaying writing system" (Uhlenbrock 1982: 29). Given the multifaceted range of potential sources (i.e., signs of Linear A, of the Cretan hieroglyphic script, symbols of Old European heritage) in the formation of the Linear B writing system, it seems appropriate "to think of Linear B as a relation of Linear A, but not a direct descendant of it" (Hooker 1980: 20).

Old European sign	Reference number	Sign of Linear B	Phonetic value
⟁	OE 105	⟁	e
⋉	OE 118	⋉	je
≡|≡	OE 229	≡|≡	te

Sign convergences in the Danube script and Linear B (excluding parallelisms in Linear A) (author's collection).

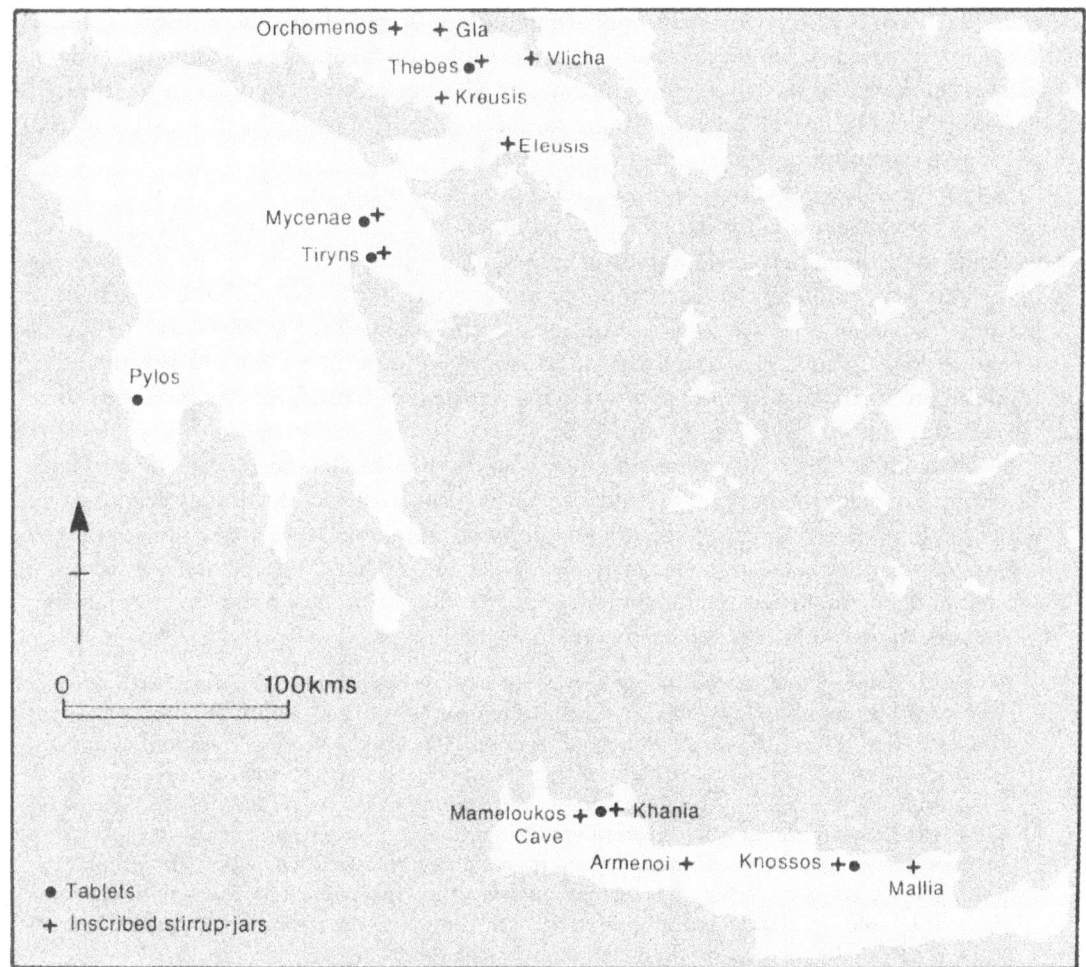

Geographical distribution of items inscribed in Linear B (originally published in *The Aegean bronze age* by Oliver Dickinson. Cambridge: Cambridge University Press, 1994).

Remembering the Past: Myths, Historicity and Concepts of Reality in the Greek Tradition

The civilization of Greek antiquity offers conditions for an embedding of mythical tradition that may serve as a sandbox model for the study of the ways the ancients perceived myth. The Greeks are said to have invented myth. Or so we believe. The historical facts, though, prove such beliefs wrong. The Greeks inherited the genre of myth from their predecessors, from the people who had lived in Greece long before the formation of a Hellenic ethnic identity. The Greeks adopted myth-making from the ancients because this vehicle of knowledge-construction had proved to be successful and useful for innumerable generations. The Greeks put myths to work in their own society, and the powerful heritage from the ancients became imprinted in the Greeks' cultural memory. So the myths persisted in the intergenerational chain as to always impress young people anew.

For Plato, the narration of myths was equal to "a search for the things of the past" (*Kri-*

tias 110a). That is a far cry from our modern understanding of myth. According to a widely held view, the notion of "myth" stands in opposition to the concept of reality, and to the kind of thinking that we call "reason." In contexts where beliefs or prejudices are confronted with facts, there is the well-known saying: "one has to search for the reality behind the myth," with myth connotating everything that is not real.

From the classical period of Greek antiquity—that is from the fourth century BCE—onward, the concept myth (Greek *mythos*) connotated the meaning "story, tale, narrative," referring to the imagined world of mortal heros and divinities. Since then, most derivations of the basic expression mythos carry those connotations: e.g., *mythologia* "a telling of mythic legends, legendary lore"; *mythologos* "a teller of legends, romancer"; *mythologikos* "versed in legendary lore"; *mythologeo* "to tell mythic tales or legends; to invent like a mythical tale; to frame an imaginary constitutio"; *mythographia* "a writing of fables"; *mythographeo* "to write fabulous accounts" (Liddell and Scott 1991: 521).

The connotations of *mythos* and its derivatives that dominated Hellenistic and later Byzantine language use have forged the wider European tradition of thinking according to which myth is related to the imaginary and opposed to reason. If we are to investigate the essence of what myth among the ancients was all about, we have to free ourselves from the burden of distorting interpretations of Greek myth that became popular at the beginning of the modern age and have persisted ever since.

> It must be stressed that the word "myth" was not used in English until the nineteenth century. The word does not occur in eighteenth-century dictionaries or encyclopedias. When a single myth was referred to, it was always as a "mythological fiction," a "poetical fiction," a "tradition," a "poetical history," or, most commonly, a "fable." ...Almost everything relating to what we now think of as myth came, for the eighteenth century, under the heading of the word "mythology." This word did not then mean primarily a collection of myths or fables; it meant, first of all, an explanation or interpretation of myths.... The most common eighteenth-century meaning of mythology is "pagan theology," and ... religious concerns constitute the usual context in which mythology was discussed. From a Christian point of view, then, mythology is the opposite of true or Christian theology. It is false theology or pagan theology [Richardson 1978: 10*f*].

And yet, there is an older meaning of *mythos* that was common in the society of archaic Greece (eighth century BCE) and not associated with notions of the imaginary or of entertainment. In this older context, *mythos* was not an opposite to logos, that is, reason and logical thinking. In the context of Homeric epic literature, *mythoi* (myths) were synonyms of holy ideas, *hieroi logoi* (Vernant 1988: 204). In archaic Greece, *mythos* referred to the cultural knowledge accumulated in society and handed down from one generation to the next. Therefore, what was considered true was concentrated into myth.

The mythic experience of the world and its origins which crystallizes in the oldest Greek myths reflects orally transmitted knowledge of past generations. According to some scholars, myth in this function is as old as the emergence of human culture itself. Arguably, the earliest genre of organized language use to develop was the explanation of the world within the framework of mythopoetic conceptions. The mythopoetic conceptualization of the world may have provided a major incentive for enhancing the use of language, and the role of mythmaking in the development of verbal skills may have been even more important than the need for verbal instructions in the teaching of tool-making.

> The myth is the prototypal, fundamental, integrative mind tool. It tries to integrate a variety of events in a temporal and causal framework. It is inherently a modeling device, whose *primary* level

of representation is thematic. The pre-eminence of myth in early human society is testimony that humans were using language for a totally new kind of integrative thought [Donald 1991: 215].

The intrinsic interplay of early mythmaking and early use of language—that is, the close interrelation of myth and speech—has been emphasized in semiotic studies (e.g., Röhr 1994: 77). There is something of a cognitive duality that characterizes the infrastructure of mythopoetic experiences in humans: "the emotional necessity of myth is constant; the forms of myth are not" (Chase 1969: 113). The oldest Greek myths find their origin in the oral tradition, and the most general meaning of *mythos* is "anything delivered by word of mouth, word, speech." The original connection of myth to knowledge, reason and truth continued to be reflected during the classical age in various meanings of *mythos:* (a) "a speech in the public assembly"; (b) "talk, conversation"; (c) "counsel, advice, a command, order, also a promise"; (d) "the subject of speech, the thing or matter itself"; (e) "a resolve, purpose, design, plan"; (f) "a saying, saw, proverb," etc. (Liddell and Scott 1991: 521). The written versions of the myths of the classical period which have come down to us are later adaptations of oral narratives transferred into the medium of written literature (Morgan 2000: 32*f*). It is appropriate to speak of the invention or creation of mythology when thinking of the tradition of fiction that was crafted as literary narrative.

The connotations which *mythos* had in archaic Greek society as a source for the transfer of traditional knowledge continued into the tradition of early historiography (sixth and fifth centuries BCE) and of philosophy of the fourth century BCE. There have been earlier approaches by some scholars to explain the continuation of myth into the era of rational thinking. According to Kirk (1970: 240*ff*) the persistence of myth is a reflection of the fact that "real myths" (rationalizing life experience) once existed. The ancestors of the Greeks might have possessed real myths in a remote past. Systematic investigation of the pre–Greek cultures started in the 1970s and the contours of the overall picture of Old Europe became known in the 1980s. Accurate dating of the pre–Greek cultural layers became available as late as the 1990s. Despite the availability of substantial facts about the early history of myths, seemingly, the value of traditional myths (without their distortions as a literary genre in the Hellenistic age) is still questioned by many scholars. However, regardless of the standpoint from which one may look at Greek myth in the pre-classical era the trajectory of historical development remains the same: both historiography and philosophy are daughters of myth.

Mythology into Historiography

In the beginnings of Greek historiography, *mythos* and *logos* were intrinsically intertwined. There was no independent training for historians. The original meaning of the Greek term for historian, *histor* (a hybrid form molded on the fusion of the verbs *oida* "to know" and *idein* "see"), is "the one who knows because he has seen" (Darbo-Peschanski 2011: 29). A prerequisite for being a historian is, then, to travel much and have a look at the world. However, this virtue was true only for a few Greek historians. Although Herodotus (ca. 484–424 BCE), the father of Greek historiography, traveled as far as Egypt, his reputation falls behind of what his work would have required. Herodotus is said to have heard too much and seen too little (Schepens 2011: 47).

There is another factor in the picture of early Greek historiography that stands against any generalization about a mythologizing trend reflected in the ways historical events are described, and this has to do with personal preferences and inclinations. Herodotus' world is imbued with the spirit of the gods while they are absent from the work of Thucydides who, being thirty years younger, represented the next generation after Herodotus. The gods are again well present in the historical accounts of Xenophon (fifteen years younger than Thucydides). There is no clear-cut distinction of generations.

> In Herodotus' own day Sophists were busy finding anthropocentric ways of explaining the world. Herodotus could have told a secular story, but he did not. Religion is everywhere in his book; no one would write such a thing were they not, at the least, profoundly interested in the gods and their role in human history. In this light the idea that he is a religious sceptic of some kind seems very hard to sustain. Though he expresses many reservations concerning various human beliefs about the gods, this is quite different from scepticism about their basic existence. Any number of passages demonstrate his belief in divinity; none suggests disbelief [Fowler 2010: 319].

The mythopoetic and narrative trend in early Greek historiography is not surprising when taking into consideration that historians were educated in the registers of the literary language, and they were trained to master style and genre. One has to keep in mind that "the Greek and Roman historians came from the schools of grammarians and rhetors: the formation of the historian was the same as that of the orator and there was no specific preparation for the writing of history" (Nicolai 2011: 21).

Writing history was equal to writing in the narrative genre. The mythic tradition had permeated literary production since the early epic literature, and it influenced historically oriented narration as much. Historiography was a literary genre rather than a science. For a long time, historiography was equal to mythography with connotations that were not tainted with attributes such as funny or fantastic. The mythical past was taken as the starting point by many an author of historical works. This is especially true for Herodotus who does not doubt the historicity of mythical abductions (of Io from Argos to Egypt, of Europa from Tyre to Greece, of Medea from Colchis to Europe, of Helen from Sparta to Troy) and "he accepted without hesitation the notion that the royal dynasties of Lydia and Persia had been established by Heracles (*Histories* 1.7.2). Indeed, he made this derivation the cornerstone of his chronological system by placing Heracles nine hundred years before his own time (2.145.4)" (Graf 1993: 122).

Dealing with myth was common for historiographers into the classical and Hellenistic periods.

> Classical historiography, which was born out of myths and invented the "mythical" as its foil, obviously did not succeed in putting myth out of business. It even paid attention to its invention. But its criticism of fabulous stories constitutes a major contribution to our understanding of what ancient historians considered as "historical" [Saïd 2011: 87].

Mythology into Philosophy

The respected genre of myth became seminal also in the domain of philosophical reasoning. The pre–Socratic philosophers are known for their breaking away from the mythic tradition. And yet, in their independent reasoning they reached the same conclusions about the origins of the world as imbued with the actions of divine powers (Haarmann 2013a: 144*ff*). Among the prominent representatives of the pre–Socratic movement, which has been called the "first enlightenment" in European intellectual history, is Parmenides (fifth century BCE) who is purported to have made the statement: "From nothing comes nothing." Parmenides' concept of Being is mythopoetic and shows resemblances to a certain type of mystical experience in which space and time seem to lose all significance and there is an acute sense of the unbroken unity of all things with each other and with the self. He actually presents his philosophy as derived from a private divine revelation. But nothing is more significant of the intellectual climate in which he lives than the fact that he does not say "the goddess showed me, and I saw," but "the goddess proved it with the following arguments." He is concerned to rationalize his vision [West 1988: 115].

Myth was a strong agent in the philosophical thought during the time of Plato (ca. 427–347 BCE) who restored the original meaning of *mythologia* as tradition, or as the useful knowledge handed down from the ancestors (Detienne 2003: 22*ff*). In some contexts, Plato equated *mythos* with *logos,* for instance, in the context of the myth of origin (Partenie 2009: 2). Plato did not present his philosophical writings in the form of reflections about abstract concepts. He made ample use of allegories and metaphors, and he chose the genre of myth as the most elementary frame to express his ideas.

In archaic societies myths were believed to tell true stories—stories about the ultimate origin of reality. For us, on the contrary, the term "myth" denotes false belief. Between the archaic notion of myth and ours stands Plato's [Partenie 2009: 1].

Plato has been credited as the father of European philosophy but the overall anatomy of his work makes him as much a "mythologist" (Janka and Schäfer 2002). Historians of philosophy hail the great achievement of Greek philosophers to detach themselves from the shackles of myth and to become enlightened by the application of reason (*logos,* respectively). And yet, this modern perspective is not very realistic.

It has been realized for some time that the picture of the irrational fading away in the face of science is flawed. Popular, traditional, and supernatural beliefs were never superseded.... It seems clear that philosophy made a difference in the way we engage in intellection. But why is the difference specified in terms of myth, and why is myth equated with irrationality? Why is the Greek miracle the freedom of *logos* from myth? Because that is what the Greek philosophers tell us to think [Morgan 2000: 33].

If we are to perceive the impact which incipient historiography and philosophy had on the cultural history of Europe we are advised to study myth and the role that myths had in Greek society of antiquity. When we engage in the study of myth under these auspices we will be rewarded with manifold insights because understanding the interrelation of Greek myth and Greek worldview takes us to the very core of ancient Greek civilization. In other words: we cannot do without the study of myth when we want to assess the place of Greek civilization and the longevity of its institutions. "'Mythological' philosophy teaches the important lesson that philosophical knowledge cannot shine transparently through the medium in which it is expressed [i.e., language]. *Mythos* is the condition of the world we inhabit" (Morgan 2000: 291).

Mythology into Architectural Sculpture (Picture Friezes)

The role of myth in Greek antiquity is readily associated with literary genres such as historiography and philosophy. And yet, myth, used as a cultural medium and even instrumentalized for ends of political self-representation, covered a wide array of social life in antiquity. Recent investigations have produced valuable insights into the implications of myth in the domain of architecture and art; e.g., the embedding of a monument adorned with picture friezes depicting mythological scenes in a given cultural environment.

> [Barringer] considers the use of myth as architectural sculpture in Classical Greece (ca. 480–323 BC) and argues that myth is not randomly selected and does not serve a purely decorative function but has meaning (the same is true for small-scale works, such as vase painting), and the interpretation of a given myth depends on context. The same myth, such as the ubiquitous Centauromachy [Heracles' fight against the centaurs], can mean different things in different contexts, and in a monumental context, the mythological image relates to the site and often to other monuments surrounding it, which redouble, resonate, or create variations on a theme [Barringer 2008:2].

It is noteworthy that one finds pre–Greek elements among the major concepts for knowledge-construction in ancient Greek society. One is *mythos* which is generally believed to be genuinely Greek. In fact, "the word is ... Pre-Greek" (Beekes 2010: 976). Another term designating refined knowledge (i.e., wisdom) is *sophia* the stem of which (*soph-*) has no cognate form in other Indo-European languages. The isolation of this expression in Greek and its sound structure "point to a substrate word" (Beekes 2010: 1374).

Mythologizing History: The Crafting of New Myths

Every era produces its own kaleidoscope of myths which means that there is a repertory of older myths that serve to transmit the overall worldview of the time (i.e., explaining eternal "truths") and, in addition, new myths are invented to meet the need for explanation of current developments. Greek historiography does not only present a multifaceted competition of elementary orientations (in the form of *mythos* versus *logos*)—with changing gravitations in the horizon of time—but also the persisting readiness of the historiographers (in their role as mythographers) to present their accounts with mythical underpinnings. For this end, new myths were crafted that claimed to be as true as the myths transmitted by the ancients.

One of these new myths which even gained political weight was the transformation of the older myth of Theseus who had slain the Minotaur in the labyrinth of the palace of Knossos (Crete). After their victories over the Persian navy the Athenians bolstered their maritime defense system with a modern naval force and they became the most important member in the Delian League that was founded in 478 BCE. The oracle at Delphi urged the Athenians to retrieve the bones of the ancient hero Theseus and establish a new cult for him as a divine hero. This task was assigned to a young general, Cimon. He set out on a search for Theseus' bones. On the Cycladic island of Skyros he unearthed bones from an ancient grave and brought them to Athens where they were kept in a sanctuary dedicated to Theseus. What followed was mythmaking.

> Athenians inherited many myths from the remote past, but when current developments, such as the rise of the navy, seemed to cry out for mythical precedents, they readily invented new ones. Cimon abetted the process. Among the creative artists whom he patronized was a genealogist and mythographer named Pherecydes. He had already traced Cimon's family tree back to the hero Ajax of Salamis. Now Pherecydes rewrote the Theseus myth. In this exciting new account, a desperate Theseus rushes back to the harbor near Knossos after killing the Minotaur and ensures a safe escape by ramming the hulls of the Cretan ships so that they cannot pursue him. A later mythographer named Demon improved the tale by transforming the Minotaur into a Cretan general named Taurus and claiming that Theseus defeated him in a naval battle—the first naval battle

in Athenian history!—at the mouth of the harbor. Thus Theseus metamorphosed into a true naval hero, with exploits that foreshadowed naval warfare of Cimon's own day [Hale 2009: 85*f*].

When the navy set out on its campaigns in the Aegean, there was a saying that became proverbial among the mariners: "Not without Theseus!" In the course of the fifth century BCE, the Athenian city-state enlarged its sphere of military and political supremacy in successive seasonal campaigns, also with the intention to secure economic resources: "desire for precious metal and ship-timber was part of the explanation for aggression against, and settlements at, Thasos, Thurii, and Amphipolis. Above all there was tribute, in ships or money (increasingly the second was preferred by all parties)" (Hornblower 1988: 127).

The irradiation of Athens' power as a city-state stood in marked contrast with the local

The Athenian maritime empire in the fifth century BCE (originally published in *Greece and the Hellenistic World*, edited by John Boardman, Jasper Griffin and Oswyn Murray. Oxford: Oxford University Press, 1988. Used by permission of Oxford University Press).

range of economic and political influence of other Greek settlements around the Aegean Sea that participated in the maritime trade network. Most of the settlements were concentrated in the coastal area, and the rural extension was rather limited. When the maritime network is mapped out in the scholarly sources, as a rule, only the geographical distribution of coastal settlements is indicated. The ideal of an integrated survey of coastal settlements showing their hinterland is an exception, found only in some maps, as in the one presented by Hornblower (1988: 128) of the Athenian maritime empire in the fifth century BCE.

At the outbreak of the Peloponnesian War (431 BCE) Athens was at the height of its might, as a military power on land and at sea. When this war ended in 404 BCE, the empire had crumbled.

4

Seafaring, Trade and Commerce
Trade Networks in the Early Greek World

The ancient Greeks are known for their mercantile endeavors in the areas surrounding the Mediterranean and the Black Sea, and in the antique sources we find much information about how they conducted business with other Greeks and foreigners. Those Greeks also founded colonies abroad already during the "Dark Ages." The first to start the colonial enterprise were the Spartans who established a trading center on the Cycladic island of Thera (modern Santorini) around 1000 BCE (Osborne 1996: 121). Those Greeks who explored the coastal areas of the Mediterranean were not the first to frequent sea routes. There had been other Greeks before them to engage in seafaring and colonization.

Many Greek settlements outside the Greek mainland had been established by the Mycenaeans hundreds of years earlier. Mycenaean-Greeks settled on the Ionian coast of the Aegean, in Asia Minor, and Mycenaean merchants explored the sea route to the west and founded trading posts in southern Italy where remains of Mycenaean pottery have been unearthed. The Mycenaeans did not only conduct trade but they also built ships to wage war. The most famous of those wars for strengthening Mycenaean political power in the region was the Trojan war whose agents, the heroes of the Trojans and the Achaians, gained immortality in Homer's epic work *Iliad*.

In the beginning, though, the Greeks were no seafarers because their ancestors, the Indo-European pastoralists, came to Greece on inland routes. The development from a pastoralist society to a seafaring nation is quite amazing and raises many questions. How come that people who originally lived in a landlocked environment set out to sea? What might have been the motivation for them to set their minds to seaborne trade? It is clear that the shift from inland orientation to seafaring did not happen overnight. In all probability, for such a process to unfold one has to take a span of time of many generations into consideration. It is unrealistic to imagine the shift to have occurred as a rapid leap. Rather, we have to do with a kind of transitional process that unfolded in a step-by-step progression.

How Did the Indo-European Migrants Accustom Themselves to a Maritime Environment?

At the time when the ancient Greeks started to build ships and explored the coastal waters there had been no contact between the Greek mainland and Egypt. Neither the know-how of ship-building nor of seaborne trade could have come from there. In fact, this know-how originated in the world where the early Greeks and the native Europeans engaged in cultural exchange. In this milieu of bicultural and bilingual contacts the agents have to be sought that are responsible for an extension of the Greek mind to explore the world beyond the mainland. The first step, though, was the exploration of the new homeland which the newcomers came to call Hellas, with its multifaceted coastline.

After the ancestors of the Greeks had arrived in the south and had begun settling down, they got to know an environment that was strange in the first place because the newcomers had not have any experience with marine conditions. The indicator that reflects the early Greeks' lack of experience is their language. The newcomers learned many words from the natives for phenomena that they did not know, starting with the most general expression for a marine environment, *thalassa* (with a variant *thalatta*). This expression, which has survived to this day in modern Greek, is the word for "sea." *Thalassa* is not related to any of the inherited expressions for sea in Indo-European languages. The original inland orientation of the early migrants is "supported by the fact that those stocks actually living adjacent to an open sea (e.g., the Greeks, the Germans and the Indo-Aryans) had borrowed words for the body of water from non-IE sources, e.g., Grk *thalatta* 'sea,' OE *sæ* ' sea' (> NE *sea*), Goth *saiws* 'sea'" (Mallory and Adams 1997: 503).

In addition to *thalassa,* the early Greeks adopted an abundance of terms, for natural phenomena relating to the sea and for marine life.

(i) The sea and related phenomena
  aigialos "sea-shore, beach"
  akte "promontory, rocky coast, rough shore, edge"
  alibduo "to sink, submerge into the sea"
  andera "raised bank of a river or ditch; dike, border of the sea"
  bythos "depth (of the sea)"
  charme "high-rising cliff in the sea"
  eïon "shore"
  Euripos "straits, narrows," especially the straights between Euboea and Boeotia
  isthmos "strait of sea (especially with respect to the strait of Corinth)"; "spit of land, small entry"
  kroke "rounded pebble on the seashore"
  laitma "depth, gulf of the sea"
  nesos / nasos / nassos "island"
  ochthe "high and rocky edge by the water," "bank, shore"
  petra (also *petros* "stone") "rock," "boulder, big stone," "rocky mountain range," "cliff, ridge," "rock cavern," "cave"
  phrix / phrike "shiver, the shivering or ruffling of the sea surface"
  plemyris / plemyridos "rise of the sea, flood"
  rothos "roar (of waves)"
  salos "turbulent movement of the sea, flushing of the waves"
  scheros "cape, shore"
  spilos / spilas "rock, reef"
  thalassa "sea"

(ii) Marine life
  abrytoi "sea urchin"
  aphareus "belly fin of the female tuna"
  astakos "smooth lobster"
  channa / channos "(kind of) sea bass (serranus cabrilla)"
  (h)eledone "octopus"
  ichla / kichla / kichle "sea-fish"
  kammaros "crab"
  kampe / kampos "sea monster"
  karis name of small crustaceans
  kauax "seamew, tern (sea-bird)"
  ketos "big sea-animal, sea-monster," "whale"
  knide "nettle; sea nettle"
  korallion / koralion / kouralion "coral"
  kordylos "seafish"
  kochlos "shellfish with a spiral-shaped shell," "sea snail, land snail," "purple snail"
  krabyzos "shellfish"

kraggon / kragon / kragge "small crustacean (squilla mantis)"
mormyros "seafish (of the family of the breams)"
ostreion / ostreon "oyster, mussel, sea snail"
pagouros "(edible) crab (cancer pagurus)"
pelamys / pelamydos / palamis "(young) tuna"
phagros / pagros / phagoros "sea bream (pagrus vulgaris)"
prason "leek (allium porrum)," "seaweed"
prethma "tentacled head of an octopus"
premas / premnas "(young) tuna fish"
salpe / sarpe / salpigx "sea fish (box salpa)"
sepia / sepie "squid"
sparos "lesser sea bream (sargus annularis)"
tethea "sea squirt (ascidia)"
thynnos / thynna "tuna fish"

The first impulse to learn from the natives about marine life seems to have been the curiosity among the early Greeks to go out fishing to catch foodstuff. Catching fish from small boats stood at the very beginning of the Greeks' experience with the sea. In the ancient Greek vocabulary, a term from the substrate language has been preserved: *aspalieus / aspalous*, "fisherman." In the specialized terminology of utensils needed for fishing one finds the following substrate terms: *gaggamon / gaggame*, "small round net for catching oysters," and *sagene*, "large fishing net, trawl." Learning the know-how of native fishermen and becoming fishermen is one thing, but setting out to sea as merchants for engaging in marine trade is quite another. The occupation of fishermen requires the knowledge to manage seaborne vessels. The native Europeans had ample experience with that. What is also required is the know-how of boat- and ship-building, and the native Europeans had much experience in this domain either.

We do not know how the ancient Danubians constructed boats and seafaring ships but they must have developed technical skills that remained unrivaled among their contemporaries. Some pictures and clay miniature models of the fifth and fourth millennia BCE show details of vessels that were used (Raduncheva 2003: 292). In the fourth and third millennia BCE boat types were developed on the Cycladic islands that were driven by up to 25 oarsmen. Images of such boats are found on Cycladic pottery and on the plates which are known as "frying pans."

> The images prevent us seeing if the hull was a tree dugout or a clinker (constructed from overlapping planks); the former is possible for the small shape, but might be difficult for the larger. A notable feature is a high stern sometimes decorated with a large fish [Bintliff 2012: 105].

The shipbuilding skills in the other ancient civilizations (i.e., Egypt, Mesopotamia) developed much later. Some of the useful know-how of Old European shipbuilders found its way—through manifold transformations—into Greek craftsmanship, and some technical terms survived in the specialized vocabulary of ancient Greek:

agkyra "anchor"
aphlaston "curved poop of a ship, with its ornaments" (cf. the decorated sterns of ancient Cycladic boats; Bintliff 2012: 105)
boutani "part of the ship to which the rudder is tied"
eune "anchor stones"
kalon "wood for building ships"
kanthelia "curved pieces of wood at the back of a ship"
kindynos "bench in the prow of a ship"

korymbos "uppermost point of a ship"
kybernao "to steer (a ship)"
kydaros "small ship"
laipha / laiphe "sail made of skin"
lenos "socket into which the mast fitted"
malthe "mix of wax and pitch, used to caulk ships"
paron "light ship"
phalkes "board, rib of a ship"
ptakana "boat mat (used in boats called *kanna*)"
selis "crossbeam of a ship"
sipharos "topsail, topgallant sail"
stamines "vertical side beams of a ship"
traphex "board of a ship"

The pictures and clay models of Old European ships do not reveal many details that would help understand the principles of how Neolithic vessels were constructed (Raduncheva 2003: 292). Since those crafts were made of organic material (i.e., wood) and this decays in time, there are no remains of very old ships. The oldest surviving evidence dates to the Mycenaean era, to a period when the Mycenaean trade network experienced its greatest expansion, reaching as far west as southern Italy and Sardinia (Cultraro 2011: 224*ff*, 228*ff*).

The oldest shipwreck so far discovered in the world is the so-called Uluburun ship, which was named after the site where it was found, off the southern coast of Turkey. According to dendrochronological dating, this ship sank around 1320 BCE. Something that strikes the eye of an experienced underwater archaeologist is the special kind of construction, reflecting a long-standing tradition of shipbuilding. "Initial indications suggest that the Uluburun Ship was a robust and ancient example of the shell-first mode of construction that was to dominate the construction of wooden ships in classical antiquity and to influence later ship construction in that region as well" (Gould 2011: 130).

It is from the Mycenaean era that we find the earliest mention of the profession of "shipbuilders" (*naudomoi*, written as na-u-do-mo in the Linear B texts, derived from *naus* "ship"). Other terms referring to seafaring are "rowers, oarsmen" (*eretai*, written as e-re-ta in Mycenaean texts) and "sailor, mariner" (*pontilos*, as po-ti-ro in Linear B). Also various personal names, recorded in Mycenaean texts, are derived from the stem *naus*: e.g., O-ti-na-wo (Ortinawos), Na-u-si-ke-re-we (Nausiklewes "One who is famous because of his ships"), Na-wi-ro (Nawilos "Sailor"), O-ku-na-wo (Okunawos "Someone possessing a fast ship"), E-u-o-mo (Euhormos "Someone possessing a good harbor"); (Ilievski 2000: 364, 369).

The Greeks became known as skillful shipbuilders in all the countries of the Mediterranean. The backbone of the Greek navy in the fifth century BCE was a special type of galley, the trireme. This is a Latin term meaning "with three banks of oars." The corresponding expression in Greek is *trieres* ("three-oarer"). The earliest evidence for the trireme comes from the seventh century BCE. The trireme was in use into the fourth century BCE when it was replaced by larger warships, the quadriremes and quinqueremes, with four and five banks of oars, respectively.

> At dawn, when the Aegean Sea lay smooth as a burnished shield, you could hear a trireme from Athens while it was still a long way off. First came soft measured strokes like the pounding of a distant drum. Then two distinct sounds gradually emerged within each stroke: a deep percussive

blow of wood striking water, followed by a dashing surge. Whumpff! Whroosh! These sounds were so much a part of their world that Greeks had names for them. They called the splash *pitylos,* the rush *rhothios.* Relentlessly the beat would echo across the water, bringing the ship closer. It was now a throbbing pulse, as strong and steady as the heartbeat of a giant [Hale 2009: XXIII].

This colorful description of the impression of a trireme in full speed may gain in profile once the source of the special terms for the collective noise the oars made is taken into consideration. The Greeks were talented pupils who honored their masters, the Pelasgian shipbuilders, by thoroughly adopting and transmitting Old European terminology. In addition to all the technical terms from the linguistic substratum also the expressions *pitylos* and *rhothios* were adopted and integrated into the Greek vocabulary of seafaring (Beekes 2010: 1198, 1290).

Trading and Commerce: The Old European Heritage in the World That Was to Become Greek

There is an additional source of motivation for the Greeks' endeavor to set out to sea, and this is the long history of trading in southeastern Europe and in the Aegean Sea. When the early Greeks started to engage in seaborne trade they exchanged commodities with the Minoans in ancient Crete who had frequented trade routes in the Aegean and beyond long before the rise of Mycenaean power. Already in the third millennium BCE, mainland communities entertained "far-reaching trading contacts" (Forsén 2010: 61).

What is little known, though, is the prehistory of Minoan and Mycenaean trade relations and maritime endeavors. The Minoans themselves did not "invent" seaborne trade as a profitable domain for their economy. Seafaring and maritime trade started out thousands of years earlier. Technological advance in building boats and ships gives the advantage to use waterways (i.e., rivers and oceans) for communication and interaction. Traffic via waterways enhances trade, and both river-borne and seaborne trade are known from earliest times in Old Europe.

In fact, seafaring was practiced even before the advent of agriculture and this can be conjectured from evidence of obsidian from the Cycladic island of Melos that was transported to the Greek mainland. Obsidian which was the preferred material for the fabrication of tools in the Stone Age has a particular structure which is locally specific. Therefore the provenance of obsidian, found on the mainland, from Melos can be accurately identified. The earliest traces for the trade with obsidian in the Aegean Sea can be dated to the tenth millennium BCE. During the seventh millennium BCE this trade increased. Obsidian continued to be transported from Melos to the Greek mainland and to Crete during the Bronze Age, and into Greek antiquity.

When looking at the map of Neolithic settlements in southeastern Europe one notices that most of the sites are located along the waterways that cross the Balkans from west to east and from north to south. The biggest and most proliferated of these waterways is the mighty Danube River, which, together with its numerous tributaries, forms an extended network of trade routes in all directions. In the formative stage of the Danube civilization Vinca (near Belgrade) assumed a prominent role, as a nodal trade center in the central Balkanic region, and it kept its importance for trade along the Danube for one and a half

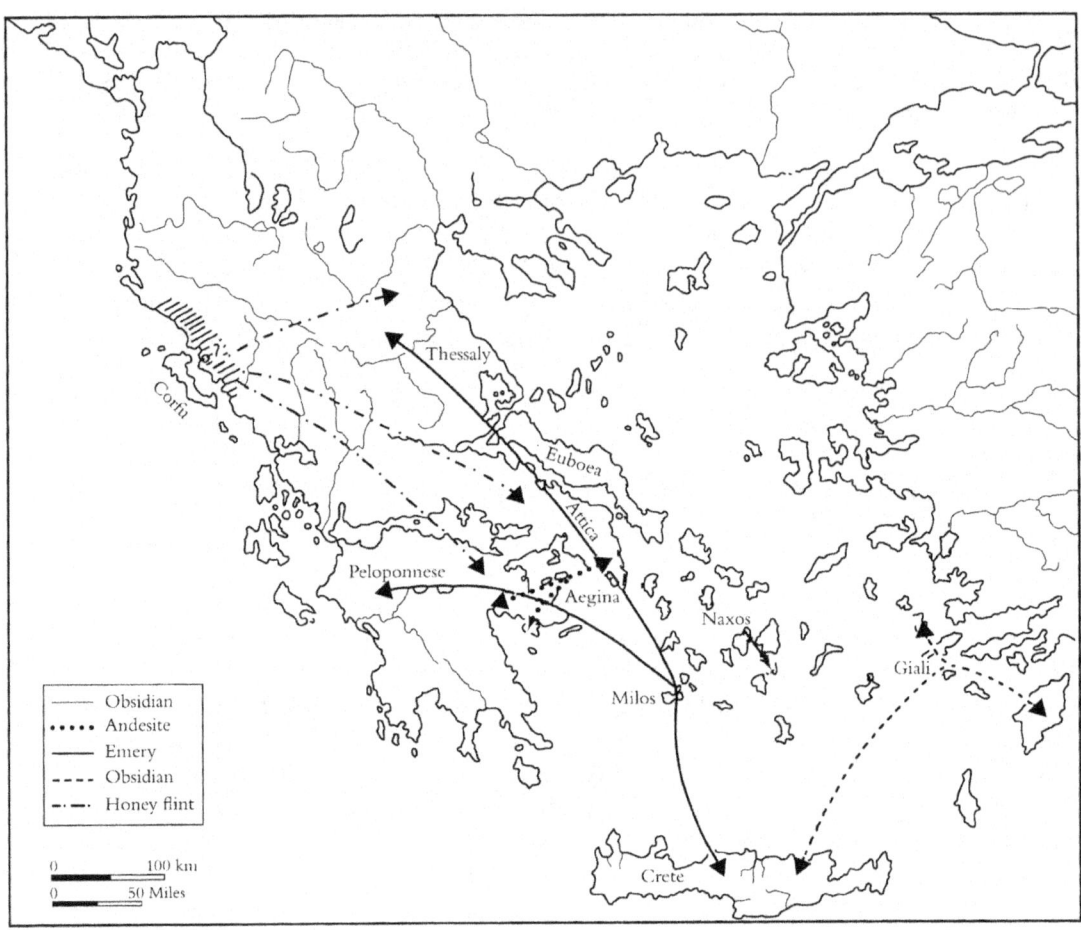

Trade networks and trade routes in the Aegean since the Neolithic (originally published in *The Early Neolithic in Greece: The first farming communities in Europe* by Catherine Perlès. Cambridge: Cambridge University Press, 2001).

thousand years. There were some other trade centers that had equal importance further east, Varna for one.

All the commodities that were produced by craftsmen in the workshops of the Old European economic centers were traded along the eastern trade route: flint blades, artifacts such as rings and beads made of spondylus, small stone axes, etc. Having been developed around 5400 BCE, the craft of smelting and working copper spread rapidly across the Old European economic zone, and objects made of copper are among the trade goods that passed through Varna. Gold was also traded, though this innovation only occurred during the era when élite power was emerging at Varna.

The people in the region of Varna had access to a resource that was in short supply elsewhere: salt. Archaeological investigations carried out since 2005 have uncovered a salt-production site at Tell Provadia-Solnitsata, some 6km southeast of the town of Provadia (Varna District), on the Provadia plateau. Analyzes of large vessels used for "dry-boiling" salt water that was collected from salt springs nearby puts the date for the beginning of salt production in the region at ca. 5400 BCE, which makes this site the earliest center for the production of salt in all of Europe (Stoyanova 2008). Those who engaged in this craft distinguished themselves by their ceramics and tools as bearers of the Karanovo III–IV culture, which extended further south into Thrace.

The advantage of the Varna region was not only that it had special resources (such as salt and metal) to offer, but it was also located pivotally at the intersection of a trade route over land and a maritime trade route along the western coast of the Black Sea. Evidence for seafaring and regular seaborne trade in that area dates to the early fifth millennium BCE.

> The direction of the main currents and winds from North to South probably acted as an incentive for the communities in the northern part of the littoral to travel along the coast to their neighbours in the South. [...] Seafaring brought most probably many of the items, whose accumulation in the communities along the sea shore and near the coastal lakes makes them so unique—sea shells [...], axes of volcanic rock, copper for ornaments and weapons and, not to be ruled out, also gold [Ivanova 2008: 237].

The trade good that produced the widest network was spondylus (spondylus gaederopus). This shell is found only in the Mediterranean. The mere presence of spondylus in the region of Varna points to long-distance trade with the south. The trade network for spondylus included all the regional cultures of Old Europe, and even extended beyond them.

> We can follow the Spondylus trade archaeologically over nearly three thousand kilometers—mirroring the trajectory of the spread of domesticated wheat, barley, legumes, cattle, and sheep northward out of Greece extending from the Aegean and Adriatic Seas, where the shells were harvested, to France, Germany, and Poland, where they are found in the archaeological remains of settlements and cemeteries, in graves, and as isolated finds [Séfériadès 2009: 181].

Finds of spondylus in the archaeological record of Neolithic Europe are usually described by archaeologists as items of "prestige." However, this description of the significance of spondylus to the people who were engaged in trade is confusing. In modern languages, the concept "prestige" is associated with social status, material wealth and the political influence that goes with it. The concept of "prestige" with its modern connotations is not relevant to the social conditions in the Old European communities.

The people from the steppe migrated to the northwestern coast of the Black Sea. The movement of the steppe people was not accidentally directed to that region. There were various reasons why the region of Varna attracted foreigners. The steppe environment that was familiar to the pastoralists extended as far as the area of the Danube delta. Beyond the river, the agricultural landscape opened up to the south, with Varna a short distance away. It was most probably its favorable location on the periphery of Old Europe that enabled Varna to develop into an important trading center. Its pivotal role becomes apparent when one looks at a map of trade routes that connected settlements in the Danube civilization. Varna is located in the middle section of a major trade route that linked the south with the north.

Many trade goods were transported along this route, and the trade via Varna also included contact with the steppe people. Certain artifacts of Old European provenance have been found as far east as the Volga basin (Anthony 2009a: 38). Among the finds are breastplates, which were items of prestige among the steppe people. The wealth of Varna as a trading center and the presence of prestige goods there may have inspired the steppe people to seek control over the region (see Cunliffe 2008: 155 for the exchange networks in southeastern and eastern Europe involving metal).

The suggestion that trade relations between the Old Europeans and the people from the steppe region were the driving force behind the movement of pastoral nomads to the west is not new. In her assessment of the sociopolitical changes that resulted from the Varna event, Gimbutas (1991: 338) gives the following explanation: "I consider this change a result of rapidly rising trade activities of the inhabitants of the Black Sea coast with the Dnieper-Volga steppe population who were wedging their way into territories west of the Black Sea." And yet, details of the process of takeover and its consequences have become available only recently.

Traders and Trade Routes: Who Traded What, Where and with Whom?

For a long time, the trading capacities of ancient societies have been underestimated and "ancient historians have tended to fall into a dichotomy of modernity or stagnation, rather than considering whether different pre-modern societies might have their own dynamics of development and laws of motion" (Morley 2007: 9). Trade relations in Old Europe have only recently been investigated with some scrutiny (Haarmann 2011a: 81*ff*), and the emergence of seaborne trade on a larger scale is a much debated issue. Extensive maritime trade is documented for the Minoans who created their high culture in the third millennium

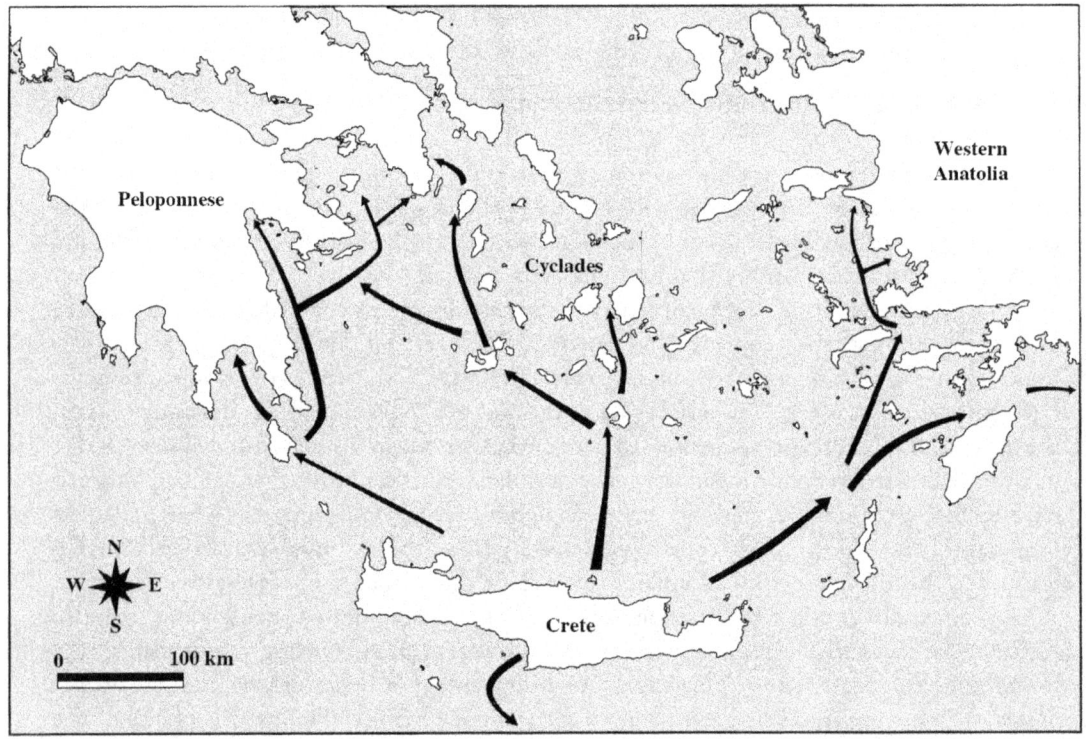

The network of Minoan trade relations and cultural contacts (originally published in *An island archaeology of the early Cyclades* by Cyprian Broodbank. Cambridge: Cambridge University Press, 2000).

BCE. An older network of trade routes existed and this was extended by the Minoans, the heirs of Old Europe, in both the technological and cultural sense. Their reign, centered on ancient Crete, has been described as a thalassocracy ("maritime power"), a term derived from *thalassa*. The Minoans frequented the major sea routes that connected Crete with the Cycladic islands and the mainland.

The early Greeks could draw on the experience of the descendants of the native Europeans, both on the mainland and from ancient Crete, in matters of seafaring and shipbuilding. They also learned how to conduct trade and soon participated in the network of trade relations in the Aegean. The Greeks must have built their own ships already in the early second millennium BCE because the oldest archaeological evidence available points to an independent Mycenaean tradition of seafaring. There is documentary evidence that the Mycenaean Greeks conducted trade overseas, and

> data about this activity of the Mycenaeans can be derived from personal names and some prosopographical qualifications: E-po-ro-jo prob. /Emporoio/, gen. of Emporos "tradesman, merchant." Ku-pi-ri-jo /Kuprios/, that occurs on tablets from nearly all the centres, is probably not a personal name but a description of a man from Cyprus, with which the Mycenaean traded. The non-monetary economy had to exchange the surplus of production for commodities which they lacked. Thus, the Mycenaeans had to export their products, and to import copper, tin, styptic, etc. from eastern countries [Ilievski 2000: 364].

Although various seafaring peoples participated in seaborne trade in the eastern Mediterranean the Mycenaean Greeks, and later the Greeks of the Dark Ages and the archaic period, had their own particular way that was not developed or practiced by others, except by the Phoenicians.

> Maritime connectivity obviously depended on the technology of ship-building and ship-related matters. Long-distance shipping represented a technology alien to the great Near Eastern empires, and the frustrated ambitions of the Persian king to rule the sea provides a good illustration of what he failed to achieve [Malkin 2011: 49].

The Greeks got acquainted with trading and commerce on the mainland and they adopted the know-how of commercial entrepreneurship from the native Europeans. Evidence for the source of know-how is encapsulated in the ancient Greek vocabulary. The general expression for trade is *kapeleia,* derived from a word stem of the substrate language. Other derivations from this same root are *kapelos* ("merchant") and a special form *kapelis* ("female merchant").

The existence of special terms for either sex raises the question of gender in trade relations. According to a widely held opinion, those who engaged in trade in Greek antiquity were men. It is true that women were barred from public life and were not allowed to conduct business, which was the domain of men. And yet, women had their niches in public life.

> We know quite a bit about the status of sellers, who were not all free men. Aristophanes' plays show free women selling bread, other food items, and flax cloth. Athenian law, legal speeches, and inscriptions demonstrate their presence as well. Women tended to concentrate on selling products that corresponded to their activities in the oikos, but also those that required little capital investment in either equipment or stock [Johnstone 2011: 16].

The occupations for men dominated the economic scene but there were certain domains where work was done by both men and women and, there was a range of occupations which were female-oriented. Results from a recent investigation show that, of 190 occupations, 174 were reserved for men while, in 9, women worked alongside men (Harris 2002). The remaining 18 occupations are of special interest since the kind of worker which is specified for each only appears in the feminine form. When viewed in a gender-oriented perspective it is reasonable to assert that these occupations were the exclusive domain of women.

Female occupations in Athens (fifth and fourth centuries BCE) (survey compiled according to the findings in Harris 2002: 68)

Textile workers:
akestria "seamstress"
amorgantinos, (gynaika) amorgantina "textile worker" (*gynaika* "woman")
erithos "wool worker"
hyphantikos "weaver"
linourgos "linen / flax worker"
talasiourgos "wool-worker"

Retail and food:
artopolis / artopoles "baker"
halapolis "salt seller"
kapelis "retailer"
libanopolis "incense seller"
pandokeutria / pandokeus "inn-keeper"
stephanopolis "wreath seller"

Service:
aleiptria "masseuse"
charitopolis "charm seller"
hetaira / etaira "prostitute"

himatiopolis "clothes seller"
kommotria "hairdresser"
pluntria / pluntes / pluneus "clothes cleaner"
porne / pornos "whore"

Child care:
maia "midwife"
titthe "wet nurse"
trophos "nurse, nanny"

Entertainment, performance:
auletris / auletes "flute player"
orchestris "dancing girl"
psaltria "harp player"

Seasonal agriculture:
trugetria "grape-picker"

Craft:
chrysotria / chrysotes "gilder"

Female occupations in Athens (fifth and fourth centuries BCE) (compiled according to the findings in "Workshop, marketplace and household: The nature of technical specialization in classical Athens and its influence on economy and society" by E. Harris. In *Money, labour and land: Approaches to the economies of ancient Greece* edited by Paul A. Cartledge, Edward E. Cohen and Lin Foxhall. London: Routledge, 2002: 68).

> The eighteen solely female occupations fall into a limited range of categories. The largest and most common of these is textile working. To an even greater degree than in Roman Italy this was a skill that all women were expected to acquire, and it was practically the only craft regularly open to women. An interesting difference from the Roman world is that almost no men in classical Greece appear to have played any visible role in the manufacture of "domestic" textiles (e.g., clothing, blankets), though some were involved in the production of "industrial" textiles (e.g., sails, sacking). Of the remaining occupations documented in texts, retail and service work (also represented occasionally in vase painting, Lewis 2002: 92) and jobs connected with child care (and in the case of midwives, childbirth) are the most common, while work connected with the preparation, serving and selling of food also appears regularly. Jobs in the sex trade were also common; prostitutes of various kinds are obviously sex workers, but musicians and dancers were regularly hired for entertainment and were assumed by men to be available for sex (Davidson 1997: 80–2), and female workers in inns and tavernas might also have been thought of in the same way [Foxhall 2013: 99].

Functionaries of public cults were recruited from the ranks of aristocratic women. This was true for the office of the priestess in the cults of the various goddesses. For instance, the status of the high priestess of the Parthenon temple on the Acropolis in Athens, dedicated to Athena, was one of the highest prestige in Greek society (Dillon 2002: 84*ff*). On the other end of the social hierarchy, slave women could conduct business for their mistresses in public.

There were also certain domains of commerce where women occupied niches and acted, on a more or less equal footing with men. A prominent commercial domain in which men and women alike were involved, was the land-based grain trade. The grain trade in the Athenian state was a major enterprise since it was the backbone of Athenian economy. In the course of the fourth century BCE, the Athenians became dependent on grain imports from abroad because the domestic economy lacked the capacity to respond to the growing demands of food supply.

> Hundreds of ship-cargoes were required annually to satisfy Attica's enormous need for grain—and many other items were imported by sea in amounts at least equal to deliveries of grain. Because of the primitive condition and high expense of overland transport [...], fourth-century Athens was entirely dependent on this maritime trade [Cohen 2005: 297].

Grain came from the Bosporan kingdom (kingdom of the Cimmerian Bosporus) on the northern shore of the Black Sea, a Graeco-Scythian state that based its power on the income from the grain trade with the Athenian state. The grain was shipped from the port of Panticapaeum (in what is nowadays modern Kertch), the ancient capital of the Bosporan kingdom, to the port of Piraeus in Attica which assumed a pivotal role for the distribution of foodstuff and commodities for the urban population of Athens and all of Attica.

In the port of Piraeus, grain dealers awaited the shipments and engaged in retail trading.

> Grain-dealers (*sitopolai*) are regarded in modern scholarship as an identifiable class of persons engaged in the particular business of retailing grain in Athens. They are assumed generally to have been low-class metics acting as small middlemen (*kapeloi*) between importers (*emporoi*) and the Athenian consumer. Their numbers are regarded as considerable, if despite their poverty they were capable by themselves of purchasing, storing, and reselling most (if not all) of the considerable amounts of grain arriving in Piraeus [Moreno 2012: 213].

The metics were foreigners, but it is very probable that also native Europeans (i.e., Pelasgians) were among them. In the literary sources, one finds allusions to the *kapeloi* of belonging to an impoverished class, and such allusions repeat themselves in a kind of stereotyping way. When taking into account that the traders did not only handle shiploads of grain but they also had to manage the financing of the loads then the allusions to poverty may rather reflect the need to downplay, on the side of the traders, their chances of profit in the business they conducted, and such a need may have been especially felt in democratic Athens.

> In communities professing egalitarian ideologies, people are reluctant to give publicity to benefits they exclusively enjoy—in particular when scarce products are involved.... Fear and desire to conform combined to make people underplay their foreign connections [Herman 1987: 82*f*].

In the course of time, the image of the *kapeloi* assumed ever more negative features. The traders became the target of writers who scorned them for cheating and accused them of corrupting wine measures; "*kapeleia* was a general badge of abuse instead of a technical term denoting a specific division of labour: it was an accusation of engaging in seemingly treasonable business practices, specifically in profiting from the perceived detriment of the community" (Moreno 2012: 233). The negative image is most clearly reflected in some well-known literary works such as the comedies *Ecclesiazusai, Lysistrata* and *Wealth* of Aristophanes (ca. 450–after 385 BCE).

The negative image that crystallized around the concept of *kapeleia* can partly be explained by the conditions of the zeitgeist in classical Greece. Fluctuations for prices of certain commodities on the markets were not perceived as resulting from abstract factors such as the balance between demand and supply. Instead, individual traders were held responsible for an increase in prices which stirred suspicions of fraud and manipulation. State officials were entrusted with the task of supervising the flow of goods and the retail trade, with the aim to control the traders' activities.

The various regulations and officials introduced by states to monitor and control the markets that took place under their jurisdiction were expressly designed to make individual traders responsible for what were, in the eyes of the state and probably of many of the citizens, the consequences of their decisions; the right to make a profit was not inalienable, if this would threaten the interests of the community (Morley 2007: 79).

By the fourth century BCE, maritime transactions preferably functioned through written agreements, and financial considerations (i.e., loans for financing shipments) played an increasing role.

> In contrast to the relatively simple retail dealings of the landed Agora, sea trade in the fourth century was extraordinarily intricate, involving multiple contingencies and disparate complex circumstances and conditions. A single ship might carry many "traders" (*emporoi*), and each of these *emporoi* in turn might be transporting disparate cargo securing separate loans [Cohen 2005: 297].

According to the traditional view, a clear class distinction existed between those who engaged in trade and those who did not. It is assumed that members of the Greek aristocracy were not involved in commerce, which was the preferred domain of people from the lower classes (see Moreno 2012: 243*f* for this agenda). When taking into account the increase in monetary transactions (along the lines "grain for money") it is inconceivable how ordinary traders could have managed bigger shiploads of grain without financial backing from a wealthy source. And this source must have been the wealthy aristocracy. So, although aristocrats might not have conducted business themselves they nevertheless lent money to others, to take care of transactions for them (or in their interest). The profits of successful trading would have been divided between the lender of money and the trader.

Greek Measures of Pre-Greek Origin and Devices for Calculation

Trade in a technologically advancing society requires precision of measurement and calculation. Since the ancient Danube civilization was the most advanced society of its time it is not surprising to find, in the archaeological record, evidence for the existence of a system of weights, an archaic calendrical system and a notational system for writing numbers (Haarmann 2011a: 181*ff*).

> For to measure—whether in the dimensionality of weight, or of distance or of time—is to develop a new kind of material engagement with the world that is at once practical and conceptual. It is an act of cognition—a cognitive act. Such an act has philosophical implications, for measurement allows us to transcend the limitations of the here and now. It involves observation, and it facilitates construction. It encapsulates the seeds of mathematics and of science. It makes possible architecture

and design. It is the basis for systematic observation and prediction. It leads on towards astronomy and cosmology. It is the basis for any complex economic system. It is one of the foundations of all urban civilisations [Renfrew and Morley 2010: 1].

A major clue for an understanding of the long-standing tradition of trading and the preservation of a network of trade relations in southeastern Europe and the Aegean Sea from earliest times is the layer of borrowings from the substrate language in the nomenclature of Greek measures and their significance for ancient Greek commerce. Systems of weights and measures were required to control the flow of commodities that were traded. The movements of goods to the markets were described with a pre-Greek term: *phoitao / phoitesai* "to go to and fro, go repeatedly, walk about," "frequent someone, come to the market (of commodities)."

The archaeological record of sites in the area of the Danube civilization yields an abundance of weights, made of stone or clay, some of which are inscribed. Apparently, the signs on the weights convey different units of weight. Weights in the form of stone disks or made of metal (i.e., lead or silver), as a typical marker of sites on the Greek mainland and in the Aegean archipelago, appear in the Late Bronze Age, and the increasing frequency of finds illustrates the expansion of the Minoan overseas trade. The finds confirm earlier assumptions that the Minoans introduced a system of conventional measures in the whole Aegean region via their trade relations. The terms for units of measures that survived from pre-Greek times and were adopted by the Greeks may well be relics of that old Minoan system.

> The fact that some of the most numerous weight systems come from these islands [Crete and the Cyclades] is a clear indicator of their economic vitality and of their convergence with the regional trade system. The spread of the system also in more remote zones, on the margins of the Minoan-Cycladic area—like Samothrace, Miletos, Vaphio (Laconia) and Thorikos (Attica)—is considered one of the most significant elements of the extended Minoan influence in the Aegean and highlights the significance of the Cretan economic primacy in the region [Alberti 2009: 22].

The metric systems that were used by the Mycenaean Greeks are known from the texts, recorded in Linear B, from the palace archives of Knossos (Crete) and Pylos (Peloponnese).

> The metric signs are a special type of ideogram. There are three series; for weight, dry measure and liquid measure. The Mycenaeans must have also had a system of linear measure, but no trace of this appears in our documents [Chadwick 1990: 165].

The Linear B system of weights and measures (originally published in *The Aegean Bronze Age* by Oliver Dickinson. Cambridge: Cambridge University Press, 1994).

Among the Mycenaean terms for metric units are *kotyle* and *choinix,* and these are elements of the pre-Greek substratum. There is a pre-Greek borrowing in the ancient Greek nomenclature for units of linear measure, *plethron* (see below). This term might well be as old as the other mentioned expressions and it might have formed part of the Mycenaean metric system although it lacks documentation. The measures in ancient Greece were not standardized in our modern sense and their value could oscillate according to changing regulations.

Anyway, the need to introduce and use measures with conventional (i.e., recognized) values (known and acknowledged by all parties engaged in commercial transactions) was felt already by the native Europeans, and they designed a system of practical measures, including containers such as cups, baskets and the like. Some of the practical systems which they had introduced persisted into classical antiquity and were extended by additional abstract units. In the Greek nomenclature of weights and measures, ancient terms of pre-Greek origin abound:

abax / abakos "board for calculating or drawing"
banotos "vase used as a measure"
daktylos "finger (also as a measure)"
drachme / darchma "drachm (weight and coin)"
gelge "frippery (petty wares and dyes, and spindles and combs)"
kalathos "basket (for transporting charcoal)"

WEIGHTS AND CURRENCY VALUES

6 obols	=	1 drachma
60 drachma	=	1 mina
100 minai	=	1 talent

In Athens a mina weighed 431 grams or about a pound.

DRY MEASURES

4 kotylai	=	1 choinix
8 choinikes	=	1 hekteus
6 hekteis	=	1 medimnos

LIQUID MEASURES

12 kotylai	=	1 chous
12 choes	=	1 metretes

For both dry and liquid measures, the kotyle usually fell between 240 and 270 ml. (depending on the city), just a bit more than a cup.

Ancient Greek weights and measures (from *A history of trust in ancient Greece* by Steven Johnstone. Chicago: University of Chicago Press, 2011: 171).

On the island of Delos, a *kalathos* was more than a basket; it was an amount of charcoal. Since Delos, a small island, uniquely had to import all its fuel, the *kalathos* may have been the customary container in which it was packaged. Here the *hieropoioi* (the officials in charge of the temple of Apollo) bought charcoal for fires on the altar by the *kalathos,* but they also recorded purchasing fractional units: "half-*kalathos*" and "eighth-*kalathos*." The half alone does not systematize a unit, but in conjunction with the *eighth* it represents an attempt to do so [Johnstone 2011: 43].

kollybos / kollybon "small change," "small gold weight," "rate of exchange"
kotyle / kotylos "bowl, dish, small cup," a measure for liquids and dry materials
kophinos "big basket," a measure of capacity

The references to *kophinoi* show it as a household container for moving things rather than storing them. The *kophinos* seems to have had a customary capacity, so that Aristotle could use it as a measure of size that he anticipated his audience would understand, as could the writers of the New Testament story of the loaves and fishes [Johnstone 2011: 44].

kotyle / kotylos "bowl, dish, small cup," a measure for liquids and dry materials

lagynos "flask with a small neck," a measure

mare name of a measure for liquids

mathalis "cup used as a measure" (cf. *batos* a measure of liquids)

mation a measure of capacity

medimnos corn measure (bushel) (equals about 52½ liters in Athens)

A *medimnos* was a measure of volume—abstract because its capacity was independent of the situations in which the grain (or any other commodity) was handled. It was not a container, and it often designated amounts that had not actually been measured. As a standardized measure, the *medimnos*'s primary virtue was abstractness rather than precision [Johnstone 2011: 40].

obelos / obolos / odelos / obellos (Thess.) bar of metal used as a coin or weight (equals obol), ("broach")

pelanos "sacrificial cake (liquid flour dough, flour pulp, honey and oil)," name of a weight or coin

plethron "measure of length of 100 feet," "square measure of 10.000 square feet" ("race-track")

psephos "small stone, pebble (used especially for counting and calculating)"

schoinos "rush, reed," "rope plaited of rush," a land measure

tryblion "drinking vessel (of unknown shape and varying size)," a measure of capacity

In the systems of weights and measures, practical means alternate with abstract concepts. The impression that one gets from the archaeological record and from ancient sources is that, in everyday life, a clear preference for practical means can be observed.

Greeks organized economic activities in households without abstract systems. Instead, to manage consumption they relied on local expertise, especially the knacks of eyeballing and thrift. Both of these depended on divvying stuff up in batches corresponding to periods of time, storing it in containers of recognized (but not standardized) sizes, and allocating it out by continually adjusting, through sight, the depletion of the container to the passage of time [Johnstone 2011: 80].

Of the pre–Greek measures that persisted into classical antiquity, the *medimnos*, *drachme* and the *obolos* are the best known and most widely spread in the ancient Greek world. The *drachme* remained the monetary unit of Greece until it was replaced by the Euro. Around the middle of the sixth century BCE Greek city-states started to mint their own coins. The most popular coin in the Athenian state was the so-called "owl," a four-drachma piece, that became the brand of Athenian coinage.

Athenian coinage was conservative in terms of its types: obverse (bust of Athena) and reverse (owl, olive branch, ATHE); the standard coin used in trade was the tetradrachm (four-drachma piece).... The brand stood for solid quality: Athenian tetradrachms were nearly pure silver and standardized in weight (17 g ±. 15 g for post–Persian War coins). A genuine "owl" (as the coins were called, after the image of Athena's owl stamped on the reverse) was thus dependable as an exchange medium.... Although Athenian owls, like all Greek silver coins, were exchanged primarily on the basis of their commodity value (the worth of the silver itself), they also possessed a "fiduciary value added" in the Athenian state's guarantee of precious metal content and standard weight [Ober 2008: 227*f*].

One finds pre-Greek terms in various sections of the nomenclature for measures. This is true for measures of width (*daktylos*), of distance (*plethron, schoinos*), of area (*daktylos, plethron*), of solids (*daktylos*), of liquids (*kotyle*), of dry material (*kotyle, kophinos, medimnos*). Like the Athenian owl coin also other units in the system of weights and measures could change their value, according to place and time. The *medimnos* was a measure of grain that corresponded to 52.6 liters in the archaic and classical periods. After the third century BCE, the value increased and one *medimnos* was equal to 57.9 liters. This unit was also used in the Greek cities of Sicily. The Sicilian *medimnos* corresponded to 43.8 liters.

In addition to a specialized meaning in terms of measures several of the terms mentioned in the foregoing have meanings outside the domain of measures. The original meaning of *daktylos* is "finger," and this meaning is retained in ancient Greek vocabulary. The use of this term as a unit of width or of area is specialized, thus secondary. The duality of primary and secondary meaning is also true for expressions such as *kotyle, kophinos, schoinos, tryblion* and others. Although all the terms are of pre-Greek origin, in some cases, the secondary meaning might have been developed by the Greeks.

The *kotyle*, as a volumetric measure (i.e., a measure of capacity) has been used throughout the ages, from Greek antiquity through the modern age. Its form has remained a cup which is called *kutel* in Slavic, a borrowing from Greek. The term itself had various meanings in different periods. In some places it was replaced by other terms, in some places its volumetric value changed. In the Balkan region, *kutel* is perhaps the most popular measure that has persisted from the era of the Mycenaeans. When taking into consideration that the term itself is much older and dates to pre-Greek times then *kutel* has a history which is more than five thousand years old. Still today, the *kutel*—like the *medimnos* measure in Greek antiquity—is used as a land measure, associated to the capacity of land to produce a certain amount of grain.

> The general measure which until recently could be found almost in every Macedonian family is a *kutel*. That is a vessel the cylinder of which is usually made from one piece of wood, often chosen with a branch on it, so that the handle can be carved from it. The volume of hand-made kutels is not absolutely equal, but in most cases it is about 10–11 l., containing about 8.5–9.8 kg. of qualitative wheat. The *kutel* is an important measure with a large use. The surface of fields is counted according to the seed measured by it (400 sqm with the seed of one *kutel*; 1 hectare, 10 000sqm with 5 osmaks, 25 kutels).... In the old water-mills, balances were not used at all; the grain and flour were measured only by kutels. Grain was also measured in kutels and osmaks for sale purposes [Ilievski 1997: 71].

5

Ingredients of Pan-Hellenic Identity
Sacred Places, Rituals and Festivities

Culture is an organic whole that provides the wrappings for our lives. This is so nowadays and it was not different in antiquity. For constructing culture and keeping it functioning a certain ingredient is needed that provides the motivation for the cultural endeavor. This crucial ingredient is identity in its widest sense. Every individual has to identify with a cultural framework in order to interact successfully with other individuals and to internalize adaptive strategies for future planning. Identity is a complex mechanism that provides an individual with the capacity to make varied choices based on role relationships. Identity is not an immutable entity. Rather, it is a dynamic process which is reactivated in everyday interactions and has the potential for change (Haarmann 1996b, 1999b).

Finding one's identity is a process, and this process of identification involves the mental construction of the Self in relation to the Other(s). The formation of a more complex overarching framework of group activities (i.e., culture) depends on the extent to which the individual Self and the others share patterns of social interaction, common systems of communication and the motivation to act as a group. Identity, the mental strategy to distinguish the self from the other, is so intrinsic that it drives and defines all interaction and cultural activities. Regardless of whether we talk about prehistoric people who produced rock art or about those who constructed ancient high cultures the preconditions for group activity are the same: "Each human society develops a unique culture, which is also to say that it constructs a unique world that includes not only a special understanding of trees and rocks and water surrounding it, but of other things, many unseen, as real as those trees and animals and rocks" (Rappaport 1999: 9).

If the process of identification is about finding a balance between the consciousness of the self as an individual and of the role played by the individual in group relations, then our social existence is characterized by manifold memberships in groups. Accordingly, constructing one's identity is naturally related to a person's kinship relations (identifying with one's descent), to specific local conditions of community life (identifying with cultural traditions), to a shared worldview and to a culturally specific value system (identifying with a local group's phenomenology). All these processes are subject to cultural diversity and ethnic boundary-marking.

In order for identity to emerge, it required a sophisticated medium in which to exist, and this was language, complex language in particular. Complex language emerged as a result of the dynamic process of identification among human beings, as they were confronted with the challenges of reconciling their cultural activities with the conditions of their natural habitat. Complex language made the construction of complex culture possible (Carstairs-McCarthy 1999).

If identity is central to the culture process, then "the theory of identity has to be regarded as the basic theory of all the humanities, on which the more specialized ethnological and other anthropological disciplines [...] would have to be based and elaborated" (Müller 1987: 391). Constructing culture means giving meaning to community life in the natural environment through symbols, and these may be signs of language or visual symbols that are not language-related such as religious icons, heraldic identifiers of group membership, particularities of dress and/or hairdo.

From the beginning of social relations among modern humans, the oral tradition has served as a prominent means of organizing the collective experience of the community in the cultural process. Spoken language served as a means for perpetuating mythical ideas, and its use was always associated with and related to the items in a given culture's environment. Orality is more than a collective body of verbal narratives. Experience with orality in traditional cultures teaches us that the memorized collective knowledge in a language community is reiterated, renewed and/or elaborated, through ritualistic performances such as storytelling, ritual chanting and dancing and other activities.

The Formation of a Pan-Hellenic Identity Among the Early Greeks

Many of the achievements of Greek civilization can be documented because they are visible (i.e., architecture, pottery, trade goods). Many other achievements are invisible but evidence can be found in the ancient written sources (e.g., Plato's philosophical works). But there are certain underlying structures that support the fabric of Greek high culture, and these structures form an invisible network that can only be made accessible through interdisciplinary investigation. An understanding of this network is necessary for assessing the formation of a "pan-Hellenic identity" among the early Greeks.

The network in question is defined by ethnic boundary-marking and by profiling self-awareness, of the kind which the early Greeks professed. Their activity of sociocultural networking was a fundamental process of collective identification. The major arbiter of membership in an ethnic group is cohesion that may be experienced through daily interaction or actively sought, for instance, through rituals enhancing in-group solidarity. Membership remains stable as long as the network of sociocultural relations within the group functions without disturbances or impediments. "Ethnic cohesion is achieved through interaction between members of intimate networks like close family and friends, effective networks such as kinship or occupation, and the extended networks of neighbourhood or social group" (Henson 2006: 19).

Collective identity in populations of the past was based on a set of elementary categories defining group membership. While the basic conditions of membership in an ethnic group may reflect universal anthropological principles (e.g., kinship relations as a stable component, the mechanism of ethnic cohesion), the concrete manifestations of group membership may vary considerably in the horizon of time and across cultures.

The need to bolster pan–Hellenic identity among the Greek tribes was persistent throughout antiquity and it was manifested in the most particular ways. One of the special features of Greek social life was the institution of the *choros* (*khoros*) which has a double meaning: "round dance" and "choir." The round dance—and its term—have lived on in Greek community life up to the present. Things are different with the institution of *choros* as choir. It is widely believed that the importance of choral singing declined after the classical period.

> But contrary to rumour, the *khoros* did not wither away at the close of the classical period. It remained for centuries a major cultural institution for social re-creation and reflection, particularly for reflection on issues of social cohesion [Wilson 2012: 165].

It is hardly surprising to learn that the institution of the *choros,* with its central role for the celebration and preservation of social cohesion among the Greeks, is of pre–Greek origin because the term forms part of the lexical borrowings from the substrate language in ancient Greek (Beekes 2010: 1644).

The formation of a pan–Hellenic identity among the early Greeks was a complex process. This process did not unfold in a vacuum as if social networking would have been only a matter of the Indo-European tribal groups that arrived in the South to become Hellenes.

> Even if we are prepared to accept that a number—be it large or small—of Indo-European speakers arrived in the Greek mainland at a certain point in time and imposed their language on the substrate language of their predecessors, that does not in itself indicate the commencement of Hellenic identity as the Greeks themselves conceived it. The history of a language or of cultural practices is not necessarily the same as the history of the people who are later identified—and identify themselves—with these markers [Hall 2002: 45].

The coming of Indo-European tribes to Greece is one thing, their becoming Greeks in the process of acculturation is quite another. The emergence of an awareness of pan–Hellenic cohesion among the local populations was closely associated with conditions of biculturalism and bilingualism. What makes a pan–Hellenic identity concerns as much the tribal groupings among the Indo-European immigrants as assimilation of Pelasgian culture and language to proto–Greek patterns. The early Greeks had their own term for "tribe," which was *phyle*.

In addition, under the impression of the ongoing bicultural interaction with the Pelasgians, they also adopted key concepts of ethnic identification that were used by the native Europeans. Some of these concepts assumed a pivotal role for the development of a pan–Hellenic identity and this is reflected in the wide functional range and frequent use of the related terminology. This is true for expressions such as *ethnos* ("people accustomed to live together as members belonging to the same cultural and linguistic community; crowd; company; nation") and *laos* ("common folk; crowd; tribe," derivation *leos* "follower"); (Beekes 2010: 377*f,* 832*f*). Both terms have persisted into modern Greek, and *ethnos* (with its adjectival derivation *ethnikos*) has entered the cultural vocabulary of many languages.

It is somehow puzzling that one finds, in the lexicon of ancient Greek, a variety of terms relating to ethnic phenomena although there is no single term that would correspond to our modern perception of "ethnic identity." This feature of ancient Greek (i.e., synonymity as contrasting with precise nomenclature) is not limited to ethnic phenomena but is revealed in other conceptual domains, too. The ancient Greeks did not know any specific terms for "gender," "social class," "culture" and others.

> They could, however, talk "around" these concepts. When they discuss how particular populations are characterized by their *diaita* (daily way of life), *ethea* (dispositional habits) and *nomoi* (regulated

norms), or speculate that mental values and physical comportment may be inculcated in the young through *paideia* (education), it is difficult to maintain that they are not talking about culture in certain senses that we are able to recognize. Similarly, in attributing the social solidarity of an *ethnos* to *genos* (birth) and *syngeneia* (kinship), the Greeks came about as close as they could to our concept of ethnicity [Hall 2002: 18].

The adoption of terms for ethnic cohesion (i.e., *ethnos* and *laos*) from the substrate language illustrates two basic aspects of the process of pan–Hellenic identity. On the one hand, the existence of specific words to express ethnic aggregation in the language of the native Europeans tells us something about their self-identification as an ethnic group. This means that the idea of ethnic self-consciousness dates to prehistoric times. On the other hand, the popularity of the basic term *ethnos* and its derivatives illustrates the basicness of the ethnic process among the Greek tribes. It is noteworthy that the concept *ethnos* is applied by some modern scholars to describe the Athenian state in terms of a nation—avoiding the somehow ambiguous term *polis* ("city-state")—with various social segments of society that were united by ethnic cohesion (Cohen 2000).

What makes ethnic cohesion an organic whole is a network of constituents which may be categorized, in their distinctiveness, as follows (according to Haarmann 2013b):

- constituents of human ecology (the relationship between natural environment and cultural space; etc.);
- sociocultural markers of ethnicity (kinship; socialization of the young generation in the context of specific cultural traditions crystallizing around the concept of Greek *paideia*; etc.);
- communication systems (visual communication such as body painting or tattooing; emblematic and heraldic systems; language-related visual communication such as writing technology; etc.);
- interaction and social behavior (in-group and out-group interaction; customs of interethnic contacts; language-related behavior such as chanting, myth-making and story-telling; etc.);
- phenomenological markers of ethnicity (self-identification; categorization of others; religion and worldview; value system; etc.).

These constituents formed an organic whole of something that may be termed a corporate design of Greekness.

Greek Myths of Origin and Differential Models of Greek Self-Identification

Nowadays, human genetics provides insights about the genetic coding of populations that may help define collective ethnic identity. People in antiquity did not know anything about genetic coding so their approach to descent (theirs and others) was permeated with mythological conceptualizations.

The most elementary layer of mythopoetic experience which we find in the world's cultures contains myths of origin, which usually explain, in ethnocentric terms, how a certain group of people (a clan or kin group) was the focus of a process of creation, for which spirits or divine beings are held responsible. For the Greeks the oldest period in the past with which they could mythically connect was the Heroic Age. During the archaic era, the visible remainders of the Bronze Age impressed people in the local communities, inspiring them to establish genealogies including their mythical predecessors in the region. This was achieved in various ways:

> [...] in the course of the eighth and seventh centuries, certain communities within the Argive Plain expressed their ethnic solidarity through a range of "ancestralizing strategies"—for instance, situating new sanctuaries in areas of Late Bronze Age activity or depositing offerings and even practising reburial in Bronze Age tombs—with the aim of establishing a direct connection with presumed ancestors and an intimate association with an ancestral territory [Hall 2002: 23].

In ancient communities, descent, as a marker of ethnicity, was mystified and associated with foundation legends. Variations of culture-related and language-related self-awareness are well documented from the classical Greek period onward. Central to this attitude toward local traditions was the perception of origin, which was conceptualized in mythical categories. In Greek mythology, the category of *aition* serves the purpose of explaining the place of humans in the world. "An *aition* served as a cult's raison d'être. It legitimated the rites which were conducted in its name by providing the priesthood who conducted it with a justification and warrant of antiquity for why it did what it did" (Garland 1992: 152).

In classical Greece, the *aition* was a basis of self-awareness in that it provided an explanation for tradition. Even after the introduction of literacy, the original oral tradition of Greek myth—and of the *aition* in particular—did not lose any of its importance in ceremonies in which prestige values of noble descent were celebrated. These ceremonies were of great symbolic importance, to enhance communal cohesion and to ritually harmonize relationships within the community. The essential elements in oral and written versions of *aition* myths—as in Greek myths generally—were heavily intermingled. The modern observer is impressed by the written records of Greek mythology. These sources, however, reflect artistic aspirations in the literary adaptation of mythological themes rather than the original motivation of oral performance (Thomas 1992: 88*ff*).

The One-ness of Greek culture and language, as a concept for Greekness or Hellenicity (self-identification as Hellenes), gradually developed in the Greek communities of the classical period. First, there were subethnic categories such as Dorians, Achaians, Aiolians, Ionians and others. To be a Hellene was a novel category of ethnic collectivity and self-identification. In the process of developing a common awareness of pan–Hellenic sameness, the colonization movement played an important role. It seems conclusive

> that colonization informed and strengthened the nascent idea of Greekness primarily because the initial colonial experience was similar and common, and its initial problems and solutions were quickly copied among colonies that had different origins and were at great distances from one another. A list of such common problems may include the role of Delphi (foundation prophecies and ongoing relationships); the negotiation with various "Others" and the unwilling or suspicious acceptance by local populations; ... the adaptation of a social order and a code of *nomima*, usually from the mother city; ... the assimilative social forces of nuclei of organized settlers for disparate groups of colonists; ... a common visual language, often expressed in similar motifs in art and architecture; and the special investment in the great Panhellenic sanctuaries and participation in the Panhellenic games [Malkin 2011: 63].

Ethnic subdivisions such as the distinction of tribes and tribal territories never vanished but were kept alive in the Greeks' self-awareness throughout antiquity. Although the original division of tribes was abandoned with the reforms of Cleisthenes in 507 BCE the concept "tribe" was retained and ten new tribes were created. This meant a redefinition of subethnic boundary lines and a revision of tribal territories. This reformed tribal division assumed political significance in the newly established democratic order of the Athenian polis (see Chapter 7).

The ancient Greeks created a variety of myths of origin to bolster their self-consciousness. Two of the Greek tribes developed particular ideologies regarding their mythic origins. Those myths that narrate Athenian origins and those explaining the descent of the Spartans are perhaps the most contrasting. The one focuses on aboriginality (the Athenian model), the other on migration and colonization (the Spartan model). It is noteworthy that, in both models, reflections of ancient memories of the era are encapsulated that is called Helladic by archaeologists, the era when Greek ethnicity emerged and concepts of Hellenicity were constructed. The Athenians remembered their pre-Greek past as a focal aspect of their self-identification while the Spartans were aware that their ancestors were Dorians (of Indo-European affiliation) who once came to southern Greece as migrants. Athens and the region of Attica were less affected by the Dorian migrations than the Peloponnese further south which may explain why aboriginality is of greater significance for Athenian self-identification.

The ancient Greeks are responsible for the articulation of two prominent variants of ethnic identification, that is, descent and tradition. Political power, when added as a binding agent, eventually produces an explosive mixture of ethnic identity: nationalism (Derks and Roymans 2009). Nationalism turned out to become a driving force for the Athenians to wage war with their neighbors, with the Spartans in particular.

According to a widely held stereotyping notion, the Greeks distanced themselves from alien peoples by instrumentalizing the image of the barbarians as everything that was non-Greek, and this was perceived as equal to being less civilized and less developed than Greek civilization. This notion was always kept alive and it was constantly fueled by intellectuals and politicians (Hall 1989).

And yet, there was another facet to the Greeks' collective self-identification and self-presentation and the distancing of the ethnic Other. In some regions of the Greek world political and economic demands called for compromise or even for the demise of Greek public rhetoric about the barbarians. One such region which became most important for the Athenian state because of its grain supply were the Greek colonies on the northern shore of the Black Sea, geographically stretching as far east as the Kerch Straits (known as the Cimmerian Bosporus in antiquity).

In the fifth century BCE, the local ruling elite established the Bosporan Empire that lasted into the fourth century BCE. The influential aristocratic families had opened their blood lines to powerful Scythian clans of the steppes and their lifeways reflected a refined blend of Graeco-Scythian culture. In the milieu of these bicultural and bilingual surroundings Scythian nobles assimilated to Greek lifeways, and Greeks adopted Scythian customs and established kinship relations with the neighbors from the steppe.

> We recall that King Scyles, whose parents were the Scythian king Ariapeithes and a Greek woman from Histria, himself took a Greek wife and built an enormous house in Olbia decorated with sphinxes and griffins. Here he visited periodically, and having left his army outside the walls, changed from Scythian to Greek clothes, and "lived in the Greek way in every other respect, and made sacrifices to the gods according to Greek custom" [Herodotus *Histories* 4.78]. If it was possible for a Scythian king to live this double life (or at least for Herodotus to hear, and by all indications believe, this story told in the Olbia of his day), we have good grounds to believe that the same was possible for a Greek [Moreno 2012: 153].

The stereotype of the barbarian completely lost any of its negative allure to the ruling elite in the Bosporan Empire since their artistic preferences illustrate their great appreciation for Scythian aesthetics. There is an abundance of luxury goods, manufactured of gold, electrum and silver, that were found in the graves of fourth-century kurgans (burial mounds).

> These masterpieces reveal a first-hand understanding not only of Scythian objects and shapes, but also of the aesthetic principles of Scythian art, and all three can be translated into Greek terms. In other words, these objects were created under the immediate demand and according to the tastes of their consumers, and at Panticapaeum the most influential of these clients were obviously not Scythians from the steppe, but members of the Bosporan aristocracy [Moreno 2012: 193].

The Athenian Model of the Greek Aition (Earth-bound Myth of Origin)

Unique among the local Greek myths was the Athenian *aition* of origin, which became the dominant model of cultural self-awareness in classical times. Athena was the protectress of Athens and, in particular, the patron divinity of the Acropolis. Although a virgin goddess, Athena became the foster mother of a boy named Erechtheus (Loraux 1981). According to the early tradition, the child was entrusted to Athena's care by the earth goddess, Gaia. In a later version of the myth, Hephaestus was named as the boy's father. According to this later version, Hephaestus sought comfort in the arms of Athena while his wife, Aphrodite, was indulging in one of her many affairs. He attempted to rape her, but Athena escaped. From Hephaestus' seed, which fell on the soil, grew a child who was raised by Athena. The specific association with the soil motivated an alternative name for Erechtheus, Erichthonius, in which the central element was popularly associated with *chthon* (earth).

> A closer look at the myth of Erichthonios' birth uncovers even more about Greek attitudes toward females, divine and mortal, and about Athenian self-representation. The myth is intriguing not only because of the autochthonous origin of Erichthonios, who went on to become king and found one of the most illustrious lines in Athenian history, but also because of the emphasis placed on Athena and Hephaistos, the two deities associated with arts and crafts or *techne* (including weaving), who are parents (indirectly in the case of Athena) of this chthonic figure, founder of the Athenians. In other words, *techne* is embedded in the Athenian character. Athena naturally resists the challenge to her virginity [...], yet she is a pivotal figure in the myth—necessary for the birth of Erichthonios and also serving as *kourotrophos* or nurse after his birth (cf. Hom. Il. 2.547–548), a position she hastily relinquishes [Barringer 2008: 102*f*].

The Athenian myth of origin was just one among a number of myths. Crucially, however, the Athenians derived their state ideology from this Athenian *action*. The mythical genealogy of the Athenians, the "House of Athens," presents itself in the following way (Gantz 1993, Appendix—genealogical table 12: p. xxxvii):

Mythical ancestor: Erichthonios
Descendant (first generation): Pandion I
Descendant (second generation): Erechtheus

Among the later descendants are Theseus and Eurynome.

The myth names Erechtheus as the first king of Athens and the surrounding Attica. The Athenians extended the myth by claiming they were direct descendants of the ancestral hero. The fact that Erechtheus grew from the earth (*gegenes* "born from the earth") was interpreted as meaning the Greek settlements in Attica were aboriginal. With Athena as the powerful protectress of the city and the historical landscape of Attica, the Athenians and their homeland were ensured of protection against destruction or defeat (Kinsley 1989: 145*ff*). Thus, a direct link between mythical ethnic origins and territoriality is established.

The Athenians knew that Athena had resided in Athens and Attica before the arrival of the Greeks and they were also aware of the high age of the Earth Mother Gaia.

> The first Athenian was born by Ge (the Earth) in Attica. That is where the Athenians had lived ever since—the city had not been founded by any single act. This is what the Athenians themselves have told us, and they are not likely to have told anything completely incompatible with what they observed round themselves [Isager and Skydsgaard 1995: 126].

Modern research in historical linguistics has confirmed that the names of all the agents involved in the Athenian myth of origin are of pre–Greek origin. This is true for Athena, Erechtheus, Gaia and Hephaestus. Markers of pre–Greek origin may be phonetical (e.g., the non–Greek suffix -*n* in Athena) or sound variations (e.g., Gaia with alternative forms such as Ge and De, as in Demeter "goddess of grain"); (Beekes 2010: 29, 255, 269). In the story of Athena and Erechtheus, genuine elements of the pre–Greek past, mythical and linguistic, fuse to form a unique matrix of cultural memory, the Athenian myth of origin.

The concepts of divine origin and aboriginality were key to the Athenians' consciousness of themselves as a civilized people. The Athenians developed a cult of their aboriginality. They hailed the pureness of their ethnic descent as a noble marker of their distinctiveness from other Greek tribes. In many of the classical sources the notion of noble aboriginality is highlighted as, for instance, in one of Plato's works:

> We [the Athenians] are pure Hellenes, who have not mixed with barbarians (*amigeîs barbáron*). For we are not like the descendants of Pelops or Kadmos, Aigyptos or Danaos, nor many others who, being barbarians by nature (*phúsis*) and Hellenes by convention (*nomos*), dwell among us (*sunoikoûsin hemîn*)—we reside here as genuine Hellenes, not as half-barbarians (*meixobärbaroi*) [Plato *Menexenos* 245d].

The idea of Greekness (Hellenicity) was related by many writers and historiographers to processes of acculturation so that being a Hellene was perceived as the final stage of a process when a foreigner adopted the Greek language and accustomed to a Greek lifeway. Greekness thus could be understood as a matter of ethnic diffusion.

> Herodotus, who believed that Hellenicity was a matter of diffusion, was only too happy to inform the Athenians that their pride in being autochthonous was double edged. If Hellenicity was a matter of becoming, that meant they could not possibly have originally been Hellenes but rather Pelasgians [Malkin 2011: 60].

The meaning of the Athenian *aition* was further developed to include elements of self-glorification and, consequently, a negative categorization of others, thus establishing the defensive mechanism of Greek ethnicity. Other Greek tribes (e.g., Dorians, Ionians, Spartans) were considered by the Athenians to be less prestigious representatives of Greek civilization simply because they were not aborigines, but immigrants in their homeland and, more specifically, "a motley rabble tainted with foreign blood" (Parker 1987: 195).

Relations between Athens and Sparta were particularly eventful. The two city-states were sometimes allies, sometimes foes. In a debate in Sparta in 432 BCE, during which the Spartans reproached the Athenians for having broken the Thirty Years' Peace which had been concluded in 446/5 BCE, the representatives of Athens responded to the reproach by glorifying their role as defenders of Greek civilization during the Persian Wars (Dillon and Garland 1994: 205*f*). During the Peloponnesian War (431–404 BCE), which saw Athens at war with Sparta, the pride of the Athenians reached unprecedented heights. Aristophanes' comedy *Lysistrata,* which was first performed in 411 BCE, is replete with invectives against the Spartans, who are ridiculed. The Athenians' use of public funerals to glorify their ethnic uniqueness was a prominent method by which they developed a patriotic mythology emphasizing autochthony (Stupperich 1977).

The funeral speeches were designed to glorify autochthonous descent, which was considered a noble quality of Greekness. In the aftermath of victory over the Persians, the Athenians indulged in public speeches which emphasized their pivotal role in the victory. Imagined qualities such as noble ancestry and innate prowess were instrumentalized to this end. Self-identification among the Athenian Greeks exhibited substantial elements of an Athenocentric, nationalistic ideology.

> The construction of Hellenicity that emerges in the late fifth century is not ... formulated in "digital," diametric and mutually-exclusive terms but represents instead what we may term an "Athenoconcentric" conception of the world. Athens, the new self-appointed arbiter of cultural authenticity sits at the centre of Hellas and the relative position of other Greek city-states on the Helleno-barbarian continuum is measured in terms of their convergence or nonconvergence with Athenian-determined cultural norms [Hall 2002: 202*f*].

Ethnicity assumed a key role in Athenian politics and in discourse about the political order in their city-state. Athenian identity had a multiple orientation and was not solely linked with the Greek language, which was only one of the major markers of Athenian-ness. The other marker was descent in the sense of blood ancestry. Belonging to an autochthonous lineage (*genos*) was a prerequisite for attaining high offices in the Athenian state, in the state bureaucracy and in the influential priesthood. This fact and the resulting patterns of political action have been described as "kinship nationalism" or "racial identity" in recent research on Greek politics (see, for example, Lape 2010: 249*ff*). The laws regulating Athenian citizenship, which changed throughout the antique period, oscillated between strict autochthony and the naturalization of foreigners into the Athenian community.

A tendency toward favoring ethnic unity over ethnic heterogeneity can be observed in Greek political discourse. For example, in his *Politics* (1303a25), Aristotle (384–322 BCE.) emphasizes that the main reason for a stalemate (*stasis*) in sociocultural development or civil war is the absence of ethnic unity because a community is not "of the same tribe" (*homophylon*). "Both in Athenian political discourse and in Greek political thought more generally, ethnic diversity within a polis is seen as pushing against political unity and as diminishing military strength" (Lape 2010: 253).

Language was one of the pillars of Athenian cultural consciousness, on which they built their self-awareness. The negative attitudes of ancient Greeks toward the ethnicity of other peoples are illustrative of their language-oriented self-glorification. The stereotype of the uncultured barbarian who does not speak Greek and thus does not share in the blessings of Greek culture emerged in the archaic period. In Homer's *Iliad* (II 867), the term *barbarophon* (of barbarian speech) is used to describe the Carians of Asia Minor. Indeed, it was the Athenians who began to refer to foreigners as *barbaroi,* and this habit persisted throughout Greek antiquity. The Spartans used a different expression to refer to foreigners: *xenioi*.

In her seminal study of Greek cultural stereotyping, Hall (1989: 121*ff*) lists the following attributes as being ascribed to *barbaroi* in Greek classical literature:

- effeminate, luxurious, highly emotional and cowardly (e.g., the Phrygian slave in *Orestes*);
- despotic and servile (e.g., the Aeschylean play *Persae*);
- savage, lawless and unjust (e.g., the Thracian Polymestor in *Hecuba*);
- unsophisticated and unintelligent (e.g., Euripides' play *Helen*).

By stereotyping the barbarian in negative terms, the Greeks accentuated the virtues which they believed to be typical of themselves (manliness and bravery, political freedom, lawfulness and justice, intelligence and reason) and which set them apart from foreigners.

Since the Greeks correctly understood their language to be the major vehicle of Greek civilization, they developed a particular pride in their language. The cult of the civilized Greek language was especially monopolized by the Athenians and the inhabitants of Attica. A command of the Greek language was a prerequisite for participation in cult life. For example, anyone who wanted to become an initiated participant in the mysteries of the goddess Demeter at Eleusis had to speak Greek.

The Spartan Model of the Greek Aition (Ideologizing Migration and Colonization)

Another model of cultural self-awareness existed among the Greek tribes. This model, which manifested itself in numerous local myths of origin, lacks an association with the concept of territoriality and the claim to aboriginality so typical of the Athenian *aition*. The Spartans' myth of descent is a classic example of this. In this myth, the historical movement of the Dorians in the Late Bronze Age is mythologized as the "return of the Herakleidai," who are identified as the descendants of Herakles.

According to the Spartan myth, the Herakleidai, having been exiled for several generations, returned to their original homeland in the Peloponnese. Their king, Kresphontes, was murdered and the mythical connection with the Spartans was established by his sons. "The remaining Herakleidai, Kresphontes' sons, then turned to the Spartans and offered the country to them" (Malkin 1994: 38).

The belief that the Spartan kings descended from the Herakleidai did not imply territorial claims. The Spartans considered their city-state to be a Dorian colony, thus acknowledging that they were the descendants of the immigrants who had occupied the land. Despite the fact that the Spartans did not claim to be indigenous to the territory, they legitimized the founding of their state on the basis of the Herakleidai's noble genealogy (Herodotus in *Histories* IX 26.2). According to their charter myth,

> the Spartans had emigrated from the north and, by force, taken possession of the land that they now controlled; but they had the right to do so because they were descendants of Herakles who, once upon a time, had had Lakonia presented to him and thereby acquired the right to Messenia; by their arrival to the Peloponnese, as Heraklidai, they had merely collected their legitimate inheritance [Isager and Skydsgaard 1995: 129*f*].

Perhaps, in the Spartan myth of origin, are reflected conditions of a hostile takeover of control, by Indo-European immigrants from the north, over territory that had been previously held by native Europeans. Seemingly, the main thrust of the immigration was directed south into the Peloponnese while Athens remained on the periphery of the migratory mainstream, and life in the communities of native Europeans in Attica was less affected by immigration.

The Spartans' attitude toward colonization may have been influenced by the Spartan charter myth. Seeing themselves as the descendants of a mythic colonizer may have encouraged them to resume the heroic deeds of their revered ancestor. In view of their charter myth and the fact that they were a landlocked city-state, it is not surprising that the Spartans were the first Greeks to establish colonies, doing so many decades before other city-states joined in the colonial enterprise (Osborne 1996: 119*ff*).

Thera, which was founded by Sparta in the southern Cyclades in the early-eighth century BCE, was the first Greek colony. The Spartans revived the older Minoan-Mycenaean trade center there (Malkin 1994: 73*ff*). The Euboians, who were another Greek tribe whose homeland was—according to their myth of origin—a Dorian colony, were the next to engage in colonization. They ventured far westward and founded Pithekoussai (the modern Ischia) in the Bay of Naples (Ridgway 1992: 31*ff*).

The Transformation of Centers of Pre-Greek Cultural Identity

When the Greeks mixed with the native Europeans, the Pelasgians, they did not overthrow or displace the rituals and festivities of the latter. On the contrary, the sacred places of the ancients were frequented by the early Greeks, too, and so the significance of pre–Greek sacred places and inherited rituals continued into Greek society, enhancing pan–Hellenic cohesion throughout antiquity. By the time of the celebration of the first Olympics in 776 BCE "Greek speakers had been settled in Greece for more than a thousand years, building upon and integrating with the earlier neolithic and bronze age cultures of Greece and the Aegean" (Phillips and Pritchard 2012: viii).

There were thousands of sacred places where the Greeks worshiped their gods, from mighty temples to modest shrines and altars in the homes or courtyards. The range of functions which the ancient Greeks assigned to their gods varied considerably. There were the Olympian gods with their pan–Hellenic significance, and there were other deities that had locally bound importance. This ambiguity in the essence of a Greek divinity makes it difficult to assess the role of individual divine figures for the formation of a pan–Hellenic consciousness.

> Gods are not limited to their local cult: there is always a kind of divine surplus, so to speak. Moreover, there is a kind of general quality that remains the same over many centuries: Dionysos who gives the wine, Artemis who helps in childbirth, Hera who presides over the marriage [Bremmer 2010: 11].

There were also sacred places where only the might and splendor of a divinity were on display, without any cult practices performed. That was the case with the Parthenon on the Acropolis where the monumental statue of Athena functioned as a visual symbol of the power of the Athenian state. Most sacred places, though, served people to express their veneration and devotion, directed to an individual divinity at a particular place. All sacred places where rituals were performed had altars for that purpose and facilities for making special offerings (e.g., the pits in Demeter's sanctuaries for piglets to be thrown into them as sacrifice).

The concept "ritual" in the context of Greek antiquity has its own specific connotation which is much more comprehensive than how we may understand it today:

> A ritual is a complex of actions effected by, or in the name of, an individual or a community. These actions serve to organize space and time, to define relations between men and the gods, and to set in their proper place the different categories of mankind and the links which bind them together.... If ... one starts from the definition of "ritual" that we have just given, Greek religion may then fairly be said to be ritualistic in the sense that it was the opposite of dogmatic: it was not constructed around a unified corpus of doctrines, and it was above all the observance of rituals rather than fidelity to a dogma or belief that ensured the permanence of tradition and communal cohesiveness [Zaidman and Pantel 1995: 27].

The native Europeans had their sacred places, and the Greeks had theirs. But since the Greeks adopted divine figures and cult practices from their predecessors, they also frequented older pre-Greek sites where popular worship continued. Evidence for this can be found in the ancient terms for cult places, elements of the pre-Greek substrate language, that were borrowed into ancient Greek: *alsos* "sacred grove," *krotaphos / kortaphos* "temple," *megaron* "inner space of a temple," *naos / nauos / neos / naios / neios* "sanctuary," *orymos / orymbos* "altar," *sekos / sakos* "enclosed sacred space." This is also true for expressions relating to cult practices: *kterea* "gifts for the dead, sacrifice," *megara* "sacrificial pits into which piglets were thrown (as part of the Thesmophoria ritual)," *orgia* "secret religious rituals," *pelanos* "sacrificial cake (liquid flour dough, flour pulp, honey and oil)," *threskeuo* "to perform or observe religious customs."

Among the sacred places that had been frequented already by the native Europeans and that continued in their original function to be used by the early Greeks there were two with paramount significance for the corporate design of pan-Hellenism: Olympia and Delphi (Scott 2010).

Olympia and the Takeover of a Pre-Greek Sanctuary by Zeus

It is easy to illustrate the continuity of culture in the region of Olympia (in the northwestern part of the Peloponnese) because, according to the archaeological record, the area was continuously inhabited since the fifth millennium BCE. This makes Olympia a place that was frequented (and settled) by the native Europeans, and because of its high age, Olympia formed part of the sociocultural network of the Danube civilization. The history of Olympia unfolded uninterruptedly during successive periods before the arrival of the Greeks there. Among the relics pointing to a former presence of the native Europeans and their descendants are the foundations of some houses, an abundance of ceramic ware of different types and some figurines. Continuity of cultural activities in the area is documented for a prolonged period, from the early Bronze Age onward.

> Whether cult was always associated with games and other competitive performances, as claimed by ancient tradition, is unclear, but at Olympia significantly legend told how the Games originated with the funeral games for the mythical hero Pelops, whose tomb was believed to lie at the locality. Minor Bronze Age activity at the site has been documented, including an Early Bronze Age ritual tumulus which could have been the kind of monument encouraging later myths of heroes buried at the sanctuary. Significant cult activity begins here in the ninth century, whilst dedications only really take off in the eighth century [Bintliff 2012: 243].

What is of special interest are the traces of the transitional phase when the site passed on from the indigenous inhabitants to the Greeks. The oldest constructions of Olympia, within the precinct of the Altis (sanctuary to the gods), are the temples of Hera, the wife of

Zeus, and of Rhea, the mother of Zeus. When interpreting the chronology that is encapsulated in the mythical tradition, a prolonged continuity of female goddesses and their cults is revealed that predates the introduction of a male god (i.e., Zeus) and its cult to the area.

Olympia is a truly mysterious place. The Olympic Games of ancient Greece, under the patronage of a male god, are known worldwide, but the much older tradition of festivals, associated with Hera, are not even known to all the visitors of Olympia, not to speak of a broader public. What is common to both traditions, the older female-dominated and the younger male-dominated, is that sportive competitions were organized there at intervals. According to a widely held view, the Olympics of antiquity were held for and by men only, with no women allowed to either participate or watch. This is a distortion of reality. Men as well as women participated in sportive games, only, the events of their festivals were segregated according to sex.

The early patron of festivities at Olympia was Hera, the pre–Greek Earth Mother, goddess of fertility and of the family. Although Hera's role in the Greek pantheon of classical times may seem somewhat marginal, this impression is misleading; "the *Iliad* nevertheless preserves traces which suggest that Hera had once been a truly powerful goddess, and of course her importance in cult continued to be very significant in later times" (Yasumura 2011: 57).

At Olympia, rituals in Hera's honor were celebrated by young women, and women were the only ones allowed to take part in the sportive competitions, called Heraia. In Greek art, we find pictures of women runners who compete with one another in the Heraia.

Once a year, the Heraia were held at the end of summer, comparable in their function to what we know as Thanksgiving. The women in the region of Olympia who gathered for the Heraia celebrated the blessing of the crops and they expressed their wishes for fertility, for themselves and for the domestic animals.

> The girl-athletes, all maidens, run three foot-races according to age groups, always of the same length, one stadion minus a sixth (probably because a stadion is 600 feet, and a woman's pace is smaller than a man's). The girls do not compete naked—they wear a short dress—but their female power is nonetheless displayed and transmitted in what

A female runner at the Heraia of Olympia (bronze figurine, ca. 500 BCE; courtesy of The British Museum).

is, without question, an ancient fertility ritual, and perhaps, in part at least, a prenuptial rite of passage. As they run, their long hair flies loose, their dresses are unhitched at the right shoulder to expose a single breast, and their bare feet pound the track in direct contact with Mother Earth. The energy of their young bodies symbolises the dynamism of life [Faulkner 2012: 85].

If it is true that sportive contests were held at Olympia in pre–Greek times then one would look for an expression from the substrate language to describe the essence of competition. Indeed, there is a key term of pre–Greek origin in ancient Greek, and this is *amilla* "a contest for superiority; a trial for strength" (Beekes 2010: 88). This word is also used in metaphorical meanings, for example, for a contest of marriage or a striving for wealth. The

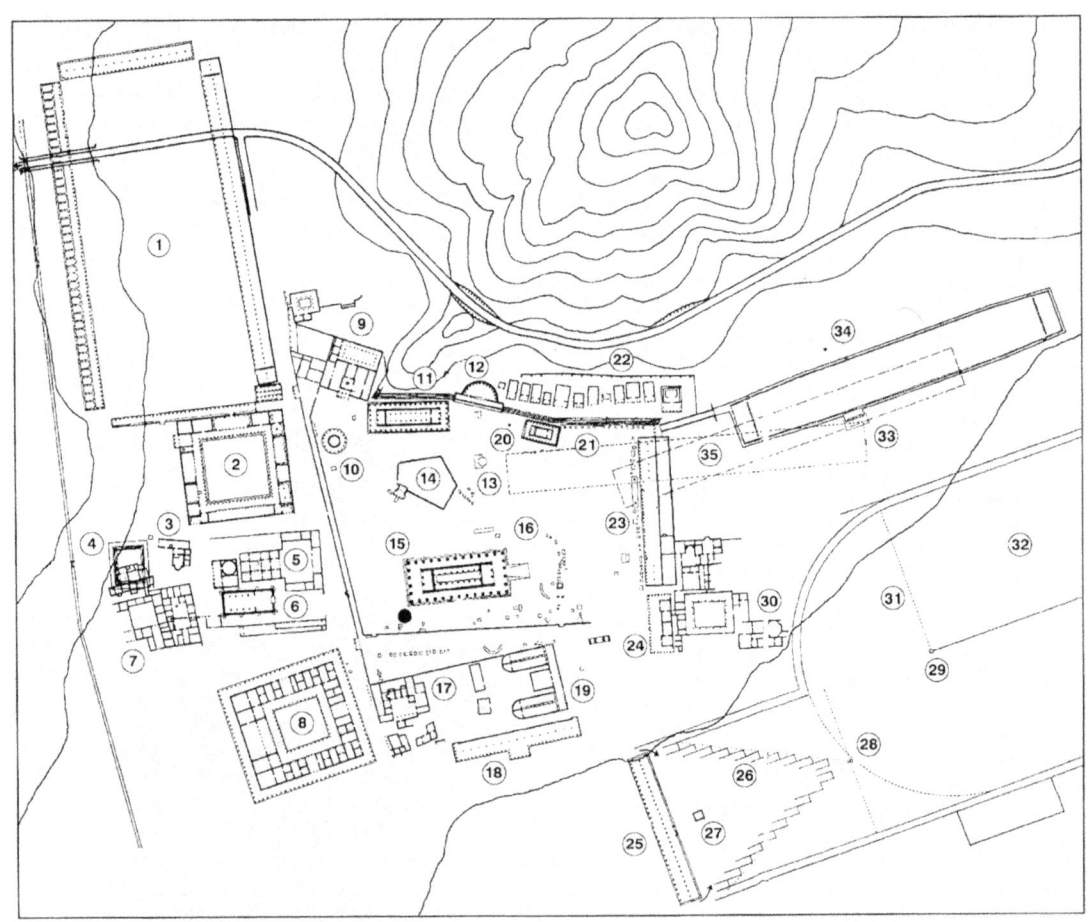

1. Gymnasium
2. Palaestra
3. Greek Baths
4. Swimming Pool
5. Theokoleon
6. Pheidias' Workshop
7. Roman Guest House
8. Leonidaion
9. Prytaneion
10. Philippeion
11. Heraion
12. Nymphaeum of Herodes Atticus
13. Altar of Zeus
14. Pelopion
15. Temple of Zeus
16. Altis
17. South Baths
18. South Stoa
19. Bouleuterion
20. Metroon
21. Zanes
22. Treasuries
23. Echo Colonnade
24. SE Building
25. Stoa of Agnaptos
26. Aphesis
27. Altar-Eagle
28. Dolphin
29. Statue of Hippodamia
30. East Baths
31. Finishing Line
32. Hippodrome
33. Tribune of the Hellanodikai
34. Altar of Demeter
35. Stadia I, II and III

Plan of the pan–Hellenic sanctuary of Olympia (courtesy of Michalis Toubis Editions).

idea of *amilla* for expressing peaceful competition is quite different from what is described as *eris* "rivalry; conflict; military campaign." *Eris* was personified as the sister and companion of Ares, the god of war. *Eris* was known as the goddess who excites war. What was organized at Olympia was *amilla,* explicitly to avoid *eris.*

If Hera symbolizes the pre–Greek heritage of the region, then Zeus stands for the Greek presence. His temple is some 150 years younger than the temple of Hera, and it was completed in 456 BCE. The dimension of this construction is monumental although its three-stepped platform—with a length of 64 m and a width of 28 m—is a little smaller than the foundation of the Parthenon temple on the Acropolis of Athens.

The native Europeans who had settled at Olympia accommodated themselves and came to terms with the Greeks who took over the site, just like Hera accommodated herself to the master of all gods by becoming his wife. The union of Zeus and Hera in Greek myth can be interpreted in metaphorical terms as marking the shift from pre–Greek to Greek cultural dominance. When this interpretation is embedded in the archaeological record of early Greece, one finds that the pre–Greek goddess Hera competed with the "first wife" of Zeus who was an Indo-European goddess.

> His wife is Hera, a pre–Greek goddess of fertility. Diwia—the Indo-European partner of Zeus— was still worshipped in Mycenaean times and had her own shrine in Pylos, but was obviously replaced by Hera who appears together with Zeus and receives offerings at Zeus' sanctuary (Ilievski 2000: 365).

Hera won the competition, and this can be interpreted as the resilience with which the pre–Greek substrate culture infused the structures of Greek civilization. At Olympia, Hera is worshipped on equal terms with Zeus, and this did not change until the advent of Christianity.

The men copied the idea of the sportive competitions from the women who venerated Hera and organized events every fourth year, honoring Zeus. According to common belief— already established in antiquity by the Greeks themselves—the first Olympic Games were held in 776 BCE. Altogether 293 games took place during antiquity, until 393 CE when the sporting event was abolished by the Roman emperor Theodosius I for its pagan association.

Myth has it that the Olympic Games were introduced by Heracles to honor Zeus. Heracles is also credited for having designed the Olympic Stadium although it is most probable that the site had been used by the female participants in the Heraia already earlier. The men who participated had to be Greeks, either as free citizens of the Athenian democratic state or as subjects in the various local kingdoms under Greek rulers. This means that the ancient Olympics were no international events in the modern sense but were restricted to Hellas, the Greek world. The victors of the Olympic contests gained fame among the whole Greek population, in their home towns in particular.

On the western side of the temple of Zeus stood a sacred olive tree. Twigs were cut from this tree to adorn the victors. In connection with the privileges granted to those who were victorious one can notice further similarities between the Heraia and the Olympics, with certain customs copied by the younger organization from the older.

> Like male athletes at Zeus's games, the female champions of the Heraia are also awarded olive wreaths, enjoy a sacrificial feast of beef, and have the right to erect victory monuments. No less telling of the hidden origins of the men's games is the fact that the gold-and-ivory table for the olive wreaths is stored in the Temple of Hera, not that of Zeus: it is the goddess, not the god, who crowns the victors (Faulkner 2012: 86).

Both women and men were engaged in sportive activities, not only at Olympia but also at other sites with pan–Hellenic significance. This raises the question of what might have been the source of inspiration for the Greeks to pay so much attention to sportive competition. Sport in ancient Greece is widely believed to have developed under the impression of Minoan cultural influence on mainland Greeks (e.g., Raubitschek 1983). And yet, the validity of this assumption has been questioned.

> Sport is one of the many aspects of Greek life often imagined to be an inheritance from the Minoans via their complex interaction with the Greek-speaking Bronze Age Mycenaeans.... There is no evidence that the Minoans took part in chariot racing (a Mycenaean pastime...). While both boxed, the protective helmets and footwear of Minoan fighters are unattested for Greece at any period.... Greek sport owes little to Minoan Crete ... the great gaps in our knowledge of the nature and role of these activities on Crete and other Minoan centres ensure that the interest in and impact of sport among the Greeks remain unusual for their time and place [Golden 1998: 32*f*].

There is no wonder that the Minoans were not interested in chariot racing. As descendants from the Palaeo-Europeans and heirs of Old European culture the Minoans lived in a world where horses were unknown while, for the Mycenaeans as descendants from the Indo-European pastoralists, the horse was an animal of great significance, both in their economy and mythology. The Greeks' drive of athletic competition might well have inspirational roots in the local Pelasgian (that is, mainland) heritage although archaeological evidence for this is not available.

Olympia lies within the territory of the ancient city-state of Elis, and the Eleans were entrusted with the maintenance of the sanctuary and the organization of the Olympic Games. The ancient Olympics lasted four days, and during this span of time all hostilities in all of Greece ceased. The Eleans were expected to remain neutral and not to take sides with any other city-state in political affairs. Elis hosted the festivities, and representatives from all Greek city-states were equally welcome, provided they did not exchange hostilities during their stay at Olympia. Paradoxical as it may seem, Athenians and Spartans contested during the Olympics that were held despite the raging Peloponnesian War (431–404 BCE) with its disastrous impact on the population in both city-states.

Both the Heraia and the Olympics had a decisive effect for engendering a pan–Hellenic spirit of cohesion and a sense of cultural sameness.

> It is often maintained that the terms "Hellas" and "Hellenes" were diffused throughout Greece via the sanctuary of Delphi.... The construction of an ethnic community of Hellenes probably had more to do with Olympia than with Delphi, though the geographical conception of Hellas was indeed articulated through Delphi [Hall 2002: 134*f*].

Like on the occasion of the Panathenaia in Athens, also at Olympia, the awareness of collective Greek identity (Hellenicity) was celebrated by the performance of a symbolic weaving together of local interests that interlace in the collective fabric of Greek self-awareness. Like at Athens, also at Olympia, maidens wove a garment (*peplos*) to decorate the statue of the goddess. In Athens, this was the statue of Athena Polias and, at Olympia, the statue of Hera.

Symbolically, sixteen women were chosen to weave the sacred garment, each representing one of the sixteen communities of which the state of Elis was comprised:

> Once in conflict, the sixteen "little cities" or "villages"—which Pausanias calls *poleis*—now find themselves reunited into a small federation thanks to the intervention of feminine wisdom....

Once its manufacture is completed, the new fabric is carried from the House of the Sixteen Women in Elis to the temple of Hera at Olympia, in order to replace the goddess's old cloak. This conveyance must have been spectacular, as it displayed to all of Elis the work of the Sixteen Women, into which the peace of the entire country was woven or rewoven.... It is to interweave what is different, contrary or hostile, in order to produce a unified, harmonious textile, worthy of covering the great goddess of Olympia herself [Scheid and Svenbro 1996: 12].

The organization of the Olympic Games lay in the responsibility of the Elean Olympic Committee (EOC). This was a board of nine judges (*hellanodikai*) who were selected from the aristocratic families in Elis. Although the election of the judges from among prominent Eleans was in itself an act of pre-selection, the electoral procedure somehow diminished the chances of patronage. Names of potential candidates for the office were written on potsherds (*ostraka*), then placed in a ceramic vessel, and lots were drawn to choose those to become members of the board.

The games that were organized at Olympia were not only a positive symbol of pan–Hellenic solidarity, they were, at the same time, a kind of valve for "letting off steam" from the pressure that was caused by constant competition among the city-states.

Competition between Greek states were not expressed uniquely in destructive organized violence: competition among rivals was played out in athletic games, in public-building projects, and in musical performances.... Competition promoted innovation in the waging of war, but also in various other domains: in performance culture, architecture, and, notably, in institutional design [Ober 2008: 84].

The idea of promoting innovation and social cohesion through contests is reflected, not only in the contests at Olympia, but also in the many competitive performances during the festivals held in Athens under the democracy and, in this context, it is noteworthy that competition produced a pleasant erasing of boundaries that existed between the social classes, and the ever-present social distinctions were felt less pressuring by the Athenian citizens.

Training and competing for these events, as Xenophon repeatedly acknowledged, involved intense and often pleasurable collaboration between the rich and the less rich, all driven by the competitive desire for collective victory. The language of *leiturgia, euergesia, charis* and *philotimia,* of individual ambition, involving reciprocal pleasures and mutual community benefits, linking together liturgists, participants and general citizen audiences, is routinely deployed in law court speeches (from the beginning of the fourth century), and in inscriptions (from the mid fourth century) as central elements in the beneficial effects of these festivals [Fisher 2011: 200].

The idea of the Olympics as a pan–Hellenic event shares with the idea of democracy that it vanished from public life for long, after the institution had been abandoned, and one could have imagined that it would have never reemerged again. But the idea of the Olympic Games never died and attempts were made, from time to time, to revive them. In the New Era, we can see various initiatives to reestablish a sportive event that would take place in regular intervals and would be dedicated to the ideals of ancient Olympia. Between 1612 and 1642, the Cotswold Games (also called the "Cotswold Olimpick Games") were organized by the lawyer Robert Dover. When the British Olympic Association applied for the Olympic Games in London (2012) it mentioned the Cotswold Games as "the first stirrings of Britain's Olympic beginnings" ("400 years of Olimpick passion").

Under the auspices of the French Revolution, the memory of the Olympic Games was revived and a national Olympic festival ("L'Olympiade de la République") was organized for several years, from 1796 until 1798.

Several approaches to the revival of the ancient Olympics were made during the nineteenth century. In Greece, a wealthy merchant (Evangelos Zappas), sponsored the first modern Greek Olympics which were held in Athens in 1859. Zappas provided funds for the restoration of the ancient Panathenaic Stadium where Olympics were hosted in 1870 and 1875. This endeavor, however, did not last. In Britain, an annual Grand Olympic Festival, organized by John Hulley and Charles Melly, took place in Liverpool, between 1862 and 1867. Although this festival was not repeated after that time, it had an impact on the later Olympics of 1896. The National Olympian Association was founded by Hulley, Brookes and Ravenstein in Liverpool in 1865. The articles of foundation of this forerunner of the British Olympic Association became a model for the International Olympic Charter (Young 1996: 24).

An exceptional case are the Wenlock Olympian Games, introduced and organized by William Brookes in 1860. This event has become a stable elements in the region of Much Wenlock (Shropshire) and has been held annually up to the present. Although regional in their organizational dimension, the Wenlock Olympian Games nevertheless inspired baron Pierre de Coubertin who had attended the Olympics at Wenlock in 1890. De Coubertin founded the International Olympic Committee (IOC), profiting from the ideas of Brookes and Zappas. On the occasion of the first Olympic Congress in Paris, in June 1894, it was decided to organize the Olympics in Athens in 1896. It is noteworthy that the program of the Olympic Games in Athens copied the program of the Liverpool Games of the 1860s (Girginov and Parry 2005: 38).

The first Olympiad was held in the spirit of the ancient Olympics, with only male contestants allowed to participate. Since the second Olympics, held in Paris in 1900, both men and women have participated in the Olympic Games. Charlotte Cooper of the United Kingdom was the first woman Olympic champion to be celebrated in Paris. In light of the presence of both sexes in the sportive competitions at Olympia (the older Heraia for women and the younger Olympics for men) one could say that, in the modern Olympiads, the spirit of the interconnected pre–Greek and Greek history at Olympia has been revived.

The goddess Hera has never succumbed to the dominance of her divine spouse but has retained vital functions associated with the sportive competitions. While the significance of her temple housing the gold-and-ivory table for the victors' wreaths vanished with the abolition of the Olympics in late antiquity, in the modern Olympics, the presence of the goddess is secured albeit somehow veiled. Among the various rituals of the opening and the closing of the games established at the Olympics of Antwerp in 1920 there was the ritual of bringing the Olympic torch into the stadium to light the Olympic flame in a cauldron. Since that event the torch has been lit at Olympia, at the altar of Hera situated in front of her temple.

The true patron of the modern Olympics is Hera who keeps blessing the Olympic torch, the flame and the spirit that goes with it. In recent years, the lighting of the torch at Olympia has gained more and more attention from the mass media. Celebrities in antique dresses pose for the cameras at Hera's altar where the torch is lit by the natural light of the sun and then carried out of the once sacred precinct. Hera's altar, with her temple in the background, is in focus, not the remnants of the temple of Zeus that remains a silent place without any function other than to be admired, as a historical monument, by visitors to Olympia.

The Oracle at Delphi, Its Prehistory and Its Role for Pan-Hellenic Solidarity

Among the innumerable sacred precincts relatively few housed oracles, that is facilities where oracular revelations were uttered. Of particular fame in the ancient world were the oracles of Dodona, Didyma, Larissa, Claros and some others. The most famous oracle of all was undoubtedly the one at Delphi, with its umbilical stone (*omphalos*), symbolizing the center of the world. This identification is widely understood as referring to all the regions populated by human beings. But such a cosmopolitan connotation is a modern projection which does not reflect realities of antiquity. For the ancients the umbilical stone at Delphi marked the center of the Greek world in particular (without taking into consideration the world of the barbarian peoples). In the archaic period, that is at the times of Homer, the world inhabited by the Greeks, known as Hellas, was relatively small.

> Between the time of the Iliad (ca. 750 BC) and the Odyssey (ca. 725 BC), the conception of Hellas has broadened from indicating a specific region south of Thessaly to designating central Greece generally. It is not, however, until the time of Alkman in the later seventh century that the term can be used to describe the whole of mainland Greece, while its broadest application to embrace the whole of the Greek world is not attested until the time of Xenophanes in the third quarter of the sixth century [Hall 2002: 156].

The popularity of Delphi and the significance assigned by worshipers to its oracle are reflected in antique sources, and there is ample literary documentation of the contents of particular oracular pronouncements (Parke and Wormell 1956 for oracles at Delphi). Famous writers of antiquity dedicated parts of their work to the description of sacred activities performed at Delphi. Those who are mentioned, in the literary sources, as visitors to Delphi are not only living people but also figures of Greek mythology. Delphi is in focus in Sophocles' play *Oedipus,* in the works of Herodotus one finds the story of Croesus, king of Lydia, and the well-known pronouncement made by the oracle at Delphi that a kingdom would fall should he cross the river Halys to engage in war with the Persians. Indeed, a kingdom fell, namely Croesus' own because he was defeated by the Persian king Kyros.

Delphi's fame reached far beyond the Greek world and, once all of Greece had been integrated into the Roman empire, also many Romans visited Delphi. Among them was Cicero (106–43 BCE), the famous orator and writer who discussed the oracles of Delphi in his work *On divination.* Plutarch (45–120 CE) wrote essays about Delphi. All great figures of Athenian history frequented the sanctuary of Delphi to consult the oracle. Among them was also Cleisthenes who, while exiled from Athens, made inquiries at Delphi about what the future might hold for him. The oracle encouraged him to remain steadfast and envisaged Cleisthenes' successful return. Cleisthenes did return to Athens and carried out his reform work which safeguarded the persistence of the principle of democratic governance on the communal and state level (see Chapter 7).

The pronouncements of the oracle have come down to us because they were recorded in writing. In their original form the oracular contents was given in spoken language, that is the oracles were uttered on site and written down later. The one who is credited with the utterance of oracular pronouncements occupied a central position among the cult personnel of Delphi. This position was held by a highly trained priestess, the Pythia. Pythia is not the individual name of any priestess but the designation of her office. In the early days of cult activity at Delphi, the pronouncements of the Pythia were made in rhymed language, and they were molded on the literary meter of the Greek hexameter which is the mold of epic literature. One may wonder how it was possible for a priestess to make oracular pronouncements in a complex literary meter. An explanation may be found in the fact that those women who held the office of the Pythia were originally elected from the circle of high aristocracy, and these women were familiar with the works of epic poets. In the classical period, ordinary women also could function as Pythia and utterances were made in ordinary language.

Part of the Pythia's special training was the experience of trance because she made her oracular utterances in an altered state of consciousness. The secret of how the Pythia transcended into trance was never revealed and modern investigations point to two alternative explanations. The Pythia sat on a tripod and near that place was a crack in the soil from where volcanic fumes rose. Some scholars assume that the fumes produced an intoxicating effect and caused the priestess' consciousness to alter while others look for intoxicating substances in the living environment of the sanctuary. The holy precinct was dedicated to the god Apollo and the laurel was his sacred attribute. Perhaps the Pythia brewed a beverage by mixing the leaves of the laurel tree with boiling water. The consumption of such a tea-like mixture could have had an intoxicating effect. "Scholars remain divided as to whether the inspiration of the Pythia was simply a psychological state, perhaps helped along by a solemn drink of holy water from the Castalian spring, while Maurizio [1995] holds to an interpretation that brings the Pythia much closer to shamanic practitioners from other cultures" (Stoneman 2011: 34).

There is unanimity among scholars that the practice of the oracle and the conditions of the priestess' office point to great antiquity of this institution and of the entire sanctuary. Already the Hellenophile representatives of the Romantic Movement in the early nineteenth century identified oracular practices and trance as part of the oldest layer of Greek religion (Lambropoulos 1993: 174). Trance as a means of ritual performance is characteristic of shamanism which has been identified by anthropologists as the oldest institution of religious beliefs among human beings. "The most ancient, the oldest and the most long-lasted institution in the northern hemisphere is shamanism. Shamanism is a family—a clan—institution and it has been present in hunting, gathering and agricultural societies right up to our day, living on in the industrial era" (Kare 2000: 104).

The significance of shamanistic practices, as a relic from the pre-agrarian age, for early agriculturalists has been emphasized recently (Lewis-Williams and Pearce 2005: 42*ff*, 62*ff*) and the presence of shamanism in Neolithic Europe is well documented, extending beyond altered states of consciousness into ritual interaction with figurines and artifacts with religious significance. For instance, this is true for certain artifacts made of spondylus, a shell that was found on the coasts of the Aegean Sea and exchanged in an extended network of trade relations along the big waterway, the Danube, and its tributaries. The special value of spondylus artifacts can be inferred from the fact that some show traces of long-term use with a duration longer than a person's lifetime. "Shamanism remains the best explanation for why certain objects made of Spondylus were transmitted from generation to generation while others, including anthropomorphic and zoomorphic figurines, were intentionally broken and/or burned" (Séfériadès 2009: 187).

The characteristics of ritual practice at Delphi speak in favor of a long duration of that sacred place. According to the mythical tradition, recorded in the works of Pausanias, the beginnings of ritual activities at Delphi are embedded in the mythical past.

Legend held (Paus. 10.5.9) that a series of eight temples had been built for Apollo at Delphi: the first was made of laurel branches from Tempe, the second was made by bees out of wax and feathers; the third temple was of bronze, destroyed by a thunderbolt as Pindar's eighth *Paean* tells us. A fourth temple was built by the heroes Trophonius and Agamedes [...], and the temple that stood in Pindar's day (and that stands now) was the eighth in the series. The long succession emphasizes how far in the distant past (or depths of the psyche) lay the ancient and terrifying oracle of Earth [Stoneman 2011: 35].

Is there material evidence available to support the general impression of great antiquity, reaching beyond Greek literary accounts and Greek presence into prehistory? The oldest architectural remains that can be identified at Delphi date to the eighth century BCE which testify to religious activities during the archaic period. Were there older structures? It is difficult to answer this question. Had there been any pre–Greek architecture at the site it would have disappeared once the Greeks started to build temples. On the other hand it may be futile to look for pre–Greek architecture at Delphi because the conceptualization of the sacred space among the pre–Greek population differed considerably from how the ancient Greeks perceived it.

For instance, there is written record of how the sacred space at Ephesus on the Ionian coast was modeled. When the monumental temple, the famous Artemision (one of the seven wonders of the ancient world) was erected there in the sixth century BCE to honor the mighty Ephesian Artemis, the holy precinct already had a long history. In the beginning it was a place of worship in a sacred grove with only one landmark which was natural, not man-made: a sacred tree (Ekschmitt 1984: 107). Therefore, at Ephesus, there are no pre–Greek architectural remains. Most probably the conditions of worship at Delphi in pre–Greek times were similar to those in Ephesus. There were no temples but rituals were performed in the open in a natural environment.

What has been discussed so far with respect to the identification of Delphi as a sacred place in prehistory is conjecture. And yet, there is circumstantial evidence, and it comes from the study of historical names and of myths relating to the sanctuary of Delphi.

In the mythical tradition of how the Greeks explained their world the sacred space at Delphi is associated with Gaia, the Earth Goddess, who was the original owner of the sanctuary. In this role, Gaia was venerated by all who visited Delphi. Gaia is no Greek name but derived from a pre–Greek word stem meaning "earth." Variations of this pre–Greek word are *ge-* and *de-* (as in Demeter, name of the Grain Goddess, with De- as a pre–Greek element and *meter*, "mother," as an Indo-European component). The Greek word for earth is *chthon* which lives on in our cultural vocabulary (i.e., in the derivation *chthonic*, "earthbound"). In the association of a pre–Greek goddess with the sanctuary of Delphi, its pre–Greek heritage is revealed.

In a scrutinous analysis of myths focusing on Gaia as a female divinity, the pivotal role of this figure has been highlighted for establishing a balanced relationship with the male gods, with Zeus in particular whose succession to become the mightiest of gods was orchestrated by Gaia.

In Hesiod's *Theogony*, physical strength is less of a *motivating* force in succession than is generational strife, in the sense that a female figure, either a wife or a mother, always interferes in the process of succession. Although the physical strength of Zeus is often mentioned in the *Theogony*, in fact it is Gaia who is the dominant figure in plotting the succession and who plays the decisive, i.e., motivating, role [Yasumura 2011: 77].

Gaia actually was not the only owner of the place but she shared ownership with Themis. This goddess was her daughter who was not the fruit of a liaison of Gaia with a male god or any of the mortal men. Gaia became pregnant "by accident." The mythical tradition has it that Hephaestus fell in love with Athena, the eternally virgin goddess, and when he was aroused he wanted to make love. Athena, though, escaped his grip and Hephaestus spilled his seed on the ground which caused Gaia to become pregnant. Themis was not any goddess but she held a most significant position in the Greek pantheon. She was the goddess of righteousness, of customary law and of social order. During the times of democratic rule in Athens, in the fifth and fourth centuries BCE, she symbolized the right of a representative of the National Assembly (*ekklesia*) to speak up freely. The name Themis is of pre–Greek origin as is the divine figure (Beekes 2010: 539). Like Athena, Themis connected two worlds, the heritage of the pre–Greek world with the innovations of the Greek world. Like Gaia, Themis was held in high esteem and was always remembered by those who visited Delphi.

Since the times of Homer and the other epic poets, Apollo was known as the owner of the sanctuary at Delphi. This god is Greek. According to myth, Gaia and Themis entrusted Apollo with the ownership of Delphi but they themselves were never ousted or abandoned but remained present throughout Delphi's long history. In their myths, the Greeks conceptualized the transition from an older culture (that of the pre–Greek population) to a younger culture (that of the Greeks) and they also kept their awareness of the ritual continuity of the sacred space.

The kind of continuity of the functions of a sacred site in association with a shift from a female divinity to a male god that we see at Delphi is known also from other famous sites, Mount Haroun (Jabal Haroun) near Petra in Jordan for one. Today, the place is frequented by Islamic pilgrims who honor Aaron, the brother of the biblical Moses who, according to Christian and Islamic tradition, was buried on the mountain that bears his name. Aaron's cenotaph is located inside the fourteenth-century Muslim shrine. The owners of Mount Haroun shifted from goddess to prophet: "The religious significance of the mountain in the Byzantine and Islamic periods is known from written sources, but evidence is now beginning to mount that the mountain was the site of an important sanctuary—probably dedicated to the goddess al-'Uzza/Isis—already in the Nabataean-Roman period" (Lahelma and Fiema 2008: 213).

There was a shift in the cultural embedding of the sanctuary at Delphi but stability of the site in terms of its function as a sacred place. And there was continuity of what concerns the ritual practices of the oracle. From pre–Greek times through late antiquity, as long as the oracle was consulted, the office of the functionary was held by a woman, the Pythia. Under the auspices of male-dominated society in ancient Greece, one could have expected a shift from priestess to priest once the ownership shifted from female owners to a male owner, but the tradition of electing a priestess for the office of the oracle was never changed.

Themis was no marginal deity and sanctuaries were dedicated to her in various parts of Greece, in Thessaly, Boiotia, Epiros, in the Argolid, on Rhodes, in Macedonia and, in Athens. There was a saying in ancient Greek and this was *themis esti* "it is the custom, it is the norm of social conduct." The mythical kinship with Gaia may be understood as an aspect of the earthbound lifeways of the early agriculturalists whose norms of social conduct and customary law were established by Themis who also functioned as patron to safeguard these norms. "If Themis did indeed start life as an aspect of Gaia, her gaining of autonomy could be understood as a reflection of a shift in emphasis, from an agrarian concern with fertility to an increasingly urban concern with law and political order" (Stafford 1997: 158).

In fact, Themis was the integrating figure at Delphi because, unlike Gaia who retained only some symbolic meaning after the shift of ownership, she held vital functions even at the times of Apollo's patronage over the sacred site. In the Greeks' perception the Pythia was no ordinary priestess but the ritual activities that she performed in her trance were imbued with divine inspiration. The Pythia was perceived as a personification of Themis and her intentions and, in this identification, scenes of the oracle were painted on Attic vases. One of those scenes shows Aegeus who seeks advice from Themis in the posture of the Pythia. Aegeus was a descendant in the royal lineage of Erechtheus, the mythical founder of the Athenian dynasty.

Themis in the posture of the Pythia (Attic red-figure cup of the fifth century BCE) (originally published in *Auserlesene griechische Vasenbilder, hauptsächlich etruskischen Fundortes* by Eduard Gerhard. Berlin: Reimer, 1839).

It is of little importance whether the Greeks perceived the Pythia as a human being, guided by divine spirit, or whether they identified the priestess with the personality of Themis. The matter of significance was the atmosphere that was created by the ritual act of making pronouncements in trance. Like her office, the Pythia represented the social order that had emerged in pre–Greek times and persisted into classical antiquity. The mentality that stood behind that order was encapsulated in the concept of *hosia*. This particular term in ancient Greek stood for customary law, the norms of social conduct handed down from previous generations based on the life experience of the ancestors, customs and traditions known from the ancients. Traditional values in cultural memory were associated with the lifeways of the native Europeans from whose institutions and achievements the Greeks immensely profited. In light of the Pythia's identification with Themis as a guarantor of ancient customs all communication of the oracle's visitors with the Pythia unfolded in the spirit of an appreciation of traditional values as maxim.

In a way, the Pythia was the guardian of a mindset oriented toward a harmonious integration of the genuine pre–Greek and the genuine Greek. The integrative spirit became manifested in a very particular way at Delphi, in the heartland of Hellas. The social order of the ancients was based on the principle of an egalitarian society, and communal self-administration in the pre–Greek settlements strengthened the self-awareness of the values of what would later be called "democratic governance." The long and successful experience with this model of political organization impressed the Greeks as much as it had impressed their predecessors. At Delphi, amidst the process of Hellenization, the idea of egalitarian governance culminated in the founding of a tribal league, an interregional network of political decision-making. This league was called the *amphiktiony*. This expression is a compound word, being comprised of the preposition *amphi-* ("around") and the verb *ktizein* ("to inhabit, settle"). The original meaning of *amphiktiony* is thus "people in the neighborhood" (Hall 2002: 148). The point of reference in this context was a central sanctuary, Delphi.

> The Delphic (Anthela) amphiktiony (a ritual network or grouping of political communities, mostly *ethnê*, supervising the Delphic sanctuary, centered on Thermopylai and with a strong Thessalian influence) undoubtedly played a significant role in the original spread of the term "Hellenism." All who joined in the Delphic network probably became Hellenes, a term originally associated with only a section of the amphiktiony [Malkin 2011: 59*f*].

The date of the founding of the Delphic amphiktiony (literally "League of Neighbors") is not known. Written records are available from the sixth century BCE onward. The tribal council is certainly much older and may have originated in the eighth century BCE or even earlier. The earliest version of this tribal network, to enhance security among the ancient tribes through the medium of diplomatic negotiations, has been associated with the Thessalians in modern scholarly investigation (McInerney 2000: 164*f*). An indication of this is the fact that the chairman of the council was always a Thessalian.

The central organ of the league was the council, in which twelve tribes were represented by two representatives (*hieromnemones*) each, bringing the number of members of the council to 24. According to the statutes of the amphiktiony, each tribe had to observe peace and war between the tribes was forbidden. Each tribe had the obligation to secure the provision of the inhabitants of towns and villages with drinking water, not only for the population on its own territory but also for other tribes. Originally a religious network that took responsibility for the maintenance of the sanctuary at Delphi, the amphiktiony gradually gained political significance. Sentences could be imposed against those who broke the statutes and sacred wars could be declared as punishment. The first sacred war was waged in ca. 591 BCE and the third (and last) in 356 BCE against the Phocians who had sacked the sanctuary at Delphi.

The Delphic amphiktiony has been celebrated as the common bond of Hellas. The Roman orator Cicero called it "commune Graeciae consilium" ("the common council of Greece"). In modern research the Delphic amphiktiony has been celebrated as a prototype of the Swiss confederation. A comparison may also be made with the confederation of the five nations of the Iroquois in North America (Bradley 1987: 181*ff*).

It is noteworthy that, in 490 BCE, the council—following a suggestion of the chairman from Thessaly—reached a majority decision how to respond to the Persians' demand that the Greeks should become vassals of the Persian empire. Most of the Greek tribes that were represented in the council voted for the subjugation of Greek cities to the Persians. The representatives of Athens and of Sparta opposed and left the council. It is well known from history books that the Athenians engaged in war against the invading Persian armies on the mainland and against their fleets operating in the Aegean. After the Persian wars that lasted for half a century the Delphic amphiktiony lost their former significance. The activities of the tribal network came to an end in 346 BCE when the Macedonian king Philip II usurped its presidency. As a counter reaction to this undemocratic act many of the other tribes' representatives left the council and abandoned the league.

The Power of Customs and Conventions: Dispute Settling and Law-Giving in a Traditional Key

The lifeline of any culture is guaranteed by the continuation of its traditions. Continuation points to a dynamic process which unfolds on the continuum of absolute time. Thus, the persistence of a culture depends on how representatives of subsequent generations instrumentalize their cultural memory to renew and modulate past traditions in the present and future. The perpetuation of cultural traditions over many generations reflects stability in the reproduction of existing models while cultural change is due to modifications effected in the cultural memory by subsequent generations. The living conditions of the younger generation may call for adjustments of older knowledge to retain its usefulness in a changing world. Whether unchanged perpetuation or modulation of useful knowledge, its transmission depends on the ways the younger generation is introduced to the knowledge of their parents, that is, instructed by the elders.

Most successful is the instruction in a community where the knowledge of the living instructors is perceived by the younger generation as valid experience of the elders or even as valued heritage transferred to the living from the times of the ancestors. Such an awareness of the value of useful knowledge as a collective body of cultural heritage gives additional weight to the instruction of its contents, like an intellectual-cultural surplus that is likely to strengthen the traditions held by a community. Throughout Greek history, the significance of customs of behavior and customary (i.e., unwritten) law was understood and their value for education emphasized. For example, in Plato's work *Laws,* it says that "the unwritten laws or customs that govern education are the bonds of the whole regime. If these unwritten laws are established in a noble way, they will save the written laws" (Lutz 2012: 96).

The earliest Greek law known to have been written down comes from Dreros (in the northeastern part of Crete) and dates to around 650 BCE, "and during the next century, laws were inscribed all over Crete (especially at Gortyn) and the rest of Greece" (Gagarin 2005: 91). The oldest law code that is known from Athens is Draco's homicide law, enacted in 621 BCE. The text itself has not come down to us but its contents was included in Solon's collection of laws that he presented together with his reforms in 594 BCE (Dillon and Garland 1994: 59*ff*).

> The aim of the [Draconian] law was to regulate and limit private revenge, which until that moment had been the habitual and unquestioned response to every wrong that a person claimed to have suffered. But although it prohibited revenge in a general way, the law established some exceptions.... Draco guaranteed impunity to the man who had killed another man caught "next to" (*epi* + dative) his wife, mother, daughter, sister, or the concubine (*pallake*) he kept for the purpose of having free children, that is, his free concubine [Cantarella 2005: 239].

Law-giving did not start with the first written law around the mid-seventh century BCE. And early laws of the Greek world recorded in writing did not cover all domains of people's lives. The oldest collection of laws, found in the Cretan town of Dreros, is comprised of regulations for cult life and for administration (concerning access to high offices in the community). The contents of later compilations of laws reveals that the major themes addressed fit in with the frame of what can be described as customary law. Customary law always precedes written law since maxims for proper social conduct and punitive measures against offenders exist in all cultures, including all those which are illiterate.

> Written laws are attested first in our evidence around the mid-seventh century, and they increase at precisely the period when the Greek city-states were developing more formal political systems in a process of state formation.... Our firmest evidence for Greek law in the archaic and early classical period remains the inscriptions recording laws; thus we know far more about those laws which were inscribed on stone (as opposed to wood or bronze) and survived to this day [Thomas 2005: 42*f*].

Most extant laws from Greek antiquity are written on stone, some text fragments on bronze have been found at Olympia (Elis) and at Argos (Argolid). No traces are left of the original codifications of the archaic period in Athens (i.e., Draco's and Solon's laws) or in other places where, according to antique sources, laws were given (i.e., Thebes, Catana, Locri).

Those who were the most diligent to codify their laws in written form were the Cretans. The civilization of ancient Crete was built up by the Minoans who were called after the prominent figure of king Minos in the Greek myths. Minos is credited as the first lawgiver. In the works of antique authors one finds allusions to Crete as the cradle of the Greek tradition of lawgiving (Thomas 2005: 43*f*). The most famous of all Greek law codes is the compilation on stone from Gortyn (Crete), known as the Gortyn Code (mid-fifth century BCE). The codification of laws in writing makes a difference (compared with orally transmitted juridical regulations) and not only with regard to its graphic representation.

> When law becomes established in the Greek world, there are a number of different aspects to it: social institutions, human practices, and mental categories, and it is these that define legal thought as opposed to other forms of thought, in particular religious ones [Vernant and Vidal-Naquet 1990: 30].

The roles of both orality and literacy in lawgiving were valued by the Greeks, and attitudes toward the written form of laws varied considerably in the Greek world. The Spartans claimed that their most famous lawgiver, the legendary Lycurgus, had forbidden writing down laws. He called the laws *rhetra* which is derived from the same lexical root as rhetoric and implies oral transmission. The contents of the *rhetra* had to be handed down from one generation to the next as oral memory (Plutarch, *Lycurgus* 13.3). The ways in which oral transmission works is not always the same in the Greek world which means that the concept "oral memory" was not always understood as relating exclusively to the spoken word. From literary sources we know that, for instance, the laws of Charondas—a lawgiver from Katane (Catania) in Sicily of the sixth century BCE—were chanted in a choral song (*paian*, a term of substrate origin); (Thomas 1995: 62*f*). Katane was a Greek colony whose mother city was Chalkis in Euboia.

The case of Lycurgus is a special one. It is unclear whether he was a historical figure (who lived in the eighth century BCE) or a fabrication of mythmaking in ancient Greece. Herodotus, the father of Greek historiography, connects Lycurgus with the Cretan tradition of lawgiving, and this may be seen as an attempt to increase his prestige. According to a pronouncement made by Plato the Spartan laws were given to Lycurgus when he visited Delphi and consulted the oracle. This again adds to Lycurgus' fame, and the authority of the Delphic oracle certainly had a bearing on the acceptance of the laws by the Spartans. The oracle, with pronouncements given by the Pythia in trance, was an institution that cherished traditional values, among them the regulations provided by customary law. What the oracle had to say in matters of lawgiving was provided in the spirit of Themis and her sense of social order, observing the ways of the ancients.

Scholars have searched for an old layer in Greek laws, for what is common to all law codifications. "The study of Attic law can be considered not only an end in itself, but also, if properly understood, as a means of recovering other Greek laws; laws, let us repeat, that are indisputably diverse among themselves but among which, nevertheless, can be found the existence of *a common substratum*" (Biscardi 1982: 9; my emphasis).

One of the aspects of a common substratum is the motivation why laws were written down. Modern research rejects the idea—advocated by the traditionalists who look for Oriental origins of all Greek institutions—that the tradition of writing laws originated in Mesopotamia and inspired the Greeks to follow the example. Such a comparison is too simplistic. Law codes in the ancient Middle East were intended as icons to glorify and celebrate the ruler, but their function was not necessarily to bring justice to his subjects.

The motivation for codifying laws was altogether different in the Greek world. The essence of Greek lawgiving is encapsulated in Greek theater plays, in fifth-century tragedy in particular. Euripides, in his *Suppliants*, makes his actors reflect on the nature of the Greek laws. Theseus uses the term *koinos* (related to *koion*, "pledge," an element of the pre-Greek substratum)

> to describe the valid law that is set in opposition to the tyrant's law. That word denotes precisely that legitimate law is public or a communal or shared possession. The laws of Greece, the laws of mortals, and the laws of the gods must all be different types of "common law" or "law of the community." These types of law are publicly possessed insofar as none can be said to have a specific, named mortal author; they seem to come from the community as a whole. In a society, whose religious laws were not based on a single divinely inspired text, even the laws of the gods took their authority from the community's valorization of religious beliefs [Allen 2005: 389].

The anonymity of the laws and the collectivity of their communal possession makes the essence of the concept *hosia*. This concept was the very foundation of the ways of Themis (see above for her association with the Delphic oracle). Both the concept *hosia* and the term itself are elements of the pre-Greek substratum, and both were adopted by the Greeks from their predecessors who had lived by the regulations of customary law since the Neolithic. The *hosia* of the ancients were common law, for mortals and gods alike, and as such they were sacred. "Many 'sacred laws' are indeed true laws, in the sense of regulations emanating from the citizen assembly or other legislative body of the city concerned, and backed by its authority" (Parker 2005: 63).

The source of what was comprised by *hosia* was readily associated with divine agency. The best quality of laws was imagined to emanate from the kind of justice that only gods can inspire. In Plato's work *Laws*, there is a lengthy passage where the philosopher—in the disguise of the "Athenian Stranger" who engages in a dialog with Kleinias—elaborates on a city "under divine law." Divine law is conceptualized by Plato in a way "that the gods rely on intellect (*nous*) to establish the laws (Laws 714a), indicating that inspired laws would reflect a wisdom that is discernable by human intellect" (Lutz 2012: 111).

There is consensus that the only way to achieve the quality of "noble laws" is

> in keeping with the principle that the lawgiver always makes law for the sake of what is best (*Laws* 628c6–7). And as a result of this agreement, they also accept that the laws of the city ought to aim not simply at overcoming conflict within the city but more importantly at introducing to it peace, goodwill, and happiness (*Laws* 628d3–7). By comparing the city that undergoes domestic conflict to a body that suffers from a disease (*Laws* 628d2–3), the Athenian Stranger suggests that the city in which citizens live harmoniously would be like a body whose parts work together, pro-

ducing a positive, glowing health in the body as a whole. And the corresponding aim of divine law would be to bring this sort of health or well-being to the civic body [Lutz 2012: 40].

There is good reason to assume that the *hosia* of the ancients were not only meant for everybody to follow, that is for members of both sexes, but that also the handling of juridical matters (e.g., dispute settling) could, at some time, be executed by both men and women. In classical Greece, women were excluded from the public domain, and law-giving and dispute-settling were the exclusive activities of men. And yet, in some regions of Greece, stories were told about wise women who engaged in dispute-settling. At Olympia this crucial role of women for the creation of a pan–Hellenic consciousness is well documented.

At Olympia, sixteen elderly women wove a robe for Hera every fourth year (Pausanias 5.16.2–6; 6.24.10). The origin of this was a board of female elders once chosen from sixteen cities of Eleia to settle differences between the towns of Pisa and Elis. The women selected, considered to be "the oldest, the most noble and the most esteemed of all," were highly successful in settling the dispute, making peace between their two cities (Pausanias 5.16.5). On the model of this group, the sixteen women of Elis were charged with supervising the festival of Hera, including girls' footraces and choral dances [Connelly 2007: 43].

In the pre–Greek tradition the oral memorizing of sacred laws was given priority, and this attitude is still reflected in the way Lycurgus manages lawgiving without the medium of writing. Other cultures know the taboo of unwritten laws, too. An example is Irish society in the early Middle Ages. Although the Ogham script had been in use for funerary inscriptions since the fourth century CE it was forbidden to record Druidic laws in writing. The Druids memorized the contents of the old Irish laws as secret knowledge. Only when Christianity had come to dominate were the restrictions lifted and the old laws were written, using the Latin script (Mytum 1992: 54*f*).

In the Greek discourse about law and justice one finds valorizations favoring unwritten over written laws. "Hippias, for instance, asked whether justice can be defined as keeping to the law, because law can be altered, but unwritten laws, such as the law that everyone must look after their parents, are divine and observed everywhere (Xenophon, *Memorabilia* 4.4.13*ff*)" (Thomas 2005: 51).

According to the worldview of the Greeks in which human beings interacted with the gods through rituals and cult practices, the usefulness of laws could be valued by the application of intellect. In the interaction of humans with gods, intellect becomes a means of communication that functions both ways.

The divine legislator needs to use intellect to make the laws. Insofar as the intellect provides the citizen with knowledge of virtue, it provides the citizen with access to the gods' thinking. To use intellect to discern virtue is to divine what the gods have in mind regarding what the citizen considers to be the most important things (*Laws* 964b, 965e, 968b–c, 969c–d). In this respect, it could be called the divine part of the soul [Lutz 2012: 175].

The most common term for law was *nomos*, whose meanings were rather ambiguous, ranging from customary unwritten law to regulations of cult practices and specialized laws for the limitations of the offices of members of the council and of the magistrate (Hölkeskamp 2000: 74*ff*). The content of unwritten customary law continued to be observed in the Greek communities, regardless of how extensively the juridical concerns may have generated ever more specialized regulations once laws were written. In short, the customary law of the ancients (the *hosia* as substratum) remained the foundation of Greek lawgiving.

There is another feature by which Greek laws distinguish themselves from any codification of Mesopotamian coinage, and this is the function of laws to serve in dispute-settling. The application of laws and their practicability for the settling of disputes of contestants was a major concern of the Greek legal system. The authority of written laws was enhanced by the specific way in which they were displayed and handled.

> These laws were inscribed ... and were displayed prominently in public areas, often in or near a temple or sanctuary. This location may have conveyed the sense that the laws had divine authority but they were not "religious" laws such as, say, the collections of laws in the Old Testament [...]. Unlike many Near Eastern law codes, Greek legislation was meant to be used in actual litigation. Even the earliest inscriptions make some effort to organize provisions in ways that are useful to users (e.g., by grouping together provisions on the same subject) and to incorporate other physical and stylistic features that make the laws easier to read [Gagarin 2005: 92].

The basic idea of dispute-settling was to persuade contestants in a law suit to seek a settlement which enhanced the development of rhetoric skills. The contestants had a chance to speak and give their arguments, and the judge would then give his verdict without any obligation to explain on which ground he made his decision. The role of the judges (*dikastai*) was central for keeping up a just balance between the regulations provided by the law and the people for whom the law was made. The *dikastai* are "asked to identify with the *demos* as the beneficiaries of the law" (Yunis 2005: 205). This means the intentions of the demos are the intentions of the *dikastai*.

Dispute-settling was one of the cornerstones for the functioning of the communal system. In the archaic period, the noble task to act as judge in dispute-settling was that of a Homeric king. There are various instances of dispute-settling, as an agenda, woven into the stories of epic literature (e.g., *Iliad* 16.542; *Odyssey* 12.440). The protagonist of one epic story is the god Hephaistos who crafts a shield for the hero Achilles which he decorates with scenes of human activity. For the overall theme of a city at peace Hephaistos chooses two scenes: one is a wedding and the other a trial (*Iliad* 18.497–508).

In the epic literature, the respectable office of the judge is often assigned to the king (*basileus*). According to the findings of modern scholarship, the *basileus* in Mycenaean times was no mighty king of a city-state but a figure invested with authority, by the local communities, to hold a tribe together (see Chapter 7). The respect he enjoyed was a function of his authority to settle disputes. In Hesiod's *Theogony* (84–103) the king, acting as supreme judge, is most respected if he is eloquent and possesses the skills to persuade the disputants to reach a settlement. In the poet's view, a judge needs the gift of the Muses, eloquence, as much as a poet does.

The badge of the judge's office was a staff, called *bakteria,* and this was a term from the substrate language. *Bakteria* symbolized authority assigned by the community, and this differed markedly from the function of *skeptron* ("scepter") which was the symbol of power. In Homer's works, *skeptron* is borne by chiefs and transmitted from father to his son, and *skeptron* also is the symbol of royalty (Dergachev 2007: 163).

The tradition of customary law occupied many niches in Greek society of antiquity, and some customs—imbued with juridical as much as moral obligations—were perpetuated in formulaic rituals. An example of this are oaths in the texts of which are preserved archaic formulas.

> When Athenian recruits submitted their oaths of allegiance they called upon a series of known deities as their witnesses, but at the end also "the boundary-stones of their native country, wheat,

barley, vines, olive trees and fig trees." The lawgivers of each city-state did in fact lay down rules as to how the distribution and exploitation were to be regulated [Isager and Skydsgaard 1995: 120].

Pre-Greek elements in the nomenclature of customary law, social conventions, religious customs, juridical offenses:

aesylos "criminal acts"
(h)osios "sanctioned, permitted (by the gods or by nature)" (derivation *(h)osia* "divine or natural law," "holy custom")
klapai "stick (as a means of punishment)"
kyrbeis "customary law, regulations" (since the fifth century BCE)
miaino "to defile through bloodcrime"
themis goddess of justice, "justice, law, custom"
threskeuo "to perform or observe religious customs"

Greek laws were a powerful means to hold society together and to regulate social interaction. The contents of the laws—of the part of customary law, in particular—entered public discourse to the extent that it was integrated into the literary genre of tragedy since, in Greek tragedy, every aspect of the existing laws was addressed and judgment was passed in theatrical performances.

> The almost obsessive use of a technical legal terminology in the language of the tragic writers, their preference for themes connected with crimes of bloodshed that fall within the competence of one court or another, the very form that some of the plays take, namely that of a judgment, make it imperative that, to understand the exact meanings of the terms and all the implications of the drama, the historian of literature step outside his own specialized field and make himself a historian of Greek law [Vernant and Vidal-Naquet 1990: 31].

Processions, Communal Rituals and the Festive Calendar

The ancient Greeks share a basic function of their ritual life with many cultures, and this is enhancing sociocultural cohesion in the communities. As for the cultural timeframe of ritualized behavior there is consensus among anthropologists that the instrumentalization of altered states of consciousness for ritualistic purposes belong to a very old layer of religious beliefs, and they are typical features of shamanistic practices (Lewis-Williams and Pearce 2005: 46*ff*). Such practices are characteristic of some of the central cults in Greek antiquity which had a ritualistic impact on community life and which were supportive of the formation of a pan–Hellenic awareness.

The cult of Dionysos is known for its uses of intoxication and for its "Bacchic revels" (the Dionysia), with ecstatic performances of ritual dancing and wine-consumption (Du Bois 2010: 36). Another cult where altered states of consciousness play an important role is the oracle at Delphi where the priestess, the Pythia, who makes an oracular utterance is in trance during her performance (Stoneman 2011: 40*ff*). It is noteworthy that, in both cults, women are in the center of ritual activities.

In light of these circumstances it is not surprising to learn that the cults in question date to pre–Greek times and are a heritage of traditions that are much older than Greek civilization itself. What is surprising is the fact that shamanistic traditions related to the Mesolithic in southeastern Europe that had continued into the Neolithic of Old Europe have persisted into the subsequent cultures of later periods, into ancient Greece, for one. In this prolonged continuity we may discern the reflection of a basic need in human beings' religiosity, and this kind of spiritual communion with the supernatural enhances techniques for the human mind to transcend into altered states of consciousness. The pre–Greek cults and the newly introduced cults of Indo-European origin fused to form the mosaic of religious life typical of the ancient Greeks. This mosaic has been studied so extensively, and yet, has remained so little understood.

The organization of processions that included rituals of various kinds lay in the hands of the priesthood. The training of priests and priestesses in antiquity was quite different from modern practices. In fact, education in religious affairs was much less bureaucratic or formalized than the path of modern priesthood and much more oriented at the transmittance of social knowledge from the community to the candidate for priesthood, to meet the needs of the community.

> A more useful lens through which to understand Greek cult service is that of the collective groups that defined communality within the polis, groups based on family, gender, age class, and marital status. Social rituals defined communality as well, through activities such as poetic recitations, sacrificial meals, and symposia [Connelly 2007: 28].

Among the most visible manifestations of cult life in the Greek city-state were ritual processions. This was a major event—known in Greek by the name *thiasos,* a term of pre–Greek origin (Hofmann 1966: 115)—with communal and also political implications. Apparently, the institution of the ritual procession and its traditional form were inherited from the pre–Greek population. The organization of processions was the responsibility of the cult personnel and the *thiasoi* were of great significance as symbols of sustained community life, and many famous representatives of Greek society participated.

> The relationships of cult, divinities, and sanctuaries were articulated through the directions in which processions traversed the cityscape. This movement could be centripetal, marching from the periphery to civic and religious center, or centrifugal, departing from city center and advancing toward places outside of it. Processions provided highly visible, dramatic displays in which leaders and participants understood their roles. Their movements reflected the structures and values of the community [Connelly 2007: 167].

In this context, an ethnographic comparison with derivational cultures of the Danube civilization may help perceive the significance of communal festivities in the annual life cycle of Old European communities. Since the times of the Mycenaeans the significance of festivities and their formal performances is documented. Greek ethnicity emerged only a few hundred years after the decline of Old European civilization, and this enhances the probability that various cults of the ancient population were adopted by the early Greeks together with the associated customs. Communal festivities, accompanied by processions, played a central role for celebrating the spirit of community life in the Greek cities. Those processions were led by female protagonists, by priestesses, respected members of their community.

> It was the priestess's responsibility to carry the holy things in sacred processions, which gave visibility, not just to the instruments of worship, but also to the priestess herself.... Women who led these processions marched in the spotlight that underscored their agency and highlighted their symbolic capital within the larger group [Connelly 2007: 167].

The institution of processions in the ritual life of the Greeks was no novelty. Religious processions are well known from the imagery of the ancient Aegean cultures, the offspring of the Danube civilization: Cycladic culture and Minoan civilization of ancient Crete (Marinatos 1987: 52*ff*, Bintliff 2012: 132*ff*).

Despite the abundant archaeological and textual evidence that gives proof of the existence of processions in ancient Greek society, with religious and, at the same time, communal significance, we modern observers cannot reconstruct any of the festivities with accuracy. This paradoxical situation has in part to do with the associated mysteries, initiation rites, that formed part of the performance but whose contents was never totally disclosed to the non-initiated. And yet, there is the basic knowledge that such processions once existed which appealed to a timeless anthropocentric need. With respect to the mindset of those who participated in antique processions the following pronouncement has been made:

> Being ignorant of the ritual and unable to reproduce it, we cannot recreate this experience, but we may acknowledge that it was there. There was a chance to "join the *thiasos* with one's soul," *thiaseuesthai psychan,* and this meant happiness [Burkert 1987: 114].

This experience that was there but cannot be substantiated was the amazing event of *sympatheia,* a constituent of the Greeks' cultural memory but no Greek invention. The *sympatheia*—as a manifestation of social and spiritual balance in community life—was a resounding echo of the experiences of previous generations and, ultimately, a reflection of the Old European spirit.

The prominence of women in ritual activities is emphasized especially in those festivities which were known by the Greeks themselves for their extraordinary antiquity. An illustrative example of a tradition that dates back to pre–Greek times are the festivities in honor of the Grain-Mother Demeter (Clinton 1993). The procession from Athens to Demeter's main sanctuary at Eleusis was led by a priestess along the *hieros dromos* ("the holy road"). Significantly, the custom to perform this procession has persisted up to the present, and it is organized nowadays to honor the Virgin Mary in the same role as Demeter in antiquity, as the one who blesses the fruits of labor in the fields, the bread.

A central part of Demeter's festivities were the Thesmophoria, the offering of piglets in special offering pits (called with a pre–Greek term, *megara*). This was a ritual activity in which only married women were entitled to participate. The worshipers gathered after the offering ceremony, sat together at the foot of the sacred hill—in Athens this was the Pnyx (see Chapter 7)—and told mythical stories of Demeter and her daughter Persephone. The Thesmophoria were a festival with exclusive significance for women, as organizers, participants and narrators of women's agenda.

> The most widely celebrated of the occasions that allowed women a temporary respite from the routines of the *oikos* was the annual festival of Demeter, the Thesmophoria. This festival recalled the motherhood of Demeter and the loss of her daughter Persephone through rape/marriage to Hades. During the celebrations, which lasted from three to ten days depending on the *polis,* married women left their homes and camped out together in a *polis* of women, while the operations of the male *polis* came to a halt. The women mourned Demeter's loss of her daughter, and, in most cities, they rejoiced in the festival of Beautiful Birth. The role reversal implicit in the creation of a *polis* of women, and the physical escape from the demands of the *oikos,* provided a safety valve for the tensions caused by the restrictions of daily life, while reinforcing community norms of marriage and childbearing. A somewhat similar acculturating role is played in modern Greece by women's reverence for the Panayia (Mother of God), who, like Demeter, embodies the ideal values of motherhood in a woman's life [Demand 1994: 24].

Processions and rituals were integrated in the festive calendar of the Greeks, which was multifaceted, and many local festivities were celebrated throughout the year. The distribution of festive events according to the months of the year may cause some confusion from the standpoint of the modern observer because the beginning of the year was set at different points of time. There was always a right time for every festival. The idea of the right point of time of the year was called *kairos* (a borrowing from the substrate language) in ancient Greek. The concept "year as vegetation cycle" was also termed with a pre–Greek expression, this being *lukabas*.

A proper calendar becomes available only once an attempt is made to connect the lunar year with the solar year, as was the case in various places in Greece in the young city-states of the seventh century.... They all had a year consisting of twelve lunar months, and most of them, for instance Athens and Delphi, had the year begin at midsummer, ideally from the first new moon after solstice. In Boeotia, on the other hand, the new year was counted from the first new moon after the winter solstice, whereas Miletos and her colonies seem to have used spring equinox as the dividing-line [Isager and Skydsgaard 1995: 165].

There was no festive event without occasions to address the gods, performing rituals, sending prayers and carrying out animal sacrifices. In the festive calendar, divinities of pre–Greek descent such as Demeter, Dionysos and Athena were celebrated alongside gods of Indo-European origin such as Zeus, Apollo and others. "While all Greek *poleis* performed public rituals, the Athenians of the classical era were renowned for their extraordinarily

Grain	Vine	Olive	Varia	Signs			Demeter (Kore)	Dionysos	Zeus (Hera)	Athene	Apollo	Artemis	Other gods
			*Harvest of figs	Sirius rising	July	Hekatombaion				Synoikia Panathenaia	Hekatombaia		Kronia
					August	Metageitnion					Metageitnia		Herakleia
	Vintage		Woodcutting	Arcturus rising	September	Boedromion	Eleusinian Mysteries				Niketeria Boedromia	Artemis Agrotera	Genesia Demokratia
Ploughing Sowing	*Harvest and pruning begins			Pleiades setting	October	Pyanopsion	Proërosia Thesmophoria	Oschophoria	Proërosia Apatouria	Apatouria Chalkeia	Pyanopsia		Theseia
				Orion setting	November	Maimakterion			Pompaia				
(Late ploughing)				Solstice	December	Posideon	Haloa	Rural Dionysia					Posidea
					January	Gamelion		Lenaia	Gamelia				
Ploughing of fallow field	Pruning finished Opening of jars			Arcturus rising at dusk	February	Anthesterion	Chloaia Lesser Mysteries	Anthesteria	Diasia				
			*Sheep to the mountains		March	Elaphebolion		City Dionysia			Elaphebolia	Elaphebolia	Asklepieia
					April	Mounychion			Olympieia	Olympieia	Delphinia	Delphinia Mounychia	Bendideia
Harvest	Digging finished			Pleiades rising	May	Thargelion				Kallyntheria Plyntheria	Thargelia	Thargelia	
Threshing Ploughing of fallow field				Solstice Orion rising	June	Skirophorion			Dipolieia Diisoteria	Arrephoria			
					July		Skira						

* Not mentioned by Hesiod.

The festive calendar in Attica (Athenian city-state). (originally published in *Ancient Greek agriculture: An introduction* by Signe Isager and Jens Erik Skydsgaard. London & New York: Routledge, 1995. Reproduced with permission).

dense ritual calendar. Athens was not only recognized in classical antiquity as a highly successful democratic community, but also as an intensely *festive* community" (Ober 2008: 194).

> One of the most important such festivals was the Panathenaia, the annual festival in honor of Athena's birthday or in commemoration of the Gigantomachy [victory over the titans], when Athenians, both citizens and *metics* (resident aliens) paraded from beyond the Dipylon gate, through the gate and into the city walls, across the Athenian Agora, up the Akropolis, and to the altar and Temple of Athena on the summit in which the ancient olive wood *xoanon* (iconic statue) of Athena was housed [...]. Sacrifices and invocations were made to the goddess, and every fourth year during a more elaborate version of this festival, the Greater Panathenaia, a new peplos [garment] was presented to the cult image, and athletic and musical contests took place [Barringer 2008: 61*f*].

On the occasion of the Panathenaia, a multitude of competitions were organized of which the athletic contests were the most dramatic. These contests were very attractive, and not only because the victors could expect to be honored by a great crowd of citizens. Winning an athletic contest at this festival was a factor of economic proportions because "individual prizes at the Panathenaea were of such a scale that even a boy winner in the wrestling, say, would earn the equivalent of eight or nine months' wages for a skilled worker—enough to pay for the training to launch a successful athletic career" (Golden 1998: 165).

The festive events were set according to the seasons of the agricultural cycle. The overall significance of the vegetation cycle, which had been observed already by the native European agriculturalists, was highlighted by many Greek writers, by Plato for one:

What I allude to is this—the arranging of days into monthly periods, and of months into a year, in each instance, so that the seasons, with their respective sacrifices and feasts, may each be assigned its due position by being held as nature dictates, and that thus they may create fresh liveliness and alertness in the State, and may pay their due honours to the gods, and may render the citizens more intelligent about these matters (Plato, *Laws* 809d).

Ritual terminology of pre–Greek origin in ancient Greek:

> *alisgeo* "to pollute (ritual term)"
> *alsos* "sacred grove"
> *aozos* "servant (of a god)"
> *balletys* festival in Eleusis during which stones were thrown
> *bretas* "wooden image of a god"
> *brualizon* "breaking (into Bacchic frenzy with a certain movement)"
> *brykos* "herald; locust" (derivation *brykainai* "priestesses [Dorian]")
> Daeira / Daira name of a chthonic goddess in Attica to whom a pregnant sheep was sacrificed
> *dithyrambos* name of a song at the festival for Dionysus
> *distropon* "vase for libation"
> *elegos* "mourning song (accompanied by flute)"
> *essen* name of the priests (-esses) of Artemis in Ephesus
> *eschara* "sacrificial hearth"
> *(h)eorte* "feast, religious festival"
> *ialemos* "lament, dirge"
> *ithymbos* "a Bacchic song with dance," "one who performs this dance"

Kabarnoi name of the priests of Demeter on Paros
kalaboutoi "songs sung of Artemis in her sanctuary"
karkadon "price paid to Charon by the dead for their passage"
kteras "gift," *kterea* "gifts for the dead, sacrifice"
konos "fruit of the pine, cone"; *kones* "stave of the Bacchantes"
laigmata "seeds, holy firstlings," "(ritual) cakes" (derivation *laitma* "sacrifice")
leitor "priest"
megaron "inner space of a temple"; *megara* "sacrificial pits into which piglets were thrown (as part of the Thesmophoria ritual)"
moriai name of holy olives in Athens (Athena Moria as protectress of olive cultivation)
morotton "wickerwork made of bark with which people used to beat each other during the Demetria"
momos / momar "stain of a sacrificial animal"
naos / nauos / neos / naios / neios "sanctuary"
nektar / nektaros "nectar," "drink of the gods"
orgia "secret religious rituals," "sacred secret services"
oulai / olai / oloai "(unground) barley corns, roasted and sprinkled between the horns of the sacrificial animal"
oulos "song to worship Demeter" (original meaning: "sheaf of corn")
pelanos "sacrificial cake (liquid flour dough, flour pulp, honey and oil"
sekos / sakos "enclosed sacred space"
sphazo "to slaughter (by cutting the throat), sacrifice"
tenella "hail," ritual exclamation from the cult of Demeter in Paros (Archilochos)
thiasos "Bacchic revel; religious guild; procession"
threnos "dirge, lament, lamentation"
threskeuo "to perform or observe religious customs"
thriambos "hymn sung at festivals for Dionysus"
thyrsos "wand (wreathed in ivy and vine-leaves with a pine-cone at the top)"
thysthla "the sacred implements of Bacchic orgies," "sacrifice"
tomouroi "interpreters (of the oracle), priests, augurs, officials (of a temple)," designation of the priests of Zeus in Dodona (cf. name of the mountain Tomaros/Tmaros)
trittys / triptys / triktys "sacrifice of three animals"

Festivities, ritual activities, processions:

chonnoi Cretan festival (Gortyn)
komos "revel, merrymaking of youths," "Dionysiac festive procession and festive songs; festival"
oschophoria name of an Athenian festive day (held in September/October)
stenia festival in Athens before the Thesmophoria where women uttered curses and insults

6

Pre-Greek Origins of the Arts
*The Muses and Their Doings
from Old Europe to Classical Antiquity*

The ancient Greeks are known for their social events, for banquets (*symposia*) and sportive competitions, for public sacrifices (*thymai*) and ritual processions (*thiasoi*). They are also known for their eagerness in dancing, playing music and in theatrical performances. Such skills were developed by the Greeks and became ever more sophisticated over time. But the Greeks did not invent such activities. Thus, they were not the first people in Greece to perform dances, music or theater plays. The Indo-European migrants who settled down in Hellas brought with them their own repertory of music and dance but they eagerly absorbed the artistic performances of the natives and created a cultural mix of both traditions.

The Greeks did not handle abstract concepts in ways we modern people are accustomed to do. Abstractness was expressed by associating the meaning of an abstract idea to a mythical being. For example, memory is an abstract concept that was personified by the Greeks as a goddess, Mnemosyne. Victory was personified as Nike, peace as Eirene, customary law as Themis. In concord with this principle of personification of abstract concepts, major mental activities were personified. The figures that the mythopoetic mindset created were the muses (*mousai*). It is widely believed that this word is derived from an Indo-European stem *men* "think." However, the vocalism cannot be explained according to regular sound changes in the history of the Greek language.

Recent investigations speak in favor of a pre–Greek source for the concept and sound structure of *mousa* whose original meaning points to poetry and singing, rather than thinking and memorizing (Beekes 2010: 972). According to Greek myth the muses inhabited the Parnassus, a mountain range with a high peak of over 2,400 meters in central Greece. The name of this mountain, home of the muses, is pre–Greek as is the name of its mythical residents. The Parnassus provides water for the sacred spring Kastalia, dedicated to the muses. On its slope is located the ancient sanctuary of Delphi whose roots reach back into prehistory (see Chapter 5). Pre-Greek origin for the muses and their name is conclusive with the assumption that the Greeks shared with the native Europeans a similar preference for the personification of abstract ideas.

The accounts about the muses and their patronage over mythology, science, literature and the arts give a diversified picture of their number, their emblems and association with various domains. Hesiod, in his *Theogony* (seventh century BCE), states that the number of the muses was originally three and their land of origin Boeotia, his homeland. The muses were associated with Mount Helikon in Boeotia.

In the second century CE, Pausanias gives the names and functions of the original muses as Melete ("practice" in the sense of cult practice), Mneme ("memory") and Aoide ("song" or "tune"). The muses were also worshiped at Delphi where three of them are distinguished: Nete, Mese, Hypate. The god Apollo is assigned the role as patron: Apollon Mousagetes ("Apollo Muse-leader").

At times the number of muses is given as four (Thelxinoë, Aoede, Arche, Melete) and also as seven (Neilo, Tritone, Asopo, Heptapora, Achelois, Tipoplo, Rhodia). Since the times of Hesiod and Homer, the number of the muses has been given as nine. The muses were commonly perceived as the daughters of Zeus and Mnemosyne. In the Hellenistic era, another version of their genealogy was advocated, namely by Pausanias in the second century CE who speaks of two generations of muses. The older generation of muses would have Uranus and Gaia as parents. This would give them a pre–Greek goddess as mother. The younger generation is associated with Zeus and Mnemosyne.

In the tradition of categorizing the muses, "there are two main lines of interpretation: one that goes back to the classics (e.g., Ausonius), identifying individual Muses with particular poetic modes, and a second, beginning with Fulgentius (Mythologies: 1.15), which identifies each Muse with a particular stage of learning" (Brumble 1998: 226).

The muses were assigned their special domains and they were given emblems as attributes (Brumble 1998: 226–230):

Calliope (epic poetry; writing tablet);
Ausonius (*Appendix to Ausonius: 3*) "Calliope commits heroic songs to writing."
Clio (history; scroll);
Ausonius: "Clio, singing of famous deeds, restores times past to life."
Erato (love poetry; cithara and sometimes also a crown of roses);
Ausonius: "Erato bearing the plectrum harmonizes foot, song, and voice in the dance."
Euterpe (song, elegies; aulos);
Ausonius: "Euterpe's breath fills the sweet-voiced flutes."
Melpomene (tragedy; tragic mask);
Ausonius: "Melpomene cries aloud with the echoing voice of gloomy tragedy."
Polyhymnia (hymns; veil);
Ausonius: "Polyhymnia expresses all things with her hands and speaks by gesture" (referring to her as the Muse of rhetoric).
Terpsichore (choral dance; lyre);
Ausonius: "Terpsichore with her lyre stirs, swells, and governs the emotions."
Thalia (comedy; comic mask);
Ausonius: "Thalia rejoices in the loose speech of comedy."
Urania (astronomy; globe and pair of compasses);
Ausonius: "Urania examines the motions of the heaven and stars."

The muses were perceived as the patrons of historiography. The editors from Alexandria who edited Herodotus' monumental work *Histories* divided the texts into nine books, each named after one of the muses.

In their artistic skills, the muses remained unrivaled among human beings. Wandering poets who offered their services to entertain the inhabitants of the various city-states presented themselves as "servants of the muses," not their equals: "by calling himself *Mousaon therapon* ('servant of the Muses') the anonymous singer not only blended himself into the poetic past, but activates a deeply traditional set of associations through which poets are equated with cult heroes" (Martin 2009: 86). There is an indicator for the ancient tradition of wandering poets, and this is the use of a pre–Greek term (i.e., *therapon*) for "servant." The only singer who dared challenge the muses in a musical competition and who strove for surpassing the muses' talents, Thamyris the Thracian, was punished for being presumptuous and blinded (Wilson 2009: 55*ff*).

And yet, there was this one exception, among human beings, who equaled the muses in their skills and that was the lyric poetess Sappho from the island of Lesbos (ca. 630–570 BCE). The original form of her name, Psappho, points to non–Greek descent, and it was simplified to Sappho. Some two hundred years after her death she was eternalized by Plato who, in one of his epigrams, stated: "Some say that there are nine Muses ... but how careless, look again ... Sappho of Lesbos is the tenth." As the "mortal Muse" Sappho was hailed by Antipater of Sidon (ca. 100 BCE). Sappho's lyrical work has come down to us only in later copies. Her original poetry was oral and first recorded in writing more than a hundred years after her death. Until the first century BCE copies of Sappho's poetry circulated in the Hellenistic world. The Roman poets Horace and Catullus knew her work from such copies.

> But fashions change, and technologies change too. Gradually it became the custom to cite the language of Athens, Attic, as the true classical Greek, and Sappho's Aeolic dialect was considered provincial. Then, when the book trade improved its materials and switched from papyrus rolls to the more durable parchment codex, it seems that scribes and their employers thought Sappho an arcane taste, not worth the labour of retranscription. Gradually all her Nine Books disappeared [Reynolds 2000: 18].

When, during the Renaissance, interest in Sappho's poetry was once again revitalized, only fragments of her work had remained. Despite the fragmentized state of Sappho's original work she has become an icon for high appreciation among female poets. In modern history, the title of "tenth muse" has been attributed to some women by French critics: Marie Lejars de Gournay (1566–1645), Antoinette Deshoulières (1633–1694), Madeleine de Scudéry (1607–1701) and Delphine Gay (1804–1855). In the short list of poets honored with the title of "tenth muse," one finds two women from the Americas. One is Anne Bradstreet (from New England) whose poems were published in London in 1650, the other Sor Juana Inés de la Cruz (Sister Joan Agnes of the Cross), a self-taught poet of the Baroque school who lived in Mexico, in the seventeenth century. Sor Juana features on a Mexican banknote, the 200 pesos bill.

The muses have never lost their attractiveness. Innumerable sculptures and paintings were created in the classical and Hellenistic periods. The popularity which the muses enjoyed among the Greeks was perhaps toppled by the Romans who readily adopted these figures. The muses and their emblems experienced a golden age in Renaissance and Neoclassical art.

In the nomenclature of various domains of the Greek arts the pre–Greek origins are reflected and preserved. In the ways dance and music (instrumental and vocal) were performed one can identify much older traditions that testify to the persistence of the Old European cultural heritage. This heritage is encapsulated in the cultural vocabulary of our modern languages, manifested in numerous derivations from the key term "muse"; e.g., music, museum (the original meaning of Greek *mouzeion* was "place where the muses are celebrated"), to amuse, amusement, to muse (upon).

The Art of Figurine-Making

The sculpting of small-size statuettes is among the oldest skills of human beings. The oldest figurine found so far dates to the Aurignacian era and its age is given as between 35,000 and 40,000 years BP (before present). This female figurine, found in the cave of Hohle Fels in Southwest Germany, has been called the "Swabian Eve" (Conard et al. 2009: 270).

In the pre-ceramic era, figurines were made of organic material (i.e., bone, wood) or of stone (i.e., marble, alabaster, sandstone). In the long record of figurine production in Eurasia we can make the surprising observation of the presence of statuettes made of low-temperature-fired clay since the Upper Paleolithic.

> We can trace them [ceramic female statuettes and animal figurines] from Central Europe across the Russian Plain to Southern Siberia and back to the Levant and Northern Africa. They are well embedded in Eurasian hunter-gatherer social contexts, and chronologically clustered within a time span from 26 000 to 10 000 years BP [Budja 2005: 61].

Clay dominates figurine-making during the advanced Neolithic and the Copper Age. During the era of metal-working, figurines are also made of metal, for instance of gold (Anthony 2009b: 162).

As for the gender marking of human figurines the abundance of female statuettes testifies to the prominence of the feminine sex. Male figurines are the exception and their number is fairly limited. Female figurines are closely associated with the space where female activities are carried out. Figurines are found next to the baking oven (either indoors or outdoors) and beside the hearth which is the focus of practical as well as ritual activities in the household. The hearth as a place for combined practical/ritual activities has a long history, dating back to Paleolithic times. Continuity is evidenced for the Mesolithic at Lepenski Vir (Bonsall 2008: 255*f*) and well documented for Old Europe in Gimbutas' works. The custom of keeping figurines, as ritual items, near the hearth points at continuity from earlier stages of cultural evolution although the location of the hearth inside a permanently occupied building is an innovation of sedentary life in Neolithic communities.

The abundance of figurines and their location at places of major female activities in the homestead (indoors as well as outdoors) is evidence for the significance of domestic rituals throughout all regions of the Danube civilization and throughout all periods of its existence. Gimbutas identified figurines as media in cult practices relating to the reverence of ancestors, and the validity of this assessment has been reconfirmed in recent pronouncements where it is stated that "the rituals represented by female figurines seem to have emphasized the dominant role of women inside the house, and perhaps were connected with ancestor cults centered on their mothers and aunts" (Anthony 2009a: 45).

Figurines are among the prominent markers of Old Europe. At some places one can observe an astounding continuity in figurine production and use, spanning periods of several thousand years. The association of figurines with the religious sphere is widely accepted. Modern scholarship has confirmed the validity of Gimbutas' fundamental insights about the significance of figurines, and there seems to be consensus among scholars that "many everyday household practices, such as sleeping, food storage, grinding, and cooking, were embedded in domestic ritual, as indicated by the figurines often deposited nearby each practice" (Chapman 2009: 82).

Also other findings from Gimbutas' works enjoy a reappraisal among modern scholars, for instance, her assessment of the function of figurines for ritual life.

> One aspect of Gimbutas' analysis that probably does reflect Old European reality is her recognition that a great many different varieties and kinds of ritual behavior and religious symbolism are represented in the figurines of Old Europe [Anthony 2009a: 45].

The layout of houses in Neolithic southeastern Europe with rooms in a linear sequence of control from outer living space to inner space underscores the prominence of women in the homesteads and as crystallizing foci of lineages (Hodder 1992: 66*f*). In this light, the role of figurines for ritual behavior is enhanced.

Scenes of human beings engaged in group activities are known from the assemblages of ritual artifacts and imagery in Old European sanctuaries, at Ovcharovo in Bulgaria, Scânteia, Isaiia and other places in Romania, but the exact role of the anthropomorphic figures in the scenes remains ambiguous. As for the particular assemblage from Ovcharovo, four different identifications may be suggested:

- the figures are worshipers performing rituals;
- the figures are priestesses performing rituals in front of a crowd of worshipers

(not seen in the assemblages);

- the figures are visualized spirits of revered ancestresses who act in the role of worshipers performing rituals, thus communing with the living;
- the figures are epiphanies of the goddess, a visual metaphor of the Principle of Life and Regeneration.

The assemblage of figurines and ritual artifacts from Ovcharovo (Bulgaria); Karanovo culture, fifth millennium BCE (originally published in *The language of the goddess: Unearthing the hidden symbols of Western civilization* by Marija Gimbutas. San Francisco: Harper & Row, 1989. Used with permission of the Institute of Archaeomythology).

The ritual character of the assemblages is emphasized by enigmatic proportions of certain categories of figurines and artifacts that form part of the cult complexes. There are striking similarities between the assemblages at Isaiia and Poduri (both in eastern Romania), concerning the number of objects and their attributes. This may point at an awareness of magical conceptualizations, with manifestations in ritual activities and/or festivities. At Isaiia and at Poduri, the assemblages illustrate the following identical conventions:

> 21 statuettes [...], 13 chairs [...], 15 decorated statuettes, 4 statuettes with stitches on legs [...] etc. The conclusion is that there was a magic of numbers in Precucuteni culture, with unitary forms of expression, as part of a unitary religious system [Ursulescu and Tencariu 2006: 136].

Some scenes in works of Old European art allow for an interpretation relating to communal festivities, for example, human figures in boats. Such assemblages seem to point at some kind of festive gathering. The river trade played an important role in Old European economy (see Haarmann 2011a, 81*ff* for a documentation), and water as the elixir of life formed an integral part of the religious symbolism (Gimbutas 1991: 246, 292, etc.). It may be conjectured that the Old Europeans knew communal festivities relating to the rivers and the sea (boat processions?); (see Chapter 4 for ship-building and maritime trade).

The connection of figurine-making with Greece is well documented. As in other regions of Old Europe, in Greece, too, there was continuity in figurine production from the Paleolithic onward through the Neolithic.

> Another mystery of the Greek Neolithic is the meaning of the immense variety of figurines in clay and stone that have tantalized, amazed, and puzzled a generation of archaeologists.... White marble, plain clay, and clay painted with red or brown abstract designs are the principal media used in the manufacture of figurines. The pure abstraction of the crosslike or violin-shaped marble figures changes in time to the startling realism of heads with detailed and recognizable features, painted red, and resembling the face of a newborn child [Runnels and Murray 2001: 58*f*].

The cultural chronology at Karanovo in eastern Bulgaria illustrates the continuous significance of figurines in community life over some 3500 years, from the Early Neolithic (ca. 6500 BCE) to the Early Bronze Age (ca. 3000 BCE). This is an enormous span of experienced time. Figurines may have been persistently attractive because they appeal to all our human senses, ranging from their visible corporeality to the most sophisticated metaphorical meaning that might be evoked in the perceptive mind (Haarmann 2009: 85*ff*).

There is something of a mystery about some elementary contours of figurines which reveal a timeless aesthetic appeal. The variety of styles and forms of prehistoric figurines in the European-Asian convergence zone—encompassing the artistic traditions in Neolithic Southeast Europe and Anatolia—is astounding. And yet, it would be futile to speculate which aesthetic features caused certain forms and styles to be more popular and widespread than others. An explanation for the seemingly coincidental persistence of certain forms may be sought in the fact that the aesthetic appeal forms part of a multi-dimensional network of features which characterize a figurine. The aesthetic features, though, may dominate the impression that figurines make on the beholder, once all information about their original role and function is lost.

The persistence of figurine production throughout the Neolithic and Copper Ages is phenomenal. When the Indo-European pastoralists began to move south they set in motion sociopolitical changes among the indigenous population. Under the impression of a reshuffling of customs certain traditions declined in the northern area and shifted to the south.

This was the case with figurine-making, which had been of constant significance for people of Old Europe during the Neolithic and Copper Ages. Around 3000 BCE, a disrupture of this tradition can be observed in the archaeological record because no more figurines were produced in the northern region. And yet, figurine-making was not abandoned in the south where figurines continued to be produced even on the mainland, for example at Lerna on the east coast of the Peloponnese, during the Helladic period (third millennium BCE). The crafting of figurines continued in the ancient Aegean cultures (i.e., in the Cyclades and in Minoan Crete). The Greeks became familiar with figurine-making in Hellas and adopted key terms for the crafting of these artifacts from the substrate language.

> [Figurines] were regularly produced throughout the Bronze Age in the Aegean, continuing an extant tradition from the Neolithic period [...]. While Cycladic and Minoan products develop continuously, the mainland tradition of female figurines with exaggerated body features dies out in the Early Bronze Age [...]. The quantity of figurines present in the archaeological record is indicative of their use. Fewer than 2,000 EC [Early Cycladic] figurines are known, produced over some 600–700 years in the third millennium BC. In contrast, at least 4,500 have been uncovered at a single site, Mycenae, dating between 1400–1100 BC [Tzonou-Herbst 2010: 211].

Among the materials from which figurines were made, the following have to be mentioned: clay, stone (marble, sea pebble), bone, ivory, metal, faïence, shell. There seems to have been also traditions to craft figurines in materials that are less durable than ceramics or stone, and these traditions persisted in the mainland settlements. These perishable materials that are recorded in ancient Greek sources are wood and wax. The oldest statue (*xoanon*) of Athena that is mentioned in the sources is made of wood. One finds references to the origins of wooden statues and that these were manufactured by the Pelasgians. In his account of southern Greece, Pausanias (second century CE) mentions Therai in the Peloponnese, the site of a sanctuary (i.e., Eleusinium) dedicated to Demeter: "Spartans say that here Heracles was hidden by Asclepius while being healed of the wounds. In this sanctuary there is also a wooden image of Orpheus, which is, they say, a piece of work of the Pelasgians" (Pausanias, *Description of Greece,* 3.20.6).

Like wood, wax decays in the course of time, and there is no archaeological evidence of figurines crafted in this particular material from the Bronze Age. And yet, one finds traces of this tradition in the oldest layer of pre–Greek borrowings in the vocabulary of ancient Greek. Though only preserved in a fragmented form a terminology of specialized technical terms can be retrieved from the ancient written sources that relate to the crafting of figurines with beeswax (see the entries for the following terms in Beekes 2010):

> *dagys* "puppet (of wax)"
> *kanabos / kinnabos* "wooden framework around which artists molded wax or clay; block figure"
> *keros* "wax"
> *koroplathos* "one who forms female figures; doll modeler"
> *plaggon* "wax figurine; doll"

The survival, in Greek antiquity, of a fragmented terminology of pre–Greek origin relating to the production of wax figurines clearly points to a long-standing tradition of figurine-making, dating from Old Europe and persisting through the Bronze Age and ancient Greece. The tradition continues throughout Greek antiquity, during times when other materials for figurine crafting were re-introduced (i.e., stone, terracotta, metal). Longevity of figurines made of wax extends into the early Middle Ages. According to legend, St. Luke is credited with having created an image of the Virgin Mary with her child (Vreffokratousa) with wax, serving as an icon for the Christian community in Jerusalem. This image was brought to the island of Lesbos by the monk Agathona of Ephesus at the beginning of the ninth century CE. Still in the Mycenaean era, imagery is imbued with the Old European spirit.

Despite the persistence of the craft itself and its terminology a fundamental change in style and form occurred during the archaic period. In the course of the seventh century BCE,

The type of figurine with raised arms: (a) Old European figurine (early fifth millennium BCE) (originally published in *The civilization of the goddess* by Marija Gimbutas. San Francisco: HarperSanFrancisco, 1991. Used with permission of the Institute of Archaeomythology); (b) Mycenaean-Greek figurine (twelfth century BCE) (originally published in *The Mycenaean world: Five centuries of early Greek culture* by Katie Demakopoulou. Athens: Ministry of Culture, 1988).

figurines assume a different aesthetic appeal, one that is characterized by imitative naturalism rather than by abstract stylization. Seemingly, the Old European spirit was altogether abandoned and never again resurfaced. The aesthetic sense of classical Greek antiquity came to dominate figurative art, first of the Roman tradition and, later, it developed into the canon of European art that is known from art history (Hersey 1996).

A specific feature in the mosaic of continuity is the custom of inscribing figurines. Inscribed figurines have been found at many sites throughout the area of the Danube civilization, for which reason the conclusion can be drawn that the custom of decorating and inscribing such objects was widespread (Haarmann 2011b: 152*ff*). Even though the popularity of figurines declined, as an expression of older worship, in cultural memory, the reminiscence persisted among the pre–Indo-European population in the Aegean. Evident traces of the old custom survived in ancient Crete, where inscribed figurines have been excavated.

The idea of dedicatory inscriptions may be considered universal in all societies that possess writing. Although basically true, the association of such inscriptions with specific objects and functions has to be regarded as culturally specific. This is true for writing on figurines and statuettes. The Old European tradition persists in the Aegean, and even beyond the period of Minoan-Mycenaean cultural supremacy. In classical Greece, the custom of inscribing human sculptures re-emerges and continues throughout Greek antiquity. The Aegean-Greek tradition of a symbiosis of figural art and decorative writing finds a reflection in Etruscan art and literacy as well (see Haarmann 1995: 150*ff* for an outline).

The symbiotic interaction between figurative art and writing, with its long-standing tradition from the Neolithic into the classical era, can be observed also in other domains of the arts and crafts, for instance, in the production of painted pottery bearing inscriptions. Here, the functions and the communicative input of writing are as varified as in the context of inscribed figurines.

Writing on pottery is revealed ... to have been, from its very inception, very variously

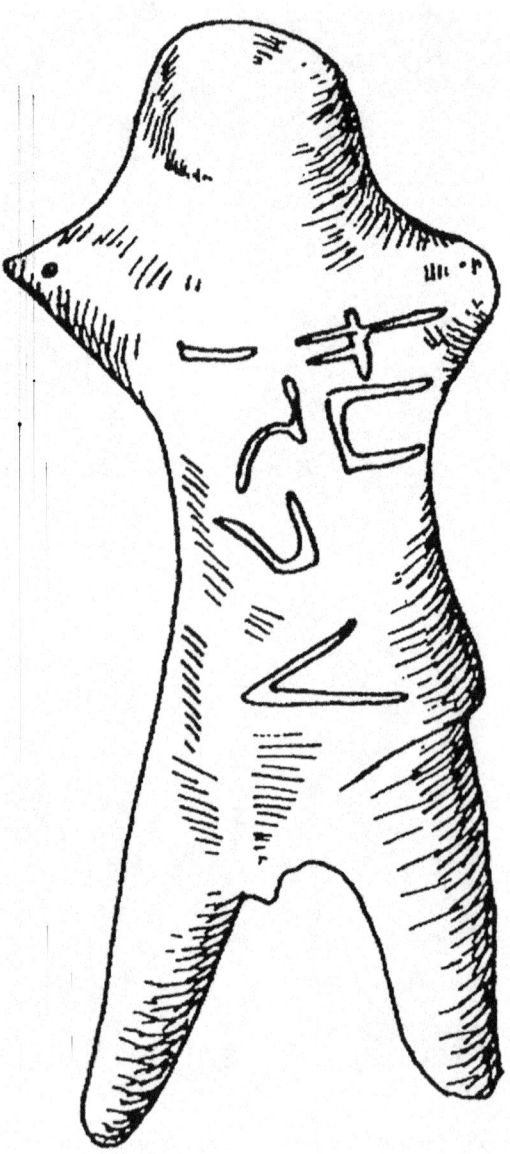

An figurine from Tylissos, inscribed in the Minoan script Linear A (author's collection).

used. It has also been revealed to have been a performance act. Writing does things on a pot, it engages with the viewer as the viewer uses the pot. The appearance of the writing was always important, and the effect of the writing on the user of the pot calculated. Inscriptions on stone stand there while viewers pass by, and their performative role is generally restricted. Writing on pots is encountered as the pot is used, and so the engagement with the viewer occurs in social contexts that are themselves closely related to, and even determined by, the shape and function of the individual pot [Osborne and Pappas 2007: 154*f*].

What inscribed figurines and pottery have in common is the interactive potential that unfolds between the artifact and its user. The meanings expressed in writing are strengthened by the associated image and the material objects engage in interaction with the human agents in their living space.

Dance

Certain customs are widespread and can be found in any culture, since oldest times. Dance is one such ingredient of social life. The native Europeans had their dances as had the immigrating Indo-Europeans. It is noteworthy that the Greeks adopted a certain type of dance that has retained its popularity, throughout the ages, from the Neolithic through our time, and this is the round dance which is known by a name adopted from the substrate language. The fact that the name for the round dance appears in variations in all the modern languages of southeastern Europe points at the spread of this tradition over the whole area where the Danube civilization once flourished. In Greek the round dance with its Neolithic origins is known as choros, in Serbian as hora, etc. Most probably, the round dance became known to the ancestors of the Greeks already at an early date, and the term choros dates to the formative period of the Greek language.

The earliest archaeological evi-

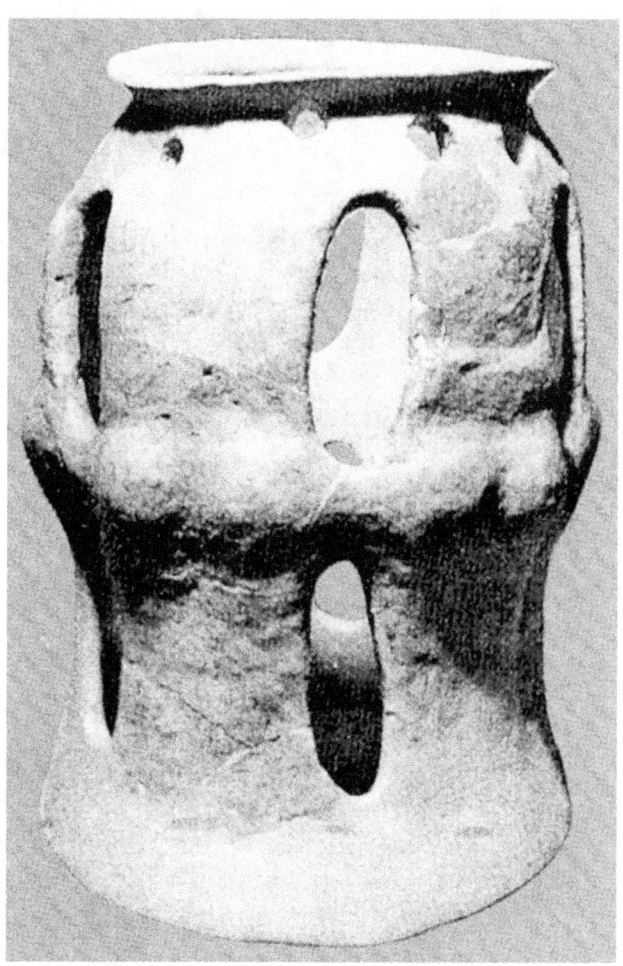

Above and following page: Dancing women in the cultures of southeastern Europe (fifth millennium BCE to the present): (a) Dancing women as constituents of a hora vase from Frumușica (Romania); Cucuteni culture, ca. 4500 BCE (originally published in *The language of the goddess: Unearthing the hidden symbols of Western civilization* by Marija Gimbutas. San Francisco: Harper & Row, 1989. Used with permission of the Institute of Archaeomythology); (b) Bronze sculpture depicting naked women dancing in a circle from Olympia (courtesy of Michalis Toubis Editions); (c) The motif of women in historical costumes dancing in a circle on a Greek 0.45 Euro stamp.

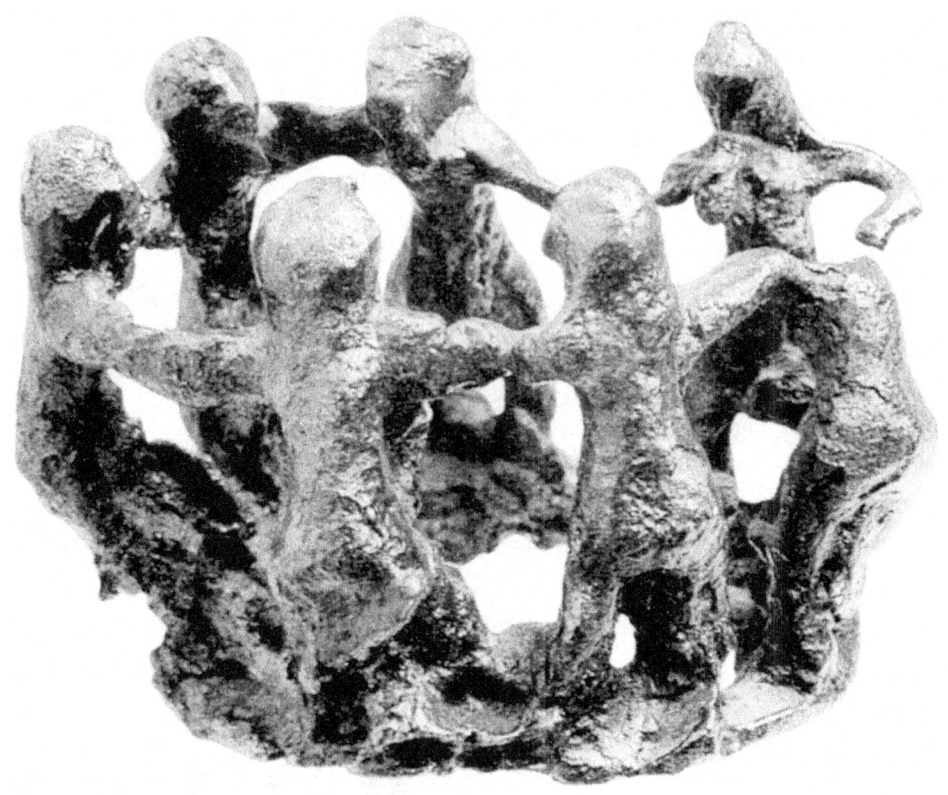

dence for dance in southeastern Europe dates to the fifth millennium BCE. Dancing women are depicted in different media, for instance, performing the ring dance as in sculptured hora vases or painted on ceramics. As part of the cultural traditions of local inhabitants in southeastern Europe the ring dance was transmitted from the Neolithic throughout the Copper and Bronze Ages into classical antiquity. One can find astounding parallelisms in the imagery, from different periods, where dancing persons are depicted. The Neolithic motif of women dancing in a circle and holding one another by the shoulders is repeated in the Bronze sculpture of a group of naked females, dating to the Geometric period and found at Olympia.

In antiquity, the round dance assumed paramount significance for Greek social life. The value of this dance for communal cohesion in ancient Greece can hardly be overestimated. Recall that, according to Plato, "choral dancing constituted the entirety of education" ("Laws" 672e; translation by Furley and Bremer 2001: 22).

Dancing played a central role in Greek theater and it never lost its original ritual function. In fact, the tragic chorus and its action (i.e., choral dancing) were oriented at the altar in every theater as a focal point.

> The triadic principle of circling one way around the altar, reversing the circle, and halting before the divine image seems an obvious way to structure a circular choral dance, and astral explanations might be accounted for as a later rationalization [Wiles 1997: 93*f*].

The intimate relationship of theatrical play and dance is particularly evident in tragedy which preserves ancient dance forms. It is possible to codify the movements of choral dancing in Greek tragedy from the visual evidence as presented in Greek iconography (Emmanuel 1987).

There are competing theories which of the media was of the greatest importance in a theatrical performance: language as the medium of the plot or dance as a medium of interaction. In any of the Greek tragedies, dance, song and music were equally integrated to produce a symbiotic interplay. In some of the terms that the Greeks inherited from their predecessors, the intrinsic relationship between dance and music becomes evident in their encompassing meaning (i.e., *kolabros, ithymbos, melpomai, tragodos*).

Dance and music were not only intertwined for the purpose of theatrical performance but these two forms of art symbiotically interacted also in the context of communal festivities. New insights about the interplay between vocal music and dance have been produced recently, and scholars "have demonstrated the central importance of collective song-dance performances in honour of the gods and the city, for the Greek cities' conceptions of their identities and as a major impetus for their stability (see e.g., Murray & Wilson 2004 and Kowalzig 2007a)" (Fisher 2011: 183).

In the dance-related vocabulary of ancient Greek a number of specific terms of pre–Greek origin have been integrated:

brualizon "breaking (into Bacchic frenzy with a certain movement)"
choros "round dance," "dancing-place"
droite name of a dance
ithymbos "a Bacchic song with dance," "one who performs this dance"
karpaia "mimetic dance (in arms) of the Thessalians"
kolea kind of dance
kordax dance (in old comedy)

krinon name of a dance (literally "white lily")
kroupezai "wooden shoes to indicate the rhythm of a dance"
lombros name of an "indecent" dance
melpomai "to celebrate with song and dance"
sikin(n)is "dance of the satyrs"
tragodos "singer and dancer in the tragic choir, tragic actor"

Music

Findings from modern musicology identify pentatonic music (with five notes per octave) as the oldest known form of its genre. It is widespread in historical and recent cultures of the world. In China, Mongolia and Japan, pentatonicism is of high age and has remained popular up to the present. In Europe, it is documented for folk music of the Saami in the North (Saami *yoiku* singing), for the musical traditions of the Mari, Chuvash and Tatar peoples in the Volga area of European Russia, for Hungary and for Celtic folk music. It is noteworthy that pentatonicism as postulated for the Paleolithic and Neolithic and inferred from musical instruments with only a few strings has persisted—over thousands of years—in southeastern Europe to the present (Baud-Bovy 1983).

Pentatonic music is attested for modern folk music in various parts of the Balkans, southern Albania for one. "In fact, in contemporary Albanian folk music, pentatonicism incontrovertibly remains the most distinctive characteristic of melodic construction" (Tole 2007: 130). The most typical genre of pentatonic folk music in Albania are pastoral songs: "Albanian shepherds play their traditional pastoral iso-polypjonic repertoire on *fyell* or *dyare* above a continuous iso background provided by these block poly-pentatonicisms" (Tole 2007: 216).

Pentatonicism has been identified also for folk music in northwestern Greece. Modern theory rejects any Near Eastern influence on ancient Greek music and opts instead for an indigenous origin of pentatonic music and its continuity into Greek antiquity and beyond. "The observation of recent pentatonic melodies on Greek territory led to the formulation of a new variant of the theory, according to which an anhemitonic pentatonic would stand behind the archaic 'Dorian,' opposed mainly to the diatonic Phrygian" (Hagel 2009: 436).

The tradition of oral music produced a multifaceted array of genres. Among the genres that became especially influential for the Greeks' performance culture is the dithyramb (*dithyrambos*), a genre typical of the Dionysiac festival. "Literary histories of the genre tend to plot its move from a primitive cult song to a hypersophisticated artistic spectacle watched by thousands in the theatres of Athens alongside the equally sophisticated performances of drama" (Wilson 2012: 165). What the literary histories have not recorded so far is the important fact that the term *dithyrambos* is an element of the lexical substratum, as is the genre itself.

Musical performance was often combined with the utterance of poetry or, to put it the other way round: the presentation of poetic texts was accompanied by music played on a string instrument, preferably the *lyra*. There are accounts about the performance of exceptionally skilled poets, with the skills to orchestrate singing, dancing and playing music. Among the most celebrated of those poets was Alcaeus from the island of Lesbos: "Alcaeus' description of public festival, with singing and dancing to the aulos [...] was balanced by one of lyre-playing, and that led into an account of music-making by winged creatures which are common as figures for a poet, the nightingale and the cicada" (Bowie 2009: 120).

Patterns of popular performance that originated in antiquity have continued, throughout the ages, in many parts of Greece into the modern era. One such pattern are the *mantinades,* compact poems (i.e., rhyming couplets) which are typical of Cretan folklore. It is noteworthy that, in the tradition of performing this song and speech genre, a marked gender distinction can be observed.

> In Crete, the western Hania and Sfakia, and generally the mountainous pastoral areas, are well-known for extreme patriarchy, as well as for the submission of female participation in public discourses. In stark contrast, in eastern Crete, in the agricultural and fishing lowland cultures, active female participation in public performance was a rule as long as the traditional performance practices were held (chiefly until the 1970s). With the contemporary transfer of the public poetic dialogues to the mass media arenas, women now have attained an equal public position as performers and poets [Sykäri 2011: 22].

To the ancient Greeks, musical performance (in close association with the utterance of literary texts and integrated in a choreography with dance) was at the very core of pan-Hellenic self-consciousness, and it has been emphasized in recent research "how collective *mousike* was held by a wide variety of Greek thinkers, including Plato (esp. Laws I–II), Aristotle (esp. Pol. VIII), Polybius (2.28), Diodorus Siculus (3.64.7), Aelius Aristeides (24.53), to be a most powerful cohesive force, mitigating the threats of stasis, and celebrating its overthrow" (Fisher 2011: 183). Certain ancient writers have explicitly elaborated on the far-reaching influence of music for the shaping of national identity and political education. One such writer is Polybius from Arcadia who lived in the second century BCE.

> Polybius' account in 4.20–1 of the savage and uncivilised nature (*agriotes*) of the Cynaetheans, the only people among the Arcadians to have abandoned the practice of musical education as introduced by their ancestors [...], includes a long and significant digression on the rôle of music in shaping human characters and, consequently, national identities in relation to natural environmental conditions. It is within this ancient version of environmental determinism that the Arcadian Polybius gives us a full account of the importance of musical training in Arcadia as a means of "a state-run system of musical socialisation" (Wilson 2000: 300) [Prauscello 2009: 189].

In Greek music, different modes were distinguished, and each mode was associated with certain mental and emotional conditions of human beings.

> Music in the "Dorian mode" was slow and temperate; such music was conducive to virtue. Music in the quick-paced Phrygian mode was thought to excite the passions. Phrygian music could excite lust, for example. But since it could also excite the wrathful passions, Phrygian music was useful and appropriate on the battlefield. It could make men bolder. Music in the Lydian mode excited joy and desire [Brumble 1998: 358].

Vocal music, accompanied by the *lyra,* was the kind of music that the Greeks liked most of all. This preference is deeply anchored in Greek mythology and associated with the performances of talented singers who traveled all over Hellas to participate in musical competitions or to entertain local people.

> Travel and "wandering" are persistent elements in both the reality and the *imaginaire* of Greek poetry, and intellectual and cultural life more generally, from the earliest days. They are, for example, central to the figure of Orpheus, usually regarded by the Greeks as the first major poet and/or holy man (cf., e.g., Aristophanes, *Frogs* 1030–32), whether in his role as a teacher of holy rites, as

an Argonaut, or as a lover grieving for the double loss of his wife Eurydice [Hunter and Rutherford 2009a: 1].

Orpheus is the singer that gained the most fame in Greek mythology. He is described as a figure of pre–Greek times, and also his name is explained as a "nom mythique pré-hellénique" (Chantraine 2009: 800):

> The earliest appearance of this figure seems to be, in fact, on the metopes of the Sikyonian monopteros at Delphi, where his name painted in guarantees him to have been one of the Argonautai [...]. One would guess that at some point his musical skills were of special use to the expedition, and indeed in Apollonios he saves the crew by drowning out the song of the Seirenes which would have lured them to their deaths.... The obvious idea that his song could charm savage beasts is first preserved in Simonides, where birds fly overhead and fish leap from the sea in time to music [Gantz 1993: 721].

According to some authors of antiquity the god Apollo was the father of Orpheus, according to others this was the Thracian river god Oiagros. Orpheus' mother is said to have been Calliope, one of the muses. There is unanimity among the ancients that Orpheus came to the Greeks from a northern region. Strange as it may seem, Orpheus experiences death like a mortal although his parents are of divine origin (Brumble 1998: 248*ff*).

What is so special about Orpheus is perhaps that this figure has inspired a field of scientific research in its own class, Orphic studies. Amazing is the vitality of Orphic traditions in some areas of the Balkans, in Oltenia, Banat and the south of Transylvania in particular.

> Significantly, richest in Orphic (and mythical–Dionysiac) elements are some of the Romanian funerary traditions. Outstanding among those are the many variants of the funeral dawn-song (Zorile, ...) and fir-song (Cântecul bradului), respectively. There is something meaningful even in the fact that those folk productions have been recorded in a peculiar geographic area, namely in certain conservative regions of southwestern Romania.... That location, besides being very close to the southern Danubian homeland of what was to become classical Orpheus, appears to have some connection with the probable Neolithic roots of what is now known as Orphism [Poruciuc 2010: 106*f*].

Musical terms from the substrate language relating to songs and singing:

dithyrambos name of a song at the festival for Dionysus
"the dithyramb, at least from the end of the sixth century BC onwards, was a choral piece sung to the accompaniment of the *aulos*" (Prauscello 2009: 180).
hymnos "song, chant, hymn, elegy"
ialemos "dirge, lament"
kalaboutoi "songs sung of Artemis in her sanctuaries"
kolabros "song (which accompanies the dance kolabrismos)"
komos "Dionysiac festive procession and festive songs"
minyrizo "to sing in a low tone, hum"
oulos "song to worship Demeter" (original meaning "sheaf of corn")
paian "choral song, hymn"
threnos "dirge, lament"
thriambos "hymn sung at festivals for Dionysus"

The majority of instruments of Greek antiquity are string and pipe instruments. As can be inferred from the fact that their names point at pre–Greek origins the shape and function of the instruments are also to be sought in the musical heritage of the pre–Greek population. Prototypes of both categories of musical instruments are known from ancient times. "Fragments of bone flutes or pipes were discovered in the author's [Marija Gimbutas'] own excavation at Anza, Macedonia, belonging to the period prior to 6000 BC" (Gimbutas 1982: 85).

As regards images of musicians playing their instruments from pre–Greek times, the marble sculptures from sites in the Cycladic Islands are the most famous. Pictures of these sculptures can be found in many publications and, sometimes, images of musicians playing different types of instruments are presented in impressive juxtaposition, as in the following setting.

The oldest string instruments are those that have few strings, such as the three-stringed pandoura and the four-stringed lyra and skindapsos, and the old pipe instruments have few holes such as the photigx and syrigx. In the course of time, more complex types of instruments were developed. Originally, the lyra had five strings; later versions have seven and even twelve strings. In Greek iconography the lyra is typically associated with female players (e.g., Sappho playing the lyra).

 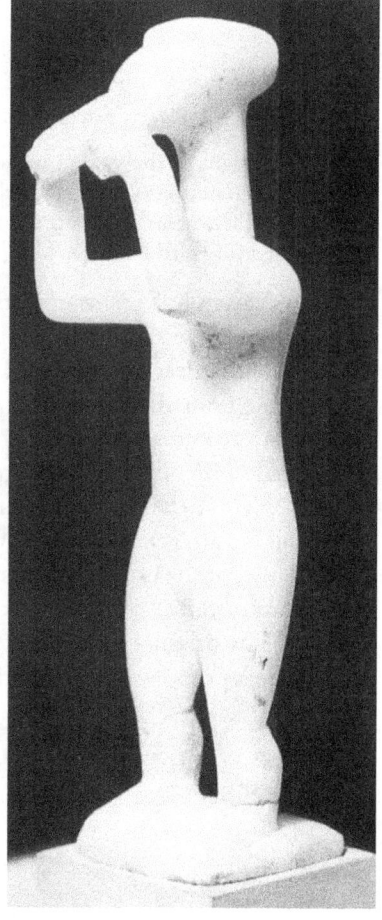

Musical instruments from the Bronze Age (Cycladic culture; ca. 2800 BCE) (originally published in *Cycladic art* by J. Lesley Fitton. London: British Museum Press, 1989. Courtesy of the British Museum): (a) Marble sculpture of a harp player; (b) Marble sculpture of a double-flute player.

The survey of musical terms of pre–Greek origin illustrates how diversified the Old European heritage is in this domain:

(i) String instruments and the music they produce
  barbitos musical instrument with many strings
  kithara "lyre"
  kollops "peg or screw by which the strings of the lyre were tightened"
  lyra "lyre, four-stringed (or seven-stringed) instrument (like the cithara)"
  pandoura "three-stringed lute"
  phoinix a stringed instrument, "a type of lyre that had long arms made from the twisted and hollow horns of a kind of antelope, the *oryx*" (Wilson 2009: 79).
  phormigx "cipher (especially as an instrument of Apollo)"
  psallo "to sing to a harp, chant praises"
  simikion musical instrument with five strings
  skindapsos "a four-stringed musical instrument with thorn-like appendices"

(ii) Pipe instruments and the music they produce
  donax "pipe (made of pole-reed)"
  elegos "mourning song (accompanied by flute)"
  photigx kind of flute
  syrigx "flute, syrinx"

The note names in ancient Greek stem from archaic lyre tunings. Two sets of notation are known, one for vocal music and another for instrumental music.

> The signs of the system come in two complete sets, which are associated with vocal and instrumental music respectively, although the extant scores do not maintain the distinction throughout. But the instrumental notation is obviously the older one, so it is very likely that it was originally used for vocal melodies also [Hagel 2009: 2].

Most parallelisms of instrumental notation can be identified when comparing the note signs with the signs of the Cypriot-Syllabic script. This system, inspired by Linear B, had been in use after the latter had declined and before the advent of alphabetic writing. Cypriot-Syllabic flourished from the eleventh to the sixth centuries BCE. So, knowledge of linear signs were known to the Cyprian Greeks and those Greeks from the mainland who engaged in trade with Greek-speaking people abroad. The Cypriot-Syllabic script served to write the local Cyprian language and Greek, spoken by the migrants to Cyprus who had fled the Greek mainland after the decline of Mycenaean power there. The inspiration to use signs of Cypriot-Syllabic for the notation of Greek music might have occurred in Cyprus and the custom was then transferred to the Greek mainland.

The original set of signs for instrumental notation also served vocal notation before a new set of signs was developed for the latter, drawing on the repertories of local Greek alpha-

$$a \quad a^\uparrow \quad a\sharp \qquad\qquad\qquad d$$
$$< \quad \vee \quad > \qquad\qquad\qquad \mathsf{Z}$$
$$\mathsf{C} \ \cup \ \mathsf{D} \qquad\qquad < \qquad\qquad \sqsubset \ \sqcup \ \sqsupset \qquad\qquad \mathsf{Y}$$
$$e \ e^\uparrow \ f \qquad\qquad a \qquad\qquad b \ b^\uparrow \ c \qquad\qquad e$$

Signs for instrumental notation in ancient Greece (originally published in *Ancient Greek music: A new technical history* by Stefan Hagel. Cambridge: Cambridge University Press, 2009).

bets. The separation of instrumental from vocal notation dates to the fifth century BCE (Hagel 2009: 366*ff*).

The association of instrumental notation with the tradition of linear writing in the Aegean world and in ancient Cyprus is in concord with the observation that key concepts of ancient Greek music are of pre–Greek origin; e.g., *pyknon,* a central term referring to the crowding of notes. This expression is derived from *pyknos,* a pre–Greek lexical borrowing whose meaning is "dense" (Beekes 2010: 1256).

Literature

The beginnings of ancient Greek literature have been extensively studied but there are still many phenomena that remain unexplained. According to a widely held—and yet outdated—view the epic genre, written in an elaborate formulaic language, rises seemingly out of nothing in the eighth century BCE. Such a scenario is quite unlikely and "modern opinion considers that epic poems in hexameter verse may have existed hundreds of years before Homer and circulated in oral form, performed by singers like Demodokos and Phemios in the Odyssey" (Shapiro 1994a: 2).

It is futile to search for the origins outside of Greece because there is no equivalent anywhere to the characteristic metrical form in which the epic works are recorded, the dactylic hexameter. The attribute dactylic ("finger-like") is derived from the word *daktylos*

Demeter I begin to sing,* the fair-tressed awesome goddess, 1 herself and her slim-ankled daughter whom Aidoneus** seized; Zeus, heavy-thundering and mighty-voiced, gave her, without the consent of Demeter of the bright fruit and golden sword, as she played with the deep-breasted daughters of Ocean, 5 plucking flowers in the lush meadow—roses, crocuses, and lovely violets, irises and hyacinth and the narcissus, which Earth grew as a snare for the flower-faced maiden in order to gratify by Zeus's design the Host-to-Many,** a flower wondrous and bright, awesome for all to see, 10 for the immortals above and for mortals below. From its root a hundredfold bloom sprang up and smelled so sweet that the whole vast heaven above and the whole earth laughed, and the salty swell of the sea. The girl marveled and stretched out both hands at once 15 to take the lovely toy. The earth with its wide ways yawned over the Nysian plain; the lord Host-to-Many rose up on her with his immortal horses, the celebrated son of Kronos; he snatched the unwilling maid into his golden chariot and led her off lamenting. She screamed with a shrill voice, 20 calling on her father, the son of Kronos highest and best. Not one of the immortals or of humankind heard her voice, nor the olives bright with fruit, except the daughter of Persaios; tender of heart she heard it from her cave, Hekate of the delicate veil. 25 And lord Helios, brilliant son of Hyperion, heard the maid calling her father the son of Kronos. But he sat apart from the gods, aloof in a temple ringing with prayers, and received choice offerings from humankind.	Δήμητρ' ἠΰκομον σεμνὴν θεὸν ἄρχομ' ἀείδειν, 1 αὐτὴν ἠδὲ θύγατρα τανίσφυρον ἣν Ἀϊδωνεὺς ἥρπαξεν, δῶκεν δὲ βαρύκτυπος εὐρύοπα Ζεύς, νόσφιν Δήμητρος χρυσαόρου ἀγλαοκάρπου παίζουσαν κούρῃσι σὺν Ὠκεανοῦ βαθυκόλποις, 5 ἄνθεά τ' αἰνυμένην ῥόδα καὶ κρόκον ἠδ' ἴα καλὰ λειμῶν' ἂμ μαλακὸν καὶ ἀγαλλίδας ἠδ' ὑάκινθον νάρκισσόν θ', ὃν φῦσε δόλον καλυκώπιδι κούρῃ Γαῖα Διὸς βουλῇσι χαριζομένη πολυδέκτῃ θαυμαστὸν γανόωντα, σέβας τό γε πᾶσιν ἰδέσθαι 10 ἀθανάτοις τε θεοῖς ἠδὲ θνητοῖς ἀνθρώποις· τοῦ καὶ ἀπὸ ῥίζης ἑκατὸν κάρα ἐξεπεφύκει, †κὦδιστ' ὀδμή† πᾶς δ' οὐρανὸς εὐρὺς ὕπερθε γαῖά τε πᾶσ' ἐγέλασσε καὶ ἁλμυρὸν οἶδμα θαλάσσης. ἡ δ' ἄρα θαμβήσασ' ὠρέξατο χεροῖν ἅμ' ἄμφω 15 καλὸν ἄθυρμα λαβεῖν· χάνε δὲ χθὼν εὐρυάγυια Νύσιον ἂμ πεδίον τῇ ὄρουσεν ἄναξ πολυδέγμων ἵπποις ἀθανάτοισι Κρόνου πολυώνυμος υἱός. ἁρπάξας δ' ἀέκουσαν ἐπὶ χρυσέοισιν ὄχοισιν ἦγ' ὀλοφυρομένην· ἰάχησε δ' ἄρ' ὄρθια φωνῇ 20 κεκλομένη πατέρα Κρονίδην ὕπατον καὶ ἄριστον. οὐδέ τις ἀθανάτων οὐδὲ θνητῶν ἀνθρώπων ἤκουσεν φωνῆς, οὐδ' ἀγλαόκαρποι ἐλαῖαι, εἰ μὴ Περσαίου θυγάτηρ ἀταλὰ φρονέουσα ἄϊεν ἐξ ἄντρου Ἑκάτη λιπαροκρήδεμνος, 25 Ἥλιός τε ἄναξ Ὑπερίονος ἀγλαὸς υἱός, κούρης κεκλομένης πατέρα Κρονίδην· ὁ δὲ νόσφιν ἧστο θεῶν ἀπάνευθε πολυλλίστῳ ἐνὶ νηῷ δέγμενος ἱερὰ καλὰ παρὰ θνητῶν ἀνθρώπων.

A specimen of epic poetry in hexameters (the beginning of the Homeric *Hymn to Demeter*; Demeter [parents: Rhea and Kronos; grandparents: Gaia and Ouranos; Aidoneus = Hades, god of the Underworld]) (from *The Homeric hymn to Demeter: Translation, commentary and interpretive essays* [3d ed.] edited by Helene P. Foley. Princeton, NJ: Princeton University Press, 1999: 2-3).

("finger"), an element of the substrate language, and refers to a snippet of rhythm, with one long syllable and two short ones. A hexameter is an alignment of six rhythmic units (*hexa* "six" + *metra* "rhythmic unit") which consist of dactyls. Actually, the last unit in a hexameter is not a perfect dactyl. Its structure is two long syllables and one short one. Thus, a hexameter is comprised of six (seven, respectively) long syllables and eleven short ones (see http://www.skidmore.edu/academics/classics/courses/metrica/).

> During the period between the beginning of high Mycenaean culture and the end of the geometric epoch, the fund of epic language formulae was developed into such a fine and highly differentiated instrument of poetic utterance that it raised ancient Greek oral poetry far above all kindred forms so far known among the Slavs, the Malayans and other peoples. Similarly, the hexameter verse form developed for this oral poetry transcends in its length, variability and its capacity for articulation all other known verse forms of oral poetry, and continued to play a dominant role in the following, written epoch of Greek literature [Dihle 1994: 9].

In fact, the metrical structure of the hexameter was not only applied for epic poetry, it became popular also for writing scientific and philosophical texts. Many of the pre–Socratic philosophers chose the dactylic hexameter as the medium for their discourse. For instance, the text of the first book on astronomy, written by Thales, is presented in the mold of hexameters. As for the domain of philosophy, the wisdom of Parmenides "is expressed in epic hexameters, which, although commonly stigmatised as clumsy and pedestrian, transport us back to the poetic and mythological realm of Homer and Hesiod" (Morgan 2000: 67).

In light of traditional teachings about the emergence of the hexameter we are to believe that the sophisticated instrument of the epic tradition is a product of purely Greek ingenuity. However, it is more realistic to associate the genre of the hexameter with the pre–Greek era, given the conditions of intensive cultural exchange, in archaic Greece, between native Europeans and early Greeks. The Old European cultural heritage had been penetrating many domains of Greek daily life. Why would oral poetry have been exempted, like an oasis of genuinely Greek fabric? Approaching the tradition of oral literature in Mycenaean times as a domain untouched by pre–Greek influences turns out to be a quite unrealistic endeavor.

Criteria for identifying the origin of the hexameter come from within the tradition of Greek literacy, of early poetic language in particular. Findings in the comparative study of local Indo-European literary traditions point to similarities, on the one hand, and to isolated phenomena in Greek poetic patterns, on the other. Similarities have been observed when comparing the line pattern of eleven syllables in the poems of the Greek poetess Sappho, from Lesbos, and in the Rigveda, first noticed by Antoine Meillet in his seminal work "Introduction à l'étude comparative des langues indo-européennes" (1937). Within the Greek poetic tradition, Sappho's pattern corresponded to a certain genre of poetry from which the other genre, the epic style, deviated.

> The Sapphic line characterized the so-called Aeolic poetry. It is important to note that both single [...] and double [...] short can come in between the long syllables. In the Homeric hexameter, to take another case, this is not so. There it is possible for two shorts to take the place of one long syllable (isochronism), something which does not occur in Aeolic or Old Indic poetry. Meillet for this reason wondered whether the hexameter had been borrowed from non–Indo-European inhabitants of Greece [Beekes 2011: 44].

When inspecting the formulaic pattern of the hexameter in relation to the linguistic structures of the Greek language one is surprised to find that this meter is somehow awkward, as if it does not really fit the syllable patterns of ancient Greek. Why would the Greeks have chosen a highly complex meter for recording oral poetry? A much simpler medium would do, as in the case of other cultures with rich traditions of oral poetry. Perhaps the hexameter is not originally Greek and was adopted by the Greeks to bolster their literary capacities. This would, at least in part, explain the awkwardness of this meter. The Greeks of antiquity believed that the idea to codify written laws originated in Crete and was adopted by the Greeks on the mainland. Could it be that also the oldest meter of Greek poetry was adopted from a pre–Greek culture?

Another approach to identify pre–Greek origin of the hexameter—thus following Meillet's line of argumentation—has been made in the 1980s. C.J. Ruijgh (1988) demonstrated that this metrical pattern was not developed by Greek poets and his conclusion is that the model for the hexameter has to be sought in a literary tradition where it had existed in pre–Mycenaean times. The only candidate for literacy that could have an impact on shaping Mycenaean oral and written literature is Minoan. No extant epic literature of Minoan has come down to us but the allusions in antique sources make it highly probable that such a literary genre once flourished in ancient Crete.

> The Minoan origin of the hexameter could explain why epic diction is such an artificial combination of dialects and linguistic stages: since Minoan is not Greek, the Mykenaian (i.e., Greek) development of the epic which Ruijgh proposes implies that the language had to be adapted to an external metrical structure. The development of epic diction is thus seen as extending from a hypothetical Minoan prehistory as far as the metrical form is concerned, via a pre–Mykenaian, a Mykenaian, an Aiolic and an Ionian phase, down to the eighth and seventh centuries in Euboia [Blok 1995: 188].

There is an additional argument that supports the assumption of pre–Greek origins of the hexameter, and this comes from recent investigations of the names of epic heroes. The fabric of many names, of persons, places or landscapes, in the epic works is non–Indo-European and points to the pre–Greek substrate language. Greeks and native Europeans did not only share the metrical structures of their epic poetry but also the heroes of their stories (see Chapter 3). If mythic tradition is the source of inspiration for epic poetry then not only mythmaking as a cultural pattern but also the narration of myth predate history and reach back into the Bronze Age or even further back in time. Modern scholarship has discovered the existence of a poetic language variety among the proto–Indo-Europeans dating to at least the fifth millennium BCE (Beekes 2011: 42f).

This means that the Indo-European migrants who came to Greece brought their tradition of the narration of myth with them and, in the course of contacts with the native Europeans (with their own mythic tradition), they adopted the originally non–Greek meter to give their epic language a formulaic frame. "Thus, the narration of myth in the epic poetry of the Greeks can be seen in a historical context extending as far back as the third millennium BC, to a time long before the height of Mycenaean civilization" (Graf 1993: 75).

Mycenaean civilization played a pivotal role for the continuity of myths and legends about the heroic deeds of the ancestors. After the decline of the Mycenaeans' political power, the cultural memory of the golden age of Mycenaean society did not vanish but its contents was transformed, in the intergenerational chain, to assume mythopoetic proportions.

> Greek epic poetry about legendary persons from Mycenaean times grew in the same way as did folk songs about mediaeval heroes in the Balkan countries during the Turkish domination. Greek legends were especially vivid among the descendants of those Mycenaean families who escaped

the Dorian violence and emigrated to the Aegean islands and to Asia Minor. Homesick for their mother country, they did not forget the famous leaders and founders of their cities and colonies. These heroic legends became the base of the Homeric poems which glorify the brave Achaeans, i.e., Mycenaeans [Ilievski 2000: 371].

And still, there is the wider perspective of mythmaking and the narration of myth the emergence of which can hardly be restricted to certain periods of cultural evolution. If myth is as elementary as to shape people's way of thinking, their attitudes and their way of life, then any investigation into the depth of mythological networks must pay attention to the prolonged continuity of this manifestation of human culture. It is not farfetched to search for the origins of the mythic tradition in the remote past of the cultures of southeastern Europe.

> The outlines of what was to become classical mythology can be perceived in prehistoric items unearthed by archaeologists, but such outlines also appear to be (paradoxically, from a chronological standpoint) "foretold" in folk productions recorded only as late as modern times. And just as certain features of prehistoric shrines eventually evolved into basic parts of Christian churches [...], much of what we know as mythology derived, more or less directly, from the ritual-cultural life of prehistoric peasants [Poruciuc 2010: xiv].

7

Old European Bases of Social Egalitarianism in Greek Society

Social Networking and the Making of Democratic Governance

The advanced stage of technological development reflected in the traces left by the substrate language in the ancient Greek lexicon is amazing. What then was the society like that supported technological advancement at a pace unknown in other parts of the world? At the beginning of our search for an answer to this crucial question, we make a very basic observation about the lifeways of the ancients in southeastern Europe.

> The general structure of Neolithic life, which was based in small, tightly clustered villages, with an economy firmly grounded in agriculture and animal husbandry, was not unlike rural life in Greece through the millennia to the present day. The Neolithic period, then, introduced and established a way of life that would support, shape, and sometimes constrain all later developments. We should always bear in mind that the glamorous monuments of the classical period in Greece, both physical (as represented by the Parthenon) and intellectual (science, philosophy, and drama) were achieved by people who lived in villages and small towns and were supported by an agricultural economy that was perfected after millennia of trial and error by the Neolithic farmers [Runnels and Murray 2001: 62].

Continuity of agrarian lifeways from the Neolithic through classical Greece and beyond is the key for understanding how technological development unfolded in an environment of sustained community life. The Neolithic village functioned as the focus of social interaction and of cultural activities and, as a center for handicraft and for the production of tools (i.e., sickles, spindle whorls, utensils for fishing and hunting). The inhabitants lived on agricultural goods, on grain, olives, vegetables, figs, wine, etc.

The wide array of domains of Greek economy and subsistence in which Old European influence is manifested has been mapped out in the foregoing. Greek culture is not only permeated with pre–Greek things and the pre–Greek names for them but the Greeks also adopted the denominations of various ancient professions in association with the farming communities and their sustained way of life: e.g., *kapelos* "innkeeper"; *kapelis* "female merchant, retailer"; *latris* "handmaid"; *pisyggos / pissyggos* "shoemaker" (*pessypte* "female shoemaker"), *skoidia* "educatress, housekeeper."

The archaeological record of the remains of settlements and the arrangement of dwellings suggests that the population in an individual village was kinship-based. Kinship in this context has to be understood as meaning "extended family," including close as well as more distant relatives and inmates. This configuration of social groups was characteristic of the many small villages where the number of inhabitants amounted to between several dozen and a few hundred. The average size of Neolithic villages ranged between 150 and 200 people. The native Europeans had a term for such village communities which is preserved, as a pre–Greek borrowing, in ancient Greek: *kome*. The high age of the word *kome* is encapsulated in its meaning which is "village, rural settlement (in opposition to an urban settlement)." This reference points to the rural village as the primary and original type of settlement, with urban agglomerations being a secondary development. *Kome*-type villages were scattered over the whole area where the Danube civilization and its high culture flourished.

Life in the villages did not unfold in isolation. On the contrary, the village communities were linked in a network of social, cultural and economic interaction. Kinship relations shifted with the integration of new inmates from neighboring villages and the circulation of goods was enhanced by intensive trading contacts. There must have been an awareness of the binding of social relations, of cultural and linguistic ties and of shared values among the villagers. Their cultural cohesion was certainly experienced on a level of collective identity.

Cooperation in the small village communities was mandatory for group cohesion, and the small groups of village population created strongly tied networks. "Strong common values, based on the intimate knowledge of one another's abilities, character, and day-to-day behavior are typical of strong-tie networks and can help to explain the workings and some of the attractions of traditional face-to-face communities" (Ober 2008: 136).

Social relations in Old Europe were not random but unfolded in an organized manner. What kind of social organization governed daily life in the villages? Is there any evidence available to identify the infrastructure of Old European society? Perhaps the most crucial point of this agenda is the question: were there social classes in Old Europe? In fact, there is substantial evidence and this comes from the study of burial customs and grave goods. There is consensus among archaeologists that grave goods are diagnostic markers which illustrate the degree of social differentiation in prehistoric society (Yakar 2011: 27*f*). If grave goods are distributed in a way which suggests that no distinctions existed between rich and poor or between men and women, the graves are interpreted as belonging to an egalitarian society without social differentiation or hierarchy. The presence of a ruling élite in a society is reflected in the grave goods of members of the upper class. Here, we find a marked difference between graves of the rich and the poor.

Analyzes of grave goods across Old Europe suggest a society with egalitarian structures, with social and economic equality, with all members of the community sharing in the profits from the agrarian surplus and trade. With good reason these socioeconomic conditions have been described as the Old European oecumene (or commonwealth) based on egalitarian principles (Haarmann 2011b: 88*ff*). In the Danube civilization, egalitarianism manifested itself in two spheres, the economic and the social.

Economic egalitarianism manifested itself in extended trade relations, where villages exchanged goods among themselves and with larger settlements. There is no evidence that any of the larger settlements dominated the economy of surrounding villages. In the context of economic egalitarianism, trade contacts evolved as relationships of mutual advantage, making the community a commonwealth. Among the preferred trade goods were obsidian, shells (spondylus, in particular), salt and copper. Objects with ritual functions, such as figurines, may also have been considered valuable goods for exchange.

Social egalitarianism is reflected in the absence of a marked distinction between the social roles of the sexes in community life, something which is typical of a society with social hierarchy. Equality between the sexes implies matrilinearity or matrifocality (with women as prominent figures in lineages). The prominent status of women in Old European society has been characterized as "matristic" by Gimbutas (1991: 324*ff*). Prominence must not be confused with dominance. Prominence in the status of women points to the fact that women had a privileged role in certain domains, such as in the household and in kinship relations. This does not mean that women would have suppressed men or marginalized their functions as husbands and fathers. According to modern anthropological research, cases of a sociopolitical dominance of women in historical societies are rare exceptions (e.g., the Naxi in southern China); (see Haarmann 2007: 162*ff* for an outline).

As far as kinship relations are concerned, the prominent status of women, as reconstructed for Old Europe, is not isolated as a social phenomenon of the past but finds its parallel in some recent cultures, Indonesia for one.

> Women's kin role in Java is important. Their parental role and rights are greater than those of men; children always belong to the woman in case of divorce. When extra members join a nuclear family to constitute an extended family household, they are much more likely to be the wife's relatives than those of the husband. Formal and distant relations between men in a family, and between a man and his children (especially his son), contrast with the informal and close relations between women, and between a woman and her children [Foley 1999: 260].

Communal Self-Governance from the Neolithic through Greek Antiquity

The villages in the Old European oecumene formed a network of socioeconomic nodes whose inhabitants engaged in plant cultivation and trade activities, and these village communities were not governed by any of the bigger trading centers with their pivotal role for the distribution of goods and for the spread of ideas. In fact, the local communities were independent administrative units that governed themselves. What made community life sustainable was the local administrative infrastructure, and this infrastructure reflected the principles of an egalitarian society. The villages were self-governing which means they created administrative bodies for their local needs of governance. Since there is no indication, in the grave goods, pointing to any distinction of prominent social status or the existence of social classes, the administrative body in a village must have corresponded to what we know as a democratic institution on the communal level, a kind of village council or committee, with members elected from within the local population and without interference or command from outside.

The ancient villages functioned as sustained economic units and the number of inhabitants tells us something about the ways of cooperation in small-size communities. In an environment where a few hundred people live together, build their homes and interact daily, there is a great amount of shared knowledge that is available to everyone. In a small community group cohesion is enhanced by an awareness that everybody's living standards depend on the ways how efficiently members in the group interact and give priority to the common good. The bigger the crowd, the greater the risk to lose the values of the common good. This insight is not new and it was articulated much earlier: "unless the number of individuals is quite small, or unless there is coercion or some other special device to make individuals act in their common interest, rational, self-interested individuals will not act to achieve their common or group interests" (Olson 1965: 2).

We can only speculate about the attitudes of the ancient Europeans and we cannot possibly know how much of a competition there was between individual interests and the values of the common good. One thing we know for sure is that all the necessary means enhancing sustainability were activated to safeguard group cohesion in the village communities because those communities prospered uninterruptedly over a long duration. Social cohesion was of vital importance to ensure the intactness of social and economic networks on a regional and interregional scale. A major medium to ritualize social cohesion among the villagers were figurines, and these were instrumentalized in

> rituals assisting intra- and inter-settlement social cohesion ... figurines, model clay furniture, and animals could be assembled in one building within the community into a dramatic scenario, where they formed an attention-focusing device for community religion [...]. After the ceremony, the set was dispersed into separate households, perhaps as a related symbolic activity linking families to the community, and to allow individual models to act as "apotropaic" (warding off evil) devices to protect or bless the household or its goods. They could also be stored in house models. Hearths, ovens, storage areas, and generally settlement domestic debris, seem typical contexts for Neolithic figurines, whilst their female dominance emphasizes a focal role for women and the home in their symbolism (Marangou 2001) [Bintliff 2012: 76].

The advantage of membership in a small community for the promotion of common benefits has been illustrated in recent sociological and psychological research. According to Gladwell (2000) the success of small-scale organizations depends on how closely members cooperate and how their personal relationships are embedded in successful face-to-face communication. What furthers cooperation is the kind of two-way communication which differs markedly from settings of bossy behavior, with one participant striving for dominance (Kopelman et al. 2002: 134$f\!f$). Small-scale organizations hold the key to interaction in an egalitarian community, thus promoting the spirit of democratic action: "real democracy works better in small places—dramatically better" (Bryan 2004: 83).

What is essential for decision-making in a small community is the fact that everybody knows about the qualities, both personal and professional, of the other members in the group. Mutual trust is furthered when decisions emerge in an atmosphere of shared knowledge about available capacities and grades of expertise among group members. This potential of active knowledge and trust may be put to work for promoting common benefits that shape the prospects of the community. Those who look for the prototype of democratic governance in the Greek communities of antiquity may find the oldest traces of a prolonged continuity in the villages of Old Europe.

Work in the administrative councils of Old European villages unfolded in an atmosphere of egalitarian two-way communication. This does not exclude the possibility that certain individuals were more active than others. Given the small scale of the local communities, the activities of individuals with more engagement and initiative were screened by everybody and their effects remained under "public" control. When talking about individuals that may stand out from the crowd of egalitarian group members the role of the chief in traditional cultures comes to mind. But is this association valid? Is the concept "chief" not associated with structures of a hierarchical society, with a headman in an elevated social status?

Many scholars have difficulties with the idea of a village council as a governing body without the presence of a leading figure, a chief who is in charge. This leaves two conflicting options: either making decisions for the benefit of the villagers or promoting selfish interests and acting against their intentions. Speculations about the existence of chiefdom in the agrarian villages blur the view on the essence of governance since the concept "chief" produces some kind of a bias. This concept is readily and one-sidedly connotated as being linked to conditions of social hierarchy. The chief is seen as representing the level of a social élite in a local population. In this view, the concept "chief" is unilaterally associated with "power" as a factor of social control over others.

However, in a comparative perspective of the world's traditional cultures, past and present, chiefdom appears in two distinct social models, one associated with the egalitarian principle, the other reflecting power relations within social hierarchy.

Arguably, the main reason why the term "chief" is widely perceived as a figure in an emerging social hierarchy lies with the confusion of expressions such as "authority" and "power." These words are often used as synonyms although they differ in meaning.

> The essential differences between authority and power lie in the ability to control. Authority rules mainly through persuasion and example, and tradition. Power, while not neglecting these, rules by compulsion. The measure of power is the sanctions it can impose. By sanctions is meant the mechanisms of restrictive and punitive social control that are available to the leaders [Donlan 1997: 40*f*].

Authority, in its original meaning, is assigned to someone, as a tenure or for fulfilling a certain task, by a group of people to whom the one with authority is responsible. If the one who enjoys authority fails, he may be relieved of his/her duty and his/her authority is withdrawn. A chief in this position may be a charismatic leader but his/her authority always remains negotiable. Assigned authority fits into the molds of egalitarian principles of governance. The possible existence of chiefdom in Neolithic Europe, thus, does not point at social hierarchy in the village communities.

To draw a comparison with current conditions of assigned authority the office of secretary-general of the United Nations may be mentioned. The current holder of the post of secretary-general, Ban Ki-moon, assumes much authority, assigned to him by the international public. His pronouncements carry much symbolic weight although he lacks any power to guarantee the implementation of sanctions or to supervise international agreements. Authority is assigned while power is taken without asking anyone for permission. Power, as a means of political control, is exercised by the major figure of a ruling élite or by someone who has usurped authority.

As for the conditions of agrarian settlements in the Neolithic Age "we may presume that in small farming communities the social system would have been more egalitarian than stratified. Even in relatively egalitarian societies, if not village chiefs, then at least heads of families would have formed councils of elders responsible for village management" (Yakar 2011: 174). If there had been village chiefs in Neolithic and Copper Age Europe their status may be compared to the office of the *demarchos,* the major functionary in a village, in Greek antiquity, with political and/or religious duties for the local council or magistrate. His authority was assigned and limited to the duration of his tenure (Rhodes 2013).

The autonomy of the village administration and the authority of the members of the council had a bearing on decision-making and on landownership. No reports about decisions made by the village councils in early agrarian society have come down to us. And yet, in communal landownership we can observe the working of the principle of the common good (in contrast to private property of land).

The Tradition of Communal Landownership and Land Lease

In the classical era, the distribution of land in the areas settled by the Greeks was quite complex. The following categories of the status of land can be discerned (Isager and Skydsgaard 1995: 121): common (or communal) land (*koine*), public or belonging to the state (*demosia*), sacred (*hiera*), private (*idia*). In a more scrutinous view of the land in terms of places and sites with specific functions, the following survey has been provided (ranging from the most specific to the most general; Pritchett 1956: 269): house site (*oikopedon*), private residence (*oikia*), tenement house (*synoikia*), garden (*kepos*), landed property, estate (*choros, chorion*), plot of ground (of which the exact meaning is uncertain; *gepedon*), land cultivated for cereals, vines (*ge psile*), field for cultivation in the countryside (*agros*), oak grove (*druinon*), pine grove (*pituinon*).

It is noteworthy that some of these terms stem from the substrate language (i.e., *ge*, "earth," *choros*). The diversification of land property and its terminology that we find in Greek antiquity is but the latest stage in a prolonged development of land use that started out in the communities of the Danube civilization. In the beginning, there was only one sole category of landownership, and this was communal. In the egalitarian society of Old Europe, private property of land was unknown. The ancient administrative infrastructure supported communal management of the soil that was used for plant cultivation. "In the smaller autonomous communities, an elected village council including a spiritual figure under an elected headman could have constituted a more egalitarian administrative system" (Yakar 2011: 29).

In the archaeological record of Neolithic and Copper Age Europe there are no traces of private ownership. Individual wealth resulting from private property of land would have been reflected in social class distinctions and, ultimately, in the grave goods. However, grave goods do not show such a divide. Private ownership of land is identifiable by the distribution of dwellings in a landscape. For example, a typical setting of houses in the countryside in a province of the Imperium Romanum was the presence of rural villas amidst patches of cultivated land. The inhabitants of those villas were the owners of the land by which they were surrounded. Such settings are uncommon in the cultivated landscapes of Old Europe. The arable land lies outside the settlements. The distance may have been considerable as computer reconstructions of the areas around the mega-settlements in southern Ukraine have illustrated.

The size of the village communities in the Bronze Age varied, in space and time. It has been assumed that the location of smaller villages in the neighborhood of bigger ones may point at hierarchical structures of the local society. Such assumptions have been rightly rejected as speculative: "Differences in land potential, or in the local history of a village, might create smaller and larger neighboring communities, without implying political dominance" (Bintliff 2012: 86).

The oldest Greek sources, of the eighth and seventh centuries BCE, hold information about communal landownership and of a system of land lease that persisted into the classical era. The land of a deme was owned by the inhabitants of the village community, and decisions about leasing land was made by members of the community council. Had the demes been under the control of private landowners then communal landownership would not have existed. The leasing system was not only in effect for the lease of arable land, for olive groves or vineyards, it also extended to include terrain rich in minerals that was given to entrepreneurs for exploitation. A well-known example of the leasing of land apt for mining are the silver mines of Thorikos in the southeastern part of Attica. The terrain of the local mines was leased to the Athenian state that was obliged to pay a share of the revenues from the mines to the local communal landowners. Thorikos was among the richest demes in the Athenian state, and the community could afford to build a theater that was the second largest in Attica, next to the Dionysos theater of Athens (Ober 2008: 205*f*).

Communal landownership was no innovation of the democratic era but it had existed long before Cleisthenes. It had been in place at the times of Solon's reforms (that is at the beginning of the sixth century BCE), and the tradition of land lease dates further back. Landholding was communal which means that the administrative body of the local community was responsible for the distribution of land for cultivation to the inhabitants. It is reasonable to assert that the distribution of the land was not gratuitous but was exercised as a source of income, responding to communal needs of the local village. One can imagine the working of a leasing system that required the delivery of a certain amount of the crops from leased land to the council or the execution of communal services by the lessee.

Assumptions about a system of land lease in Old Europe are not farfetched when taking into consideration that a communal leasing system was still functioning in the Mycenaean period. And the system of Mycenaean land lease was no novelty but had been perpetuated from more ancient times. The land owned by the village community was divided into plots that were then given out as lease. There is a distant echo of the ancient leasing system in the Greek language. The key term relating to the plotting of land was *kleros* (with a variant *kleirion*), "an allotment of land assigned to citizens; piece of land, a portion, farm." This expression is an element of the substrate language. There is an old land measure, *schoinos*, this too of pre–Greek origin.

Communal land lease which may be postulated for the communities of the Danube civilization (i.e., for the fifth and fourth millennia BCE) is documented for the Mycenaeans in the second millennium BCE. The documents which describe communal landholding as a major economic factor in Mycenaean society are the Linear B tablets that have been retrieved from the archives of some of the Mycenaean palaces. Those texts which contain the most information about landholding are from Pylos on the western coast of the Peloponnese. The Pylian state was among the most prominent of the Mycenaean city-states. As the base for communal landholding, the village community is identified which is called *damo* in the tablets. The Mycenaean *damo* corresponds to the demos of the archaic and the classical periods. What the Linear B texts reveal about status and function of the *damo* recalls the status of the Neolithic village in Old Europe. "The Linear B scribes appear to mean by *damo* a local organ of administration, considered in its corporate capacity" (Hooker 1995: 18).

Communal landholding (called *kekemena kotona* in the Linear B texts) stands in contrast to private ownership (called *kotona kitimena*). The society of the Mycenaean Greeks knew both kinds of landholding. In addition to communal land ownership there was also private property. Both these systems of landholding, communal on the one hand and private on the other, are documented in the written sources of the period. It is noteworthy that, in the Linear B texts, one notices an awareness, on the side of the scribes, that the system of communal land lease had a long tradition while private property is a more recent phenomenon.

> Since the two types of landholding are mutually exclusive and since the *damo* is entirely dissociated from *kotona kitimena,* we may surmise that the pattern seen in the tablets represents the superimposition of a later system of tenure upon an earlier; it is possible, furthermore, that land long settled lay at the disposition of the *damo,* whereas land more recently acquired by individual enterprise was in the hands of "private" owners [Hooker 1995: 16].

While there is good reason to assume continuity of a system of communal land lease from Old Europe into Greek civilization the emergence of private land ownership is shrouded in the mist of prehistory. Since there are no traces of it during the period when the Danube civilization prospered its beginnings must be related to the Bronze Age (starting in the late fourth millennium BCE). The Bronze Age in southeastern Europe was a time of sociopolitical turbulences. It can be inferred from the conditions of migrations directed from the Eurasian steppes to the Balkan region that settlements of the Old Europeans and their descendants, the Pelasgians, were taken over by the invading Indo-European tribes (including the Greeks) and that land previously owned by local communities turned into the property of those who established themselves as the elite. And yet, the process of takeover was not total and remained fragmentary in certain areas where the influx of migrants was minimal. Seemingly, the region of Athens and the part of Greece that is known by the name Attica were areas where the Old European communities persisted mostly intact.

The Mycenaeans are known for their mighty kings and their rich kingdoms. This is a myth and there is good reason to search for the reality behind this myth. It is true that the Mycenaeans were the first Greeks to engage in seafaring. Mycenaean merchants explored the coasts of the Aegean and reached out as far as Sicily and southern Italy in the west, and into the Black Sea in the north. At school we are taught that the Mycenaean city-state was a kingdom with a feudal society, with a strong leader, the king (called *wanaka* in the Linear B texts), supreme master and owner of the lands which he distributed to his followers as fiefs. When the historians in the nineteenth century read the works of Homer and made an attempt at reconstructing Mycenaean society from the context of the *Iliad* and *Odyssey* the feudal system of medieval kingdoms in Europe came to mind as the only political system for comparison. The structures of Mycenaean society were identified according to the analogy of a feudal system and this notion was introduced to the canon of Western education.

Recent research in the social history of the Mycenaean Greeks has produced insights that call for a revision of the older and outdated stereotype, still widely held, about a rigidly hierarchical society with a feudal king at the top of the hierarchy. In the written sources that have come down to us from the second millennium BCE, different conditions of political governance are revealed. The village communities (*damo*) were the backbone of the settled land in all the regions where Mycenaeans left their traces. Communal landholding was the foundation of organizing cultivated land, and land leased "from the local community" (*paro damo*) was the major factor for a sustained economy. Private property was present, but on a more moderate scale than the widely practiced system of communal landholding. The owners of private land (*tereta* in Linear B texts for later Greek *telestai*) were people who held offices in the palace bureaucracy (Ilievski 2000: 360).

> Our documents disclose nothing of the status of the "Great King" of the Pylian state. In particular, they give us no right to believe that a *wanaka* at Pylos owned lands and made grants of them to

noblemen. For all we know, the *tereta* held their estates by hereditary right, while the *wanaka* might have been a newcomer or a kind of figure-head who, far from granting land to others, was dependent on them for his own tenure [Hooker 1995: 18].

The contrasting models of landownership, of communal land lease (*kekemena kotona*) with its longstanding tradition, and of more recent private landholding (*kotona kitimena*), are manifested in a major document from Pylos, the so-called "land register tablet."

In this document, the names of the communities are listed in the register of communal land lease and, in a separate register, the personal names of the *tereta* as owners of private land are given (Ilievski 2000: 154*ff*).

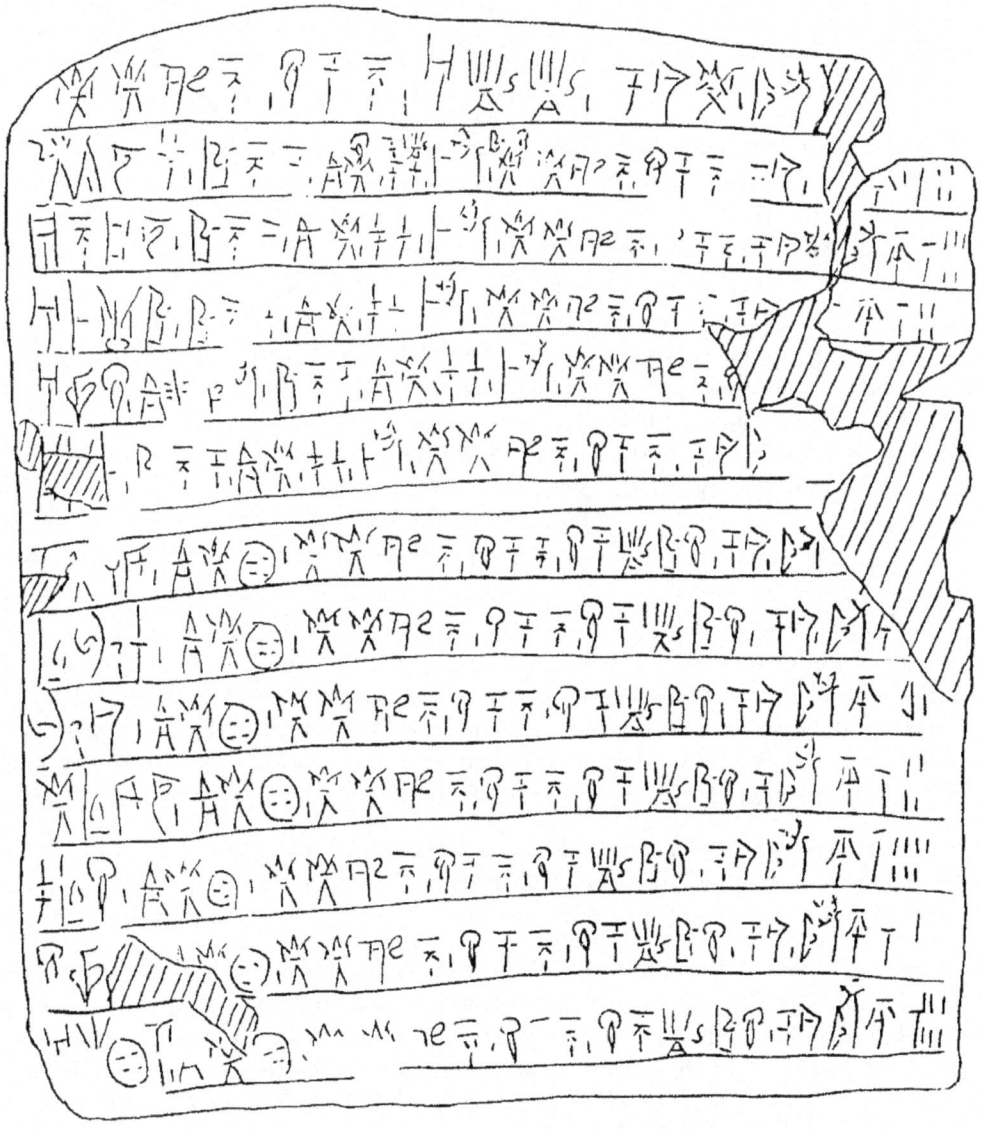

The oldest land register (cadastral list) in European history (thirteenth century BCE) (Linear B document PY Ep 301).

These two socioeconomic systems, that of communal land lease and private landholding, continued into the post–Mycenaean era and, during the Geometric period (ninth and eighth centuries BCE), they assume ever more features of contrasting worldviews. The representatives of the two mainstreams of Greek landownership develop attitudes that diverge markedly (Bintliff 2012: 212):

> One faction, the "elitist," favored retaining traditional hierarchy, emphasizing the heroic status of the aristocrats and their external contacts, the latter being a combination of gift-exchanges and more commercial ties within their regions and abroad (this attitude can be associated with private landowners);
>
> The other, the "middling" mentality, often expressed in later Classical city-states as the basis for their moderate forms of democracy, seems to have wished to level class into a single citizen community, inclusive of the serf population. It emphasized the value of local agriculture and pastoralism as well as a desire to internalize social life within the focus of an exclusive city-state (this attitude can be associated with the villagers and their control over communal land property).

The boundaries between land leasing and private landownership were never fixed. Since private landownership is a derivation from an original leasing system of communal land the conditions of how the former may have emerged from the latter should be looked at with some scrutiny. Modern scholarship has chosen the term "leasing" for the kind of land lease in antiquity because this concept implies the option, for the lessee, to purchase the lease from the owner (the lessor); (see Tuomisto 1994: 431 for this option). A patch of land that was leased to someone could remain in use with a lessee by continuously renewing the leasing contract. If successful the lessee held the privilege to obtain the leased land through purchase, provided the village council, the lessor, agreed. There must have been continuous shift of leased land to become private property already during the late Bronze Age since the Mycenaean records from Pylos make a clear distinction between the two types of landownership.

It can be assumed that those who developed private ownership were the early Indo-European immigrants to Greece for whom communal land leasing was an unfamiliar custom. The possibility cannot be excluded that, in certain areas, the immigrants simply occupied land for themselves without negotiating about ownership with the local villagers. Once private landownership had been established another domain of economic privacy opened. The beginnings of a labor market are to be sought in the aspirations of private landowners to expand the production of their lands. Those who leased communal land and later purchased it from village councils hired workers for payment. In the pre–Greek vocabulary of social relations several terms make reference to hiring laborers:

> *erithos* "day-laborer (of reapers, sheaf-binders)," "spinner," "servant"
> *latron* "payment, hire" (derivation *latris* "handmaid, hired servant")
> *thes* "serf, bondsman; hired laborer"

Are distinctions in social relations of the late Bronze Age reflected in these concepts? Were the first laborers that the private Greek landowners hired native Europeans (i.e., Pelasgians)? If so then the distinction between land as communal property and private landownership would, at the same time, signal distinctions of social groups in early Greek society. The pre–Greek term *thes* ranges among the central categories of social groups in Solon's reforms of 594 BCE. Each group is associated with a certain measure (*medimnos,* of pre–Greek origin) of yearly agricultural production. This tradition reaches back to the Mycenaean era:

The surface of the land in Mycenaean times was measured by the quantity of seed required for sowing. That practice is in use up to the present day in the Near Eastern, Mediterranean and Balkan countries, and in some places in Macedonia too. At the end of every line of the Pylos cadastral list the quantity of seed is indicated by the phrase to-so, pe-mo, -ma /tos(s)on spermo, -ma/, the ideogram 120 which very likely represents a monogram of si+to (si-to) *sitos* "grain" ... then by parts of the basic unit for dry measure, and the numerical signs of the decimal system [Ilievski 2000: 358].

In Solon's scheme of taxation, there are the *pentakosimedimnoi* "the male citizens who produce five hundred bushels of wheat," the *hippeis* "horsemen" (with an income of three hundred bushels), the *zeugitai* "yoked men" (with an income of two hundred bushels) and the *thetes* "laborers" (with an income less than two hundred bushels). The *thetes* did not have access to governmental offices. The *thetes* would have to wait for many decades before they were granted the right to public offices by Cleisthenes, in his reforms of 507 BCE.

Administration in the Village Communities (Demes) as a Model for Democratic Governance in the Polis

The conditions under which political changes occurred in Athens toward the end of the sixth century BCE were fairly complex and rather confusing (Osborne 1996: 292*ff*, Ober 2008: 57*ff*). Until 510 BCE the Athenian state was ruled by representatives of the Peisistratid family. After one of the sons of Peisistratos had been assassinated in 514 BCE autocratic rule turned into merciless tyranny. The Athenians called Sparta for help, and Spartan troops occupied the city. In 510 BCE, backed up by the Spartan military, the Athenians overthrew the last of the Peisistratid tyrants, Hippias. The Spartans who had supported the revolt with a military unit withdrew from Athens and left it to its citizens to establish a new leadership. In the state of disorder that followed the aristocratic families could not reach any agreement and factional opposition caused negotiations to end in a deadlock. Isagoras, leader of the pro–Spartan faction, called for Spartan support and a detachment of the Spartan army came to back up Isagoras' campaign.

Isagoras used his power to have the opposition expatriated. Around 700 families of the anti–Spartan faction had to leave Athens, among them the Alcmaeonids to which Cleisthenes belonged. When Isagoras tried to dissolve the Council of 400 the Athenians feared he could assume control over the city and rule, as an autocrat, like Hippias before him. The Athenians called Cleisthenes who had been exiled back to Athens and appointed him leader of a movement, with the intention to cope with the threat of governance in the Athenian state to degenerate anew into tyranny. When Cleisthenes, with the help of the Athenians, overthrew Isagoras, in 507 BCE, the outcome of his endeavor was everything but certain. This rebellion under the leadership of Cleisthenes quickly turned into a massive movement which neither Isagoras' followers nor the Spartan military managed to control. Things got out of hand, and Isagoras, his followers, together with the Spartans, withdrew to the Acropolis where they took defensive positions against the armed Athenians. Within a few days, after running out of food and supplies, Isagoras and the Spartans gave in and they were driven out of the city by the enraged Athenian citizens.

The Athenian rebellion under the leadership of Cleisthenes was blessed by good luck (Dillon and Garland 1994: 121*ff*). The endeavor could have easily failed, had the Spartans called in a relief force from their home city to crush the rebellion and reinstall their sphere of political influence. But everything happened so quickly that there was no time for thorough reflection on tactic maneuvers or strategic planning on the side of the military that had supported Isagoras. And there was not much time either on the side of the victorious Athenians who backed up Cleisthenes, investing him with the task to carefully map out a new system of governance, to take precautions against the scourge of a renewed tyranny. Time was in short supply because everybody was aware of the imminent danger of an external threat, an invasion by the Spartan army, profiting from the weakness of its adversary at a time when Athens was busy reorganizing its society and state.

This threat was real, not imagined. Sparta had formed a strong alliance with several other Greek tribes, with the Euboeans and Boeotians, and with the pro–Spartan forces in Athens. The balance had tilted after the rebellion by which Athens had cut off contact with Sparta. It could well be expected that Sparta—as the spearhead of the alliance and in the prime of its military might—would act by sending an army to reinforce its political hegemony in the region. Cleisthenes foresaw the danger of a Spartan military intervention and he therefore focused on the Athenian military, for his first major reform to materialize. In practice this meant the application of the newly devised division of Greek tribes to the divisions of military units. The ten tribes became represented by ten generals, and also the soldiers in the various units were gathered according to their membership in a particular tribe. This new form of organization was intended to enhance ethnic cohesion by furthering the fighting spirit among kinfolks. Indeed, this reform paid off in the wars that started soon after the army had been restructured.

The year 507 BCE marked a radical change and the beginning of a new era. In an historical retrospective the change from autocracy to democratic governance is explained as a development associated with the expectations of the Athenian public: "Cleisthenes' comrade-constituents, the demos that had recalled him from exile, expected a system of government suited to their newly expressed identity as participating members of a political community" (Ober 2008: 139). Here, the projection of modern reasoning about democracy into the world of ancient Athens is evident. Cleisthenes' comrades enjoyed solidarity within the anti–Spartan faction but they were hardly conscious of being members in a participating political community. Cleisthenes' followers were much interested in him taking the lead and control of state affairs. At the same time, it lay in the vital interest of the anti–Spartan faction to oust Isagoras' followers and prevent them from taking influence in Athenian politics. It was precisely the exclusion of Cleisthenes' opponents that occupied the minds of his followers rather than the membership in a political community of equal citizens.

"The constitution established by Kleisthenes was definitely democratic in character, though the four Solonian census classes remained in use as the determinant for qualification to office" (Dillon and Garland 1994: 122). Cleisthenes laid the foundation for a system of participatory democracy meant for male citizens, aged 18 and older. This was not a natural consequence of the political upheaval under Cleisthenes' leadership. Cleisthenes could have assumed authority as the supreme archon and exercised political power in the form of covert autocracy. For his political reforms to flourish he did not choose that alternative but a truly democratic order. This act of establishing a new administrative order in the Athenian state is generally hailed as Cleisthenes' creation, and democracy as a genuine invention of world history, of a truly Greek fabric (e.g., Raaflaub et al. 2007, Meier 2012: 182*ff*).

Such an assessment is in line with the canon of the Hellenophile tradition, engendered in the nineteenth century, that takes the appraisal of antique writers who celebrate Greek (and, in particular, Athenian) achievements of civilization at face value. According to the self-exaltation of Hellenistic writers:

> The Athenian *demos* had been the originator of all good things, bringing humans from animal life to civilisation; the Athenians had established bonds of community among the humans by introducing the tradition of the mysteries; thus, they had taught the Greeks that the greatest benefit for humans is intimacy and trust among each other; after receiving from the gods as gifts the cultivation of crops and the laws concerning humanity and education, the Athenians shared these presents with the Greeks [Chaniotis 2009: 256].

The notion of democracy as a product of Greek ingenuity is rooted in the interpretation of Greek history that was initiated by the German Romantic Movement in the early nineteenth century. Political events such as the Greeks' war of independence of 1823, waged against the colonial rule of the Ottoman Turks, fueled a wave of Hellenophile empathy among European intellectuals for the Greek cause, and this empathy was associated, in the minds of many idealists, with the strive for a renewal of the model of democratic governance in nineteenth-century Europe. Democracy has been addressed as the prime achievement of Greek antiquity and, as such, it is hailed in the tradition of European school education up to the present. There is nothing wrong with calling democracy an achievement of Greek antiquity. What is wrong, though, is its identification as a Greek invention. This is not only a gross generalization but also an incorrect statement based on false evaluation of historical facts or, rather, based on ignorance of historical facts.

The model of democracy that Cleisthenes introduced was no invention. Cleisthenes did not devise democratic governance out of the blue but he could look back on ample experience with communal self-administration in the village communities in the region of Attica. The innovative changes that were brought about by Cleisthenes' reforms are widely misunderstood as relying on a newly organized system of village communities, the demes as basic political units (sing. *demos*, "village (community)," plur. *demoi*). The demes existed before the times of Cleisthenes and even in pre–Greek times.

The groupings of earlier extant demes according to tribes were an innovation because Cleisthenes reshuffled the network of tribes anew, dissolving the historical four tribes and creating ten new ones. However, the division of each tribe into "thirds" was, most probably, no innovation devised by Cleisthenes. Instead, he could draw on an ancient (i.e., pre–Greek) model of deme division (see below for the concept *trittys*).

> These new tribes would play important roles in the new political system. They would also become key markers of Athenian identity.... The tribes and their constituent "thirds" were the institutional bridges by which a stable local identity [...] was linked to a desired national identity (participatory citizen of Athens) [Ober 2008: 140*f*].

According to Aristotle, it was not Cleisthenes who chose the names for the new tribes but these were selected from a longer list by the Pythia in the oracle at Delphi (*Constitution of the Athenians* 21.6). Cleisthenes did not abolish the tribal system as such but gave it a new infrastructure which served to strengthen specifically local (i.e., earthbound) ties in the network of demes. What was new from the standpoint of the demes was their association with a particular tribe. In the new order, tribes were activated in terms of overarching political units.

> The Ionian tribal names had no local reference, but the new tribal names were derived from eponymous tribal heroes who are important figures in Athenian Myth-history: Erekhtheus, Aigeus, Pan-

dion, Akamas, and Kekrops were among the legendary kings of Athens; Leos, son of Orpheus, sacrificed his daughters to save Athens at time of plague; Hippothoon was son of Poseidon; and Aias is the great hero of the *Iliad* from Salamis. To institute these new tribal names was to make all the various actions which Athenians performed in tribes, whether military, festival, or political, redolent of an Athenian past [Osborne 1996: 300].

Cleisthenes achieved something that Solon, many decades before him, did not. Cleisthenes succeeded in uniting the demes of Attica to form a state organization that was based on the same principles as communal governance. The model of communal self-administration as manifested in the local demes was transposed to the political level of the polis. Cleisthenes engaged in weaving the interests of the numerous demes together into the fabric of an overarching city-state.

Among the representations the Greeks made of society, of the bonds between men and the cohesion of human groups, or even of the city, there is one that seems to fabricate society more than any other: weaving. Domestic or political, profoundly ritualized, weaving brings into play an ensemble of notions capable of being inscribed in the collective memory, gestures that allow one to grasp, to touch, social organization. As much as sacrifice, whose gestures of sharing and distribution define the society in terms of commensality, the practice of weaving—furnishing men and gods with clothing and blankets—offers a simple model to the mind seeking ideas about the nature of social cohesion: how is it that the human group, the family alliance, and the city can hold together? [Scheid and Svenbro 1996: 9].

Cleisthenes succeeded in providing the inhabitants of Attica and the urban population of Athens with a corporate design of Greekness on the foundation of a democratic order, that is with a set of customs which was comprised of traditional (including pre–Greek) and innovative constituents. This design has been identified as nomina.

In general, nomina constituted a set of practical, organizing data for society, such as names and numbers of tribal divisions or magistracies and their terminology. They also regulated society's relations with the gods through sacred calendars, festivals, and the constitution of a polis pantheon [Malkin 2011: 189].

Cleisthenes, in his reforms, took a clear stand what concerns people's rights to participate in political decision-making. The system of governance that Cleisthenes devised for the Athenian polis was based on three pillars, the basic virtues of democracy (Haarmann 2013a: 185):

isegoria ("equal speech," referring to the right of every Athenian citizen to speak freely about political affairs);
isonomia ("equality before the law," regardless of social status);
isopoliteia ("equal participation in political activities," regardless of membership in social groups).

The achievement of *isopoliteia* on the level of political governance of the polis was a novelty in Cleisthenes' reforms because the *thetes* (members of the lowest social class in Greek society) had not been granted equal participation in political activities before. In Solon's model of democracy, devised in the 590s BCE, the *thetes* had been barred from public offices.

The ritualistic character of the ingredients that made Athenian democracy echoed far into successive periods and various approaches were made to explain what actually held the community of Athenian citizens together. In Plato's works one finds a statement about the role of musical education for enhancing stability in a democratic society. In Plato's *Laws,* the "Athenian Stranger," taking the part of the analyst, reflects on this issue.

> The Athenian Stranger finishes his examination of Megillus by discussing democracy in ancient Athens. He says that the ancient Athenians placed great emphasis on music and music education. Moreover, those who had knowledge regulated the sacred music very carefully and forbad innovations and misuse. When the music was performed, the people listened reverently, in solemn silence, and lived in an orderly way (*Laws* 700a–d) [Lutz 2012: 87].

Cleisthenes was celebrated by European republicans of the seventeenth century and, later, by the representatives of the Enlightenment in the eighteenth century and of the romantic movement in the early nineteenth century for having highlighted the basic democratic virtues. "In the seventeenth and early eighteenth centuries Athens provided a heartening model to many English republicans seeking instructive analogues for increasing the accountability and moral tone of government in their own day" (Roberts 1994: 156).

It is true that Cleisthenes was the first to formulate these key concepts of democratic governance but, in practice, these virtues already existed and were observed in the village communities. *Isegoria* meant the right of each villager to talk about communal matters, *isonomia* guaranteed equal treatment in juridical matters according to customary law and the obligation for everyone to respect the behavioral norms of the ancestors, and *isopoliteia* referred to the equal right to be elected as a member in the village council. Cleisthenes' request meant in fact a confirmation of a system of communal governance that had been in place before his time (including self-determination in juridical affairs). These implications have to be inspected with further scrutiny.

If the demes existed before the introduction of democracy what then was their mode of governance? How can one identify the mode of administration in village communities during the "Dark Ages," in Mycenaean times and even before the Greeks established themselves in the land they called Hellas? Is it reasonable to assume continuity of political governance from the Bronze Age onward or to look for even older origins of the Greek deme system? Indeed, there is good reason to dig deep into pre–Greek history to find out about the early sources of what was developed as democratic governance by the ancient Greeks. The sense of communal cohesion and the trust in the values of communal self-administration clearly pre-date the Greeks and was present in the communities of the pre–Greek population.

There has been much debate in classical studies about the nature of the demes in early Greece. There are those who advocate the idea that a Greek deme, at the time when democracy was introduced, was a densely populated village community (e.g., Osborne 1985), and others who assume that demes consisted predominantly of scattered farmsteads (e.g., Jones 2004: 17*ff*). In light of recent archaeological surveys of the region of Attica there were demes of various sizes and with differing populations. Of the 139 demes that were registered for the implementation of Cleisthenes' reforms 76 were smaller and 46 larger demes.

The average size of a deme at that time was a community with a total amount of some 700 residents, with about 180 to 200 adult native males who had the right to vote and were eligible as candidates for the National Assembly (*ekklesia*). In the larger demes there was an urban center with an agglomeration of houses while, in the countryside around that economic and cultural center, farmsteads were scattered. This means that the categories of densely settled villages and scattered farmsteads did not necessarily stand in opposition for defining a deme.

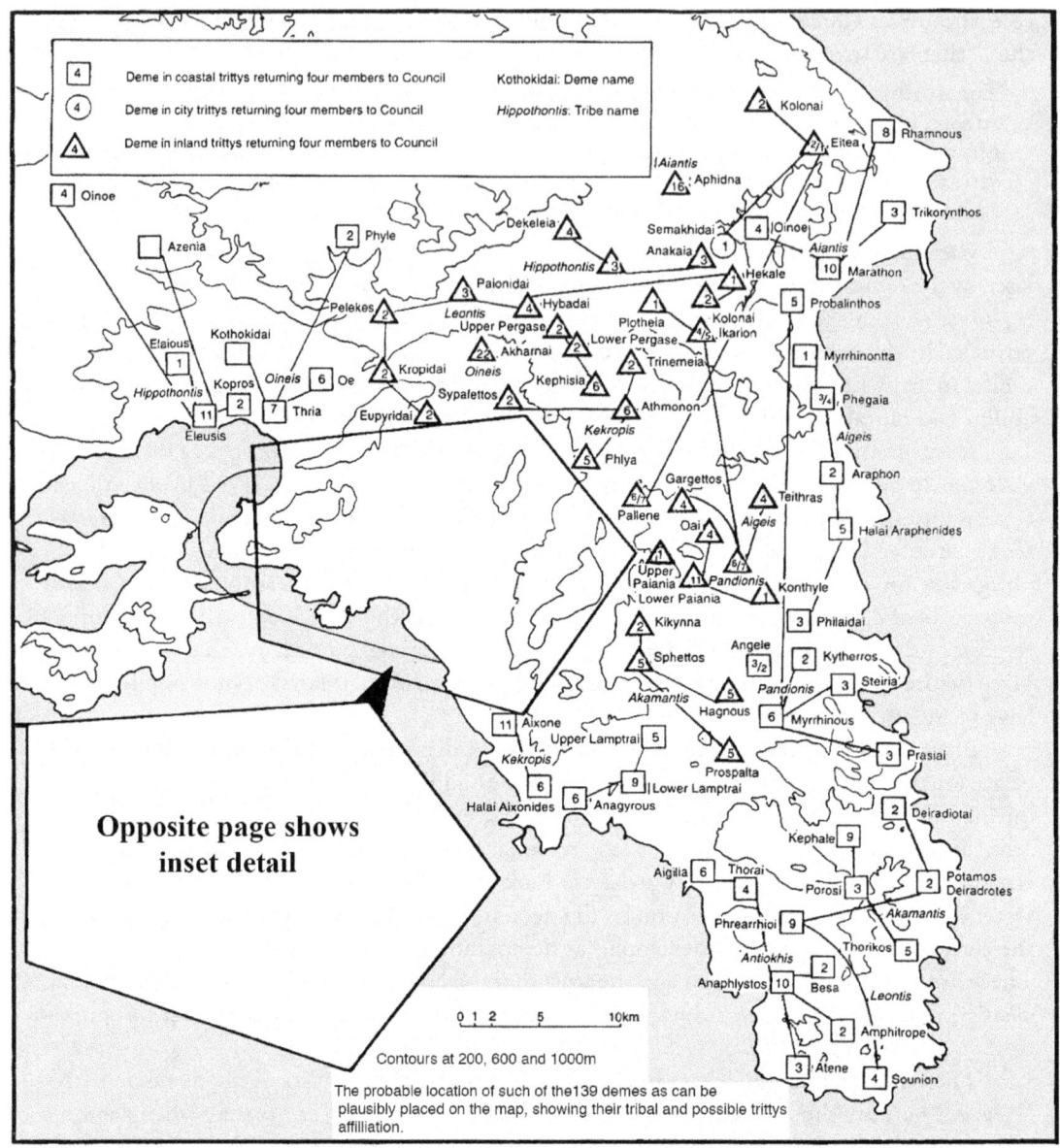

Above and opposite: The demes of Attica according to the reforms of Cleisthenes (507 BCE) (originally published in *Greece in the making 1200–479 BC* by Robin Osborne. London & Routledge, 1996. Reproduced with permission): (a) The demes of Attica; (b) The distribution of demes in the city of Athens.

The tribal division of the Greek population that had existed since the times of immigration persisted although in a revised form. Every deme was associated with one of the ten tribes so as to form a complex network of tribal and communal boundary-marking. As for communication between demes and tribal regions, priority lay with the demes because

> of the two, only the deme could function as a face-to-face society. Given that oral news disseminates more easily and accurately among the members of a small community, it is conceivable that the deme provided an ideal social context for the development of participatory democracy within

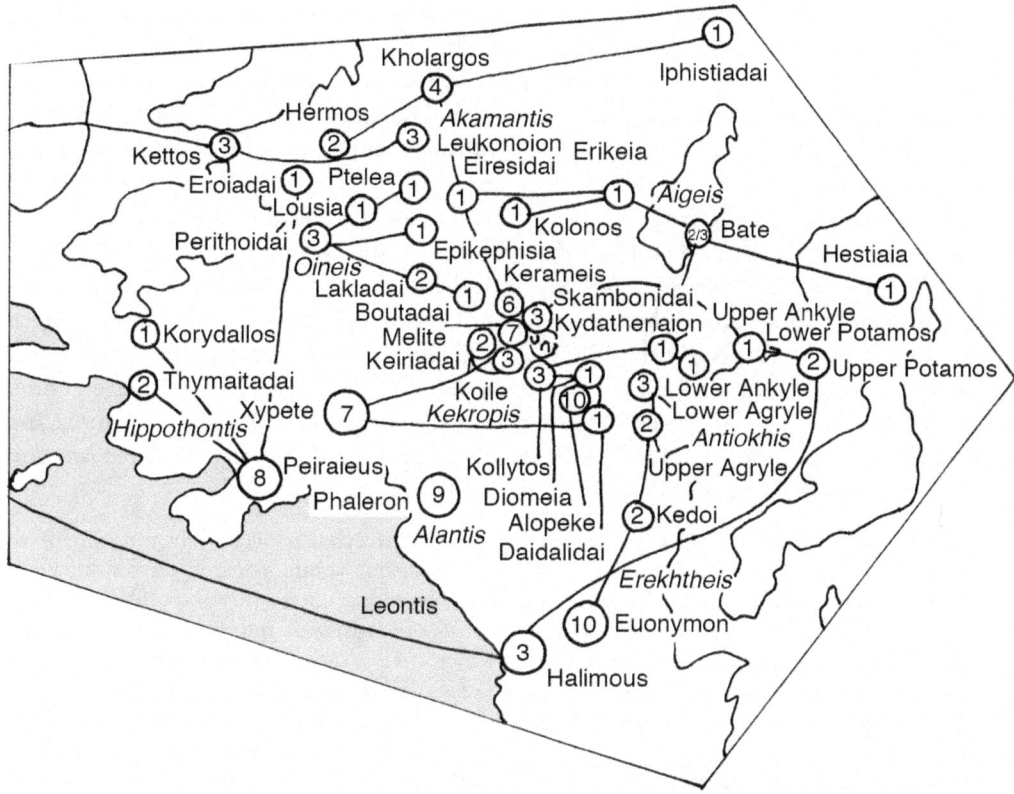

itself; in a face-to-face society, intelligently and publicly shaped opinion may rely on the spoken word alone. The members of a deme, for example, would remember decisions or appointments of local magistrates [Missiou 2011: 20].

Cleisthenes mastered the organizational challenges, posed by the application of the principle of self-administration in the deme system to governance in the Athenian polis. This network of communal governance which united the villages, the deme system, was the foundation for Attica's political system and Cleisthenes formalized administration in the demes, "requiring each of them to appoint a leader (demarch) annually, and giving them a role in determining their own members, and hence the membership of the citizen body, as well as their own cultic activities, finances, and even to some extent their judicial arrangements" (Osborne 1996: 296).

The vital importance of the village communities (i.e., demes) and their principle of communal self-administration for the success of participatory democracy in the Athenian city-state has been duly emphasized.

At the time of the Kleisthenic reforms, Athens, like the rest of the Greek world, was indeed a fundamentally agrarian community, to which Aristotle's dictum "most men make their living by farming the land and by eating the fruits of cultivation" (*Politics* 1256a, 39–41, my translation) was clearly relevant. The majority of the estimated 30,000 Athenian citizens in 500 BC were smallholders. Although there is no direct evidence available on the percentage of people living in the city as opposed to the countryside, it is widely accepted that the vast majority—perhaps 85 per cent—of Athenian citizens lived outside the civic centre [...], farming their fields dispersed all over the large peninsula of Attika [Missiou 2011: 13].

The Athenians always remained aware of the religious implications of their governmental affairs as an organic whole. Athena was celebrated as the patron of all the major institutions of the Athenian state. According to the mythic tradition, the goddess had founded the Areopagus, the high court of Athens. The National Assembly convened under the patronage of Athena and the elected representatives of the local demes held speeches and made decisions with a mindset that put the goddess in the position to preside over the sessions.

There was nothing comparable in all of Greece to the grandeur with which the Great Panathenaia was organized and performed. Everything was on display, the worship of Athena as patron of Athens and the celebration of political union because this was "a festival which highlighted the actions of the Athenians as a political body and exhibited their preparations to face the outside world" (Osborne 1987: 172). It is noteworthy that the role of Athena for self-identification of the political body of Athenians was not only vital for the period under democratic governance, but also in the earlier context of tyrannic rule. The two contexts are investigated by Connor (1987: 47*ff*) in terms of a relationship between civic ceremony and politics, based on two episodes in Herodotus' *Histories:*

> The first was Peisistratos' return to power in the 550s with which is associated the tradition of his entry into Athens in a chariot accompanied by a statuesque young woman (*parthenos*), Phye, dressed as Athena (Hdt. 1.60.2–5). Connor dismisses Herodotus' incredulity and offers a plausible explanation based upon the shared religious *mentalité* of Peisistratos and the Athenians and the involvement of the populace in a "shared drama" which, *inter alia,* was familiar with the traditions of Athena riding in the chariots of her favoured heroes and mortals. The second episode was the establishment by Solon of a census system based on agricultural production and wealth expressed in *medimnoi* (pentakosiomedimnoi, hippeis, zeugitai and thetes, Aristotle Ath. Pol. 7.4) from which Connor argued that one of the roles of festival processions was to provide a means for both the display, and perhaps the determination, of the wealth of its citizens, especially its rich citizens [Phillips 2012: 204].

The overall significance of the Panathenaic festival can hardly be overrated. "In its inclusiveness, it exemplified the city's participatory democracy; in its contests it demonstrated the competitive spirit of its people; with its prizes it displayed the skills of its artisans and the wealth of its produce; and above all it celebrated Athena as the divine protectress of a glorious city" (Neils 1992a: 27).

The religious tradition, mythical beliefs and the political reality of participatory democracy were intrinsically intertwined to create a network of sociopolitical cohesion, and this cohesion was celebrated in intervals, in the four-year rhythm of the Panathenaia. During the golden age of Athenian imperial power, in the course of the fifth century BCE, "the Panathenaia had evolved into a kind of recapitulation of the history of democratic Athens" (Shapiro 1994b: 128). In the course of time, democratic Athenian society became a "performance culture," and the sequence of performances of the Great Panathenaia was accompanied by changing political conditions and the input of memorable events steadily increased (Kavoulaki 1999).

When setting the dates (in intervals) of the Great Panathenaic festival in perspective and associating them with political events of the sixth and fifth centuries BCE, the following historical panorama unfolds (Phillips 2012: 205*f*, 208*f*):

> 594/3 BCE (Solon is archon in Athens), 590/89—every four years—566/5 (reorganization of the Great Panathenaia by Peisistratos), 562/1 (Peisistratos strategies: war against Megara), 558/7—every four years—546/5 (third, successful attempt at tyranny by Peisistratos), 542/1—every four

years—514/3 (assassination of Hipparchos), 510/09 (first Great Panathenaia after the tyranny; Great Panathenaia becomes linked to anti-tyrant sentiments), (508/07—Cleisthenes' tribal reforms), 506/05 (first Great Panathenaia after tribal reforms), 502/01—every four years—490/89 (battle of Marathon), 486/5—every four years—462/1 (reforms of Ephialtes), 458/7, 454/3 (transfer of the Delian League treasure to Athens), 450/49—every four years—438/7 (completion and dedication of Pheidias' statue of Athena Parthenos at the Great Panathenaia), 434/3, 430/29 (plague epidemic at Athens), 426/5—every four years—410/09—every four years—402/01 (first Great Panathenaia of the restored democracy).

The grandeur of the Panathenaia that became one of the most prestigious festivities in all of Greece can partly be explained by the popularity of contests and competitive performances associated with it. Competitiveness was a significant ingredient in Cleisthenes' new arrangement of the tribal and communal divisions which has been emphasized by Aristotle (*Politics* 1319b, 19–27) as a kind of "mixing-up" of the population in order to erase encrusted factionalism and rivalry between the ancient tribes in pre-democratic society. Competitions (athletic, musical, dramatic or other) were instrumentalized, by the architects of Athenian democracy, to enhance citizens' solidarity with their city and its democratic governance.

> Kleisthenes and his successors, through their creative use of expanded and carefully regulated competitions, achieved a transformation in co-operative social relations between elite and less elite members of the community [...], which came to make a significant contribution to lessening the dangers of *stasis* arising both from geographical and status divisions [Fisher 2011: 183].

If sporting competitions played a pivotal role for the interaction between members of different social groups then these events needed specially designed spaces to accommodate larger crowds of people. The idea was to provide open space for contests similar to the center in all Greek cities—on the Greek mainland, in Magna Graecia in southern Italy and in the colonies around the Mediterranean and the Black Sea—which was the agora serving as a space for conducting business, for convening in political gatherings and for participating in ritual processions.

> Lefebvre once characterized the space of the Greek agora as one left physically open so as to allow for the gathering of the citizen body (Lefebvre 1991: 237).... This Classical model of open, unelaborated space can be paralleled in other types of civic space, particularly areas of sporting competition and preparation; even the famous gymnasia of Athens were, for the most part, unmonumentalised park spaces for the majority of the Classical Period [Scott 2013: 161].

The Agora of Athens was the center of all the activities typical of Greek lifeways under the democracy:

> On any given day, the fifth-century B.C. Athenian Agora was peopled with Athenian adult males attending the democratic assembly; worshipers making offerings at shrines and altars; merchants hawking their wares to a mixed populace of freeborn and slaves, both male and female; young aristocratic men talking and walking with their philosopher mentors; civic officials hurrying to and fro, conveying documents and information to the Council House, the Assembly, and the Archives; bronzeworkers forging metal for armor, utensils, and votive dedications; and citizens consulting the latest news on the "bulletin board" of the Eponymous Heroes Monument. On special festival days, this same space was filled with crowds cheering young male athletes competing in athletic games in honor of the patron goddess Athena, processions of hundreds of the city's men and women bringing offerings and animal sacrifices to the Akropolis, or would-be initiates gathering to make the 14-km walk to Eleusis to be inducted into the Mysteries of Demeter and Persephone [Barringer 2008: 110].

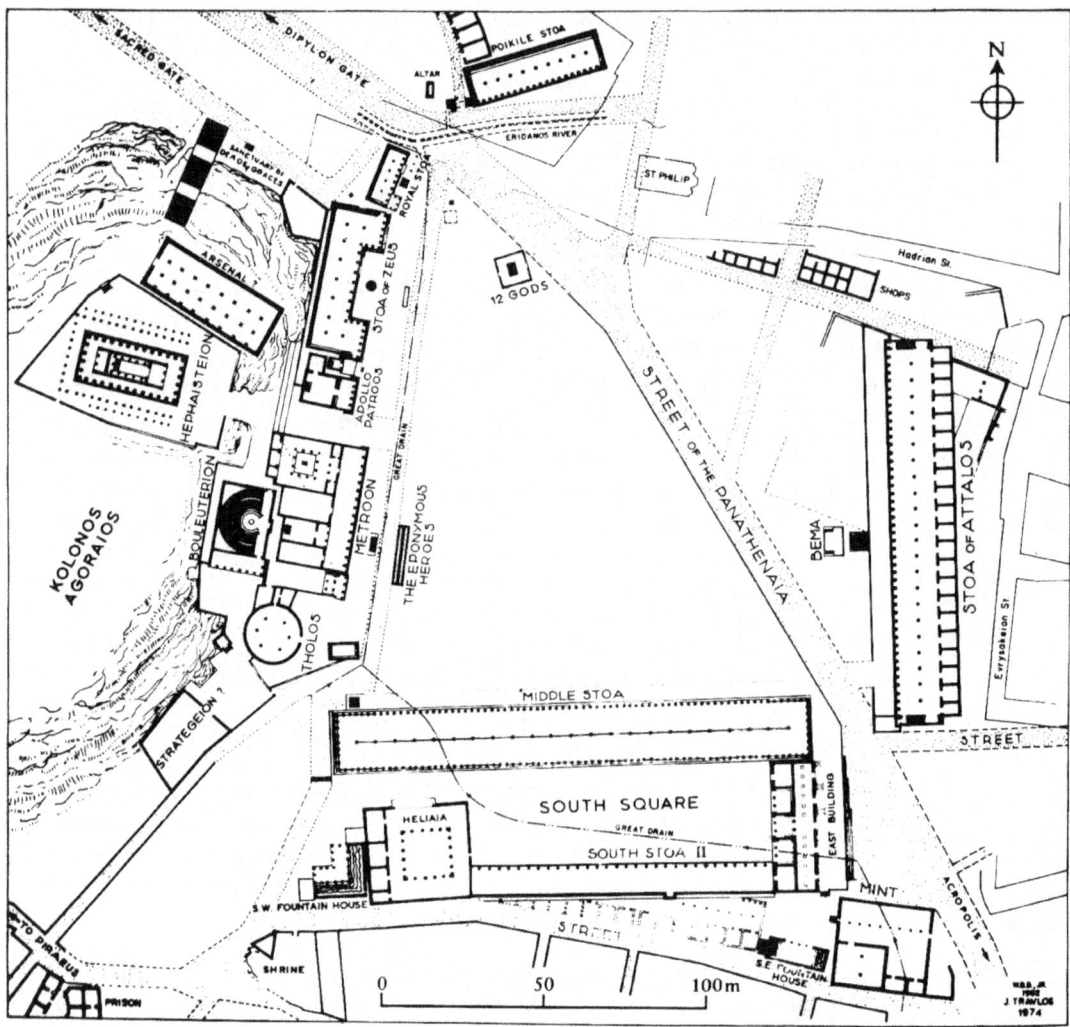

The Athenian Agora in the fifth century BCE (used with permission from the American School of Classical Studies: Agora Excavations).

The Major Democratic Institutions of the Athenian City-State

The citizen Assembly and the People's Courts are generally regarded as signature institutions of the Athenian democracy, and their effective functioning is certainly among the most mysterious aspects of Athenian political organization [Ober 2008: 161].

THE NATIONAL ASSEMBLY (*EKKLESIA*)

This democratic institution was founded by Solon in 594 BCE. Its elected members were representatives of their local communities (demes), and these were adult male citizens who had served two years in military service. Since the times of Cleisthenes' reforms (507 BCE) all social groups were represented, including the *thetes*. Whether the latter group had representatives in the Assembly before the reforms of Cleisthenes is as yet unclear. The number of members of the Assembly ranged from a minimum of 6,000 to more than 8,000. The Assembly was the main decision-making body and it also nominated members of the magistrates (Hansen 1987). Decisions were made according to the principle of majority votes by a show of hands. The agenda of the Assembly was set by the Council. Decisions were recorded in writing, the debates that preceded decision-making were not. Sessions of the Assembly were originally held once a month (during the times of Solon). In the fifth century BCE, after the Persian Wars, the Assembly convened three or four times per month.

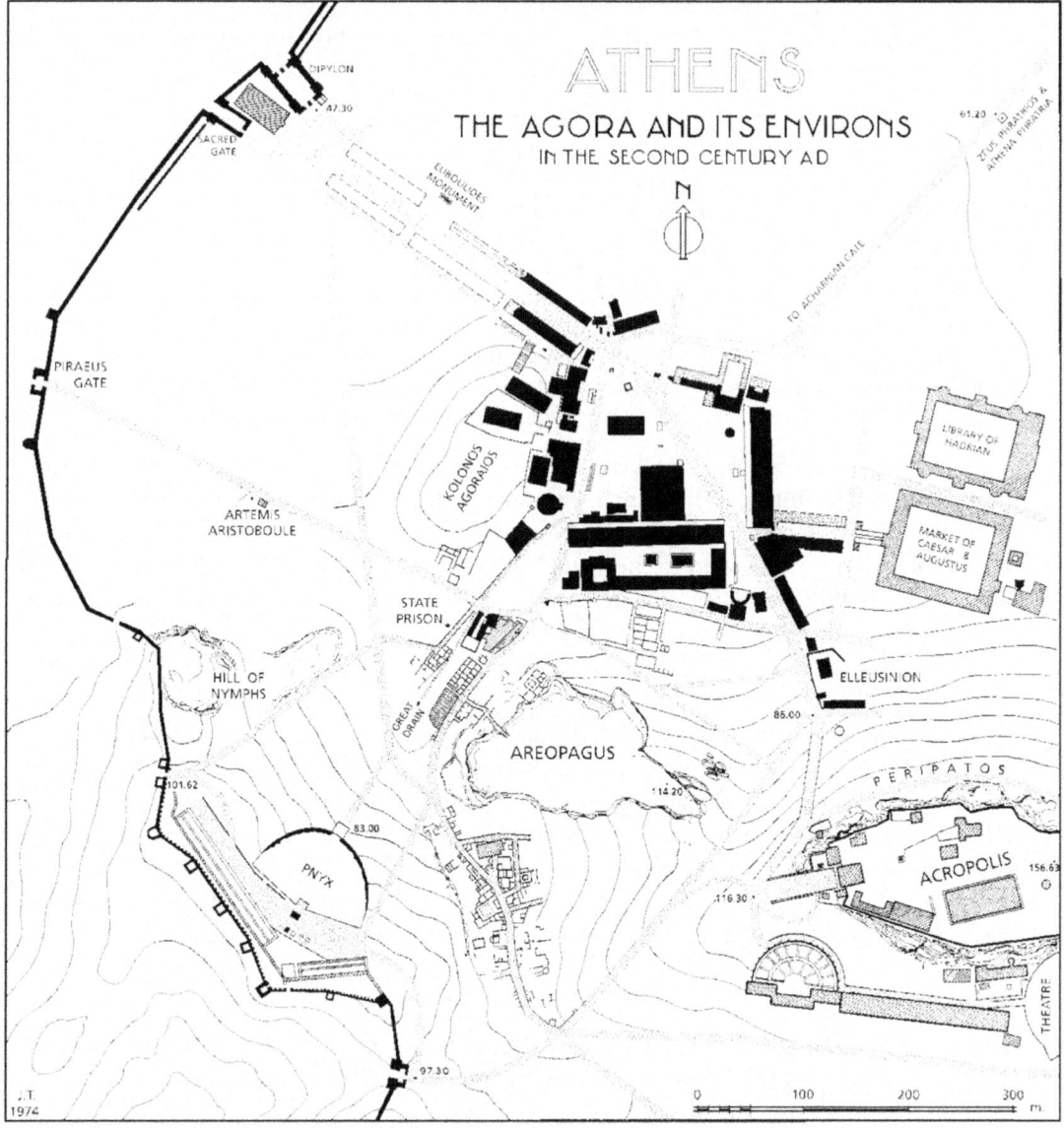

The Pnyx and its location in the ancient city of Athens (used with permission from the American School of Classical Studies: Agora Excavations).

The elected representatives of the citizens of Athens, the National Assembly, convened on the plateau on the top of a hill, some 500 meters west of the Acropolis. The name of this hill is Pnyx, dating from pre–Greek times, and its original meaning might have been "rock with a flat top." The hill has preserved its name up to the present.

The Greeks learned the name Pnyx from the "native" Athenians, that is the pre–Greek inhabitants of the city. The perseverance of the name form among the Greeks may well be a reflection of the significance that the Pnyx had, as a meeting place, for the native Europeans. Since only male citizens could be elected to the Assembly, the hilltop was reserved for men only. The flat hilltop, the original meeting-place for the members of the Assembly, was remodeled in several phases (Forsén and Stanton 1996) until, in the mid-fourth century BCE, the round retaining wall created conditions of intervisibility as in the other circular structures of the Athenian democracy.

> In the fifth century the people of Athens looked down on their politicians, and saw as a backdrop the Agora spread out beneath. Symbolically, the politician was in a subordinate position vis-à-vis the populace, and the focus of debate was not the individual politician but the needs of the city that lay constantly in view. In the fourth century, all changed: the politician was on a level with the people, and against the backdrop of rock the people could focus pin his personality.... In the mid fourth century the Pnyx attained its present form. More of the hill-side was cut away, the retaining wall moved outwards, and a harmonious fan-shaped auditorium was created, symmetrical save for the sanctuary of Zeus on the left-hand rock face. The speaker stood on a high rock podium in front of a semi-hewn square of rock of uncertain purpose. An axial line passes from the single central entrance-way through the speaker and the unhewn rock to a huge altar placed on the crest of the slope above, used for sacrifice at the start of an assembly [Wiles 1997: 35*f*].

And yet, also the women of Athens, convened at the Pnyx, but the place and the function of the women's meeting differed fundamentally from those of the men. The women convened at the foot of the Pnyx to celebrate the Thesmophoria and the Stenia which formed part of the cult of the goddess Demeter. These ritual activities took place in autumn (in the month of Pyanopsion, corresponding to September/October). The participation in these festive events was exclusive for women.

The Pnyx was the only place in the Athenian state where both men and women performed in public: the men on the hilltop taking care of communal-political affairs, and the women at the foot of the hill engaging in earthbound rituals with their roots in the pre–Greek past. During the classical era, one could see the focal points of Athenian life from the top of the Pnyx: the Agora in the northeast, the Areopagus (seat of the Supreme Court) at a short distance to the northeast, the Acropolis with the monumental Parthenon temple in the east and the theater of Dionysus on the southeastern slope of the Acropolis. All the mentioned sites have their own pre–Greek history, except for the theater. There had been no theaters as a genre of architecture in pre–Greek times, and this for a reason (see below).

The Council (*Boule*)

Originally, the boule had 400 members (according to Solon's reforms). Later, the number was set at 500. "According to Cleisthenes' plan, the new Council of 500 was to be made up of ten fifty-man delegations—one delegation from each of the ten newly created tribes. The members of each tribal delegation were in turn selected at deme level, serving for one year. Each year every deme sent forward a certain number of councilors, based on the deme's citizen population" (Ober 2008: 143). In the fifth century BCE, the *boule* functioned as the main administrative and judicial body of Athenian democracy (Rhodes 1972). The members of the *boule* (*bouleutai*) supervised the finances of the Athenian state and examined officials before and after their terms in office. The leading body of the *boule* was comprised of 50 men, selected from the overall 500. The 50 men who presided over the Council were called *prytaneis* (a pre–Greek term). The seat of the *boule* was on the western periphery of the Agora.

The Council maintained an archive where the written recordings (i.e., laws and regulations, decisions of the Assembly and of law suits) were kept. This was the older building of the Council (*bouleuterion* I) which was dedicated to the Great Mother (Megale Meter), Rhea, the mother of the gods. The archive building was known as the Metroon.

The High Court of Appeal (*Areopagos*)

At some distance from the Acropolis in the northwest rises a rock formation that became the seat of the Athenian High Court of Appeal. The Greek name *areopagos* or Areios Pagos literally means "Rock of Ares." According to Greek myth, Ares, the god of war, had to stand trial on this rock for the murder of Alirrothios, Poseidon's son. The institution of the *areopagos* itself is linked to Athena who organized the court and presided over it. One of the episodes of the *Iliad* is associated with the *areopagos*, the story of Orestes which is best known from the trilogy *Oresteia*, Aeschylus' tragedy (Agamemnon, the Choephori or Libation-Bearers and Eumenides) that was performed first in 458 BCE (Graf 1993: 157*ff*). After returning home from Troy, Agamemnon, Orestes' father, is murdered by his wife, Klytaimnestra, and her lover, Aigisthos. Inspired by the god Apollo, Orestes kills his mother and the murderous intruder into the family. Orestes is tried at the *areopagos*. When the judges cannot reach a majority verdict Athena gives her vote, which is a vote of acquittal (Dihle 1994: 102*ff*). In Greek juridical terminology the saying "the vote of Athena" was used to refer to a vote of acquittal. This was the custom in the voting process of the *heliaia* (see below).

Membership in the *areopagos* was restricted to persons who had held high offices and, after retiring, could be elected to serve, as judges, in the *areopagos*. The court was comprised of nine members who were called archons (*archontes*). Solon, himself an archon, was given authority by the other members of the *areopagos* to carry out the first democratic reforms in the city in 594 BCE. Judging from these conditions of membership and the association with the goddess Athena, it is reasonable to assume that the *areopagos* was the meeting place for the council of the elders of pre–Greek Athens.

While, in the network of democratic institutions devised by Solon, the *areopagos* held a top-level supervising function, its role changed with the introduction of Cleisthenes' reforms. The supervising function was assigned to the Council (*boule*) and the *areopagos* retained its function as high court. A radical change occurred in 462 BCE with the reforms of Ephialtes through which the role of the *areopagos* became marginalized. The only domain for this court that was retained was homicide.

The Court (*Heliaia*)

Neither the origin of the institution nor its name have been explained with certainty. It is not known whether the *heliaia* was introduced by Solon or by Cleisthenes, although it is assumed that Solon might have inspired the National Assembly to dedicate some of their sessions to agenda of trials and lawsuits. Some derive the name for this democratic institution from the verb *heliazesthai* ("to congregate") in ancient Greek. Others associate the name with the ancient custom to convene outdoors, that is, under the sun (i.e., *helios*, "sun"). The seat of the *heliaia* was a building in the south part of the Agora.

The *heliaia* was comprised of 6,000 members who were elected by the lot. Six hundred each were chosen by each of the ten tribes. The tenure of the court members (called *heliastai* "heliasts" or *dikastai* "dikasts") was one year. Six hundred was also the number of members in the chambers into which the *heliaia* was divided. In each chamber, some 500 served as regular members, the others as alternate jurors. The chambers were in session every day, with the exception of the last three days in a month. There were no meetings of the judges either on the days when the Assembly convened (Lanni 2006). Central offices in the *heliaia* were held by the *hegemon*, a kind of supervisor who was in charge of the registration of complaints, and by the herald (*keryx*) whose role was that of a coordinator of the formal procedures (i.e., calling on heliasts and witnesses to act, supervising the casting of the votes and announcing the results). The name for this official, *keryx*, is an element of the pre–Greek substratum (Beekes 2004: 112*ff*).

The role of the *heliaia* changed significantly in the course of time. As long as the *areopagos* was the top-level supervising body the *heliaia* functioned as ordinary court. With the reforms of Ephialtes the *heliaia* assumed most of the former functions of the *areopagos*.

The Old European Imprint on the Language of Greek Public Life and Athenian Democracy

One cannot expect to find a complete set of pre–Greek borrowings in ancient Greek, covering the whole range of the democratic endeavor, from the infrastructure of communal self-administration in the demes to institutions of public life in the Athenian state. The survival of substrate elements in Greek democratic terminology is fragmentary as it is in other domains (in agriculture, pottery, in the arts and with respect to social relations). And yet, in the nomenclature of Greek democracy a number of key terms point to a prolonged persistence of ideas about egalitarian society from Old Europe through classical antiquity.

Athenian democracy had its public institutions from which irradiated the values of democratic governance and which displayed the Athenians' pride in their political system. The most influential of these institutions are, at the same time, reminiscent of their pre–Greek past. One is the Great Panathenaia festival that was held every fourth year in summer (in the Athenian month of Hekatombion which corresponds to June/July). The Panathenaia was celebrated to honor the patron of Athenian democracy, the goddess Athena of whose pre–Greek origin the Greeks were well aware (see Chapter 1). The other is the meeting place of the National Assembly, the decision-making body of elected citizens, the Pnyx (see in the foregoing).

The institution of places for communal gatherings and speaking is no innovation of Greek society. The Agora in Athens is perhaps the best known of such places in the Greek world. The native Europeans had their meeting places long before the arrival of the Greeks. Remnants of the related terminology have been preserved, as substrate elements, in ancient Greek (i.e., *apellai, eire*).

At first sight it seems as if terminology of democratic institutions and procedures—as far as it stems from the substrate language—is somehow scattered throughout the democratic vocabulary. And yet, in a closer inspection of the lexical items, a concentration of pre–Greek terms in certain domains is revealed (Haarmann 2013a: 59*ff*). A procedure of central significance in the democratic system was the casting of lots. In this domain, the relatively high number of pre–Greek terms strikes the eye. There were two key terms for the lots, each associated with a different context. One was *kuamos* ("bean"). Beans were used in communal elections while small pebble stones were cast by the members of the areopagus and the *heliaia*. The word for "pebble stone" in ancient Greek is *psephos* which is an element borrowed from the substrate language. The vote of acquittal, "Athena's vote" was called *psephos Athenas*. The urn into which the stones were thrown was called *kethis,* and the lid to cover the opening also had a pre–Greek name, *kemos*.

Pre-Greek elements in the domains of community life, communal governance and political order in the city-state:

(i) Administrative units; places for communal gatherings
  apellai "enclosed space, meeting place, (people's) assembly" (Apella was the name for the National Assembly in Sparta)
  eire "place of speaking or gathering"
  kome "village," "district" (as opposed to a strengthened polis)
  oie "village"
  teramna / teremna "home, residence (lyre)"

(ii) Relationships of authority and power:
  aisymnao "to be ruler"
  brabeus "judge at the games, arbitrator; leader"
  (h)eros "hero; lord"; several feminine formations (*heroïne, heroïssa*, etc.)
  kybernao "to steer, head for," "to govern, rule (metaphor)"
  peos / paos (Aeol. Dor.) "kinsman by alliance"
  phylax / phylakos "watcher, guardian, protector"

(iii) Administration and its personal, modes and requisites of governance
  epissophos "a yearly changing official in Thera"
  kemos "plaited lid of the balloting urn"
  keryx "herald, messenger"; In Athens under the democracy, *keryx* was an office in the court (see above). It is possible "that he had a religious function in Mycenaean times [...]. If he had, it would not be very surprising: in ancient times religion was so dominant that it could hardly be expected not to be the case" (Beekes 2004: 114).
  kolakretai (*kola + ageiro*) "financial officers in early Athens, chairmen of the main treasury"
  maiomai "to investigate, search," name of an Athenian officer, financial officer
  prytanis / protanis (Aeolic) "foreman, chief of affairs, prytan (title of a leading official, in Athens member of the governing committee of the council)" (derivation *prytaneuo / brytaneuo* (Cret.) "to be prytan")
  psephos "stone for casting a lot (in elections for public offices; when finding a verdict in trials)"
  rabdos "staff, magic wand" (cf. *rabd-oukhos* "staff-bearer," name of an official)
  trittys / triptys / triktys "third of a tribe (phyle)"

The concept *trittys* refers to a distinction of forms of landscape, and the original meaning is "three-fold division, division according to thirds." When the new tribal order—with the distinction of ten Greek tribes—was established by Cleisthenes, he determined that the demes were grouped according to a threefold division so "that in each tribe demes from the city would constitute one third, demes from the inland region another third, and demes from the coastal region the final third" (Osborne 1996: 299). In all probability, the division into thirds was no innovation devised by Cleisthenes but he drew on a habit of dividing demes into overarching groupings that was practiced by the native Europeans. A clear indication of this is the pre–Greek origin of the concept and the word *trittys* (Beekes 2010: 1510).

(iv) Symbols of authority, power or honor
bakteria "staff, stick, scepter (as a symbol of judges)"
eiresione "an olive or laurel twig adorned with red and white bands and decorated with fruits," as a symbol of fertility; "a song when carrying this twig around," "wreath (of honor)"
kigklis "latticed gate," especially those through which counselors entered the court of justice or the meeting hall
thronos "throne, seat," "chair of state, judge's seat"

(v) Public communication in the city-state
kyrbeis "rotating pillars or columns (in the form of a three-sided pyramid) on which the laws of Solon were inscribed," "inscribed tablets"
peteuron / petauron / penteuron "public noticeboard," "high platform"
pinax / pinakos "writing table," "public statement"

While the rise of democracy in Athens was dramatic, the decline of democratic governance was not. The formalized political order that was established by Cleisthenes lasted into the 340s BCE when the Athenian state succumbed to the imperial expansion of Macedon. During the epoch of democracy, the Athenians experienced three major wars. In the first of these wars, the Persian Wars (490–479 BCE), the Athenians were victorious and laid the foundation for their empire. They were at the height of their imperial power in the latter half of the fifth century BCE.

The prosperous era ended when the Athenians engaged in the Peloponnesian War (431–404 BCE) against Sparta which had disastrous effects for the region and brought the Athenian state to the brink of collapse. The Athenians never truly recovered from the war against Sparta and their state experienced social unrest and financial crises.

It is noteworthy that the Athenians commemorated their ideal of democratic governance when this model of society was already on its decline. The end of the Peloponnesian Wars (404 BCE) meant for Athens surrender to Sparta's demands. An oligarchic regime, political puppets of Sparta, was installed in Athens, called the "Thirty Tyrants". Some exiled Athenians revolted under the leadership of Thrasybulus (Buck 1998). The renegades occupied Phyle, on the border between Boeotia and Attica, from where they set out to battle the Spartan garrison in Athens. After the liberation of Athens and the ousting of the tyrants, democracy was restored and celebrated thereafter in a special festival, the "Celebration of the return from Phyle" (Schwenk 1997: 10*ff*). This day of commemoration was celebrated in autumn, in the month of Boedromion (corresponding to August/September).

In the 350s BCE, Athens had to cope with the rising power in the north, Macedon, and, in the third war of its history (338 BCE), Athens fell victim to the expansionist pressure of the Macedonian kingdom. The Athenians tried to free themselves of Macedonian supremacy after the death of Alexander the Great in 323 BCE and organized military resistance. In the Lamian war that followed, the Athenians were defeated.

> After the Lamian war, Macedon mandated the end of democracy in Athens. Although a deep cultural commitment to democracy remained, and for the next two generations the Athenians would use every opportunity presented them to seek to restore democratic institutions, notably in 317

and 307, democracy would never be securely reestablished. Oligarchic governments mandated by Macedonian kings eliminated the People's Courts and other key democratic institutions, and disenfranchised and expelled large numbers of lower-class citizens [Ober 2008: 69].

The deconstruction of the former civic institutions in Athens was only the last step toward the abolition of democracy. Some scholars describe the political situation before the outbreak of the Lamian war as a virtual "implosion" or collapse of democratic governance (Scott 2012: 92*ff*).

It took the Greek people more than two thousand years before their independence was restored in the nineteenth century and even longer before democratic rule was reestablished in the twentieth century.

Theater as a Mirror of Greek Democracy

All cultures of the world, whether historical or recent, operate with a certain category of behavioral strategies that enhance in-group solidarity, maintain the rigidity of the knowledge obtained from previous generations, and reassure the sustainability of society. These strategies are called "rituals." The existence of "ritual as culture's symbolic nexus" (Doty 2000: 335) is not only universal in the global geography of human cultures, it can also be assumed for all stages of human evolution. Rituals encompass all things that there are, both in the "visible and invisible realms" (Wiener 1995).

> Rituals are performative: they are acts done; and performances are ritualized: they are codified, repeatable actions. The functions of theatre identified by Aristotle and Horace—entertainment, celebration, enhancement of social solidarity, education (including political education), and healing—are also functions of ritual. The difference lies in context and emphasis. Rituals emphasize efficacy: healing the sick, initiating neophytes, burying the dead, teaching the ignorant, forming and cementing social relations, maintaining (or overthrowing) the status quo, remembering the past, propitiating the gods, exorcising the demonic, maintaining cosmic order [Schechner 1994: 613].

There is consensus among scholars that ritual preceded theater, that ritualistic performance provides the mind frame for the reworking of eternal human matters (i.e., love, hatred, liberty, power, death) projected into the fictitious world of theater. If this is true, then it is reasonable to assert that theater is ritualistic healing and that the impression of a play goes far beyond entertainment, for example, with the experience of "drama as therapy" (Jones 1996).

> In general a ritual is an act involving performative uses of language (for example, in blessing, praising, cursing, consecrating, purifying) [...] and a formal pattern of behaviour either closely or more loosely followed. Religious ritual has as one of its major forms what may be called focused ritual, in which the ritual activity is addressed to sacred beings, such as gods or ancestors. Another major form of religious ritual is what may be called harnessing ritual or yogic ritual in which patterns of behaviour are used as part of a process of self-control that seeks attainment of higher states of consciousness [Smart 1997: 72].

The linkage between ritual and theatrical performance has been investigated with some scrutiny (e.g., Kowalzig 2007b). However, the historical depth of this linkage has not yet been fully perceived by classical scholars. Some would look for the origins of theatrical performance but, following Vernant and Vidal-Naquet (1990: 23) "it would be better to speak of antecedents." The symbiotic interplay between drama and ritual can be reconstructed for a world where the early Greeks vividly interacted with the native Europeans. Processions in the archaic period were more comprehensive than in the classical era since they included theatrical performances in which both men and women participated. In ancient Athens, processions ended on the Agora which played an important role as a political meeting place and cult center. Theatrical performances, in the archaic period, marked the final phase of processions, and it is important to perceive "the position of the 'theatre' as end-point of a procession. The procession was the core of the rural Dionysia, and theatrical performances an addendum" (Wiles 1997: 26). That was before theaters were constructed.

Theater as Performance

The sixth century BCE saw a breaking away from older ritual traditions and a remodeling of cultural life. The major occurrence was the separation of the theatrical performances from the organization of the processions that continued to be held. The consequences of the separation were of a formal rather than of a contextual nature. The performances remained ritualistic and religiously connotated. Inferring from observations in the study of oral literature in a traditional culture, one may conclude that the impact of the verbal strategies that came to bear in theatrical performances in archaic Greece were most probably characterized by similar functions and structures, both in the context of processions and in the newly devised space, the theater. This means that the texts were oriented at formulaic language use typical of rituals. The use of formulaic language made it easier for the spectators in the theater to identify with the contents of the scenes since they were accustomed to formulaic presentations from previous events of processions.

> Structural familiarity and conventionality are those factors in the process of memorisation which are also apparent when studying the complex composed of formulaic systems and families of formulae, typical scenes and themes. The supply of formulaic vocabulary, scenes and plots is structured with the help of interconnecting links in the same way as information stored in the memory generally. Particular formulae and the systems formed from them are grouped together thematically, some image elements and ideas link up with each other, some scenes have a tendency to attract certain details, etc. Tradition-oriented members of a culture (both performers and listeners) are thus more easily able to assimilate and reproduce elements organised formulaically [Harvilahti 2000: 59*f*].

Another conclusion is evident. In the early stage of development of theatrical performance, independent of processions, the spoken texts and the scenical arrangements were much simpler than what the Greek theater produced in the classical period. Elaboration and sophistication of language use and narrative lay in the future, with great names such as Aeschylus, Aristophanes, Sophocles and Euripides (Mastromarco and Totaro 2012: 68*ff*, 94*ff*, 120*ff*, 192*ff*).

Even when theatrical performance had been separated from the performance of ritual processions it remained associated with the tradition of mythical narration.

Fifth-century Attic tragedy, like archaic epic poetry, took its subjects almost exclusively from myth. Tragedies on nonmythical themes were never more than experimental.... Tragedy was also influenced by the treatment of myth in epic poetry. Even ancient authors called Homer the father of tragedy, and Aeschylus reportedly said that he worked with the crumbs from Homer's table (TrGF vol. 3, T 112a–b). The tragic poet deliberately situated himself in the epic tradition of mythical narration (Graf 1993: 142).

The ancient links with ritual processions can be readily identified in the genre of Greek tragedies. Aeschylus who is regarded by many to be the father of European drama carefully preserves the memory of the old roots of Greek theater, that is ritualistic performance of dance and song. He is the writer who most attentively interconnects satyr motifs with other elements of drama.

Dramatists competing at the Athens festival had to present three serious plays and one satyr-play; Aeschylus normally made the three plays a connected "trilogy" in which each part, though a complete unity, was a coherent part of a larger unity. This gave his drama the amplitude which his vast conceptions needed (Hartnoll and Found 1992: 7).

In the theaters that were constructed for performances there always was an altar near the stage which assumed a crucial function for the movement of the actors. The theater as a space with specific functions of performance is a secondary innovation. This can be illustrated by the etymology of the Greek term *theatron*. The stem *thea* points at a word of the pre–Greek substratum, meaning "theatrical performance" (Beekes 2010: 536). The suffix -*tron* (denoting a means for achieving an effect—in this case devising a space for display) was added later, once the architectural form of theaters was introduced. "As a literary genre with its own rules and characteristics tragedy introduces a new type of spectacle into the system of the city-state's public festivals" (Vernant and Vidal-Naquet 1990: 23).

In addition to the key concept *thea(tron)* the terminology of Greek theater contains other core expressions of pre–Greek origin:

brikeloi characters in tragedy
kerkis "wedge-shaped division of the seats in the theater" (metaphorical after the original meaning "weaver's shuttle")
kokyma "lamenting (tragedy)"
mimos "mime (name of an actor)"
pitylos "rhythmical, heavy beat (tragedy)"
thea "sight, theatrical spectacle"

Theater as Architectural Form

The layer of pre–Greek terms in the lexical domain of house construction is extensive. And yet, there are no known borrowings relating to the construction of theaters. This is not surprising since there were no theaters in Greece before the sixth century BCE, and there are no architectural remains of earlier periods that would resemble Greek theaters. According to the traditions of the pre–Greek era, there was no need for a separate architectural form since theatrical spectacles were performed along the routes of processions.

It is not clear whether the rectangular shape of theaters is older than the theater with a circular space for the audience. In any case, it has been emphasized that the round shape was the preferred model since the period when democracy was introduced (i.e., since the fifth century BCE), and this form originated in Athens (Ober 2008: 200*ff*).

The circular shape of the space for the audience offers a practical as well as a symbolic advantage over rectangular constructions. "An inward-facing circle allows maximum eye-contact; each person knows that other people know because each person can visually verify that others are paying attention" (Chwe 2001: 5). Each spectators has a chance, not only to follow how the plot unfolds but to also observe the reactions of other spectators to what happens on the stage. Intervisibility is given priority, not only in the construction of theaters, but also of other public buildings.

There is a historical association between democracy in Athens and architecture promoting intervisibility. Like the Greek theater, the *ekklesiasterion* (theater-like public meeting place for gatherings of a city assembly; in Athens, the Pnyx), the *bouleuterion* (large-scale roofed public building for a large probouleutic council), and the *prutanikon* (public building intended for public gatherings of several dozen magistrates; in Athens, the Tholos) may be Athenian architectural innovations [Ober 2008: 209].

Above and opposite: **Plan of the Theater of Dionysus and its environment (photograph and drawing by Hans R. Goette): (a) Photograph of the theater from the southeast; (b) Drawing of the architectural complex.**

7. Old European Bases of Social Egalitarianism

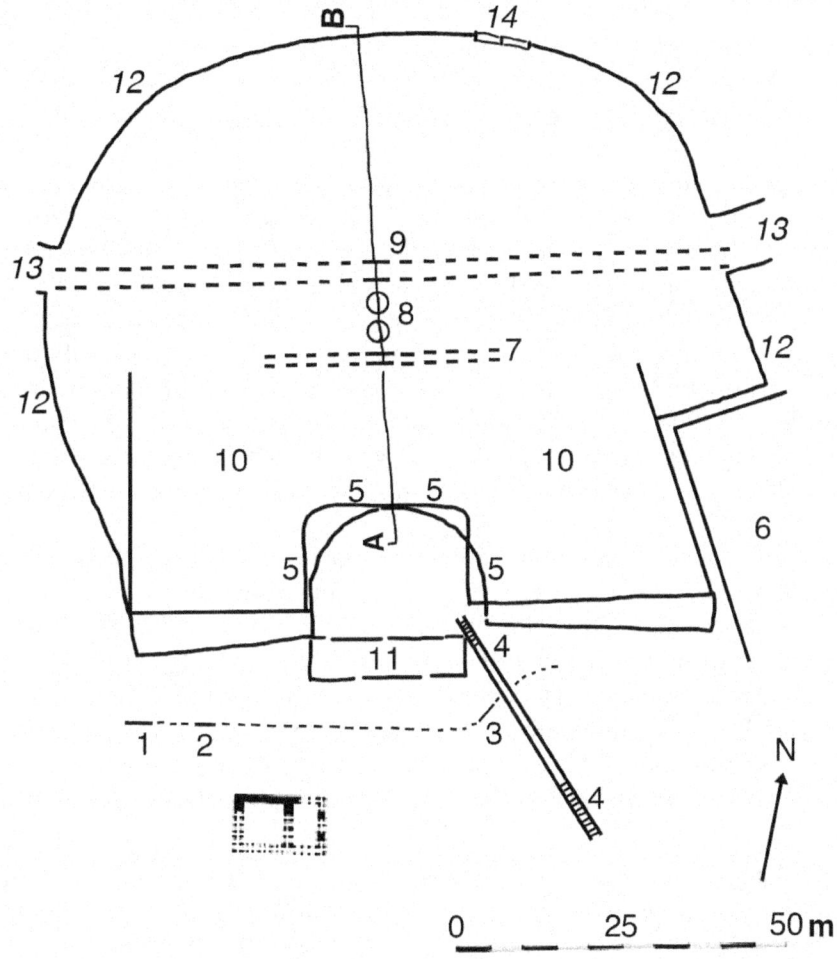

1–3: late Archaic terrace wall: 1: wall SM 4; 2: wall SM 2; 3: wall SM 1
4: water channel (drainage for the orchestra)
5: *prohedria*
6: Odeion of Perikles
7: rock cutting for theatre access (or foundation for back wall of theatre)
8: two wells belonging to a house
9: ancient road (later Peripatos)
10: reconstructed *theatron* of the Classical theatre
11: reconstructed *skene* of the Classical theatre
A–B: Doerpfeld's excavation trench through the *theatron*
12: outline of the 'Lykurgan' *theatron*
13: entry points of the Peripatos
14: choregic monument of Thrasyllos (320/19 BC) at the 'katatome'

The most perfectioned form of the circular theater is the amphitheater. Most of the amphitheaters of antiquity were constructed by the Romans (Bomgardner 2000). The best-known amphitheater of the Roman world is perhaps the Colosseum in Rome. This monumental building, erected between 72 and 80 CE, ranges among the greatest works of Roman architecture. At the same time it is the biggest building which Jewish people have ever constructed. Those who built the Colosseum were Jewish prisoners of war who had been brought to Italy by Vespasian after his victory over the Jewish army in Iudaea, ending the first Jewish-Roman war.

The popularity of the theater—as a place of social contact and an environment for a reaffirmation of Greek cultural traditions through artistic interaction—increased in the course of time, and this can be inferred from the growing capacities to accommodate spectators. The history of the Theater of Dionysus, located on the southern slope of the Acropolis, is quite informative in this regard. The original version of this particular theater, built in the classical period (fifth century BCE), had seats for some 4,000 spectators while the enlarged version of the Hellenistic era (fourth century BCE) offered space for a maximum of 17,000 spectators (Gogos 2008). "The Classical theatre of Dionysos was almost completely built over by the new, greatly enlarged building that was finished during the time of Lykurgos, perhaps in 329 BC. Little evidence remains with which to reconstruct the Classical theatre" (Goette 2007: 116).

The development that has been outlined for the transition from pre-Greek religious activity to Greek performance in a specific architectural form, the theater, repeated itself, once again, in the renewal of the genre of theater plays in medieval Europe. The theaters of antiquity with their pagan tradition of performances were abandoned by the Christians. And yet, the idea of dramatizing plots and performing them for a public that was in need of spiritual guidance did not die but was revived. The pagan agenda of human drama was replaced by stories from the Bible. And just like among the Pelasgians and early Greeks, theatrical performances served the purpose to enhance group cohesion also among medieval people.

> In traditional guild theater, which was performed in, by, and for specific local communities, actors and audience were known to one another. On religious holidays a series of plays based on stories from the Old and New Testaments was performed sequentially at various stations or places within a medieval town. Rather than formal theaters, the place of performance was often a pageant wagon. Numerous members of the community were involved in these productions, each of which was sponsored by one of the town guilds. Those who were not actors in the performance helped with preparation or participated as audience members watching the enactment of the timeless truths of biblical history [Howard and Rackin 1997: 31].

And just like the Greeks designed a specific form of architecture—as a space reserved for theatrical performances (i.e., rectangular and semi-circular theaters)—in the sixth and fifth centuries BCE, special buildings for theater plays were constructed, once again, in the sixteenth century. The oldest theater in western Europe was the Theatre, built by James Burbage on the south bank of the Thames in 1576. That was some ten years before Shakespeare came to London.

Theater and the Agenda of Gender

When addressing the agenda of gender in Greek theater we are left with a kind of void that has so far not been satisfactorily explained. Women occupied various niches in Greek society of antiquity. They could act as priestesses in public cults and they could actively engage in commercial transactions (see the role of the *kapelis* as described in Chapter 4).

Women were manipulated in Athenian legislation in their roles as mothers of Athenian citizens and as heiresses (see Chapter 5). But, otherwise, women had no socially acknowledged role in public life. This automatically excluded them from one of the most popular cultural institutions, from theatrical performances. There were no female actors and women's parts in theater plays were executed by cross-dressing men, a situation that has been called "classic drag" (Case 1985) in modern scholarship. And this lack of proportion in gender representation created a long-term imbalance in Europe's cultural history.

> European theatre has been criticized as male-generated, with one-sided male cross-dressing, and for excluding women from the stage for two thousand years (Ferris, *Acting Women,* [1989]). It was not until the seventeenth century that actresses were gradually accepted on the stage, yet they were often commodified as objects of desire for the pleasure of the male audience [Leung Li 2003: 29].

The exclusivity of male actors and the phenomenon of cross-dressing to play female parts has a parallel in the history of the Chinese opera. In the Far East, too, theatrical performances lay in the responsibility of male actors and choreographers. And just like in ancient Greek theater, the audience in Chinese theaters was male dominated. The lack of female representation on the stage of Greek theaters found its parallel in the absence of women in the audience. The deficiency of ancient Greek democracy—the exclusion of women from public life—echoed strongly in the masses of spectators who crowded the theaters in the thousands.

Aristophanes whose works have been categorized as "political comedies" ridicules the issue of women as spectators, and Plato warns of some kind of cultural collapse should women and slaves be allowed to attend theater performances. Chauvinism and prejudice about women's mental capacities and social roles produced even more radical scenarios of rejection of female spectators.

> In a famous (and apocryphal?) story from the anonymous *Life of Aeschylus,* there is mention of women in the audience at the performance of the poet's *Oresteia.* In the final tragedy, Eumenides, Aeschylus randomly introduced the chorus of the eponymous chthonic divinities, who so terrified the demos that children passed out and women miscarried [Roselli 2011: 160].

Although women always remained unrepresented in ancient Greek theater, the female agenda was present in the theater plays, at the mercy of male perceptions of women's roles in society. Examples of this abound: the plays *Women of Aetna* by Aeschylus, *Assembly Women, Lysistrata, Thesmophoriazusae* and *Women seizing the Skênas* by Aristophanes, *Iphigenia in Tauris* and *Trojan Women* by Euripides, *Women Lunching Together* by Menander, *Antigone, Oedipus Rex* and *Women of Trachis* by Sophocles.

How Democratic Was Democratic Governance in the Athenian City-State?

At first sight, this question may seem odd. If the kind of political order in antiquity which the Greeks themselves called *demokratia* ("governance of the deme system" and, in a wider sense "political power of the people") was a Greek institution developed on a pre–Greek foundation, then it was democratic by self-definition. The question "how democratic was democracy in antiquity?" can be (and is) addressed as viewed from our modern standpoint. This certainly involves the risk of distorting sociopolitical realities of the past in light of modern conceptualizations and priorities of political culture.

Any discussion about the virtues of democracy in our days includes certain a priori standards that were either unknown or otherwise little developed in societies of the past. In a functioning modern democracy, members of either sex have the right to vote and be elected for parliament, and there is no infringement of this right as regards membership in a religious community or in a social group. In ancient Athenian society, there were numerous restrictions as to the basic rights of the citizens to act politically. Human rights were not on the agenda in classical Greece, neither among intellectuals nor among politicians.

It is often claimed that the Athenian city-state, once it had risen victoriously from the Persian Wars and once democratic governance had been secured, lived a "golden age" of peace and prosperity. As for the latter this holds true, but for the former it does not because peace was in short supply. In fact, democratic governance did not stop the violence between Athens and states that were considered rivals.

Athens under the democracy was a bellicose state that waged war with almost all the other states, of which Sparta is only the best known. The Athenian national army set out on its summer campaign every year. While the members of the National Assembly enjoyed their summer "vacation," the army conquered and sacked ever new cities and ports around the coasts of the Aegean, subdued their inhabitants, took many as slaves and women as concubines for the soldiers. The wealth of Athens and its growing might as a maritime power was built on the political suppression of rival cities and on the continuous collection of spoils.

The Exclusion of Slaves from Citizenship

There was no abolition movement of slavery in antiquity, and there existed no consensus regarding all human beings to be equal. On the contrary, a clear distinction was always made between free citizens and others who spent their lives in serfdom or slavery. Slavery was perceived as part of a social system that had been devised by the gods. And although members of the lowest social class, poor citizens, were not much appreciated in the political discourse, these nevertheless belonged to a different category than slaves.

> In general, rather than any impetus to grant to slaves the political freedom attained by the poor citizen, we find that the opposite attitude predominated. The slave served as the "Other" against which all citizens, from rich slaveholders to poor artisans, defined themselves as a unity. Thus, although the philosophers consider slave and master a natural pair, in popular discourse the opposite of slave was citizen—despite the fact that at least half of the citizen body did not own slaves and artisans sometimes worked next to slaves at identical jobs [Hunt 2011: 25].

Despite the fact that the dichotomy of slave and master was deeply rooted in the ancient Greeks' mentality some historiographers and philosophers entertained the idea that slavery had not always been a marker of society but that, in the past, people enjoyed the fruits of their own labor, without the participation of slaves. When the time came that rich landowners could afford to buy slaves was not known to the Greeks in classical antiquity, nor has modern scholarship produced any reliable timeframe.

> According to local traditions, this way of acquiring slaves [buying slaves in quantity] was a novelty of the archaic age (cf. Timaeus in Ath. 6.264c). It was generally believed that there was a time when free people had to perform all the required tasks, without assistance from slaves (Herodotus

6.137; Pherecrates in Ath. 6.263b). Before the sixth or, possibly, the seventh century, almost all slaves in the Greek world were either natives or captives [Kyrtatas 2011: 92].

This observation of the conditions of the early phase of slavery in the Greek world can be corroborated by linguistic evidence. In classical antiquity, the general term for "slave" was *doulos,* this being a word of Cretan origin. In the ancient Greek vocabulary, some older expressions for "slave" and "slavery" survived which stem from the pre–Greek substrate language: *atmen* "servant, slave," *latmeneia* "slavery." These expressions clearly differ in meaning from another substrate borrowing which refers to a free person in relation to someone else: *therapon,* which can mean "attendant, servant" and "companion." Apparently, the native Europeans were among the first slaves of the Greeks, and they coined terms for their servitude in their native language. The Greeks adopted these expressions for marking the social status of subjugated locals.

The Role of Women as Passive Citizens

While slaves, by their social status, were excluded from citizenship in the Athenian state, women possessed citizenship, but they were doomed to passivity. Female citizens had no right to vote, nor were they allowed to speak in public or address political issues (Lee 2011). It has always been known that women had no voice in public in ancient Greek society, but the gender issue was addressed systematically as late as the 1970s.

> The widespread discovery of women in antiquity in the Anglo-American world belongs mostly to the 1970s and 1980s, following on the rise of the women's movement in the late 1960s and early 1970s, in the atmosphere of so-called "second-wave" feminism. A key feature of the scholarship that arose in the wake of this feminism was its interdisciplinarity: scholars in all academic fields had discovered it as a political and social movement, shared ideas with one another and drew heavily on the same core body of literary and social theory [Foxhall 2013: 6].

The stereotyped image of the woman as a passive member in Greek society had been advocated in the works of epic literature long before the first written laws were compiled.

> From poetic performances, the Greeks learned that there were two categories of women: the "honest" ones and "the others." They also learned the criteria—objective, not subjective—that placed women into one or the other: honest women lived in an *oikos,* that is to say, in a household, governed by a man (*anax oikoio,* in Homer: the sovereign of the house). The others lived alone. Their different style of life determined the way their sexual behavior was perceived: if an "honest" woman protected by the *oikos'* walls and by bonds of family affection had illicit sexual relations, she was either seduced by a man or induced by a force that she could not resist. "The others," instead, had sexual relations by seducing their partners, often overcoming their resistance [Cantarella 2005: 238].

When reducing the number of slaves and passive citizens (i.e., women without the right to vote) from the demographic record in the Athenian state, then only between 15 and 20 percent of the total population had the right to vote and be elected for the National Assembly, and these active citizens were all adult men, aged 18 years and older. All decision-making of political governance in Athens lay, thus, in the hands of a minority. Democracy in classical antiquity was a manifestation of an elite, of a kind of extended oligarchy whose members executed political power over a majority of inhabitants of the region, and the voices of these people were not heard in public.

Restrictions for Foreigners (Metics) in the Athenian State

The more powerful the Athenian state became the more its territory—the city of Athens in particular—attracted foreigners to reside there. Thousands of foreign residents, called metics (after Greek *metoikos* "resident alien settled in a foreign city, immigrant") settled down in Athens and other urban centers. Most of these metics were merchants who were engaged in trade with Greeks or who traded for Greek aristocratic families. Another group of metics were mercenaries who served under Greek command, artisans and specialized craftsmen.

> Although there was considerable variation over time in Athens' desirability as an immigration destination, if it could be averaged over the course of the democratic era (508–322), Athens would probably rank at the top of the list of all *poleis* as a chosen destination. That would not be the case in the two centuries preceding or following the democratic era [Ober 2008: 43].

Metics had no right to own property, they had to pay taxes (while Athenian citizens would be exempted), and they were not allowed to vote for or be elected into the National Assembly. Before a metic could settle down he/she had to be assigned an Athenian citizen as guardian. While Athenian citizens who committed a criminal offense were either fined or imprisoned, metics, once found guilty, were fined and extradited. These conditions of foreign residents in democratic Athens do not seem surprising since they resemble the restrictions of the rights of foreign residents in many modern democracies.

In many modern democratic societies, foreigners are allowed to participate in public festive events, just like the metics in Athens who could join the sacred procession on the occasion of the Panathenaia. Maurizio (1998: 302) has categorized the metics who joined the Athenian citizens in the procession: (i) metic girl parasol bearers (*skiadephoroi*), (ii) metic girl stool bearers (*diphrophoroi*), (iii) metic men tray bearers (*skaphephoroi*), (iv) metic girl water bearers (*hydriaphoroi*), (v) representatives of other cities who brought offerings, (vi) non-citizens and freed slaves (with oak branches).

While the exclusion of metics from processes of political decision-making seems a natural and somehow timeless limitation of their sociopolitical status, slaveholding and the exclusion of women from public life are properties that do not meet the standards of our modern understanding of democracy.

Timeless Virtues of Athenian Democracy

And yet, democracy in classical Greece offered much that has stood the test of time and is valid today as it was two and a half thousand years ago. The virtues of the traditional deme system were confirmed by Cleisthenes and safeguarded (see for *isegoria, isonomia, isopoliteia* in the foregoing) through his reforms. The representatives of the local demes were elected to become members of the National Assembly through direct vote, and candidates for all public offices were directly elected by the voters.

There were clear limitations as to the tenure of someone in office. Public offices were limited to a tenure of one year, thus preventing the rise of a dominant technocracy. The generals of the national army served only during one summer season. They were elected during the last session of the National Assembly before the summer break, and their number was ten, each representing one of the Greek tribes. After the military campaigns of summer the generals had to step down and become ordinary citizens again. This procedure was a precaution against any attempt of a military coup d'état.

Especially the technical procedure of direct election to the National Assembly and to offices made Athenian democracy highly transparent and its mechanism controllable (Çakmak 2011), something that is not even present in many modern democratic systems. If we leave out the major deficiencies of non-participation, of women and slaves, in the political process, then Athenian democracy corresponded to the standards set by Abraham Lincoln in his definition of democracy as "government of the People, by the People and for the People." Democracy in classical antiquity was a much easier business than in any of our modern models of democracy. There were no political parties that would have formed pressure groups in the National Assembly. The elected members represented their local demes, and they, as individuals, made decisions for the benefit of their village communities, of the city (polis) as well as for the state. There was no danger of political parties blocking or boycotting parliamentary decision-making or of rivalry of parties instrumentalizing their power of partisanship to outsmart ruling governments (as manifested in confrontations of Congress and Senate in the USA).

The ancient Greeks, above all the Athenians, were not shy when it came to hailing their cultural achievements. They boasted with their superiority over non–Greeks (i.e., "barbarians"), with their victories over their enemies, the Persians in particular, and with the perfection of their democratic institutions. A rare document is preserved for posterity, a text that was produced at the height of the political power of the Athenian state, at the beginning of the Peloponnesian War (431–404 BCE). In this text, the virtues of democracy are celebrated, by which Athens sets itself apart from other city-states, from their worst enemy, Sparta, in particular. This text is a funeral oration, delivered by Pericles (ca. 495–429 BCE) after the first year of war to commemorate the Athenian soldiers who had lost their lives in the fights with the Spartans. Pericles was perhaps the most influential representative of Athenian democracy in the fifth century BCE and he set in motion various reforms to stabilize the political system. He was not only a far-sighted statesman, he was also a brilliant orator, and the oration, attributed to him by the historiographer Thucydides, is a model text highlighting the virtues of democratic governance.

> Our constitution does not copy the laws of neighboring states; we are rather a pattern to others than imitators ourselves. Its administration favors the many instead of the few; this is why it is called a democracy. If we look to the laws, they afford equal justice to all in their private differences; if to social standing, advancement in public life falls to reputation for capacity, class considerations not being allowed to interfere with merit; nor again does poverty bar the way, if a man is able to serve the state, he is not hindered by the obscurity of his condition. The freedom which we enjoy in our government extends also to our ordinary life. There, far from exercising a jealous surveillance over each other, we do not feel called upon to be angry with our neighbor for doing what he likes, or even to indulge in those injurious looks which cannot fail to be offensive, although they inflict no positive penalty. But all this ease in our private relations does not make us lawless as citizens. Against this fear is our chief safeguard, teaching us to obey the magistrate and the laws, particularly such as regard the protection of the injured, whether they are actually on the statute book, or belong to that code which, although unwritten, yet cannot be broken without acknowledged disgrace [Thucydides 1914: 121–22].

What makes Athenian democracy significant for posterity is that it serves as a precursor for all other known models of democratic governance throughout history. It is not so much the reality of democratic rule in the Athenian city-state that has impressed subsequent generations and cultures. Rather, it is the image of a model of governance that highlights virtues and values of timeless significance which makes democracy's popularity. The Roman orator Cicero (first century BCE) elaborates on the virtues of democracy in a special section ("Scipio's dream") of his work *On the Republic*. Cicero evokes the vision of a dream in which Scipio Africanus, the Roman commander who had won a glorious victory over Hannibal at the battle of Zama toward the end of the Second Punic War (202 BCE). Scipio Africanus did not destroy Carthage; history left this task to his grandson who was also called Scipio. In a fictitious conversation, Scipio Senior spoke to Scipio Junior about how to achieve immortality. According to Scipio Senior, the key to immortality lies in professing the virtues of democracy: fulfilling his duty to the gods and, above all, to the state (i.e., to the Roman Republic), honoring the forefathers and their wisdom and respecting customary law.

Cicero's work was not much appreciated by recent posterity. And yet, his visionary story became popular—and even famous—starting in the Middle Ages. There is a painting of Scipio's dream by Raphael and a literary remake by Chaucer (in his poem *The Parliament of Fowls*). When Mozart was sixteen years of age he composed an opera in one act in which the dream travel of the two Scipios is enacted. Unbelievable as it may seem, the theme of Scipio's dream is found at the end of the major work of Karl Marx, *Das Kapital,* in the version of a visionary poem by Alfred, Lord Tennyson.

> We have adopted some high principles from Athens and Rome: tolerance, and civility and equality and democracy. And we have picked up some agreeable habits. But we seem to have mislaid Scipio's dream. And the search parties are still out there looking for it [Mount 2010: 378].

Epilogue
The Long Trail of Old Europe and Its Aftermath in Western Civilization

The ancient Greeks were smart. They adapted successfully to an environment with manifold features. When the Helladic tribes, as migrants, arrived in the land they came to call Hellas, they were land-bound pastoralists. Within the span of a few generations they had accustomed to live in divergent ecological surroundings, in the plains, in the mountains and on the seashore.

The ancient Greeks were smart. Upon their arrival the early Greeks got to know the achievements of their new neighbors, the native Pelasgians, and they soon became aware how much they could learn from them and how much they would profit from their newly obtained knowledge. The early Greeks set their minds to learning from those who had developed standards of a high culture, and there was so much to learn in so many domains: agriculture, weaving, pottery making, metallurgy, etc.

The ancient Greeks were smart. They surpassed their masters in manifold ways. Since they did not have to start from scratch but could rely on the long-term experience of those from whom they received instructions, they could focus on the improvement of existing technologies and on innovations derived from them. The early Greeks learned the craft of shipbuilding from the natives and developed it further until they reached the standards of international seafaring. The Greek ships of the Mycenaean era were a match for the Levantine competitors, with respect to their loading capacities and to their technical aptitude for long-distance voyages.

Certain domains were newly explored by the Greeks although the initial inspiration came from the native Europeans. This is true for the world of theater which ultimately roots in concluding rituals associated with the processions of the pre-Greek population. The Greeks virtually "set the stage" for theatrical performances with architectural spaces (i.e., theaters) designed for hosting such activities. The Greeks took over many sacred places of the native Europeans, extended the space and adorned them with elaborate buildings, thus furnishing them with imperial splendor. And yet, the spirituality with which Olympia, Delphi, Dodona and other sacred places are imbued did not change its character and it was not increased because of the glorious architecture. The sacred vitality of the space continued uninterruptedly, from pre-Greek times onward.

The ancient Greeks were smart. They managed to put a veil over the pre-Greek impact on their civilization that we admire so much. Who wants to remember one's masters if you have the intention to surpass them? In the antique sources there is no mentioning of pre-

Greek high culture or of the achievements of the native Europeans, not to speak of concessions how much the Greeks profited from the Old European cultural heritage. On the contrary, the Greeks celebrated their ingenuity and the quality of their civilization, which they thought was superior to others.

The only other civilization, in addition to their own, that they held in great esteem was the high culture of ancient Egypt. All other cultures were less valued and associated with barbarians. Literacy was highly valued by the Greeks and illiterate cultures were considered inferior. The Greeks did not understand that, for instance, the reluctance of the Celts to write down their wisdom had to do with religious constraints and was not due to a lack of intellectual capacity. For instance, "the Celtic religious proscription on writing down a corpus of knowledge prior to the start of the Christian era has been the cause of much misunderstanding and allowed the Greek and Roman writers to spread their prejudicial interpretations about Celtic society without any necessary checks, balance or correctives" (Ellis 1997: 47*f*).

The ancient Greeks were smart. They hailed their "Greek" achievements so decisively and celebrated their cultural superiority over others so convincingly that those who came after them bought the myth of a sudden rise of civilization as an expression of Greek ingenuity. Just like the early Greeks, after occupying the land of the native Europeans, had shown themselves impressed by their achievements, the Romans took the role of those who profited from the high quality of a conquered people's culture; they absorbed Greek cultural influence and cherished Greek traditions. Just like the early Greeks had visited the sacred sites of the pre–Greek population, the Romans "also had long associations with Greek religious sites.... They allegedly went to Delphi to consult the Panhellenic oracle; and they continued to be attracted to the Panhellenic sanctuaries, perhaps in part for religious reasons but surely also for the broad draw of the religious sites and their related sacred games" (Boatwright 2012: 69*f*).

In his *Epistles* (2.1.156–63), the Roman writer Horace (65–8 BCE) gives an assessment of the Greek impact on Roman culture:

> Captured Greece [*Graecia capta*] has taken its fierce captor and brought the arts to rustic Latium. Thus that crude Saturnian meter [a native Italian one] has become obsolete, and dainties have driven away the heavy stench of the farm.... For only recently has the Roman moved his wits to Greek writings, and, at leisure after the Punic Wars, has he begun to inquire what [the great Greek playwrights] Sophocles, and Thespis, and Aeschylus have usefully offered [quoted after Boatwright 2012: 66].

Romans became the mediators of the Greek cultural heritage in Western Europe. In the east, foreigners helped to preserve the Greek heritage that was in danger of being lost during the turbulences of the great migrations (of Huns, Germanic and Slavic tribes), experienced by the Eastern Roman (i.e., Byzantine) Empire as the "Barbarian Invasions" (Davies 1996: 217*ff*). In the Near East, Greek civilization of the Hellenistic era had affected local cultures, including that of the Nabataeans and other local communities of Arab affiliation. Greek had spread far and wide as a cultural vehicle, and, among the inscriptions, one finds many bilingual texts. "The most common combination is Nabataean-Aramaic and Greek, which represented the two languages of international prestige in this part of the Near East during the Hellenistic and Roman periods" (MacDonald 2003: 49).

Texts in Greek abound. The texts of late antiquity and the early Christian era became the source of knowledge-construction for the Arab tribes that set out on their quests of Islamic expansion in the seventh century CE (Trombley 1994/2: 134*ff*). Many written sources of Greek antiquity would be lost without the biggest intercultural project of the Middle Ages, the Graeco-Arabic translation movement. This movement was initiated within the framework of the cultural revolution affected by the Abbasid dynasty.

Soon after the foundation of Baghdad in 762 CE, the first ruler of the Abbasid dynasty, Al-Abbas, a relative of the prophet Muhammad, engaged in the monumental project of translating virtually every Greek manuscript that was available in western Asia. There had been translating activity in earlier centuries when Christian literature was translated from Greek into Syriac (Syrian Arabic). But the Abbasid translation project exceeded earlier campaigns by its sheer magnitude. For more than two centuries, hundreds of Greek works on astrology, alchemy, physics, mathematics, medicine, and philosophy were translated into Arabic. The project was completed toward the end of the tenth century.

Among the preserved Greek sources were several works of Aristotle and other known authors of classical antiquity. There was a lively enough reception of Aristotelian ideas among the Arab intellectuals to produce a philosophical tradition in its own right, one inspired by Greek thought and molded by Arab cultural disposition.

> The massive infusion of translated works was decisive in the formation of classical Arabic culture in the ninth and tenth centuries. Like any movement in history, it was ... initiated, favored, and promoted from within the early Abbasid society by certain social groups and strata for the advancement of their causes, interests, and policies; without such internal sponsorship translation activity, the talented and learned Syriac-speaking Christians notwithstanding, would have remained the incidental scholarly occupation of the eccentric few, socially and historically insignificant [Gutas 1998: 155].

The ideas of Greek origin that had lived, in their Arabic translations, a life of their own amidst Arabic-Islamic culture "returned" to Europe. Graeco-Arabic learning was transferred to al–Andalus, the territory in Spain that was controlled by the Arabs and it also reached the Christians in the North in the region of Spain that had been reconquered. There, in a bicultural and multilingual milieu, the sources in Arabic were re-translated, mostly into Latin. In Toledo, where, under the patronage of archbishop Raymund, a school for translators was founded in 1130, Arabic texts were translated into Latin by Christian translators, into Hebrew and Latin by Jewish scholars. This translation work "is the beginning of what has been called the twelfth-century Renaissance of ancient Greek thought in the west" (Coleman 1992: 328).

The ancient Greeks were smart. They acted as mediators of cultural heritage in two directions. They have to be credited for having absorbed Old European technologies, traditions, customs and cult practices which means they preserved the heritage and the knowledge of the ancients and profited from it to build their own civilization. What the ancient Greeks could not foresee was that they became the mediators of their own heritage for subsequent cultures. Those intellectuals who gave profile to the Enlightenment in the eighteenth century and to the Romantic movement at the beginning of the nineteenth century took interest in classical studies, in Greek history, culture and language in particular. They studied the works of antique writers, and it is through the lens of their interpretation of the ancient sources that our modern picture about Greek antiquity was formed. One of the institutions with which the ancient Greeks blessed us is a successful model of governance, democracy. The Greeks did not invent it but adopted the concept and practice of it from their predecessors. We, in the modern age, have profited from this recursive model which has stood the test of time.

In this study, a corrective to the traditional picture of ancient Greek civilization is offered. We have to accustom to a new paradigm in antiquity research. In light of the novel scholarly perspective that is being formed the values of what the Greeks achieved are not diminished, only that we have to cope with the reality that their achievements were inspired by an advanced civilization, Old Europe, that was much older than that of the Greeks and any of the other ancient civilizations. Once we realize the longevity of intercultural relations between the Greeks and the native Europeans, and once we recognize the afterglow of the Danube civilization in classical Greek antiquity, we can truly put things in perspective and accurately assess the pivotal role of the Greeks and their cultural heritage, not only for European history but for world history.

Bibliography

Adams, J.N., Mark Janse, and Simon Swain (Eds.). (2002). *Bilingualism in ancient society: Language contact and the written word*. Oxford: Oxford University Press.

Alberti, M.E. (2009). "Pesi e traffici: influenze orientali nei sistemi ponderali egei nel corso dell'età del bronzo." In Camia and Privitera 2009: 13–41.

Alcock, Susan E., and Robin Osborne (Eds.). (1994). *Placing the gods: Sanctuaries and sacred space in ancient Greece*. Oxford Clarendon Press.

Allen, Danielle. (2005). "Greek tragedy and law." In Gagarin and Cohen 2005: 374–393.

Allen, Nicholas J., Hillary Callan, Robin Dunbar, and Wendy James (Eds.). (2011). *Early human kinship: From sex to social reproduction*. Malden, MA: Wiley-Blackwell and Royal Anthropological Institute.

Anthony, David W. (2007). *The horse, the wheel and language: How Bronze-Age riders from the Eurasian steppes shaped the modern world*. Princeton, NJ: Princeton University Press.

———. (2009a). "The rise and fall of Old Europe." In Anthony 2009b: 28–57.

——— (Ed.). (2009b). *The lost world of Old Europe: The Danube Valley, 5000–3500 BC*. New York: The Institute for the Study of the Ancient World; Princeton, NJ: Princeton University Press.

Antonaccio, Carla M. (1994). "Placing the past: The Bronze Age in the cultic topography of early Greece." In Alcock and Osborne 1994: 79–104.

Assmann, Jan. (1990). *Ma'at: Gerechtigkeit und Unsterblichkeit im Alten Ägypten*. Munich: C.H. Beck.

———. (2007). *Das kulturelle Gedächtnis: Schrift, Erinnerung und politische Identität in frühen Hochkulturen*. (6th ed.). Munich: C.H. Beck.

Auberger, Janick. (2010). *Manger en Grèce classique: La nourriture, ses plaisirs et ses contraintes*. Québec: Presses de l'Université Laval.

Bachvarova, Mary R. (2009). "Hittite and Greek perspectives on travelling poets, texts and festivals." In Hunter and Rutherford 2009b: 23–45.

Bader, F. (1989). "Pan." *Revue de Philologie* 63: 7–46.

Bailey, Douglass W. (2000). *Balkan prehistory: Exclusion, incorporation and identity*. London: Routledge.

Bailey, Geoff, and Penny Spikins (Eds.). (2008). *Mesolithic Europe*. Cambridge: Cambridge University Press.

Bammesberger, Alfred, and Theo Vennemann (Eds.). (2004). *Languages in prehistoric Europe*. (2nd ed.). Heidelberg: Winter.

Barber, Elizabeth J.W. (1991). *Prehistoric textiles: The development of cloth in the Neolithic and Bronze Ages (with special reference to the Aegean)*. Princeton, NJ: Princeton University Press.

Barnhart, Robert K (Ed.). (2002). *Chambers dictionary of etymology*. (Reprint of the 1988 ed.). Edinburgh: Chambers.

Barringer, Judith M. (2008). *Art, myth, and ritual in Classical Greece*. Cambridge: Cambridge University Press.

Barthelmas, Della Gray. (2003). *The signers of the Declaration of Independence*. Jefferson, NC: McFarland.

Baud-Bovy, Samuel. (1983). *Essai sur la chanson populaire grecque*. Nauplion: Fondation ethnographique du Péloponnèse.

Beekes, Robert. (2004). "Indo-European or substrate? Phatne and keryx." In Bammesberger and Vennemann 2004: 109–115.

———. (2010). *Etymological dictionary of Greek, 2 vols*. Leiden: Brill.

———. (2011). *Comparative Indo-European linguistics: An Introduction*. (2nd ed.). Amsterdam: John Benjamins.

Berger, Ernst. (1976). "Parthenon-Studien: Erster Zwischenbericht." *Antike Kunst* 19: 122–142.

———. (1977). "Parthenon-Studien: Zweiter Zwischenbericht." *Antike Kunst* 20: 124–141.

Bernabé, Alberto. (2010). "The gods in later orphism." In Bremmer and Erskine 2010: 422–441.

Bernal, Martin. (1987). *Black Athena: Afroasiatic roots of classical civilization, vol. 1: The fabrication of ancient Greece, 1785–1985*. Piscataway, NJ: Rutgers University Press.

———. (1991). *Black Athena: Afroasiatic roots of classical civilization, vol. 2: The archaeological and documentary evidence*. Piscataway, NJ: Rutgers University Press.

———. (2006). *Black Athena: Afroasiatic roots of clas-*

sical civilization, vol. 3: The linguistic evidence. Piscataway, NJ: Rutgers University Press.

Bevan, Elinor. (1986). *Representations of animals in sanctuaries of Artemis and other Olympian deities*, 2 vols. Oxford: B.A.R.

Biegel, Gerd (Ed.). (1986). *Das erste Gold der Menschheit. Die älteste Zivilisation in Europa*. (2nd ed.). Freiburg i. Br.: Karl Schillinger.

Biehl, Peter, François Bertemes, and H. Meller (Eds.). (2001). *The archaeology of cult and religion*. Budapest: Archaeolingua.

Bikaki, A.H. (1984). *Ayia Irini: The potter's marks*. Mainz: Philipp von Zabern.

Bintliff, John. (2012). *The complete archaeology of Greece: From hunter-gatherers to the 20th century A.D.* Malden, MA: Wiley-Blackwell.

Biscardi, Arnaldo. (1982). *Diritto greco antico*. Milan: Giuffrè.

Blok, Josine H. (1995). *The early Amazons: Modern and ancient perspectives on a persistent myth*. Leiden: E.J. Brill.

Boardman, John, Jasper Griffin, and Oswyn Murray (Eds.). (1988). *Greece and the Hellenistic world*. Oxford: Oxford University Press.

Boatwright, Mary T. (2012). *Peoples of the Roman world*. Cambridge: Cambridge University Press.

Boedeker, D., and K.A. Raaflaub (Eds.). (1998). *Democracy, empire, and the arts in fifth-century Athens*. Cambridge, MA: Harvard University Press.

Bomgardner, David Lee. (2000). *The story of the Roman amphitheatre*. London: Routledge.

Bonsall, Clive. (2008). "The Mesolihic of the Iron Gates." In Bailey and Spikins 2008: 238–279.

Bouissac, P (Ed.). (1998). *Encyclopedia of semiotics*. New York: Oxford University Press.

Bowie, Ewen. (2009). "Wandering poets, archaic style." In Hunter and Rutherford 2009b: 105–136.

Boyle, Katie, Colin Renfrew, and Marsha Levine (Eds.). (2002). *Ancient interactions: East and west in Eurasia*. Cambridge: McDonald Institute for Archaeological Research.

Bradley, James W. (1987). *Evolution of the Onondaga Iroquois: Accommodating change, 1500–1655*. Syracuse, NY: Syracuse University Press.

Bradley, Keith, and Paul Cartledge (Eds.). (2011). *The Cambridge world history of slavery*, vol. 1: *The ancient Mediterranean world*. Cambridge: Cambridge University Press.

Bragadin, Marc'Antonio. (2010). *Storia delle repubbliche marinare*. Bologna: Odoya.

Breazu, Marius, and Alin Suteu (Eds.). (2007). *A history lesson: Pottery manufacturing 8000 years ago*. Alba Iulia: Aeternitas Publisher.

Bremmer, Jan N (Ed.). (1987). *Interpretations of Greek mythology*. London: Routledge.

_____. (2010). "Introduction: The Greek gods in the twentieth century." In Bremmer and Erskine 2010: 1–18.

Bremmer, Jan N., and Andrew Erskine (Eds.). (2010). *The gods of ancient Greece: Identities and transformations*. Edinburgh: Edinburgh University Press.

Brice, W.C (Ed.). (1961). *Inscriptions in the Minoan linear script of class A (edited on the basis of the notes from A.J. Evans and J. Myres)*. Oxford: Oxford University Press for the Society of Antiquaries.

Broodbank, Cyprian. (2000). *An island archaeology of the early Cyclades*. Cambridge: Cambridge University Press.

Brown, Ben. (2012). "Homer, funeral contests and the origins of the Greek city." In Phillips and Pritchard 2012: 123–162.

Brumble, H. David. (1998). *Classical myths and legends in the Middle Ages and Renaissance*. London: Fitzroy Dearborn Publishers.

Bryan, Frank M. (2004). *Real democracy: The New England town meeting and how it works*. Chicago: University of Chicago Press.

Buck, Robert J. (1998). *Thrasybulus and the Athenian democracy: The life of an Athenian statesman*. Stuttgart: Franz Steiner.

Budja, Mihael. (2005). "The process of Neolithisation in South-Eastern Europe: from ceramic female figurines and cereal grains to entoptics and human nuclear DNA polymorphic markers." *Documenta Praehistorica* XXXII: 53–72.

Burkert, Walter. (1985). *Greek religion: Archaic and classical*. Cambridge, MA: Harvard University Press; Oxford: Blackwell.

_____. (1987). *Ancient mystery cults*. Cambridge, MA: Harvard University Press.

Butrimas, Adomas (Ed.). (2001). *Baltic amber*. Vilnius: Vilnius Academy of Fine Arts.

Çakmak, Cenap. (2011). "The Greek city-states were 'democratic' by our modern American definition." In Danver 2011: 21–32.

Camia, Francesco, and Santo Privitera (Eds.). (2009). *Obeloi-Contatti, scambi e valori nel Mediterraneo antico (Studi offerti a Nicola Parise)*. Paestum: Fondazione Paestum (Tekmeria 11).

Cancik, Hubert, and Helmuth Schneider (Eds.). (2013). *Brill's New Pauly* (antiquity volumes available online: <http://www.encquran.brill.nl/entries/brill-s-new-pauly>).

Cantarella, Eva. (2005). "Gender, sexuality, and law." In Gagarin and Cohen 2005: 236–253.

Cartledge, Paul A., Edward E. Cohen, and Lin Foxhall (Eds.). (2002). *Money, labour and land: Approaches to the economies of ancient Greece*. London: Routledge.

Case, Sue-Ellen. (1985). "Classic drag: The Greek creation of female parts." *Theatre Journal* 37.3 (October 1985): 317–327.

Cavalli-Sforza, Luigi Luca. (1996). "The spread of agriculture and nomadic pastoralism: insights from genetics, linguistics and archaeology." In Harris 1996: 51–69.

_____. (2000). *Genes, peoples, and languages.* New York: North Point Press.
Cavalli-Sforza, Luigi Luca, Paolo Menozzi, and Alberto Piazza. (1994). *The history and geography of human genes.* Princeton, NJ: Princeton University Press.
Chadwick, John. (1990). "Linear B and related scripts." In Hooker 1990: 137–166.
Chaniotis, Angelos. (2009). "Travelling memories in the Hellenistic world." In Hunter and Rutherford 2009b: 249–269.
Chantraine, Pierre. (2009). *Dictionnaire étymologique de la langue grecque: Histoire des mots.* Paris: Klincksieck (2nd ed.).
Chapman, John. (2009). "Houses, households, villages, and proto-cities in southeastern Europe." In Anthony 2009b: 74–89.
Chase, Richard. (1969). *Quest for myth.* New York: Greenwood.
Chi, Jennifer Y (Ed.). (2008). *Wine, worship, and sacrifice: The golden graves of ancient Vani.* Princeton, NJ: Princeton University Press.
Chwe, Michael Suk-Young. (2001). *Rational ritual: Culture, coordination, and common knowledge.* Princeton, NJ: Princeton University Press.
Cline, Eric H (Ed.). (2010). *The Oxford handbook of the Bronze Age Aegean.* Oxford: Oxford University Press.
Clinton, Kevin. (1993). "The sanctuary of Demeter and Kore at Eleusis." In Marinatos and Hägg 1993: 110–124.
Cohen, Edward E. (2000). *The Athenian nation.* Princeton, NJ: Princeton University Press.
_____. (2005). "Commercial law." In Gagarin and Cohen 2005: 290–302.
Coleman, Janet. (1992). *Ancient and medieval memories: Studies in the reconstruction of the past.* Cambridge: Cambridge University Press.
Conard, Nicholas J., Harald Floss, Martina Barth, and Jordi Serangeli (Eds.). (2009). *Eiszeit: Kunst und Kultur.* Ostfildern: Thorbecke Verlag.
Connelly, Joan B. (2007). *Portrait of a priestess: Women and ritual in ancient Greece.* Princeton, NJ: Princeton University Press.
Connor, W.R. (1987). "Tribes, festivals and processions in ancient Greece." *Journal of Hellenic Studies* 107: 40–50.
Cook B.F. (1990). "Greek Inscriptions." In Hooker 1990: 259–319.
Coulson, William D.E., et al. (Eds.). (1994). *The archaeology of Athens and Attica under the democracy.* Oxford: Oxbow Books.
Craik, Elizabeth. (1995). "Diet, *diaita* and dietetics." In Powell 1995: 387–402.
Crouwel J.H. (1973). "Pot-Marks on Grey Minyan Ware." *Kadmos* 12: 101–108.
Csapo, Eric, and Margaret C. Miller (Eds.). (2007). *The origins of theatre in ancient Greece and beyond.* Cambridge: Cambridge University Press.

Cultraro, Massimo. (2011). *I Micenei: Archeologia, storia, società dei Greci prima di Omero* (5th ed.). Rome: Carocci editore.
Cunliffe, Barry. (2008). *Europe between the oceans 9000 BC–AD 1000.* London: Thames and Hudson.
Daniels, Peter T., and William Bright (Eds.). (1996). *The world's writing systems.* New York: Oxford University Press.
Danver, Steven L. (Ed.). (2011). *Popular controversies in world history*, 4 vols. Santa Barbara, CA: ABC-CLIO.
Darbo-Peschanski, Catherine. (2011). "The origin of Greek historiography." In Marincola 2011: 27–38.
Darkevič, Vladislav Petrovič. (1986). "Ostslawen, Rus und Araber." In Herrmann 1986: 228–232.
David, Rosalie. (1986). *The pyramid builders of ancient Egypt: A modern investigation of Pharaoh's workforce.* London: Routledge & Kegan Paul.
Davidson, James. (1997). *Courtesans and fishcakes: The consuming passions of classical Athens.* London: HarperCollins.
Davies, Norman. (1996). *Europe: A history.* Oxford: Oxford University Press.
Demakopoulou, Katie (Ed.). (1988). *The Mycenaean world: Five centuries of early Greek culture 1600–1100 BC.* Athens: Ministry of Culture.
Demand, Nancy. (1994). *Birth, death, and motherhood in classical Greece.* Baltimore: Johns Hopkins University Press.
Dement'eva, Vera V., and Tassilo Schmitt (Eds.). (2010). *Volk und Demokratie im Altertum.* Göttingen: Edition Ruprecht.
Dergachev, Valentin A. (2007). *O skipetrakh, o loshadiakh, o voine. Etiudy v zashchitu migratsionnoi kontseptsii M. Gimbutas.* St. Petersburg; Nestor-Istoriia.
Derks, Ton, and Nico Roymans (Eds.). (2009). *Ethnic constructs in antiquity: The role of power and tradition.* Amsterdam: Amsterdam University Press.
Detienne, Marcel. (2003). *The writing of Orpheus: Greek myth in cultural contact.* Baltimore: Johns Hopkins University Press.
Develin, Robert. (1989). *Athenian officials, 684–321 BC.* Cambridge: Cambridge University Press.
Dexter, Miriam Robbins. (1997). "Goddesses." In Mallory and Adams 1997: 231–232.
Dickinson, Oliver. (1994). *The Aegean Bronze Age.* Cambridge: Cambridge University Press.
Dihle, Albrecht. (1994). *A history of Greek literature from Homer to the Hellenistic period.* London: Routledge.
Dillon, Matthew P.J. (2002). *Girls and women in classical Greek religion.* London: Routledge.
Dillon, Matthew P.J., and Lynda Garland. (1994). *Ancient Greece: Social and historical documents from archaic times to the death of Socrates (c. 800–399 BC).* London: Routledge.

Dolukhanov, Pavel M. (2002). "Alternative revolutions: hunter-gatherers, farmers and stock-breeders in the northwestern Pontic area." In Boyle et al. 2002: 13–24.

———. (2008). "The Mesolithic of European Russia, Belarus, and the Ukraine." In Bailey and Spikins 2008: 280–301.

Donald, Merlin. (1991). *Origins of the modern mind: Three stages in the evolution of culture and cognition.* Cambridge, MA: Harvard University Press.

Donlan, Walter. (1997). "The relations of power in the pre-state and early state polities." In Mitchell and Rhodes 1997: 39–48.

Doty, William G. (2000). *Mythography: The study of myths and rituals.* Tuscaloosa: University of Alabama Press (2nd ed.).

Drachmann, A.G. (1938). "Pflug." In *Paulys Realencyclopädie der classischen Altertumswissenschaft* (Ed. by Wilhelm Kroll) 21: 1461–72.

Dumézil, Georges. (1958). *L'idéologie tripartite des Indo-Européens.* Brussels: Latomus.

Ekschmitt, Werner. (1984). *Die sieben Weltwunder: Ihre Erbauung, Zerstörung und Wiederentdeckung.* Mainz: Philipp von Zabern.

Ellis, Peter Berresford. (1997). *Celt and Greek: Celts in the Hellenic world.* London: Constable.

Emmanuel, Maurice. (1987). *La danse grecque antique d'après les monuments figurés.* Geneva: Slatkine Reprints (reprint of the original; Paris: Hachette 1896).

Faulkner, Neil. (2012). *A visitor's guide to the ancient Olympics.* New Haven: Yale University Press.

Fine, John V.A. (1983). *The ancient Greeks: A critical history.* Cambridge, MA: Belknap Press of Harvard University Press.

Fisher, Nick. (2011). "Competitive delights: The social effects of the expanded program of contests in post–Kleisthenic Athens." In Fisher and Van Wees 2011: 175–219.

Fisher, Nick, and Hans Van Wees (Eds.). (2011). *Competition in the ancient world.* Swansea, Oxford, Oakville, CT: Classical Press of Wales.

Fishman, Joshua A (Ed.). (1999). *Handbook of language and ethnic identity.* Oxford: Oxford University Press.

Fitton, J. Lesley. (1989). *Cycladic art.* London: British Museum.

Foley, Helene P (Ed.). (1999). *The Homeric Hymn to Demeter: Translation, commentary, and interpretive essays* (3rd ed.). Princeton, NJ: Princeton University Press.

Forsén, Björn, and G.R. Stanton (Eds.). (1996). *The Pnyx in the history of Athens.* Helsinki: Foundation of the Finnish Institute at Athens.

Forsén, Jeannette. (2010). "Mainland Greece." In Cline 2010: 53–65.

Fowler, Robert L. (2010). "Gods in early Greek historiography." In Bremmer and Erskine 2010: 318–334.

Foxhall, Lin. (2013). *Studying gender in classical antiquity.* Cambridge: Cambridge University Press.

Furley, William D., and Jan Maarten Bremer. (2001). *Greek hymns, vol. 1: The texts in translation.* Tübingen: Mohr Siebeck.

Furnée, Edzard J. (1972). *Die wichtigsten konsonantischen Erscheinungen des Vorgriechischen.* The Hague: Mouton.

Gagarin, Michael. (2005). "Early Greek law." In Gagarin and Cohen 2005: 82–94.

Gagarin, Michael, and David Cohen (Eds.). (2005). *The Cambridge companion to ancient Greek law.* Cambridge: Cambridge University Press.

Gantz, Timothy. (1993). *Early Greek myth: A guide to literary and artistic sources, 2 vols.* Baltimore: Johns Hopkins University Press.

Garland, Robert. (1992). *Introducing new gods: The politics of Athenian religion.* Ithaca, NY: Cornell University Press.

Georgiev, V. (1966). "Was stellt die Pelasgertheorie dar?" *Lingua* 16: 263–273.

Gerhard, Eduard. (1839). *Auserlesene griechische Vasenbilder, hauptsächlich etruskischen Fundortes.* Berlin: Reimer.

Gheorghiu, Dragos (Ed.). (2010). *Neolithic and Chalcolithic archaeology in Eurasia: Building techniques and spatial organisation.* Oxford: Archaeopress.

Gimbutas, Marija. (1982). *The goddesses and gods of Old Europe 7000 to 3500 B.C.: Myths, legends and cult images* (2nd ed.). London: Thames & Hudson.

———. (1989). *The language of the Goddess.* San Francisco: Harper & Row.

———. (1991). *The civilization of the Goddess: The world of Old Europe.* San Francisco: HarperSanFrancisco.

Girginov, Vassil, and Jim Parry. (2005). *The Olympic Games explained: A student guide to the evolution of the modern Olympic Games.* London: Routledge.

Giurova, M (Ed.). (2008). *Praistoricheski prouchvaniia v Balgariia: Novite predizvikatelstva/Prehistoric research in Bulgaria: New challenges.* Sofia: National Archaeological Institute and Museum.

Gladwell, Malcolm. (2000). *The tipping point: How little things can make a big difference.* Boston: Little, Brown.

Gligor, Mihai et al. (2007). "A history lesson—general data on Neolithic, manufacturing techniques and analysis methods for ancient pottery." In Breazu and Suteu 2007: 110–133.

Godart, Louis. (1995). "Una iscrizione in Lineare B del XVII secolo A.C. ad Olimpia." *Rendiconti dell'Accademia nazionale dei Lincei. Classe di*

Scienze morali, storiche e filologiche, s 9, v: 445–447.

Godelier, Maurice. (2011). *The metamorphoses of kinship*. London: Verso.

Goebl, Hans, Peter H. Nelde, Zdenek Stary, and Wolfgang Wölck (Eds.). (1996–97). *Kontaktlinguistik/Contact Linguistics/Linguistique de contact*, 2 vols. Berlin: Mouton de Gruyter.

Goette, Hans R. (1995). "Griechische Theaterbauten der Klassik—Forschungsstand und Fragestellungen." In Pöhlmann 1995: 9–48.

———. (2001). *Athens, Attica and the Megarid: An archaeological guide*. Abingdon-on-Thames: Taylor & Francis.

———. (2007). "An archaeological appendix." In Wilson 2007: 116–121.

Gogos, Savas. (2008). *Das Dionysostheater von Athen: Architektonische Gestalt und Funktion*. Vienna: Phoibos.

Golden, Mark. (1998). *Sport and society in ancient Greece*. Cambridge: Cambridge University Press.

Goldhill, Simon, and Robin Osborne (Eds.). (1999). *Performance culture and Athenian democracy*. Cambridge: Cambridge University Press.

Gould, Richard A. (2011). *Archaeology and the social history of ships* (2nd ed.). Cambridge: Cambridge University Press.

Graf, Fritz. (1993). *Greek mythology: An introduction*. Baltimore: Johns Hopkins University Press.

Gutas, Dimitri. (1998). *Greek thought, Arabic culture: The Graeco-Arabic translation movement in Baghdad and early Abbasid society (2nd–4th/8th–10th centuries)*. London: Routledge.

Haarmann, Harald. (1989). "Writing from Old Europe to ancient Crete: A case of cultural continuity." *Journal of Indo-European Studies* 17: 251–277.

———. (1995). *Early civilization and literacy in Europe: An inquiry into cultural continuity in the Mediterranean world*. Berlin: Mouton de Gruyter.

———. (1996a). *Die Madonna und ihre griechischen Töchter: Rekonstruktion einer kulturhistorischen Genealogie*. Hildesheim, Zürich: Olms.

———. (1996b). "Identität." In Goebl et al. 1996: 218–233.

———. (1998). "Writing technology and the abstract mind." *Semiotica* 122: 69–97.

———. (1999a). "Schriftentwicklung und Schriftgebrauch in Südosteuropa vor der Verbreitung des Alphabets." In Hinrichs 1999: 185–209.

———. (1999b). "History." In Fishman 1999: 60–76.

———. (2006). *Weltgeschichte der Sprachen: Von der Frühzeit des Menschen bis zur Gegenwart*. (2nd ed. 2010). Munich: C.H. Beck.

———. (2007). *Foundations of culture: Knowledge-construction, belief systems and worldview in their dynamic interplay*. Frankfurt: Peter Lang.

———. (2009). *Interacting with figurines: Seven dimensions in the study of imagery*. West Hartford, Vermont: Full Circle Press.

———. (2010). *Einführung in die Donauschrift*. Hamburg: Helmut Buske.

———. (2011a). *Das Rätsel der Donauzivilisation: Die Entdeckung der ältesten Hochkultur Europas*. Munich: C.H. Beck.

———. (2011b). *Writing as technology and cultural ecology: Explorations of the human mind at the dawn of history*. Frankfurt: Peter Lang.

———. (2012). *Indo-Europeanization—day one: Elite recruitment and the beginnings of language politics*. Wiesbaden: Harrassowitz.

———. (2013a). *Mythos Demokratie: Antike Herrschaftsmodelle im Spannungsfeld von Egalitätsprinzip und Eliteprinzip*. Frankfurt: Peter Lang.

———. (2013b). "Language and ethnicity in antiquity." In McInerney 2013:17–33.

Haarmann, Harald, and Joan Marler. (2008). *Introducing the mythological crescent: Ancient beliefs and imagery connecting Eurasia with Anatolia*. Wiesbaden: Harrassowitz.

Hagel, Stefan. (2009). *Ancient Greek music: A new technical history*. Cambridge: Cambridge University Press.

Hale, John R. (2009). *Lords of the sea: The epic story of the Athenian navy and the birth of democracy*. London: Penguin Books.

Hall, Edith. (1989). *Inventing the barbarian: Greek self-definition through tragedy*. Oxford: Oxford University Press.

Hall, Jonathan M. (2002). *Hellenicity between ethnicity and culture*. Chicago: University of Chicago Press.

Hansen, Mogens Herman. (1987). *The Athenian Assembly in the age of Demosthenes*. Oxford: Blackwell.

Harris, David R (Ed.). (1996). *The origins and spread of agriculture and pastoralism in Eurasia*. London: UCL Press.

Harris, E. (2002). "Workshop, marketplace and household: the nature of technical specialization in classical Athens and its influence on economy and society." In Cartledge et al. 2002: 67–99.

Hartnoll, Phyllis, and Peter Found (Eds.). (1992). *The concise Oxford companion to the theatre*. Oxford: Oxford University Press.

Harvilahti, Lauri. (2000). "Variation and memory." In Honko 2000: 57–75.

Helms, M.W. (1988). *Ulysses' sail: An ethnographic Odyssey of power, knowledge, and geographical distance*. Princeton, NJ: Princeton University Press.

Henrichs, Albert. (2010). "What is a Greek god?" In Bremmer and Erskine 2010: 19–39.

Henson, Donald. (2006). *The origins of the Anglo-Saxons*. Hockwold-cum-Wilton, Norfolk (England): Anglo-Saxon Books.

Herman, G. (1987). *Ritualised friendship and the Greek city*. Cambridge: Cambridge University Press.

Herrmann, J (Ed.) (1986). *Welt der Slawen: Geschichte—Gesellschaft—Kultur*. Munich: C.H. Beck.

Hersey, George L. (1996). *The evolution of allure: Sexual selection from the Medici Venus to the incredible hulk*. Cambridge, MA: MIT Press.

Hester, D.A. (1966). "A reply to Professor Georgiev's 'Was stellt die Pelasgertheorie dar?'" *Lingua* 16: 274–278.

Higgins, Charlotte. (2010). *It's all Greek to me: From Homer to the Hippocratic oath, how ancient Greece has shaped our world*. New York: HarperCollins.

Hinrichs Uwe (Ed.). (1999). *Handbuch der Südosteuropa-Linguistik*. Wiesbaden: Harrassowitz.

Hodder, Ian. (1992). *Theory and practice in archaeology*. London: Routledge.

Hölkeskamp, Karl-Joachim. (2000). "(In-)Schrift und Monument. Zum Begriff des Gesetzes im archaischen und klassischen Griechenland." *Zeitschrift für Papyrologie und Epigraphik* 132: 73–96.

Hoepfner, Wolfram (Ed.). (1997). *Kult und Kultbauten auf der Akropolis*. Berlin: Archäologisches Seminar der Freien Universität Berlin.

Hoeppe G. (2006). "Kolams: Technologie der Verzauberung." *Ethnomathematik—Spektrum der Wissenschaft* 2006: 52–59.

Hofmann, Johann B. (1966). *Etymologisches Wörterbuch des Griechischen*. Darmstadt: Wissenschaftliche Buchgesellschaft.

Honko, Lauri (Ed.). (2000). *Thick corpus, organic variation and textuality in oral tradition*. Helsinki: Finnish Literature Society.

Hooker J.T. (1980). *Linear B: An introduction*. Bristol: Bristol Classical Press.

_____ (Ed.). (1990). *Reading the past: Ancient writing from cuneiform to the alphabet*. London: British Museum Publications.

_____. (1995). "Linear B as a source for social history." In Powell 1995: 7–26.

Hornblower, Simon. (1988). "Greece: The history of the classical period." In Boardman et al. 1988: 118–149.

Hornblower, S., and A. Sprawforth (Eds.). (1996). *The Oxford classical dictionary* (3rd ed.). Oxford: Oxford University Press.

Howard, Jean E., and Phyllis Rackin. (1997). *Engendering a nation: A feminist account of Shakespeare's English histories*. London: Routledge.

Hunt, Peter. (2011). "Slaves in Greek literary culture." In Bradley and Cartledge 2011: 22–47.

Hunter, Richard, and Ian Rutherford (2009a). "Introduction." In Hunter and Rutherford 2009b: 1–22.

_____ (Eds.). (2009b). *Wandering poets in ancient Greek culture: Travel, locality and pan–Hellenism*. Cambridge: Cambridge University Press.

Iakovidis, S.E. (1985). *Mycenae—Epidaurus—Argos—Tiryns—Nauplion: A complete guide to the museums and archaeological sites of the Argolid*. Athens: Ekdotike Athenon.

Ilievski, Petar Chr. (1997). "Some parallels between Balkan popular and Mycenaean measures of volume for dry materials." *Ziva Antika—Antiquité Vivante* 47: 63–86.

_____. (2000). *Zhivotot na mikencite vo nivnite pismeni svedoshtva, so poseben osvrt kon onomastickite i prosopografski izvodi*. Skopje: Makedonska Akademija na Naukite i Umetnostite.

Ingold, Tim (Ed.). (1994). *Companion encyclopedia of anthropology. Humanity, culture and social life*. London: Routledge.

Isager, Signe, and Jens Erik Skydsgaard. (1995). *Ancient Greek agriculture: An introduction*. London: Routledge.

Israel, Jonathan I. (2012). *Democratic enlightenment: Philosophy, revolution, and human rights 1750–1790*. Oxford: Oxford University Press.

Ivanov, Ivan S. (1986). "Der kupferzeitliche Friedhof in Varna." In Biegel 1986: 30–42.

Janka, Markus, and Christian Schäfer (Eds.). (2002). *Platon als Mythologe: Neue Interpretationen zu den Mythen in Platons Dialogen*. Darmstadt: Wissenschaftliche Buchgesellschaft.

Janse, Mark. (2002). "Bilingualism in the history of Greek." In Adams et al. 2002: 332–390.

Jasanoff, Jay H., and Alan Nussbaum. (1996). "Word games: The linguistic evidence in *Black Athena*." In Lefkowitz and MacLean Rogers 1996: 177–205.

Jenkins, Ian. (1994). *The Parthenon frieze*. London: British Museum Press.

Johnstone, Steven. (2011). *A history of trust in ancient Greece*. Chicago: University of Chicago Press.

Jones, Nicholas. (2004). *Rural Athens under the democracy*. Philadelphia: University of Pennsylvania Press.

Jones, Phil. (1996). *Drama as therapy: Theatre as living*. London: Routledge.

Karageorghis, V. (1962). "Notes On Some Mycenaean Survivals in Cyprus during the First Millennium B.C." *Kadmos* 1: 71–77.

Kare, A (Ed.). (2000). *Myanndash: Rock art in the ancient Arctic*. Rovaniemi: Arctic Centre Foundation.

Katičić, R. (1976). *Ancient languages of the Balkans, vol.1*. The Hague: Mouton.

Kavoulaki, A. (1999). "Processual performance and the democratic polis." In Goldhill and Osborne 1999: 293–320.

Kinsley, David, (1989). *The goddesses' mirror: Visions of the divine from East and West*. New York: State University of New York Press.

Kirk, G.S. (1970). *Myth: Its meaning and function in ancient and other cultures*. Berkeley: University of California Press.

Kljuchevskij, V.O. (1994). *Bojarskaja duma Drevnej Rusi: Dobrye ljudi Drevnej Rusi*. Moskau: Ladomir.

Knight, Chris (2011). "Early human kinship was matrilineal." In Allen et al. 2011: 61–82.

Kopelman, Shirli, J. Mark Weber, and David M. Messick. (2002). "Factors influencing cooperation in common dilemmas: A review of experimental psychological research." In Ostrom et al. 2002: 113–156.

Kowalzig, Barbara. (2007a). *Singing for the gods*. Oxford: Oxford University Press.

_____. (2007b). "And now all the world shall dance!" (Eur. Bacch. 144): Dionysos' Choroi between drama and ritual." In Csapo and Miller 2007: 221–254.

Kruta, Venceslas. (1993). *Die Anfänge Europas 6000–500 v.Chr.* Munich: C.H. Beck.

Kyrtatas, Dimitris J. (2011). "Slavery and economy in the Greek world." In Bradley and Cartledge 2011: 91–111.

Lacoue-Labarthe, Philippe, and Jean-Luc Nancy. (1990). "The Nazi myth." *Critical Inquiry* 16/2: 291–312.

Lahelma, Antti, and Zbigniew T. Fiema. (2008). "From goddess to prophet: 2000 years of continuity on the Mountain of Aaron near Petra, Jordan." *Temenos* 44: 191–222.

Lambropoulos, Vassilis. (1993). *The rise of eurocentrism: Anatomy of interpretation*. Princeton, NJ: Princeton University Press.

Lang, Mabel. (2004). *The Athenian citizen: Democracy in the Athenian Agora*. Athens: American School of Classical Studies at Athens (2nd ed.).

Lanni, Adriaan M. (2006). *Law and justice in the courts of classical Athens*. Cambridge: Cambridge University Press.

Lape, Susan. (2010). *Race and citizen identity in the classical Athenian democracy*. Cambridge: Cambridge University Press.

Lazarovici, Gheorghe, and Cornelia-Magda Lazarovici, (2010). "Neo-Eneolithic cult constructions in southeastern Europe: Building techniques and space management—A brief overview." In Gheorghiu 2010: 117–125.

Lee, John. (2011). "The Greek city-states were not "democratic" by our modern American definition." In Danver 2011: 32–42.

Lefebvre, Henri. (1991). *The production of space*. Oxford: Blackwell.

Lefkowitz, M., and Guy MacLean Rogers (Eds.). (1996). *Black Athena revisited*. Chapel Hill: University of North Carolina Press.

Leung Li, Siu. (2003). *Cross-dressing in Chinese opera*. Hong Kong: Hong Kong University Press.

Lewis, Sian. (2002). *The Athenian woman: An iconographic handbook*. London: Routledge.

Lewis-Williams, David, and David Pearce. (2005). *Inside the Neolithic mind: Consciousness, cosmos and the realm of the gods*. London: Thames & Hudson.

Liddell, H.G., and R. Scott. (1991). *An intermediate Greek-English lexicon, founded upon the seventh edition of Liddell and Scott's Greek-English lexicon*. Oxford: Oxford University Press (impression of the first ed. of 1889).

Logan, R.K. (1986). *The alphabet effect: The impact of the phonetic alphabet on the development of Western civilization*. New York: William Morrow.

Loraux, Nicole. (1981). *Les enfants d'Athéna: Idées athéniennes sur la citoyenneté et la division des sexes*. Paris: Maspero.

Lutz, Mark J. (2012). *Divine law and political philosophy in Plato's Laws*. DeKalb, IL: Northern Illinois University Press.

MacDonald, M.C.A. (2003). "Languages, scripts, and the uses of writing among the Nabataeans." In Markoe 2003: 37–56.

MacLean Rogers, Guy. (1996). "Quo vadis?" In Lefkowitz and MacLean Rogers 1996: 447–453.

Maddicott, J.R. (2010). *The origins of the English Parliament, 924–1327*. Oxford: Oxford University Press.

Malkin, Irad. (1994). *Myth and territory in the Spartan Mediterranean*. Cambridge: Cambridge University Press.

_____. (2011). *A small Greek world: Networks in the ancient Mediterranean*. Oxford: Oxford University Press.

Mallory, J.P. (1989). *In search of the Indo-Europeans: Language, archaeology and myth*. London: Thames and Hudson.

Mallory, J.P., and D.Q. Adams (Eds.). (1997). *Encyclopedia of Indo-European culture*. London: Fitzroy Dearborn Publishers.

_____. (2006). *The Oxford introduction to Proto-Indo-European and the Proto-Indo-European world*. Oxford: Oxford University Press.

Manning, Sturt W. (2010). "Chronology and terminology." In Cline 2010: 11–28.

Marangou, C. (2001). "Sacred or secular places and the ambiguous evidence of prehistoric ritual." In Biehl et al. 2001: 139–160.

Maranti, Anna. (1999). *Olympia and Olympic Games*. Athens: Michalis Toubis Editions.

Marazov, Ivan. (2005). "Art in ancient Thrace." In Marazov et al. 2005: 7–21.

Marazov, Ivan, Gergana Kabakchieva, Gavril Lazov, and Tatyana Shalganova. (2005). *Vassil Bojkov Collection*. Sofija: Thrace Foundation.

Marinatos, Nanno. (1993). *Minoan religion: Ritual, image, and symbol*. Columbia, South Carolina: University of South Carolina Press.

Marinatos, Nanno, and Robin Hägg (Eds.). (1993). *Greek sanctuaries: New approaches*. London: Routledge.

Marincola, John (Ed.). (2011). *A companion to Greek and Roman historiography*. Malden, MA: Wiley-Blackwell.

Markoe, Glenn (Ed.). (2003). *Petra rediscovered: Lost city of the Nabataeans*. London: Thames & Hudson.

Marler, Joan (Ed.). (2008). *The Danube script: Neo-Eneolithic writing in southeastern Europe*. Sebastopol, CA: Institute of Archaeomythology.

Marler, Joan, and Mirjam R. Dexter (Eds.). (2009). *Signs of civilization: Neolithic symbol system of Southeast Europe*. Sebastopol, CA: Institute of Archaeomythology.

Martin, Richard P. (2009). "Read on arrival." In Hunter and Rutherford 2009b: 80–104.

Mastromarco, Giuseppe, and Piero Totaro. (2012). *Storia del teatro greco*. Milan: Mondadori (2nd ed.).

Maurizio, Lisa. (1998). "The Panathenaic procession: Athens' participatory democracy on display." In Boedeker and Raaflaub 1998: 297–317.

_____. (1995). "Anthropology and spirit possession: A reconsideration of the Pythia's role at Delphi." *Journal of Hellenic Studies* 105: 69–86.

Maxim, Zoia. (1999). *Neo-Eneoliticul din Transilvania*. Cluj-Napoca: National History Museum of Transylvania.

McCarthy, E. Doyle. (1996). *Knowledge as culture: The new sociology of knowledge*. London: Routledge.

McInerney, Jeremy. (2000). *The folds of the Parnassos: Land and ethnicity in ancient Phokis*. Austin: University of Texas Press.

_____ (Ed.). (2013). *A Companion to ethnicity in the ancient Mediterranean*. Oxford: Wiley-Blackwell.

McLuhan, Marshall. (1962). *The Gutenberg galaxy*. Toronto: University of Toronto Press.

Meier, Christian. (2012). *Athen: Ein Neubeginn der Weltgeschichte*. Munich: Pantheon.

Meillet, Antoine. (1937). *Introduction à l'étude comparative des langues indo-européennes*. Paris: Hachette.

Merlini, Marco. (2009). *An inquiry into the Danube script*. Sibiu & Alba Iulia: Editura Altip.

Mesmer, Beatrix. (2007). *Staatsbürgerinnen ohne Stimmrecht: Die Politik der schweizerischen Frauenverbände 1914–1971*. Zürich: Chronos.

Millet, N.B. (1996). "Meroitic." In Daniels and Bright 1996: 84–87.

Missiou, Anna. (2011). *Literacy and democracy in fifth-century Athens*. Cambridge: Cambridge University Press.

Mitchell, Lynette G., and P.J. Rhodes (Eds.). (1997). *The development of the polis in archaic Greece*. London: Routledge.

Mokyr, Joel. (2002). *The gifts of Athena: Historical origins of the knowledge economy*. Princeton, NJ: Princeton University Press.

Montanari, Enrico. (1981). *Il mito dell'autoctonia: Linee di una dinamica mitico-politica ateniese*. Rome: Bulzoni Editore.

Moreno, Alfonso. (2012). *Feeding the democracy: The Athenian grain supply in the fifth and fourth centuries BC*. Oxford: Oxford University Press.

Morgan, Catherine. (1990). *Athletes and oracles: The transformation of Olympia and Delphi in the eighth century BC*. Cambridge: Cambridge University Press.

Morgan, Kathryn. (2000). *Myth and philosophy from the pre–Socratics to Plato*. Cambridge: Cambridge University Press.

Morley, Neville. (2007). *Trade in classical antiquity*. Cambridge: Cambridge University Press.

Morley, Iain, and Colin Renfrew (Eds.). (2010). *The archaeology of measurement: Comprehending heaven, earth and time in ancient societies*. Cambridge: Cambridge University Press.

Morpurgo Davies, Anna, and Yves Duhoux (Eds.). (1988). *Linear B: A 1984 survey*. Louvain-la-Neuve: Peeters.

Mount, Ferdinand. (2010). *Full circle: How the classical world came back to us*. London: A CBS Company.

Müller, Klaus E. (1987). *Das magische Universum der Identität: Elementarformen sozialen Verhaltens—Ein ethnologischer Grundriss*. Frankfurt: Campus.

Murray, Oswyn. (1988). "Life and society in classical Greece." In Boardman et al. 1988: 198–227.

Murray, Penelope, and Wilson, Peter J (Eds.). (2004). *Music and the muses*. Oxford: Oxford University Press.

Mytum, Harold. (1992). *The origins of early Christian Ireland*. London: Routledge.

Neils, Jennifer. (1992a). "The Panathenaia: an introduction." In Neils 1992b: 13–27.

_____ (Ed.). (1992b). *Goddess and polis: The Panathenaic festival in ancient Athens*. Princeton, NJ: Princeton University Press.

_____. (2011). *Women in the ancient world*. London: British Museum Press.

Newby, Zahra, and Leader-Newby, Ruth (Eds.). (2007). *Art and inscriptions in the ancient world*. Cambridge: Cambridge University Press.

Nicolai, Roberto. (2011). "The place of history in the ancient world." In Marincola 2011: 13–26.

Nikolov, Vassil (Ed.). (2008). *Provadia-Solnitsata: Prehistoric salt-producing center. The 2005–2007 excavation seasons*. Sofija: National Institute of Archaeology and Museum.

Nissen, Hans J. (1988). *The early history of the ancient Near East 9000–2000 B.C.* Chicago and London: University of Chicago Press.

Nutton, Vivian. (2013). *Ancient medicine*. London: Routledge (2nd ed.).

Ober, Josiah. (2008). *Democracy and knowledge: Innovation and learning in classical Athens*. Princeton, NJ: Princeton University Press.

Osborne, Robin. (1985). *Demos, the discovery of classical Attika*. Cambridge: Cambridge University Press.

_____. (1987). *Classical landscape with figures: The ancient Greek city and its countryside*. London: George Philip.

———. (1996). *Greece in the making 1200–479 BC*. London: Routledge.
Osborne, Robin, and Alexandra Pappas. (2007). "Writing on archaic Greek pottery." In Newby and Leader-Newby 2007: 131–155.
Ostler, Nicholas. (2007). *Ad infinitum: A biography of Latin*. New York: Walker.
Ostrom, Elinor et al. (Eds.) (2002). *The drama of the commons*. Washington, D.C.: National Academy Press.
Otkupshchikov Y.V. (1973). "Balkano-maloaziyskie toponomicheskie izoglossy." In *Balkanskoe Yazykoznanie* 1973: 5–29.
Parke, H.W., and R.O.W. Wormell. (1956). *The Delphic oracle*. Oxford: Oxford University Press.
Parker, Robert. (1987). "Myths of early Athens." In Bremmer 1987: 187–214.
———. (2005). "Law and religion." In Gagarin and Cohen 2005: 61–81.
Parpola, Asko. (1994). *Deciphering the Indus script*. Cambridge: Cambridge University Press.
Partenie, Catalin (Ed.) (2009). *Plato's myths*. Cambridge: Cambridge University Press.
Perlès, Catherine. (1992). "Systems of exchange and organization of production in Neolithic Greece." *Journal of Mediterranean Archaeology* 5: 115–164.
———. (2001). *The Early Neolithic in Greece: The first farming communities in Europe*. Cambridge: Cambridge University Press.
Pernicka, Ernst, and David W. Anthony. (2009). "The invention of copper metallurgy and the Copper Age of Old Europe." In Anthony 2009b: 162–177.
Phillips, David. (2012). "Athenian political history: A Panathenaic perspective." In Phillips and Pritchard 2012: 197–232.
Phillips, David, and David Pritchard (Eds.). (2012). *Sport and festival in the ancient Greek world*. Swansea: Classical Press of Wales.
Pöhlmann, Egert (Ed.). (1995). *Studien zur Bühnendichtung und zum Theaterbau der Antike*. Frankfurt, Berlin, Oxford: Peter Lang.
Poruciuc, Adrian. (1995). *Archaeolinguistica*. Bucharest: Institutul Român de Tracologie.
———. (1997). "Aegeo-Balkan onomastics and Fertile-Crescent roots." In Roman et al. 1997: 218–235.
———. (2006). "Palaeo-Balkan elements in Romanian and Southeast European anthroponymy." *Orpheus: Journal of Indo-European and Thracian Studies* (Sofia) 16: 69–78.
———. (2010). *Prehistoric roots of Romanian and Southeast European traditions*. Sebastopol, CA: Institute of Archaeomythology.
Powell, Anton (Ed.). (1995). *The Greek world*. London: Routledge.
Prauscello, Lucia. (2009). "Wandering poetry, 'travelling' music: Timotheus' muse and some case-studies of shifting cultural identities." In Hunter and Rutherford 2009b: 168–194.
Puhvel, Jaan. (1978). "Victimal hierarchies in Indo-European animal sacrifice." *American Journal of Philology* 99: 354–362.
Raaflaub, Kurt A., Josiah Ober, and Robert W. Wallace. (2007). *Origins of democracy in ancient Greece*. Berkeley: University of California Press.
Raduncheva, Ana. (2003). *Kasnoneolitnoto obshtestvo v balgarskite zemi*. Sofia: Bulgarian Academy of Sciences.
Rappaport, R.A. (1999). *Ritual and religion in the making of humanity*. Cambridge: Cambridge University Press.
Raubitschek, A.E. (1983). "The agonistic spirit in Greek culture." *Ancient World* 7: 3–7.
Renfrew Colin. (1972). *The Emergence of Civilisation: The Cyclades and the Aegean in the Third Millennium B.C*. London: Methuen.
———. (1973). *Before civilization: The radiocarbon revolution and prehistoric Europe*. London: Penguin Books.
Renfrew, Colin, and Iain Morley. (2010). "Introduction: Measure: Towards the construction of our world." In Morley and Renfrew 2010: 1–4.
Reynolds, Margaret. (2000). *The Sappho companion*. London: Chatto & Windus.
Rhodes, Peter J. (1972). *The Athenian Boule*. Oxford: Clarendon Press.
———. (2013). "Demarchos." In Cancik and Schneider 2013 (online) <http:// www.encquran.brill.nl/entries/brill-s-new-pauly/demarchos-e314030>.
Richardson, Robert D. Jr. (1978). *Myth and literature in the American Renaissance*. Bloomington, IN: Indiana University Press.
Ridgway, David. (1992). *The first western Greeks*. Cambridge: Cambridge University Press.
Ritner, Robert K. (1996). "The Coptic alphabet." In Daniels and Bright 1996: 287–290.
Robb, Kevin (Ed.). (1983). *Language and thought in early Greek philosophy*. La Salle, IL: The Hegeler Institute.
Roberts, Jennifer T. (1994). *Athens on trial: The antidemocratic tradition in Western thought*. Princeton, NJ: Princeton University Press.
Röhr, Heinz Markus. (1994). *Writing: Its evolution and relation to speech*. Bochum: Norbert Brockmeyer.
Roman, Petre et al. (Eds.). (1997). *The Thracian world at the crossroads of civilizations I*. Bucharest: Vavila.
Roselli, David Kawalko. (2011). *Theater of the people: Spectators and society in ancient Athens*. Austin: University of Texas Press.
Rudgley Richard. (1999). *Lost civilizations of the Stone Age*. London: Arrow Books.
Ruijgh, C.J. (1988). "Le mycénien et Homère." In Morpurgo Davies, and Duhoux 1988: 143–190.

Runnels, Curtis, and Priscilla M. Murray. (2001). *Greece before history: An archaeological companion and guide.* Stanford: Stanford University Press.

Saïd, Suzanne. (2011). "Myth and historiography." In Marincola 2011: 76–88.

Salway, Peter. (1993). *The Oxford illustrated history of Roman Britain.* Oxford: Oxford University Press.

Sampson, Adamantios. (2009). "Incised symbols in Neolithic and Bronze Age Greece and their relation to the Old European script." In Marler and Dexter 2009: 187–192.

Schechner, Richard. (1993). *The future of ritual: Writings on culture and performance.* London: Routledge.

———. (1994). "Ritual and performance." In Ingold 1994: 613–647.

Scheid, John, and Jesper Svenbro. (1996). *The craft of Zeus.* Cambridge, MA: Harvard University Press.

Schepens, Guido. (2011). "History and historia: Inquiry in the Greek historians." In Marincola 2011: 39–55.

Schwenk, Cynthia. (1997). "Athens." In Tritle 1997: 8–40.

Scott, Joan Wallach. (1996). *Only paradoxes to offer: French feminists and the rights of man.* Cambridge, MA: Harvard University Press.

Scott, Michael. (2010). *Delphi and Olympia: The spatial politics of Panhellenism in the archaic and classical periods.* Cambridge: Cambridge University Press.

———. (2012). *Dalla democrazia ai re: La caduta di Atene e il trionfo di Alessandro Magno.* Rome: Editori Laterza.

———. (2013). *Space and society in the Greek and Roman worlds.* Cambridge: Cambridge University Press.

Seaford, Richard. (2004). *Money and the early Greek mind: Homer, philosophy, tragedy.* Cambridge: Cambridge University Press.

Séfériadès, Michel L. (2009). "Spondylus and long-distance trade in prehistoric Europe." In Anthony 2009b: 178–190.

Servi, Katerina. (2011). *The Acropolis: The Acropolis Museum.* Athens: Ekdotike Athenon.

Shanks, Michael. (1996). *Classical archaeology of Greece: Experiences of the discipline.* London: Routledge.

Shapiro, H.A. (1994a). *Myth into art: Poet and painter in classical Greece.* London: Routledge.

———. (1994b). "Religion and politics in democratic Athens." In Coulson et al. 1994: 123–129.

Shearer, Ann. (1996). *Athene: Image and energy.* London: Viking Arkana.

Sherratt, Andrew. (1976). "Resources, technology and trade: An essay in early European metallurgy." In Sieveking et al. 1976: 557–581.

Shore, Bradd. (1998). "Cultural knowledge." In Bouissac 1998: 157–161.

Sidrys, Raymond Vytenis. (2001). "Roman imports among the West Balts: Commerce or 'beads for the natives?'" In Butrimas 2001: 157–169.

Sieveking, G. de G., I.H. Longworth, and K.E. Wilson (Eds.). (1976). *Problems in economic and social archaeology.* London: Duckworth.

Sinn, Ulrich. (2004). *Das antike Olympia: Götter, Spiel und Kunst.* Munich: C.H. Beck.

Slavchev, Vladimir. (2009). "The Varna Eneolithic cemetery in the context of the late Copper Age in the East Balkans." In Anthony 2009b: 192–210.

Smart, Ninian. (1997). *Dimensions of the sacred: An anatomy of the world's beliefs.* London: Fontana Press.

Spikins, Penny. (2008). "Mesolithic Europe: Glimpses of another world." In Bailey and Spikins 2008: 1–17.

Spretnak, Charlene. (1997). *The resurgence of the Real: Body, nature, and place in a hypermodern world.* Reading, MA: Addison-Wesley.

Stafford, Emma J. (1997). "Themis: Religion and order in the archaic *polis*." In Mitchell and Rhodes 1997: 158–167.

Stevenson, Tom. (2012). "The Parthenon frieze as an idealized, contemporary Panathenaic festival." In Phillips and Pritchard 2012: 233–280.

Stoneman, Richard. (2011). *The ancient oracles: Making the gods speak.* New Haven: Yale University Press.

Stoyanova, Polina. (2008). "Keramichni sadove za proizvodstvo na sol." In Nikolov 2008: 135–154.

Stupperich, Reinhard. (1977). *Staatsbegräbnis und Privatgrabmahl im klassischen Athen, 2 vols.* Münster: Westfälische Wilhelms-Universität zu Münster.

Sykäri, Venla. (2011). *Words as events: Cretan mantinades in performance and composition.* Helsinki: Finnish Literature Society.

Thomas, Rosalind. (1992). *Literacy and orality in ancient Greece.* Cambridge: Cambridge University Press.

———. (1995). "Written in stone? Liberty, equality, orality and the codification of law." Bulletin of the Institute of Classical Studies 40: 59–74.

———. (1996). "Bilingualism." In Hornblower and Spawforth 1996: 240–41.

———. (2005). "Writing, law, and written law." In Gagarin and Cohen 2005: 41–60.

Thommen, Lukas. (2012). *An environmental history of ancient Greece and Rome.* Cambridge: Cambridge University Press.

Threatte, Leslie. (1996). "The Greek alphabet." In Daniels and Bright 1996: 271–280.

Thucydides (1914). *History of the Peloponnesian war* (done into English by Richard Crawley). New York: Dutton.

Tole, Vasil S. (2007). *Enciklopedia e iso-polifonisë popullore shqiptare—Encyclopaedia of Albanian folk iso-polyphony*. Tirana: Shtëpia Botuese Uegen.

Tomasello, Michael. (2004). "The human adaptation for culture." In Wuketits and Antweiler 2004: 1–23.

Tomkins, Peter. (2010). "Neolithic antecedents." In Cline 2010: 31–49.

Tritle, Lawrence A (Ed.). (1997). *The Greek world in the fourth century: From the fall of the Athenian Empire to the successors of Alexander*. London: Routledge.

Trombley, F.R. (1994). *Hellenic religion and Christianization c. 370–529, part two*. Leiden: E.J. Brill.

Tuomisto, J. (1994). "Leasing." In *Encyclopaedia Iuridica Fennica*, pp. 431–434.

Tylecote, R.F. (1987). *The early history of metallurgy in Europe*. London and New York: Longman.

Tzonou-Herbst, Ioulia. (2010). "Figurines." In Cline 2010: 210–222.

Uhlenbrock, J.P. (1982). "A dipinto from Tiryns." Kadmos 21: 26–29.

Ursulescu, Nicolae, and Felix A. Tencariu. (2006). *Religie și magie la est de Carpați acum 7000 de ani: Tezaurul cu obiecte de cult de la Isaiia*. Iași: Casa Editorială Demiurg.

Valavanis, Panos. (2013). *The Acropolis through its museum: Wandering among the monuments on the Sacred Rock and the great achievements*. Athens: Kapon Editions.

Vance, Norman. (1997). *The Victorians and ancient Rome*. Oxford: Blackwell.

Vernant, Jean-Pierre. (1988). *Myth and society in ancient Greece*. New York: MIT Press.

Vernant, Jean-Pierre, and Pierre Vidal-Naquet. (1990). *Myth and tragedy in ancient Greece*. New York: Zone Books.

Vickers, Michael. (2008). "Vani, rich in gold." In Chi 2008: 28–49.

Videiko, Mikhail J. (2003). *Trypil´s´ka tsivilizatsiia* (2nd ed.). Kiev: Industrial´nii soiuz Donbasu.

_____. (2008). *Ukraina: Ot Tripol´ia do Antov*. Kiev: KVITS.

Watt, W.C. (1989). "Getting writing right." *Semiotica* 75: 279–315.

Webber, Chris. (2011). *The gods of battle: The Thracians at war 1500 BC–AD 150*. Barnsley, South Yorkshire: Pen & Sword Books.

Werness, Hope B. (2006). *The Continuum encyclopedia of animal symbolism in art*. New York: Continuum.

West, Martin Litchfield. (1988). "Early Greek philosophy." In Boardman et al. 1988: 107–117.

_____. (2007). *Indo-European poetry and myth*. Oxford: Oxford University Press.

Wiener, Margaret J. (1995). *Visible and invisible realms: Power, magic, and colonial conquest in Bali*. Chicago: University of Chicago Press.

Wiles, David. (1997). *Tragedy in Athens: Performance space and theatrical meaning*. Cambridge: Cambridge University Press.

Willard, Dallas. (1983). "Concerning the 'knowledge' of the pre–Platonic Greeks." In Robb 1983: 244–254.

Wilson, Peter. (2000). *The Athenian institution of the khoregia: The chorus, the city and the stage*. Cambridge: Cambridge University Press.

_____ (Ed.). (2007). *The Greek theatre and festivals: Documentary studies*. Oxford: Oxford University Press.

_____. (2009). "Thamyris the Thracian: The archetypal wandering poet?" In Hunter and Rutherford 2009b: 46–79.

_____. (2012). "The politics of dance: Dithyrambic contest and social order in ancient Greece." In Phillips and Pritchard 2012: 163–196.

Wilson, Stephen. (1998). *The means of naming: A social and cultural history of personal naming in western Europe*. London: UCL Press.

Winn, Shan M.M. (1981). *Pre-writing in southeastern Europe: The sign system of the Vinca culture ca. 4000 B.C.* Calgary: Western Publishers.

Wuketits, Franz M., and Christoph Antweiler (Eds.). (2004). *Handbook of evolution, vol. 1: The evolution of human societies and cultures*. Weinheim: Wiley-VCH Verlag.

Yakar, Jak. (2011). *Reflections of ancient Anatolian society in archaeology: From Neolithic village communities to EBA towns and polities*. Istanbul: homerkitabevi.

Yalouris, A., and N. Yalouris. (1998). *Olympia*. Athens: Ekdotike Athenon.

Yasumura, Noriko. (2011). *Challenges to the power of Zeus in early Greek poetry*. London: Bristol Classical Press.

Young, David C. (1996). *The modern Olympics: A struggle for revival*. Baltimore, Maryland: Johns Hopkins University Press.

Yunis, Harvey. (2005). "The rhetoric of law in fourth-century Athens." In Gagarin and Cohen 2005: 191–208.

Zaidman, Louise Bruit, and Pauline Schmitt Pantel. (1995). *Religion in the ancient Greek city*. Cambridge: Cambridge University Press.

Index

acculturation 53, 74, 130, 136
Acropolis (of Athens) 10–12, 29, 32, 62, 69, 71–2, 76, 125, 134, 141, 148, 193, 204, 206, 214
Afrocentric speculations 30
Agora (of Athens) 122, 167, 202–4, 206–8, 215
alloying (of metal) 34, 63–4
ancestors 45, 88
ancestresses 168
ancient Aegean 22, 30, 42, 46, 52, 99, 103, 105, 162, 171
ancient Crete 22, 32–3, 38, 40, 45, 115, 121, 152, 163, 174, 187
ancient customs 12, 156
ancient Egypt 1, 25, 22, 27, 39, 42, 46, 101, 222
ancient Greece 13, 23, 27, 30, 55, 62, 72–3, 77, 123, 126, 145, 142, 152–3, 161, 172–3, 182
ancient Greek (language) 2, 9–10, 14, 19, 22–7, 32, 41, 57, 62–3, 66, 68, 73, 76, 83, 85, 86, 88, 91–2, 94, 98, 112–4, 121, 124, 126, 128, 130, 143, 147, 153, 155, 163, 165, 167, 171, 173, 175, 181, 183–6, 208–10, 215, 219, 224
ancient traditions 10
Apollo 72–3, 126, 149, 151, 153, 155, 163, 165, 178, 181, 206
architecture 26–7, 35, 40, 42, 45, 114, 123, 128, 134, 144, 151, 204, 212, 214, 226
archon (high official) 195, 205–06
Argonauts 67
aristocratic families 132, 144, 193, 221
Aristophanes 121, 138, 177, 215
Aristotle 75–6, 127, 138, 197, 204, 205, 207, 214, 224
art 25, 34, 36, 45, 56, 63, 65, 94, 114, 131, 134, 145, 165, 169, 173–4, 180
Artemis 27, 141, 151, 167, 169, 178
artifacts 36, 43, 45, 50, 62–3, 68, 65, 67, 103, 117–8, 149, 168, 169, 171

Asklepios 72–3, 97
assimilation 14, 53, 73–4, 82, 130
Athena 9–14, 22, 25, 27, 29, 29, 30–6, 62, 69, 71, 81, 88, 97–8, 125, 128, 134, 136, 141–2, 153, 165, 167, 169, 171, 205–8, 210
Athenian coinage 65, 128
Athenian maritime empire 116, 118
Athenian naming system 97
Athenian owl 130
Athens 1–2, 4, 5, 8, 10, 12, 28, 34–5, 40, 54, 69–73, 76, 90, 96–7, 103, 114, 116, 118, 123, 125, 128, 132, 134–8, 140, 142, 144, 146–8, 152–3, 157, 159, 163, 165, 167, 169, 173, 175, 193–7, 199, 201, 203–8, 210, 212–5, 217, 219, 221, 223, 225
athletes (at Olympia) 69, 145, 148, 208
Attic law 154

barbarians 14, 41, 55, 74, 94, 132, 136, 222
beliefs 45, 50, 52, 55, 92, 104, 106, 110, 112, 149, 154, 159, 205
biculturalism 83, 130
bilingualism 74, 82–3, 130
body-painting 94
Bronze Age 9, 11, 20, 23, 25, 36, 32, 36, 45–6, 52–3, 64, 76, 83, 92, 94, 97, 101–2, 105, 115, 124, 134, 139, 142–3, 169, 171–2, 180, 187, 192, 196, 201
bucrania 37
bull games 38
burial customs 184

cadastral list *see* land register
calculation 122
calendrical system 122
census classes 195
ceramic ware 40, 66, 143
charter myth 139, 141
choral dancing 173
choral song 73, 152, 178
Cicero 94, 97, 157, 225
citizenship 70, 90, 219
classical antiquity 1, 4–5, 11, 23, 27, 29, 33, 36, 54, 69, 114, 126, 128, 155, 167, 173, 208, 217, 219, 223, 224
Cleisthenes 2, 8, 97, 135, 147, 193–5, 195, 197, 199, 201–4, 206–7, 210, 212, 221
code-switching 83
cognomen *see* names
Colchis 67, 110
colonization 15, 39, 40, 119, 132, 134, 141
commerce 34, 121–2, 125, 124
communal elections 210
communal festivities 161, 169, 173
communal landownership 192, 194
communal self-administration 2, 197, 199, 201, 204, 208
communication systems 132
community life 26, 50, 60, 80, 128, 130–1, 159, 161, 163, 169, 183, 186, 210
complex language 131
copper 29, 34, 43, 55, 62–3, 65, 67–8, 76, 117, 118, 121, 185
Copper Age 9, 12, 25, 43–5, 68, 167, 190, 192
Coptic alphabet 44
corporate design of Greekness 132, 199
Council (*boule*) 193, 203, 205, 206–7
Court (*heliaia*) 205–6
cult life 27, 139, 159, 161
cult practice 163
cultural chronology 11, 22, 29, 169
cultural continuity 9, 23, 36, 50, 105
cultural drift 22, 67, 100
cultural heritage 9, 27, 32, 50, 159, 165, 185, 222, 224
cultural history 9, 25, 36, 65, 112, 215
cultural memory 10, 12, 35, 41, 48, 50, 66, 77, 101–2, 105, 104, 136, 155, 159, 163, 174, 187
customary law 26–7, 34, 152–6, 158, 159, 170, 201, 225

237

Cypriot Syllabic 107
Cyprus 20, 36, 40, 103, 121, 181, 183

dance 62, 72, 83, 85, 124, 130, 168, 170, 163, 165, 173–6, 178, 217
Danube civilization 29, 41, 43, 45–6, 60, 65, 76, 94, 101, 107, 115, 118, 122, 124, 143, 161, 163, 167, 176, 184, 192, 194, 196, 224
dedicatory inscriptions 174
Delphi 114, 134, 142–3, 147, 149, 151, 152–3, 155–7, 159, 163, 165, 170, 178, 197, 222
demes *see* village communities
Demeter 27, 33–5, 57, 86, 136, 139, 141, 151, 163, 165, 169, 171, 178, 183, 204, 208
democracy 1, 2, 4–5, 7–9, 11, 50, 54, 69, 90, 144, 188, 192, 195, 197, 199, 200–8, 210, 212–7, 221–5
democratic institutions 206, 209, 213–4, 223
democratic terminology 208
descent 27, 81, 83, 94, 131–2, 134, 136, 138–9, 165
Dionysia 85, 159, 215
Dionysiac festival 175
Dionysos 57, 59, 141, 159, 165, 194, 214
direct election 223
dishes 98-9
dispute settling 156
divinities 12, 26–7, 30, 32–6, 55, 72, 80–1, 88, 97, 106, 161, 165, 215
domestic economy 125
domestic ritual 167
Draco's homicide law 159
Dreros 159

economic egalitarianism 185
Eirene 27, 97, 170
élite power 55, 65, 81–3, 117
epic literature 14, 97, 106, 110, 149, 158, 187, 219
epic poetry 163, 183, 185, 187–8, 215
Erechtheus 97, 134–6, 155
ethnic boundary-marking 128, 131
ethnic cohesion 94, 128, 132, 195
ethnic group 12, 21, 128, 132
ethnic identity 14, 104, 130, 132
euphemisms 85
Eurasian steppe 23, 30, 53, 76
Euripides 57, 139, 154, 215
Eurocentrism 27, 29
European tradition 99, 106, 174
Eurynome 33, 134

female occupations 123

festive calendar 165
festivities 33, 39, 141–2, 145, 161, 163, 165, 169, 207
formulaic language 183, 215
founding myth 8

Gaia 97, 134, 136, 151–3, 155, 163, 183
gastronomy 98
gender 69, 75, 90, 121, 123, 131, 161, 167, 176, 214–5, 219
genealogies 134
gentilicium *see* names
goddess cult 12, 33
goddess of fertility (Hera) 148
gold 29, 63, 65, 67–8, 74, 118, 126, 134, 146, 149, 167
Graeco-Arabic translation movement 224
grafting (of olive trees) 67
Grain Mother (Demeter) 27, 33, 57
grain trade 125
grave goods 65, 68, 76, 80, 184, 186, 192
Greek alphabet 25, 36, 42, 44
Greek civilization 1–2, 10–1, 22–3, 25, 27, 29, 32, 34, 42, 53, 55, 72, 112, 128, 132, 136, 138–9, 148, 159, 196, 222
Greek institutions 3, 11, 154
Greek mythology 9–10, 27, 30–1, 33, 35, 55, 57, 62, 92, 97, 134, 147, 176, 178
Greeks 1–2, 4–5, 8–12, 14, 16, 19, 21, 23–7, 30, 32, 35–6, 42, 45–6, 52–9, 64, 67, 69, 72–7, 83, 85–6, 88, 90, 92, 94, 96–8, 101–2, 104, 108, 119, 112–5, 121, 124, 128, 130–3, 135–6, 138–9, 141–4, 147–8, 151–7, 159, 161–3, 165, 165, 170–1, 176–8, 181, 183, 185–7, 192, 194, 196–7, 199, 201, 204, 208, 214–5, 217, 219, 221–4

hair fashion 92
handicraft 45, 60, 97, 183
headdress 94
Helene 183
Helladic tribes 226
Hellas 2, 11, 14, 53, 55, 76, 112, 138, 142, 147–8, 156–7, 170–1, 176, 201, 226
Hellenes 11, 14, 73, 134, 136, 142, 157
Hellenistic era 43, 163, 214, 222
Hellenophiles 25
Hephaestus 134, 136, 153
Hera 32, 36, 62, 97, 141–2, 144–6, 148–9, 156
Heraia 69, 142, 145–6, 148–9
Herodotus 11–2, 14, 73, 108–10, 133, 136, 139, 147, 152, 163, 205, 218

heroes 8, 34, 76, 92, 97, 119, 143, 151, 165, 187–8, 198, 205
Heroic Age 95, 134
Hesiod 33, 55, 151, 158, 163, 170, 185
Hestia 27, 34, 97
hexameter 149, 183, 185, 187
hierarchical society 188, 196
hieroglyphs 42
High Court of Appeal (*areopagos*) 206
high culture 2, 29, 41, 46, 103, 120, 128, 184, 222, 226
Hippocrates 75, 77
Hippocratic oath 72
historicity 110
historiography 1, 5, 11–2, 14, 108, 110, 112, 114, 152, 163
Homer 33, 57, 67, 72–3, 79, 88, 97, 119, 138, 147, 153, 158, 163, 183, 185, 196, 215, 219
household (*oikos*) 27, 32, 88, 123, 127, 167, 186, 188, 219
hymn 2, 73, 169, 178, 183

Iliad 14, 32–3, 57, 67, 72, 79, 119, 138, 145, 147, 158, 196, 199, 206
Indo-European 11–2, 14, 16, 20–3, 25, 27, 30, 32–3, 35, 52–5, 57, 62–6, 73–6, 79–81, 83, 86, 88, 92–6, 99, 105, 107, 112, 114, 119, 130, 139, 142, 148, 151, 161, 165, 170, 174, 185, 187, 196
instrumental notation 181–3
intercultural relations 1, 224
intergenerational chain 48, 50, 77, 104, 187
intervisibility 204

Karanovo culture 168
kinship relations 45, 90, 92, 128, 131–2, 186
Kleisthenes *see* Cleisthenes
Knossos 38, 40, 42, 73, 85, 114, 124
know-how 2, 12, 33–4, 40, 42, 48, 52, 57, 69, 98, 113, 121
knowledge 1–2, 8–9, 11, 22, 27, 32–4, 41, 45, 48, 50, 52, 54, 63, 73, 76, 83, 102–3, 112–4, 128, 142, 156, 159, 161, 163, 181, 184, 186, 188, 201, 226, 222–3
knowledge-construction 2, 50–1, 54

land lease 2, 192, 194, 196, 198
land register 198
law-giving 80, 156
laws 120, 138, 152, 154–6, 158–9, 187, 197, 206, 212, 219, 223
lexical borrowings 14, 21, 25, 57, 130
lineages 86, 168, 186
Linear A 42, 101–3, 105, 107, 175

Index

Linear B 27, 36, 42, 52–3, 59, 85, 92, 101–5, 107, 114, 124–5, 181, 194, 196, 198
linear signs 101–3, 181
linguistic community 130
literacy 36, 42, 52, 54, 83, 101–3, 107, 134, 152, 174, 185, 187
loom *see* warp-weighted loom
loom weights 60, 61, 62, 102
Lycurgus 57, 152, 156

Macedonians 4, 96, 99
marble 30, 68, 74, 167, 169, 171, 180
marine life 112–3
markers of ethnicity 132
measurement 122
measures 28, 124–6, 128, 130, 160
Medea 67, 110
medicinal knowledge 73
medicine 72–3, 75, 77, 224
Mediterranean 14–7, 20–2, 35, 36, 40, 52–3, 67, 92, 118–9, 121, 193, 207
mentifacts 32, 45, 50
Mesolithic Age 54
Mesopotamia 1, 22, 41, 46, 65, 68, 101, 113, 154
metal-working 25, 29, 167
metallurgy 2, 23, 35, 53, 62–4, 68, 226
metrical form 183, 187
migration 16, 62, 76, 85, 132
Minoan civilization 22, 32–3, 108, 163
Minos 42, 152
Mnemosyne 170, 163
muses 163–5, 170, 178
museum (*mouzeion*) 165
music 45, 73, 165, 170, 173, 175–6, 178, 181–3, 201
Mycenaean civilization 92, 187
Mycenaean-Greek 9, 22, 36, 173
myth 1–2, 8–9, 12, 14, 32–3, 35, 41, 52, 79, 104, 106–8, 110, 112, 114, 132, 134–6, 139, 141, 148, 153, 170, 182, 187, 196, 206, 215, 222
myth-making 104
myth of origin (*aition*) 136
mythical legitimization 81, 83
mythology 12, 26, 30, 33, 45, 55, 57, 74, 79, 92, 106, 108, 138, 142, 170, 182

names 11–2, 20–1, 25–7, 32, 55, 57, 59, 67, 82, 85, 92–4, 96–7, 107, 114–5, 121, 135–6, 151, 163, 178, 181, 183, 187, 197–9, 215
National Assembly (*ekklesia*) 153, 202
native Europeans *see* Paleo-Europeans

natural law 159
Neolithic Age 60, 190
nomenclature 27, 90, 98, 124, 126, 130, 159, 165, 208
nomenclature of weights and measures 124, 130
norms of social conduct 154–5
notational systems 30, 45, 46
numbers 16, 30, 46, 122, 126, 169, 199, 214

obsidian 68, 115, 185
Odyssey 14, 32, 67, 73, 97, 147, 158, 183, 196
oecumene (commonwealth) 184, 186
Old Europe 11, 22, 29, 32, 35, 37, 41, 43, 45–6, 48, 52–3, 55, 62, 76, 92, 99, 103, 107–8, 115, 118, 120–1, 161, 167–71, 184, 186, 188, 192, 194, 196, 208, 226, 224
olive cultivation 9, 12, 53, 69–70, 169
Olympia 25, 62, 69, 102, 107, 142–8, 152, 156, 173, 226
Olympics 69, 141–2, 142–6, 148
oracles 147
oral poetry 185–7
orality 54, 128, 152
Orpheus 171, 177–8, 199
Orphic studies 178
out-migrations 23, 30, 55, 99
owl (Athena's attribute) 13–4, 28, 65, 98, 128

Palaeo-Europeans 2, 45, 55, 142
Panathenaia 12, 62, 69, 142, 167, 205–8, 221
pan-Hellenic identity 128
Parthenon 28–9, 35, 71, 125, 141, 148, 183, 204
pastoral god 30, 55
Pelasgians 2, 11–2, 14, 21–2, 26, 32, 69, 73–4, 82–3, 86, 125, 136, 141, 171, 196, 214, 226
pentatonic music 175
performance culture 144, 175
Pericles 73, 90, 223
personal names 95–6, 198
philosophy 25, 108, 112, 183, 185, 224
Phoenicians 121
phratries (brotherhoods) 88
phyle (tribe) 130, 210
place-names 25
Plato 74–5, 77, 98, 105, 112, 128, 136, 152, 154, 159, 165, 167, 173, 176, 200, 201, 215
Pnyx 163, 203–4, 208, 212
polis (Greek city) 5, 12, 90, 96, 132, 138, 161, 163, 199, 204, 210, 223
political power 39, 65, 69, 81–2, 119, 187, 195, 215, 220, 223

potter's wheel 64
pottery 23, 25, 27, 29, 34–6, 40, 53, 64, 66, 76, 101–3, 119, 128, 175–6, 208, 226
praenomen *see* names
prehistory 27, 29, 85, 115, 151, 170, 187, 196
priestesses 161, 167–8, 214
priests 79, 161, 167, 169
private landownership 192
procession (thiasos) 33, 57, 69, 161, 163, 169, 178, 215, 221
public rituals 165
purple snail 63, 112
Pythia (at Delphi) 147, 149, 152–3, 155–6, 159, 197

religious authority 65
religious symbolism 168–9
religious symbols 49
remembering the past 34, 214
resident aliens (metics) 167
rituals 2, 25, 39, 45, 83, 88, 128, 141, 143, 145–6, 151, 156, 158, 161, 165, 167–9, 188, 204, 214–5, 226; food 99
Romans 1, 10, 39, 55, 66, 82, 96–7, 147, 165, 213, 222
round dance (*choros*) 130, 176

sacred grove 77, 143, 151, 167
salt 98, 117–8, 123, 185
sanctuaries 27, 32, 36, 44–5, 69, 134, 141, 153, 161, 168, 178, 222
Sappho 165, 180, 185
Sarasvati 80–1
Scythians 55, 134
seafaring 119, 1135, 118, 121, 196, 226
self-awareness 134–5, 138–9, 156
shamanism 149
shells 68, 118, 185
ship-building 23, 28, 34–5, 113, 120–1, 169
slaves 5, 72, 88, 207, 215, 217, 219, 221, 223
smelting (of metal) 2, 66–8, 117
snake (Athena's attribute) 30, 33, 72, 74
social cohesion 130, 144, 188, 199
social egalitarianism 55
social hierarchy 68, 80, 125, 186, 190
social networking 83, 86, 130
Solon 8, 152, 159, 192–4, 199–200, 202–7, 212
Sophocles 215, 222
Spartans 83, 85, 119, 132, 136–9, 141, 142, 152, 171, 193, 223
spices 98–9
spondylus (shell) 117–8, 149, 185
sport *see* Olympia
sportive competitions 69, 145–6, 148, 170

state organization 199
steppe pastoralists 66, 83
string instruments 180
Suvorovo culture 62
symbols 42–3, 45, 49, 74, 77, 94, 102–3, 105, 128, 161, 168, 177
symposia 161, 170

tattooing 94, 132
technological advancement 34, 48, 183
thalassocracy (Minoan maritime power) 85, 121
theater 2, 154, 170, 173, 194, 204, 212–5, 217, 226
theatrical performances 2, 159, 170, 215, 214–5, 226
Themis 27, 33, 97, 153–5, 170
Theseus 92, 114, 116, 134, 154
Thesmophoria 33, 99, 143, 163, 169, 204
Thracians 65, 73
trade 29, 34, 39–40, 42, 55, 68–9, 76, 113–5, 117–25, 128, 141, 149, 165, 169, 181, 184, 186, 221; relations 39, 121, 124; routes 115
traditional cultures 188, 190

traditional healing 75
tragedy 25, 77, 154, 159, 163, 173, 206, 215, 217
tribes 2, 14, 20, 26, 54, 57, 62, 73, 82, 85, 88, 94, 96, 129–30, 132, 135–6, 139, 157, 195–7, 199, 203, 205, 207–8, 210, 222–3; Achaeans 73, 182; Arcadians 176; division 132, 203; Dorians 14, 73, 131, 134, 136, 139; Ionians 96, 136; names 94, 198; Phocians 157; territories 132, 135; Thessalians 99, 173
tripartition (in society and mythology) 79
trireme (ship type) 114–5
trittys (three-fold division) 169, 197, 210, 212
Trojan war 79, 119

units of weight 124
urbanization 46

values (shared values) 45, 50, 73–5, 102, 126, 132, 134, 152, 155–6, 161, 164, 184, 187–8, 201, 208, 224–5
Varna necropolis 65

village communities (demes) 2, 8–9, 11, 45, 184, 188, 190, 192, 196–7, 201, 204, 223
virtues of democracy 225; *isegoria* 199, 221; *isonomia* 199, 221; *isopoliteia* 199, 201, 221
visual communication 132
visual metaphor 168

warp-weighted loom 60, 64
warrior class 76, 79, 80, 88
weaving 28–9, 33, 53, 60, 62, 64, 142, 199, 226
wine cultivation 2, 55, 57, 59
worldview 26–7, 30, 41, 45, 48, 50, 52, 61, 80, 112, 114, 131–132, 156
wreath (of olive twigs) 72, 123, 212
writing: alphabetic 42, 44, 52, 181; linear 102–3, 107, 183; logographic 46; technology 27, 42, 46, 52, 103, 105, 132
written laws 158–9

zeitgeist 25, 27, 29, 76, 122
Zeus 33–4, 55, 57, 59, 73, 88, 97, 145–6, 148, 151, 163, 165, 169, 204

www.ingramcontent.com/pod-product-compliance
Lightning Source LLC
Chambersburg PA
CBHW081551300426
44116CB00015B/2838